"*A long time ago, when I was a youngster, I read Pirsig's* Zen and the Art of Motor-cycle Maintenance. *It introduced a Metaphysics of Quality, which aimed to go beyond the subject/object split that stood at the birth of our modern times and has eventually left Western people splintered into many pieces. A healing of the split between the individual, the community, and the society at large is more needed than ever. It is nothing less than the urgent task of our time, which is suffering from a terrible meaning crisis in a deteriorating physical world. This book is a deep but pragmatic exploration of this triple problem: can we be whole and free persons (not just individuals), anchored in real communities that can support their members in a solidary environment and (also just as crucially) in a society that we can mean-ingfully contribute to? That is the circle that needs to be squared. Don't expect here yet another new utopia by neo-hippies or techno-dystopian dreams but a mature and anchored 'heterotopia' by two authors with ample life and work experience and skin in the game. A high-tech world needs high touch. You will find it here.*"

—Michel Bauwens, Founder of the P2P Foundation

"*This book delivers a most practical and straightforward tutorial, introducing the reader to innovative ideas about how to increase our quality of life in a very acces-sible way, making it tangible and actionable.*"

—Dr. Ann Berens, Psychiatrist, Chief Physician,
and Medical Director at UPC Duffel

"*Finally a book that highlights the need to break free of the economic, social, and governmental systems we're in, toward an opt-in environment that would allow for a radical new way of cooperation.*"

—Oana Bogdan, architect and CEO
at Bogdan & Van Broeck

PERSON
TO
PERSON

CHANGE YOUR LIFE
AND FIX THE WORLD

JOERI TORFS & PIM AMPE
WITH GRETA MYERS

FOREWORD BY VITALIK BUTERIN

QOL.WORLD
PUBLISHING

PERSON to PERSON
Change Your Life and Fix the World

Illustrations by Laura Click

ISBN 978-1-5445-2916-5 *Paperback*
     978-1-5445-2917-2 *Ebook*
     978-1-5445-2880-9 *Audiobook*

For Lola and Enrico, who embraced me as their mother and
inspired me to make the best out of everything that crosses our path.
And for all future generations, may this book inspire you.

—P.A.

For "the crazy ones. The misfits. The rebels.
The troublemakers. The round pegs in the square holes."
May this book inspire you on your journey
toward breaking the status quo.

—J.T.

For my favorite collaborators:
Jeff, Ramona, and Gloria

—G.M.

CONTENTS

PART ONE
PERSONAL QUALITY OF LIFE

PART FOUR

OPPORTUNITIES CREATED BY THE PERSON TO PERSON ENVIRONMENT

Here's to the crazy ones. The misfits. The rebels.
The troublemakers. The round pegs in the square holes.

The ones who see things differently.
They're not fond of rules.
And they have no respect for the status quo.
You can quote them, disagree with them,
glorify or vilify them.

About the only thing you can't do is ignore them.
Because they change things. They invent. They imagine.
They heal. They explore. They create. They inspire.
They push the human race forward.

Maybe they have to be crazy.

How else can you stare at an empty canvas and see a work of art?
Or sit in silence and hear a song that's never been written?
Or gaze at a red planet and see a laboratory on wheels?

While some see them as the crazy ones, we see genius.
Because the people who are crazy enough to think they can
change the world, are the ones who do.

—Apple Inc.'s "Think Different" advertising slogan,
created by advertising agency TBWA\Chiat\Day in 1997

FOREWORD

By Vitalik Buterin

Over the last ten years of my life, I have had the privilege of being at the forefront of one of the most fascinating and promising technological and social movements that could transform how we interact with each other: the blockchain space (or "crypto," or "Web3").

Blockchains as a technology are by now increasingly familiar and need little introduction. Described in one sentence, blockchains are a new way of publicly agreeing on and updating a store of data without any central controller. The easiest application to understand is Bitcoin: the Bitcoin network publicly agrees on how many bitcoins everyone has, and anyone can generate and send a "transaction," which the network processes and verifies, to transfer bitcoins that they have to someone else. Of course, the value of blockchains is far broader than Bitcoin: they have given rise to non-fungible tokens (NFTs) that artists have used to fund their work, decentralized autonomous organizations (DAOs) to collectively manage funds and transform how people work, and much more. Altogether, I prefer to think of blockchains as a "Lego of social organization" and not just a currency. (Similar to Leon and Alex, as they brainstorm in Chapter 7 of *Person to Person*!)

But behind these technologies, there is also at the same time a fascinating culture. It is a culture that still holds the idealist spirit of the early internet, seeking more decentralized, egalitarian, free, and inclusive ways for people to collaborate, bypassing corporate gatekeepers and national borders. It's a culture that has created and cultivated a surprising internal diversity: East Asians and Latin Americans, leftists and libertarians, programmers and social thinkers, and of course both sides of the dichotomy that any new technology so easily attracts: people who just want to make money and people who have bigger dreams of changing the world. It is to these pioneers—whether they be self-interested or altruistic—that Joeri Torfs and Pim Ampe primarily address their message, with practical ideas about how we can use these new technologies and their associated cultural momentum to transform the world.

The blockchain culture is one that also tries to genuinely live its values. It features truly global organizations, like the Ethereum Foundation itself: an organization that has never had a true "head office," even from its beginning at a time when the software and venture capital elites still thought that any serious software project needed to have one. Most contributors work remotely from many countries around the world, spanning from Rio de Janeiro to Vancouver to Taipei. Most meetings happen at 1400 UTC, a time slot we call "eth o'clock" because it's literally the only time when a meeting can easily happen because all our researchers and developers are awake.

It also features cross-organizational collaboration: most of the deep science and technology, including fresh new constructions like "verifiable delay functions" and "zk-SNARKs," that powers our ecosystem is developed by researchers from a number of organizations spontaneously coming together and building out what needs to be done. Entire projects within Ethereum are often governed by biweekly calls and Telegram channels, a "flash organization" of anyone who can contribute to make the project happen. In essence, these are people in the early stages of forming organic collaboratives—to use the *Person to Person* term. They are aligning around a common purpose and seeking frictionless collaboration, for the good of the individual, the ecosystem, and the world.

2022 is a fascinating year because it's the year when this budding new culture is being thrust into contact with a big outside world that is both curious and skeptical. Can things really be done decentralized? Is openness something that people will go for in a bigger world where so many are worried about commercial competitors or even political adversaries and enemies? Even putting aside the problems with people, can decentralization achieve the efficiency and scale that people want on a purely technical level? *Person to Person* posits ways we can actually leverage our human instincts to form an environment that leads to a best-case scenario, guidance that may reassure skeptics and excite the early believers.

Along with this book's authors, there are many hardworking people focused on all of these problems: solving the deep technical challenges of efficiency, privacy, and scalability, dealing with politicians and regulators, and coming up with applications that the mainstream public will love and accept. Will they succeed? We're about to see and find out!

January 11, 2022
Vitalik Buterin
Co-founder of Ethereum
Co-founder of *Bitcoin Magazine*
Russian-Canadian software developer

INTRODUCTION

Utopia is a place where everything is good;
dystopia is a place where everything is bad;
heterotopia is where things are different.

—Walter Russell Mead,
American academic and columnist

We had to push past the boundaries to enter the property. Years ago, caretakers had surrounded the ancient buildings with a high fence, but in some stretches, the fence gave way to thick bushes serving as a barrier. That's where we pressed our way through. Thankfully, the caretaker was out of town.

It was supposed to be a bit of fun, an afternoon adventure to help us unwind. Joeri had just completed a stressful sale of his father's company in the adjacent village in this region of Southern France. Now, as we prepared to cut ties with Ginoles les Bains for good, we took ourselves on an impromptu date, visiting some of Joeri's old childhood haunts as a way of saying goodbye.

But any plans to keep our trespassing adventure confined to a single afternoon vanished when we got through the bushes into the stunning expanse of the property. It was desolate but beautiful. Lush vegetation, fed by the natural cold and hot springs, grew upward, backed by the neighboring Pyrenees.

Much of it was tropical—there were palm trees and exotic flowers—so that we felt transported somewhere far away.

The stone buildings looked ancient. We wondered if any of them dated back to the property's first genesis, when it was a park with a mill where farmers came to grind their grains. In the 1800s, it had seen new life as a thermal institute, thanks to its natural hot springs. We found the old bathhouse, built in a Roman style, with arches. The hotels, dating to the property's tourist resort days in the 1920s, had fallen into disrepair but still maintained the dignity of their old grandeur. The structures sat within a six-acre park with two old pools. It was in these pools that Joeri had come swimming as a boy, when the property had been converted to a public swimming pool. However, it had been nineteen years since he had last seen the property. It had been abandoned for years now, and the pools had filled in with seedlings and bushes. Something about the place made us feel as though we were playing a scene out of *Romeo and Juliet*. We felt giddy.

Then we became serious. It felt like such a shame that a property this beautiful—with so much potential as a destination for community gatherings and rest and connection—was going unused. The beauty of the place inspired us to begin imagining what it might become. Could this place once again be restored to become a sustainable environment and meaningful destination for future generations?

Maybe we should buy it, we said, half-joking, half-serious. We were fortunate enough to be in the financial position where that was a possibility. But—could we transform it?

There was no question that the place would need a good deal of renovation—and *innovation*—which would require a huge amount of capital. The most obvious way to make the property profitable was to turn it into luxurious, exclusive apartments—but that seemed like a waste of the special opportunities this unique property offered. Was there a way to support the nearby community, we wondered? The large elderly population in the nearby town, perhaps, or the decrease of young families due to the lack of employment opportunities? Perhaps the park could be reopened and made into a gathering place.

Joeri came at the conversations from a business perspective. After the complicated and drawn-out experience with the sale of his father's business— which involved a legal mess with the shareholders and co-owners—he felt put off by any business enterprise that was focused on money, power, and relentless promotion. We *could* have made money off of it by turning it into a luxury destination, but we didn't want to create an exclusive playground for the rich; we wanted to preserve the inclusive, inviting, peaceful atmosphere that we experienced when we trespassed on the abandoned property. However, transforming the property into a place that suited our preferred vision seemed like a financial impossibility.

Pim came at the conversations from her therapist background. She knew there were so many people in the immediate vicinity who would benefit from the lush and peaceful environment of the property, if only it could be made useful again. This could be a healing haven, a sanctuary of retreat where people could experience a greater quality of life. It could be amazing.

Perhaps, we agreed, we just needed to think outside the box.

The first iterations of our brainstorming occurred *just* outside of the box, thinking about crowdfunding as a possible solution. But we knew that would eventually lead to co-ownership and co-management, which—as Joeri had so recently experienced—are difficult and financially troublesome. When making decisions as a co-op or with co-managers, the majority rules. However, this often leaves the minority out in the cold: if you don't win the vote, well then—you're a loser. Could a project really be successful if the minority was doomed to be ruled by the majority? Is a person in the minority less entitled to quality of life than one who conforms to the norm? We wanted to avoid the pitfalls of group thinking by finding a way to allow people to think for themselves, take ownership, and exert personal agency according to their own passions and vision.

So we tried to think further outside the box. Then we decided we should discard the box entirely.

We asked: is there a way to break free of the economic, and social, and governmental systems we're in without being destructive? Could we build an opt-in environment that would coexist alongside the current one, but one that would allow for a radical new way of cooperation? Not a utopia, where all current systems must be replaced, but a *heterotopia*, a different environment altogether, where people and economics could relate in an entirely "other" manner. Was that even possible?

The giddiness of our romantic inspiration was weighed down by these sober considerations. To do this properly, you'd have to practically *invent* a new socioeconomic environment that would enable all people—not just the rich ones—to participate in bringing this place back to life, to pursue monetary gain in equal balance with quality of life, to allow for sustainability and connection across social divides.

There was no inventing that occurred that afternoon. And we didn't leave the property that day with any clear plan.

"We'll think of a plan later," we said to each other as we whacked our way back out through the bushes. "Let's buy it first."

LOSS OF PERSONAL AGENCY, LOSS OF COMMUNITY

In the beginning, we were discussing theoretical problems. But slowly, we realized we were dealing with real problems, and the impact of those problems went far beyond a picturesque property in Southern France.

It was a problem, for instance, that there was a need, and there were ways to meet that need, but no economically viable way to accomplish that. For example, in the local French village, there were many groups of people who would benefit from gathering in a place where they could exchange skills and connect with one another—lonely elderly people could connect with orphaned children in need of grandparent figures, for instance—but there was no way to make that profitable. That problem exposed many others: most societies function mainly on what will drive a profit, not what will afford people the greatest quality of life—a problem. Increasing individualism and isolation: that was a problem. The fierce competition that characterized the business world: another problem.

Those problems, in turn, led to more: because of relentless corporate competition and all the attitudes associated with it, you see an increasing number of people burning out; you see a widening gap between the rich and the poor; you see models that prioritize short-term economic gain instead of long-term environmental sustainability; you see increased polarization and division instead of people connecting and sharing ideas.

Likewise, the economic challenge of transforming the property was like turning over a rock and finding a crawling mess of problematic business models. When we approached potential collaborators whose businesses would be a good fit for the property, their first question was, "How are we going to deal with shares? And who is going to be the owner and the boss?" We didn't want that: shareholder-ship often results in zero-sum "winners or losers" power plays.

A cooperative model was also logistically challenging. The values that are the foundation of a co-op in the beginning can easily get trampled on when you're talking about the best financial move. When a nonprofit or co-op first begins, there is only the vision and the collaboration—there is no money. But as money comes, the twin monsters of fear and greed can hijack the conversation and cause people to lose their focus on the founding principles, in favor of what will be best financially. That can lead to compromising those founding values. Although this model around the world *can* lead to great community work, it only functions well when everyone shows up with the right mindset and is aligned with the same vision. That can be a real challenge.

The simplest way to organize an enterprise is the most common one we see in the corporate Western world: there's an exclusive director who determines the company's course, there's relentless marketing and promotion, and then—ideally—the organization is sold for an enormous profit. But that model also seemed antithetical to real quality of life: it leads to a concentration of power, it often panders to the rich to the exclusion of the poor, and it can kill any real collaboration. It also puts an emphasis on short-term goals at the expense of long-term vision. "Ownership," and all the related efforts to protect the *stuff* that we own, seems like the root of most of the world's evils: tribal conflicts, wars, inequality, and so on. Plus, it isn't good for the vast majority of people who work in this kind of environment. In a hierarchical power structure, employees often feel like they don't have a voice. They stop putting in their energy and best efforts. They forfeit their personal agency because it doesn't feel needed or wanted.

In fact, we realized, there seemed to be a loss of personal agency across the board, partly because of the increasing distance people experience between their effort and outcome. In most first-world countries, when you want to fill up your refrigerator with food, you don't have to plant and cultivate and harvest. You don't even have to spend an hour at the grocery store anymore; you just type an order into a smartphone and the food shows up. With almost no effort, you get an easy outcome. When a worldwide pandemic hits, we wait for our government to tell us what to do and how they're going to provide, and sometimes, we wait for some printed-out money. A needed outcome arrives, but it's one that comes completely independently of our effort. Sometimes, the *opposite* occurs: you put enormous effort into your job, but it goes completely unnoticed, and you decide you'll just put in less effort next time. In most developed countries, we find ourselves in an "easy to get" environment, but as a result, our efforts don't feel meaningful anymore. That can lead to feelings of futility, depression, and frustration.

At the same time that we are lowering our effort, we're raising our expectations. Many of us have evolved sky-high expectations of what we're entitled to but have a low estimation of what we should be expected to contribute. For instance, previous generations tended to have lower expectations of the choices life would offer. Their options were generally limited to opportunities and goods available in their local community, and they expected to work to earn them. Now—thanks to technology and social media—our options appear limitless. We want *everything*. However, we increasingly expect that other entities should deliver those things to us: we are entitled to a universal basic income or a free college education; at the very least, we're entitled to free shipping. Not all of these expectations are bad. There's no question that social services are important and even vital. However, many social services make blanket assessments about what people need; they don't encounter each person as an individual, considering their strengths and weaknesses, tailoring services to how that person most needs support and empowerment. As a result, these blanket offerings can create a complacent sense of entitlement instead of motivating personal growth. We as humans inherently have abilities to deal with danger and stress, but when someone else tells us that it's all taken care of, we can easily become complacent in exerting our own effort.

When we live with high expectations of where we "should" be, but depend on others for our outcomes, there's an unfortunate result: blame. When the groceries arrive, but all the fruit is bruised—well, we blame the delivery person. When inflation spikes in our country in part because of all the printed-out money—we blame the government. When our boss ignores our efforts at work—we blame the boss. When we don't feel any power or agency to change our situation, we blame other people for anything we perceive as bad. As a result, entire communities develop an ethos of blame: blame the opposing political party, blame the migrants, blame the educational system, blame the government. Instead of exerting personal agency to solve our problems, we create enemies.

Unfortunately, this culture of blame is pulling us away from the one thing that is truly real, the one thing that research has shown is the key to a happy life: relationships.[1] Person to person relationships are the core of everything.

---

[1] Liz Mineo, "Good Genes Are Nice, But Joy Is Better," *Harvard Gazette*, April 11, 2017, https://news .harvard.edu/gazette/story/2017/04/over-nearly-80-years-harvard-study-has-been-showing-how-to-live-a-healthy-and-happy-life.

How did humans survive in their earliest days, before they had fire, before they began to evolve? They were tightly connected to their community and tribe. Relationships have been at the center of human evolution for millennia, and they're one of the most crucial aspects of what it means to live a fulfilling and joyful life. They've kept us as a species alive. But in these recent digital years, we've started to *lose* authentic connections to other people. The systems simply do not support those close relationships anymore: we're becoming more isolated and divided. When we buy a cup of coffee, we don't think about the person who farmed it or the person who roasted it. When we scroll through social media posts or debate with people online, we easily forget that these are real people with their own complicated stories and challenges. Many people are seeking the sense of those relationships through escapism: video games, simulated worlds, fantasy novels, TV shows, movies, social media, and so on. But most find those forms of escapism a poor substitute for the real thing. Escapism is not real life.

So the question becomes: how can we make real life something more beautiful? How can we remove the blame, restore personal agency, and help build real connections between people?

We wanted to come up with a structure that was truly collaborative—one without an all-powerful director or owner—but one where people showed up, worked together, and put in their best efforts to make something beautiful, sustainable, and equitable for a community. We dreamed of an environment that was people-centric, aimed at building greater quality of life. We wanted people to feel real personal agency—where they could make their own decisions and experience the outcome of their own best efforts. And we wanted an environment that would allow for real connection—not mediated by banks or governments—but defined by connections from person to person.

That environment didn't seem to exist. But could it?

PERSON TO PERSON

It was time to start inventing. We threw out all of the "boxes" and started with what we could perceive as people's primary needs. Those needs seemed to fall into three categories: personal, community, and economic. What's more, we realized that one seemed to build on the other: motivated and inspired people were necessary to create healthy working communities, which were a necessary prerequisite to a quality of life economic environment. Here are the needs we identified:

- **Personal**: People need to know what conditions lead to quality of life, and they need more opportunities to achieve those conditions in their own lives. They need more opportunities to take personal agency, where their creativity, entrepreneurial work, and effort have a real impact on the outcome they experience.
- **Community**: People need opportunities to connect and collaborate with one another, rather than blame, compete, and divide. They need to understand what kind of mindset is required for frictionless collaboration and commit to that.
- **Economic environment**: People need a way to make money that encourages collaboration, while at the same time allowing for personal autonomy. People need a way to store long-term value but also need freedom from owning the "stuff" that so often weighs them down and causes envy, divisiveness, and inequality between people.

This book is the fruit of our years of brainstorming as to how people can actually address these needs and create a "Quality of Life World." It describes a people-centric economy, built with innovative socioeconomic tools, employing a global network. Its Person to Person environment is focused on long-term sustainability—in the human sense, financially, and environmentally—rather than having a sole focus on profits.

There's plenty of theory in this book, which we recognize can be challenging to digest without an example to pin it on. For that reason—and because we believe that a Person to Person society is best illustrated with people—we have crafted a fictional narrative to support each chapter's concepts, to show how all these principles could practically work. We have tried to make these fictional characters recognizably human—with dreams, flaws, hopes, and real desires for connection—so that our readers can see themselves taking this journey too.

The journey starts small: within the heart and mind of the individual. The journey travels outward from there, into the groups of people we interact with most frequently. Then we start traveling fast and far, exploring the far reaches of how our economic environments could be transformed to allow for a Person to Person society, a world built around quality of life.

Part 1: Personal Quality of Life

Chapters 1, 2, and 3 address our *personal* needs.

- Chapter 1: We start with research into what human beings actually require to thrive. There are eight "quality of life" domains, which collectively help lead to a person's flourishing. By identifying those needs, we know the conditions required for a world that prioritizes quality of life.
- Chapter 2: We make the case for connecting with other people in a Person to Person fashion—whether that's among friends, family units, or workplace teams. When we remove competition and divisiveness and instead build awareness of our own values and needs along with our other group members, then we can connect with others in a healthier way. By recognizing our part in a bigger whole, we sense that we belong. That increases our self-esteem, making us more inclined to collaborate and contribute our best.
- Chapter 3: A key part of collaborating with others well requires

that we show up with the right mindset. This chapter explores the unhealthy mindsets that lead to the "tragedy of the commons" and identifies the Core Design Principles that can help shape the required mindset for frictionless collaboration to thrive.

Part 2: Community Collaboration

Chapters 4 and 5 discuss tools to support our *community* needs.

- Chapter 4: This chapter discusses Troubleshooting tools and Commitment Sessions, which are key elements of creating an environment where people feel valued and heard, and can contribute their best. Since conflict and tension are an inevitable part of working with others who are different than us, we need tools to help aid us toward frictionless collaboration.

- Chapter 5: A Collaborative Agreement can help colleagues maintain their commitment to each other, ensuring that groups work together in a healthy way. By taking care of each other, pursuing our shared values and needs, and using all of our skills and abilities, we can collaborate and co-create more effectively, strengthening each other instead of competing against each other. This creates more equity and enables interaction between groups, resulting in more social cohesion and sustainable communities.

Part 3: Economic Environment

Chapters 6 through 9 address our *economic needs*, exploring the sort of financial environment that would best suit a world focused on quality of life. They also identify the technologies required to facilitate those needs.

- Chapter 6: What does collaborative finance look like? We explore ways to separate money from power: measuring effort with

Collaborative Points instead of currency; choosing your own compensation; and finding ways to incentivize long-term investment in balance with short-term needs. If people are to fully engage in their work, they need to trust that they will be fairly compensated and will benefit from their efforts.

- Chapter 7: Private property often works against quality of life—it can promote inequality, violence, and corruption, and has historically been the basis for war. It's long been assumed to be a necessary way of life—but perhaps that assumption should be questioned. This chapter explores ways to reinvent the concept of private property and introduces the book's most revolutionary concept: Sovereign Assets, which separate ownership from value. Sovereign Assets enable people to save up the financial value attached to assets without actually owning them. This can lead to greater freedom and flexibility, level the playing field for historically disadvantaged demographics, and incentivize long-term investment.

- Chapter 8: A world that prioritizes quality of life needs to find ways to get around the human tendency of manipulating systems of control for selfish gain. Thankfully, there are many pioneering technologies that allow for safe, transparent financial transactions to occur directly between people, ones that can enable the Person to Person environment to globally scale. This chapter explores and explains those technologies in simple, straightforward terms, such as Web3, blockchain, smart contracts, DAOs, and cryptocurrency.

- Chapter 9: When the Person to Person concepts are facilitated by the technologies described in the previous chapter, there are profound opportunities generated. Specifically, we see how a Web3 community DAO, the Collaborative Cloud, can be used to help collaborative groups operate, conduct personal finance, and seek out investment from a community of other users.

Part 4: Opportunities Created by the Person to Person Environment

Our last two chapters explore some of the aspects of real-world living that could be transformed through the possibilities available through the Person to Person environment.

- Chapter 10: In order for people to buy, invest, and trade without the interference of banks or the stock market, you need an environment where people can provide all those financial services to each other directly. This chapter explores what that might look like and what tools would be required.

- Chapter 11: Housing and shelter are some of our most basic needs—and this chapter explores how a Person to Person environment would look when applied to housing. What if renters could earn equity while paying their monthly rent instead of "throwing it away"? What if they didn't face the barrier to entry usually posed by homeownership: needing a down payment and a lengthy credit history? What if, instead, they could start earning long-term value with their monthly housing payments? We examine ways this could practically work, building on the Sovereign Assets concept.

The world needs something different—and that's what we have tried to envision. This book does not attempt to describe a utopia, but rather a *heterotopia*—an environment that provides a different sort of place, that invites a different way of living. It doesn't seek to replace the systems already at work in the world, but it does seek to imagine an alternative. Many of the concepts are ones that would take years to pursue; many of the concepts are ones that you could start applying today, in your own personal life.

THE TRESPASSERS

We are not specialists in macroeconomic or social environments. However, we are observers. We try to pay attention to how things work—and how things may *not* be working—especially people and systems. Rather than responding to problems with despair or escapism, we seek to respond to problems with ideas for a solution. We are hopeful; we believe that people are capable of doing great things when they are equipped to function at their best. However, we also try to be realistic, basing our ideas on research and workable tools. We are doers, implementing specific solutions that have the potential to lead to a workable viable alternative. And we are life partners, which might explain the romantic trespassing adventures.

Pim's Introduction of Joeri Torfs

I'll tell you the basic facts first. Joeri started off as a software developer and now works as an IT enterprise architect, meaning he helps organizations build entirely new IT systems that function with the latest technology, according to each organization's unique needs. He tells me that he likes the work because it allows him to build structure out of chaos and challenge the status quo. He is "allergic" to rules and authority; in fact, even though he loves learning, he was a terrible student in school—he hated being told what to do. That's why he prefers working as an entrepreneur; however, he's also functioned as a VP, a manager, and developer, in addition to being CEO of several startups. Joeri is also the operational director of the Quality of Life World Foundation, based in Belgium.

Joeri is the most brilliant person I know. He's constantly reading and is interested in how everything works—whether that's in the area of physics, technology, or the psychology of humans. He looks for ways to make systems more flexible for people to use so that there are no limitations to what they can try, while still being able to remain true to themselves. That's something incredibly important to Joeri, and it's the way he lives: he is true to himself in all contexts. He doesn't feel the need to be socially accepted into different groups. He's always friendly, but he doesn't pretend to be anything other than who he is. I really admire that in him.

Joeri's mind for inventing new systems, his passion for learning, and his desire to promote greater freedom in everyday living have all come together in his vision for a Person to Person world. He's convinced that, together, we can increase our quality of life by accepting life's challenges, building trust, letting go of control, and relying on frictionless collaboration to build a framework that can evolve with societal needs.

Joeri's Introduction of Pim Ampe

Pim has worked in a wide number of people-centric roles: she's been a psychotherapist, drama therapist, family worker, team leader, care coordinator, staff member, supervisor, teacher, and manager. She's currently working within mental healthcare and the welfare sector, where she's reminded every day of people's need for greater quality of life. She is educated in and employs various methodologies and frameworks, including drama therapy, solution-focused therapy, dialectical behavioral therapy (DBT), the Holacracy© framework, and Prosocial. She is also the constitutional director of the Quality of Life World Foundation.

Now let me tell you a few things you wouldn't learn from her CV. Pim loves learning and she's incredibly driven. She loves empowering people and is always focused on the well-being of others. To me, she is the most caring and empathic person I know. In the same way I can intuitively understand systems, Pim intuits people. She can read the ins and outs of how humans work, think, and feel. That has fascinated me from the start; she's taught me a tremendous amount about how people function. She's also provided helpful explanations to enable me to understand why people reacted to me a certain way, when I would have been clueless!

Because she understands the mechanics of people, Pim has a keen sense of what will help people communicate better, collaborate better, and engage in a more caring way. She's there for her neighbors, for her family and friends, for our neighborhood; she's there for me and our kids. Her purpose is to increase people's quality of life by expanding their ability to adapt and self-manage in the face of life challenges, whether they are emotional, social, physical, intellectual, or economic. I think she's a beautiful soul.

ANCIENT PATHS TO GREATER BEAUTY

We believe that people need a path forward to unlearn all the unhealthy habits we have developed over time. The problems that exist in our world will only continue to worsen as issues like climate change or social unrest exacerbate the challenges we're faced with. The only way out of this is by coming together and forming new ideas. We need humans to function with their utmost imagination, innovation, and entrepreneurship. The way to cultivate that is to build an environment that will help people function at their best, taking their quality of life seriously.

The Person to Person vision puts people's quality of life at the center of every process. It lays the basis for a new way of structuring society, one that honors our human needs and enables humans to connect authentically with each other. The last one hundred years have created layers upon layers of inefficiency; societies have tried to patch existing structures, such as government and financial systems—but we need more than a patchwork if we as a species are going to survive the imminent challenges ahead and thrive. We need to envision, create, and implement a radically new environment to replace the obsolete structures we have today. We believe this is necessary if we are to free the latent potential of humans, restore the relational connectedness we long for, and thrive in a just and sustainable economic environment.

In this book, we have described a vision of what a Quality of Life World could look like and how it might enable Person to Person collaboration. However, the book isn't merely a description; it's also meant to function as a guide. For anyone who desires to open the door to this new environment, the journey charted in the chapters ahead will enable you to apply these concepts to your personal life.

As we found when exploring the stunning property in France, there are ancient paths worth exploring—paths that can teach us what it means to be human. By bringing the tools and innovations of modern day to those ancient paths, we can chart a new path toward greater beauty.

The two of us have whacked our way through the bushes to try to start charting one such path—with hope, sober-mindedness, and admittedly, some clumsiness: we still have twigs in our hair and leaves caught on our clothes. We don't believe these efforts to be final, and we recognize that other people—other collaborators—will be needed to evolve these ideas.

Still, as the branches and leaves part to open a view into what's beyond— we find something stunningly beautiful.

Won't you explore with us?

PART ONE

PERSONAL QUALITY OF LIFE

*You can't think yourself into new ways of acting;
you can only act yourself into
new ways of thinking.*

–Marsha Linehan

CHAPTER ONE

QUALITY OF LIFE AS A DRIVING FORCE

Searching Out the Real Needs

*Striving for the good life involves the
arduous work of becoming, of trying to live a life
that one deems worthy, becoming the sort
of person that one desires.*

—Edward F. Fischer, researcher and author of *The Good Life*

What is it that humans really need? That was the question we arrived at during those first conversations at the Experience Center.

We coined the property the "Experience Center" before we even bought it because of the feeling of quietness, calm, and peace that we experienced there, surrounded by nature with the fostering mountains surrounding us. It was that experience that we wanted to share with others. Now, while standing in one of the property's empty pools, overgrown with vines, bushes, and weeds, we asked: what factors are contributing to this peaceful experience right now? *This* feels like quality of life. So how could we replicate this experience and share it?

For two hours, we stood and paced in that pool, a place that seemed to epitomize the entire property's combination of decay and new growth; of both breakdown and possibility. Beyond the speculations about how we could transform the property, we kept coming back to that central question: what, most of all, was needed?

As the two of us exchanged ideas about *this* demographic or *that* approach, we realized that we needed to probe deeper. Before we could address any single demographic, we had to study the issue on a deeper human level. What do humans really need to experience quality of life?

The obvious place to start would have been Maslow's hierarchy of needs, a concept familiar to many. Maslow's hierarchy identifies five categories of essential human needs; the most foundational physiological and safety needs must be met before the higher needs of belonging, esteem, and self-actualization can be met. But if so many people were familiar with Maslow's hierarchy of needs—then why were there still so many unhappy, dissatisfied people? What information was missing?

We sought greater specificity within these categories of need. For instance, we wondered: can human beings truly satisfy their needs for love and belonging via social media—or is deeper connection needed? What kind of self-actualization will bring real happiness? Is climbing to the top of the corporate ladder the surest way to life satisfaction—or not?

Maybe, we reasoned, it's different for everyone.

But then that consideration brought a new question: should these categories of needs be understood as being totally objective and universal, or are some of them subjective? And if human needs *are* universal and objective—well then, shouldn't we all get better acquainted with what those personal needs are? For instance, maybe we would all be healthier and happier if we could become more aware of our emotions, what they tell us, and how we can provide a proper response to our emotional needs. In other words, we asked, how much of a role did our conscious mindset play in shaping our quality of life?

Thankfully, we didn't have to explore these questions on our own. We were acquainted with two researchers who were both studying quality of life and factors of well-being. One of them, an anthropologist, was specifically studying people who played the virtual-world-building game *Second Life*, where the goal is to create a virtual life for yourself. As we discussed her research, we began to identify many connections to our own recent conversations. For instance, our friend had pointed out that many *Second Life* players enjoyed building and decorating houses for themselves in the virtual world because they couldn't afford home ownership in real life. These were people who wanted to create another world that could more readily meet their needs. We had that same goal, only we wanted to find a way to do it in actual life.

Our researcher colleagues agreed to combine their efforts and study what scientific literature had to say about the needed ingredients for true quality of life. They probed literature on the psychology of quality of life,[2] the anthropology of well-being,[3] the importance of self-compassion, nature connectedness, and so on. They also studied research on life domains,[4] literature identifying the five essential elements that impact well-being the most,[5] and integrative studies of quality of life, looking at how different demographics

---

[2] M. E. P. Seligman, *Authentic Happiness: Using the New Positive Psychology to Realize Your Potential for Lasting Fulfillment* (New York: The Free Press, 2002); M. Joseph Sirgy, *The Psychology of Quality of Life: Hedonic Well-Being, Life Satisfaction, and Eudaimonia* (Second Edition) (Berlin: Springer Science+Business Media, 2012).

[3] Edward F. Fischer, *The Good Life: Aspiration, Dignity, and the Anthropology of Wellbeing* (Stanford: Stanford University Press, 2014).

[4] World Health Organization Quality of Life (WHOQOL) Group, *WHOQOL-OLD Manual* (2006), https://www.who.int/mental_health/evidence/WHOQOL_OLD_Manual.pdf.

[5] Tom Rath and Jim Harter, *Well Being: The Five Essential Elements* (New York: Gallup Press, 2010).

might experience well-being differently.[6] At the end of all their reading, they brought us their comprehensive conclusions.

While they were busy researching, we also continued to engage this question personally. Throughout Pim's work as a therapist, she had found a tremendously powerful counseling tool that seemed to help even the most psychologically vulnerable clients, pioneered by behavioral therapist Marsha Linehan.[7] We will discuss Linehan's dialectical behavioral therapy method more thoroughly in Chapter 3, but essentially, the tool involved asking clients to develop a clear idea of a life that would be worth living. Clients were asked, "What kind of a life would make this therapy worth the effort to do the work and commit to life? What would quality of life mean to you?" In many cases, that question helped clients see past their difficulties, their troubled relationships, and their emotional burdens. Not only did the vision of a qualitatively rich life help them *stay* alive; it helped motivate their action to build a better life for themselves.

Pim found the tool equally effective with youth, healthcare teams, and members of the blind community. In some settings, she tweaked the conjecture: "Imagine that, in ten years, you're living the life you truly want. Think about what that life would be. Does that vision make you want to make any changes in your present life?" The vision of living into true quality of life consistently seemed to inspire hope in the future and, equally as important, motivate action in the present. If this concept of quality of life could so profoundly help people going through challenging periods in their lives, it seemed logical that the concept should be used as a foundational method for *everyone* in building their lives.

---

[6] Rocío Fernández-Ballesteros, "Quality of Life in Old Age: Problematic Issues," *Applied Research in Quality of Life* 6 no. 1 (2011), DOI: 10.1007/s11482-010-9110-x; Robert A. Cummins, "Subjective Wellbeing, Homeostatically Protected Mood and Depression: A Synthesis," *Journal of Happiness Studies* 11 no. 1 (2010), DOI: 10.1007/s10902-009-9167-0; Ömer Faruk Şimşek, "Happiness Revisited: Ontological Well-Being as a Theory-Based Construct of Subjective Well-Being," *Journal of Happiness Studies* 10 no. 5 (2009), DOI: 10.1007/s10902-008-9105-6.

[7] Marsha Linehan, *Building a Life Worth Living: A Memoir* (New York: Random House, 2021).

But how exactly should we understand, define, or explain quality of life? That's the point where our research colleagues began their presentation, once they had completed a massive review of the scientific literature on the topic. Their presentation of "key takeaways" was seventy-one slides long and referenced eighty-five different studies. Whew! No wonder we had a lot to look over when it came to this first point.

DEFINING QUALITY OF LIFE

We were initially surprised to discover just how many ways different philosophers and researchers have sought to define quality of life. When presented with all those definitions, we had to consider which description of quality of life seemed to resonate most truly with the human experience. Was it simply the experience of pleasure and the absence of pain, also known as hedonic happiness? And if so—did that happiness count if it was momentary and transient, or did it have to be long-lasting? Did quality of life refer to a kind of homeostasis—the idea that life is best when it's calm, comfortable, and balanced?

There were ultimately three descriptions of quality of life that we found to be the most compelling and actionable. We have used these foundational understandings of quality of life to guide us in everything that follows.

1. **Quality of life can be understood as happiness.** In a nutshell, "happiness" is what we're aiming for. However, this happiness is more than just hedonic moments of everyday contentment. Quality of life depends even more on *eudaemonic* happiness. The Greek word *eudaimonia* translates to being in a state of, literally, "good spirit." It refers to life satisfaction, a sense of fulfillment, and feeling a sense of control over where your life goes. It also accepts that painful experiences do happen and are sometimes even necessary

for growth, in contrast to the hedonic perspective, which seeks to avoid pain altogether. It is this deeper *eudaemonic* sense of satisfaction that is long-lasting and the most powerful in leading to abundant quality of life.

2. **Quality of life is dynamic.** One of our favorite quality of life theories states that well-being is actionable.[8] They say people usually go through six different stages of processing, involving identifying ways to initiate positive change in life, planning, taking action toward that change, experiencing positive outcomes, and then feeling a sense of satisfaction and increased meaning as a result. This understanding of quality of life means that humans have real power to take action over their well-being. We are not stuck with negative circumstances or a negative outlook: we have agency in our happiness.

3. **Quality of life is both objective and subjective.** Our team of researchers helped spotlight this key point. They wrote, "Material resources, physical health and safety, family and social relations are crucial elements of wellbeing. But those more *objective* factors are not sufficient. According to Fischer (2014), it is important to gain 'a *subjective* understanding of what people value, what their view of the good life is and could be, and the pathways they see for realizing their aspirations.'"[9] In other words, humans certainly do have objective needs, like shelter, food, and so on. Without those needs being met, quality of life will be low. However, being able to assess our lives as fulfilling, meaningful, and happy is a *subjective* evaluation. You can have an impoverished man in Manila who could

---

[8] Paul Dolan and Matthew White, "Dynamic Well-Being: Connecting Indicators of What People Anticipate with Indicators of What People Experience," *Social Research Indicators* 75 no. 2 (Jan 2006), DOI: 10.1007/s11205-004-6298x.

[9] Elise Torfs and Molly Goodman, "Quality of Life Introduction," (presentation, Research Nomads, Antwerp, Belgium, May 7, 2017 and July 22, 2017), slide 35.

honestly claim to have greater quality of life than a billionaire on Wall Street, exactly for this reason. Because of this subjective element, we can once again recognize that we have real agency in adopting a mindset that chooses to see the good.

In fact, all three of these definitions of quality of life imply that personal agency is a requirement for experiencing well-being. And if that is the case—then the question becomes one of how. *How* can we take action toward greater happiness in our lives?

SELF-STEERING YOUR QUALITY OF LIFE

Imagine a steering wheel with eight spokes, then imagine placing both your hands on the wheel. At the center of that wheel are core purpose and core values. The eight spokes branching off are eight domains that all contribute toward quality of life. When taken together, this information can equip you for *self-steering*.

When people are able to embrace an attitude of self-steering toward greater quality of life, we are better able to move past the problems of a high sense of entitlement, low personal agency, and a culture of blame. Instead, these concepts invite us to take agency over our own quality of life and to put our hands on the wheel, and encourage our active participation in realizing our own chosen purpose. We call this "being your own case manager."

Step 1: Identify Core Purpose and Core Values

The first step in being your own case manager is to identify your core purpose and core values. As you prepare to "self-steer" using the eight domains, you need to understand *why* you do the things you do and *where* you're going (purpose), along with *how* you would like to see yourself getting there (values).

Core Purpose

Your core purpose is your *why*. It's the reason you get up in the morning; it's your sense of a higher calling; it's confirmation of a life being well lived. It helps you clarify your direction in life and motivate your growth, learning, healing, and contribution. Importantly, it also can serve as a guiding star, helping you evaluate which actions in your life are helping you achieve your purpose and what, if anything, is holding you back. In order to experience true quality of life, people need to identify their core purpose and have a sense that they're making gradual progress toward this central objective.

"Progress" is an important word in understanding purpose because, ideally, we will always be progressing toward this aim. In fact, a helpful way to understand purpose is to think of it in terms of a direction: your purpose is similar to north on a compass. It's not necessarily a place where you "arrive"— although there may be many milestones along the way, as you travel in the direction of your core purpose. Throughout your life, your expression of your purpose may take different forms, but ideally, it will always be something you strive toward.

Here's an example. Let's say that a hypothetical woman named Rosa has the purpose to nurture the people and places around her. That purpose might encompass many goals—when her kids are young, she mainly lives out her purpose by nurturing her kids' development and well-being. She might also try to nurture her small vegetable garden. Perhaps she seeks to nurture her community by volunteering or by looking after her elderly neighbor. In different seasons of life, Rosa's *activity* related to her purpose will change, but she will always be pursuing the same higher calling: to nurture others. That's her purpose, her calling, her life's direction.

On the road that progresses toward your purpose, there may be goals. Those serve as milestones. A goal can be achieved, but a purpose never stops. Sometimes a goal dresses up like a purpose; for instance, Rosa may believe for a long season that her purpose is to raise happy, healthy, successful kids.

But what happens when that goal is achieved and the kids grow up and leave the house? Raising great kids was a goal—a milestone—within the larger purpose of nurturing others.

The need for a purpose was famously identified in Viktor Frankl's *Man's Search for Meaning*, in which he describes how he found the strength to endure the atrocities of a German concentration camp by identifying his purpose.[10] Other researchers have also identified a life purpose as a key component of quality of life.[11] One such researcher wrote, "Having such a larger purpose and being part of meaningful projects that go beyond narrow self-interest are central to wellbeing among both the affluent and the poor. What constitutes 'meaningful' is defined through cultural values and a sense of purpose based on what matters most in life."[12]

⟨ formatting ornament ⟩

Having a larger purpose and being part of meaningful projects are central to wellbeing. "Meaningful" comprises cultural values and a sense of purpose, based on what matters most in life.

Some people seem to have an innate sense of their purpose from childhood. For others, identifying a purpose is more of a journey. In either case, the research makes clear that working toward a guiding purpose is a central element of living a life that feels satisfying and meaningful. For those still journeying to discover a purpose, the following questions can provide helpful direction. (These questions are also available on our website for the reader's own processing; please see the QR code at the end of this chapter.)

---

[10] Viktor Emil Frankl, *Man's Search for Meaning* (Boston: Beacon Press, 2006).

[11] Michael F. Stenger et al, "The Meaning in Life Questionnaire: Assessing the Presence Of and Search For Meaning in Life," *Journal of Counseling Psychology* 53 no. 1 (2006), DOI: 10.1037/0022-0167.53.1.80.

[12] Fischer, *The Good Life*.

- What is my desired vision for the future? If I could describe my ideal life in ten years, what would it look like?
- What do I want to stand for? Put differently, what values would I like to be known for?
- In what contexts do my skills align with my passions? In other words, what "work" feels fun, exciting, and fulfilling to me?
- What will I strive for during the short time I spend on this planet?

These questions can help shed light on a person's core purpose, especially if there are reoccurring themes in your responses.

Core Values

If your purpose is your *why* and helps dictate your *where*, then your values are your *how*. Your core values will determine *how* you make choices; they will guide your behavior while you pursue your core purpose. The name signals their meaning: values are things that are valuable to you. They're beliefs and principles worth paying attention to, prioritizing, and honoring with your choices.

Imagine you're traveling in the direction of your purpose, and you come to a fork in the road. You can go this way or go *that* way. Both paths might presumably continue to take you in the direction of your purpose. Therefore, it's your *values* that will help you determine the best road to take. Will you take the quickest route or the more scenic route? It depends on what you value.

Let's revisit Rosa, for instance, whose core purpose is to nurture the people and places around her. She might get a job offer to work full time at an after-school program. Accepting the job would give her the opportunity to nurture many kids who come through the program. It would also provide her with more money to nurture her family's material needs. However, the full-time job might mean she has less time to invest in her immediate family, her garden, and her elderly neighbor. Rosa's choice about whether or not to take the job will be guided by her beliefs about what matters most, that is, her values.

A richly qualitative life pursues goals guided by values. The famous philosopher Aristotle said, "The highest of all human goods is not happiness, feeling good or satisfying appetites. Instead, it is about activities of the soul that are in accord with virtue, striving to achieve the best that is within us. Research needs to encompass the meaning-making, self-realizing, striving aspects of being human."[13] So it is not enough simply to strive to achieve one's best; one must do so while living according to one's values.

The highest of all human goods . . .
is about activities of the soul that are in accord with virtue,
striving to achieve the best that is within us.

By identifying your core values, you can ensure that your choices in pursuing your purpose remain aligned with your values, including any purpose-related goals that you may have established for yourself. For instance, Rosa's goal to raise happy, healthy kids will be guided by her values of what it means to be a loving parent: showing patience, care, and presence and offering guidance.

It's important to commit to pursue and respect these values at all times, especially because—remember—quality of life has a *subjective* element. One researcher makes the point that a subjective perception of well-being requires not only participating in the life domains that we're about to describe, but doing so according to "value-laden belief[s] about the totality of one's life."[14] In other words, it's participating in all areas of life in ways that you can feel good about, in accordance with your purpose and values. Think critically about the values you choose to live by. Many of us have absorbed motivations

---

[13] Aristotle, *Nichomachean Ethics*, trans. L. H. G. Greenwood (Cambridge: University Press, 1909).

[14] Sirgy, *The Psychology of Quality of Life*.

from people or outside pressures that are not truly authentic to who we are—for instance, to get a high-paying job, even if it's not truly what you want to do. Take another example: let's say that you grew up with the model that the needs of the group were always more important than the needs of the individual. Maybe as an adult, you overextend yourself trying to serve the needs of the group, at the expense of your own welfare. You might realize that you would actually be a better helper to others if you set boundaries to take care of yourself first—even if that goes against what you witnessed in your own role models when growing up. It's important to make a distinction between "learned desirable behavior"—the values you internalized from others while growing up—and the values that are inherently important to you. Identifying your innate values will enable you to express yourself in life and find a balance that supports your quality of life.

It's also important to distinguish emotions from values. Emotions do not define a person; they only characterize a person's experience of a given moment. As humans, we often mistakenly let emotions guide us, assuming that anything that makes us feel good *is* good and anything that makes us uncomfortable is bad. However, putting too much stock in emotions can sometimes make us drift away from our values. Emotions are reactive and temporary. Values, on the other hand, are rooted. You can't choose how you feel in a given moment, but you can choose how you respond and behave afterward. That choice is guided by *values* and strengthened by skills that you can learn. (We will discuss those skills in later chapters.) Values can help clarify when your emotions are serving you (are they leading you toward your core purpose, in alignment with your values?) and when, if ever, they need to be managed with tools for self-control so that they don't hinder your progress toward your goals.

The following questions can help you form an idea about some of the key values that guide you. (You're invited to process these questions using the tools available on our website; please see the QR code listed at the end of the chapter.)

- Why does my core purpose matter so much to me? Put differently, what motivations are behind my core purpose?
- Who is most important to me?
- What is most important to me?
- What drives me as I pursue my goals?
- What values do I prioritize in how I engage with others, with my work, and in my free time?
- What values would I *like* to guide me? How close am I to living out those values on a regular basis?
- How do I want people to remember me?

Identifying your core purpose and values is an essential step for a meaningful life. It's also critical for effective collaboration with others. Later in this book, we'll discuss healthy ways to form a collaborative group. An important first step involves each person sharing what is important to them, identifying shared values, creating a collective identity, and forming a group purpose (this is done during the group ACT matrix, discussed in Chapter 3). The *group's* shared identity and purpose will be informed by each person's core purpose as they come together to work toward a common aim. Group members need to be able to voice their own core purpose and values in order to contribute to the formation of a healthy, aligned group.

Likewise, a consciously values-driven approach ensures that everyone who works with you knows what truly matters to you. By identifying your core values, you can ensure that your behavior aligns with those standards, which will characterize your interactions with others. We describe both your purpose and your values as "core" because they should inform every other aspect of your life. They are at the center, the foundation—the core.

Introducing Jake

Throughout this book, we will be introducing a number of abstract concepts that will make the most sense when applied and illustrated in a real context.

For that reason, we'll be illustrating how all of these concepts could be applied through the journey of a hypothetical character named Jake Ramirez. So, what kind of a person is Jake? How can we understand him in terms of his core purpose and core values?

Jake is a nineteen-year-old college freshman, the first person in his family to ever attend college. His parents run a mom-and-pop convenience store in a rough area, about two hours away from Jake's new college. Money is usually tight for Jake's family. Although Jake was awarded a few scholarships to help cover the costs of school, the vast majority of his tuition and housing has been covered by loans. This is a point of stress for Jake and his parents.

In his early teens, Jake started getting into trouble with a neighborhood gang. Thankfully, a favorite teacher helped convince Jake to plug into an after-school program to stay focused on his studies and build friendships in a safe context. As Jake got older, he began tutoring at the same after-school program. He discovered that he loved working with kids. Not only did Jake find the kids fun and interesting; he also loved helping them make learning connections. The work also felt meaningful; Jake was able to see kids similar to himself getting off the streets and thriving in a safe context. During his senior year, Jake started coaching some of the older kids to play basketball. Once he moved to college, Jake had to stop his work at the after-school program. He misses it.

The experiences at the after-school program made Jake decide he wanted to become a teacher. His parents feel some concerns about this, given the amount of loans they've taken out; they know that Jake won't ever make much money as a teacher. They tend to vacillate in their support of Jake—recognizing his gifts in teaching—and pressuring him to, instead, seek out a more lucrative job. As a result, Jake is trying to pursue a double major in both biology and chemistry. He figures this will set him up to be a science teacher, and it also appeals to his parents as a good premed combination—although Jake is really not interested in becoming a doctor.

In addition to studying, spending time in class, and hanging out with friends, Jake works as an Uber driver. He's feeling increasing stress about the fact that this job isn't making him as much money as he feels he needs. He could try to work more or work nights when rates go up, but he knows this would cause his academic performance to take a hit.

Jake would identify his **core purpose** as becoming a teacher. He likes helping others, using his skills, and working toward greater social justice; he also values his family and wants to make his parents proud. These are some of Jake's **core values**.

We're going to pick back up again with Jake soon. But first, let's examine step 2 of self-steering: the eight life domains.

STEP 2: THE EIGHT LIFE DOMAINS

After identifying the "why" and "where" (core purpose) and the "how" (core values), it's time to examine the eight domains that, together, lead to a high quality of life. When most of our life domains are going well, quality of life feels easier to grasp; when a majority of them are in bad shape, quality of life feels out of reach. In this way, the subjective *and* objective evaluations of quality of life work together.

This is important because—for people like us, who are interested in world changes that could help people experience more quality of life—it points to the fact that quality of life is informed by our circumstances, in addition to our mindset. It's not quite enough to have a purpose and live according to your values. Take Viktor Frankl, for example: although he was able to identify a purpose within the concentration camp and did his utmost to live by his values under the constraints, he still was miserable. He maintained the will to survive, yes—but he was miserable. That's because he was starving, abused, and exposed to brutally inhumane conditions. His experience in essentially every single one of his life domains was appalling.

Sometimes we willfully allow our life domains to get horribly out of balance, but this can actually hinder us from fulfilling our purpose and experiencing real quality of life. For instance, let's say that Rosa becomes so consumed with nurturing others that she begins to neglect herself in various life domains. She stops getting physical exercise, sacrifices her own material comfort to make others more comfortable, and gets so wrapped up in her neighbor's crisis that her own emotional well-being becomes jeopardized. In this case, her neglect of her own life domains will compromise her ability to carry out her purpose. Therefore, it's crucial to maintain *balance* between maintaining health in the life domains while pursuing your core purpose and values. By growing awareness of those potential pitfalls and finding a helpful balance, you will be more capable in pursuing your purpose while expressing your values, thereby increasing your quality of life.

Think again of the steering wheel that we described in the "self-steering" section of this chapter. Core purpose and core values are at the center: the core. But without the spokes stretching out from the center, representing the eight life domains, the wheel can't turn. There's no self-steering, and therefore no progress, without health in most domains. So we must hold these domains as an equal priority alongside purpose and values while pursuing greater quality of life.

There are objectively good and objectively bad conditions that do influence our quality of life. When we know what those are, we can start building a life and a world that prioritizes those conditions.

So—what are our essential life domains? And what does it look like to experience real well-being in each of them?

The eight life areas we describe were largely identified, according to the World Health Organization Quality of Life Group's research, as the chief domains that influence our subjective experience of well-being.[15] However, they have been informed and tweaked by other researchers' work as well to

---

[15] WHOQOL Group, *WHOQOL-OLD Manual.*

reflect the most complete picture we could gather from research about what conditions can help produce abundant quality of life.[16] Each domain can be scored to describe the degree to which a person experiences abundance in that category.

When you understand these eight domains, you're able to take hold of the wheel and steer your efforts toward your core purpose, in alignment with your values. Scoring your quality of life in each area gives you the ability to discover what needs to be adjusted, what needs to be adopted, and what simply must be accepted. We all must walk a fine line between *what is* and *what might be*, balancing the unchangeable facts of our current reality with the desired changes of the future. In some of these domains, you may realize there isn't much you can do to change your circumstances. However, in many domains, you may have more agency than you think you do to pursue change or growth.

We all must walk a fine line between what is and what might be, balancing the unchangeable facts of our current reality with the desired changes of the future.

1. Learning and Personal Growth

Think of watching a child age from year to year. If the child didn't grow, mature, develop, and change, that would be extremely concerning. In fact, there's a name for that stasis: "failure to thrive." Similarly, if you planted a tree in the ground, but in the months to come, that tree began to droop and wasn't growing, that lack of growth would be viewed as a sign the tree wasn't thriving. You might assume it was gradually dying.

---

[16] Rath and Harter, *Well Being*.

Thriving means *growing*. Having opportunities to learn, develop, discover your abilities, grow in your talents, and put your skills into practice is one of the first ingredients for quality of life. In fact, for one researcher, this area encapsulated his entire definition for quality of life: Sen's capability theory says that quality of life depends on conditions that will allow people to become capable of helping themselves and enriching their own lives.[17] Another seminal researcher, Fischer, writes, "A capacity for aspiration and agency and opportunity to realize those aspirations is essential to wellbeing."[18]

Our growth is not meant to stop after childhood; we are meant to continue learning and growing throughout our adulthood as well. What's more, there are a number of different areas in our life that warrant growth: intellectual, emotional, physical, relational, cultural, and spiritual.

Here are some key considerations to evaluate where you are in this first domain:

- Am I regularly exposed to new ideas and concepts (intellectual growth)?
- Am I building more self-awareness about my emotions (emotional growth)?
- Do I have regular opportunities to grow physically and try out new forms of movement (physical growth)?
- Am I growing relationally, learning more about the people I care about and how I interact with them (relational growth)?
- Am I learning more about other cultures and my own culture (cultural growth)?
- Do I have opportunities to develop my beliefs and values (spiritual growth)?

---

[17] Amartya Sen, "Capability and Well-Being," in *The Quality of Life*, ed. Martha Nussbaum and Amartya Sen (Oxford, UK: Oxford University Press (1993), 30–35.

[18] Fischer, *The Good Life*.

It's likely that you're experiencing growth in some areas more than others. Consider where you could pursue more growth and learning. If you're in a season where certain areas of growth simply aren't possible, accept that current limitation and trust that your current season won't last forever. However, if most of us get really honest with ourselves, we can recognize that we have far more agency than we realize in pursuing learning and personal growth.

2. Self-Determination, Meaning, and Basic Rights

When the Taliban took over Afghanistan in August of 2021, Afghani women experienced a radical change in this "self-determination" life domain. Before the takeover, women were allowed to pursue an education, work in a career, and wear the clothing they wanted: they largely had the ability to determine the course of their lives. Immediately after the takeover, however, women hid in their homes, afraid to go out because of the Taliban's history of oppressing women.[19] They turned bedsheets into burkas, lest they be targeted for attack. Many despaired that they would have to give up their jobs and educational pursuits—that, in almost every capacity, they would no longer have the ability to direct their own lives.[20] The tragedy of this shift spotlights the importance of this domain.

People long for the ability to direct their own life and to be able to shape their own values, norms, and routines. Doing so offers reassurance and a sense of competence. It's also through self-determination that people are able to live a life they consider to be meaningful. Researchers Ryan and Deci stated that we have three major subjective needs in our pursuit of quality of life:

---

[19] Ahmad Seir et al, "Taliban Vow to Respect Women, Despite History of Oppression," *AP News*, August 18, 2021, https://apnews.com/article/afghanistan-taliban-kabul-1d4b052ccef113adc8dc94f965ff23c7.

[20] Maggie Astor, "A Taliban Spokesman Urged Women to Stay Home Because Fighters Have Not Been Trained to Respect Them," *The New York Times*, August 25, 2021, https://www.nytimes.com/2021/08/24/world/asia/taliban-women-afghanistan.html.

competence, autonomy, and relatedness.[21] In other words, people need to experience a sense of belonging and attachment to other people. All of these needs can only be met in a context where people are allowed to pursue the goals that feel meaningful to them.

Within this domain, consider evaluating how and to what extent you engage in self-determination, meaning, and basic rights:

- In what way and to what extent do you try to strengthen your autonomy? In other words, do you typically rely on others for direction and provision, or do you try to make your own way?
- Do you try to live purposefully?
- Do you feel respected in your basic rights?

3. Productivity and Activity

Related to self-determination is self-realization—the productive action of creating the life you want. When people are able to realize themselves in an activity—performing work or practicing a craft, art, or other discipline that feels meaningful and fun—there's an experience of pleasure and competence that helps lead to quality of life. Being productive and active in the areas that excite us helps us to experience our competencies, strengthen our talents, and expand our possibilities. It also gives us the opportunity for self-expression. Researcher Seligman argued that we long for a *pleasant* life, an *engaged* life, and a *meaningful* life.[22] This domain encompasses all three.

Perhaps you enjoy boat building, or playing music, or software coding. Maybe you feel the greatest satisfaction by investing in a community of children or by healing people in a healthcare context. Feelings of satisfaction, fulfillment, and greater quality of life are able to come to fruition when we

---

[21] Richard M. Ryan and Edward L. Deci, "Self-Determination Theory and the Facilitation of Intrinsic Motivation, Social Development, and Well-Being," *American Psychologist* 55 no. 1 (January 2000), DOI: 10.1037/0003-066X.55.1.68.

[22] Seligman, *Authentic Happiness*.

are productive and active in areas that feel meaningful. Consider evaluating in what way and to what extent you experience productivity and activity:

- What do I love to do most?
- What work feels meaningful to me?
- How much time do I spend doing either or both of the above activities?

Your answers to the questions above can shed light on where you experience productivity and activity, but they can also help reveal your core purpose. Take note: *these* are the areas where you experience a sense of real meaning in your work.

4. Leisure and Social Interactions

Relationships are enormously important for any fulfilling, meaningful life. This domain is all about finding your place in society and your relational connections within; it acknowledges the importance of community connections and time spent doing leisure activities that can help build social connections. This involves participating in society, investing in friendships, and engaging in roles where you bear some responsibility and also experience joy, belonging, or meaning (like parenthood, leading a volunteer group, or participating in a sports team). Leisure activities—in other words, activities we choose to participate in with others during our spare time—create a significant boost for our subjective quality of life. It means we're doing things we enjoy, with people we like, and improving our skills. That's good for us![23]

These sorts of connected social experiences can help people feel part of a meaningful, greater whole. There's no shortage of research attesting to our

---

[23] Michael Argyle, *The Psychology of Happiness* (New York: Winston & Sons, 2001); Mihaly Csikszentmihalyi, *Finding Flow: The Psychology of Engagement with Everyday Life* (New York: Basic Books, 1997). See also Mihaly Czikszentmihalyi, *Beyond Boredom and Anxiety* (San Francisco: Jossey-Bass, 1975); "Towards a Psychology of Optimal Experience," in *Review of Personality and Social Psychology, Volume 2*, ed. L. Wheeler (Beverly Hills, CA: Sage, 1982); and *Flow: The Psychology of Optimal Experience* (New York: Harper Perennial, 1990).

human needs for belonging and loving.[24] One researcher wrote, "People are happiest when they are involved in the community."[25] Research also shows that marital and romantic relationships positively correlate with happiness. This can be explained by the need to belong, attachment, the buffering effect of family, and the impact of social and marital well-being on adjacent life domains.[26]

Consider evaluating in what way and to what extent you create or experience opportunities for integration and participation or to build relationships with others.

- What do I do in my leisure time? Do I seek out activities with other people or stay isolated?
- What are some of the most meaningful relationships in my life? How am I investing in those relationships?

5. Emotional and Physical Well-Being

Physical well-being is a relatively obvious life domain impacting quality of life. Our health and physical wellness impacts everything we do. Robust well-being in this domain means you are actively working to optimize your health. You have the tools, opportunities, and willpower to improve or maintain your physical capabilities, and you are actively working to prevent physical deterioration. Aspects of well-being in this domain include access to healthcare, welfare services, and sports facilities.

Emotional well-being is less obvious and slightly more complex. How does a person experience emotional well-being when life gets hard? Does

---

[24] Erik Allardt, *About Dimensions of Welfare: An Exploratory Analysis of a Comparative Scandanavian Survey* (Helsinki, Finland: University of Helsinki, Research Group for Comparative Sociology, 1973); Dennis Rafael et al, "Quality of Life Indicators and Health: Current Status and Emerging Conceptions," *Social Indicators Research* 39 (1996), DOI: 10.1007/BF00300833.

[25] Robert D. Putnam, *Bowling Alone: The Collapse and Revival of the American Community* (New York: Simon & Schuster, 2000).

[26] Torfs and Goodman, "Quality of Life Introduction."

the "emotional well-being" only occur when circumstances are good and it's easy to feel positive emotions? No: emotional well-being refers to a person's ability to weather the bad times alongside the good, with hope and optimism.

Researchers describe the attitude of "self-compassion" as being key for maintaining this kind of emotional equilibrium. Self-compassion is not simply looking on the bright side during hard times; actually, it involves facing suffering head-on and being kind to yourself in moments that are hard and painful. For instance, if you got laid off during the worldwide pandemic, *instead* of thinking, "This is my fault. I'm such a loser," a self-compassionate attitude would express kind internal dialogue: "I feel scared and upset about this, and those feelings are legitimate. But I also know that this is a really common experience—especially right now. Even if I got fired because of my failure—well, failure is something that happens to a lot of people. I don't need to let this define me." Self-compassion researcher K. D. Neff wrote, "With self-compassion, instead of replacing negative feelings with positive ones, positive emotions are generated by embracing the negative ones."[27]

A self-compassionate mindset can make it easier to experience gratitude and life satisfaction[28] and build resilience,[29] and can even improve cognitive functioning and intrinsic motivation.[30] In all these ways, it can be a powerful tool for emotional well-being, especially in generating the positive perceptions required for subjective quality of life. This attitude looks for growth out of struggle. It acknowledges that life will often be hard and that painful

---

[27] Kirstin D. Neff, "The Development and Validation of a Scale to Measure Self-Compassion," *Self and Identity* 2 no. 3 (2003), DOI: 10.1080/15298860309027.

[28] William E. Breen et al, "Gratitude and Forgiveness: Convergence and Divergence on Self-Report and Informant Ratings," *Personality and Individual Differences* 49 no. 8 (2010), DOI: 10.1016/j.paid .2010.07.033.

[29] David A. Sbarra, Hillary L. Smith, and Matthias R. Mehl, "When Leaving Your Ex, Love Yourself: Observational Ratings of Self-Compassion Predict the Course of Emotional Recovery Following Marital Separation," *Psychological Science* 23 no. 3 (January 2012), DOI: 10.1177/0956797611429466.

[30] Neff, "The Development and Validation of a Scale to Measure Self-Compassion"; Kristin D. Neff, Ya-Ping Hsieh, and Kullaya Dejitterat, "Self-Compassion, Achievement Goals, and Coping with Academic Failure," *Self and Identity* 4 no. 3 (2005), DOI: 10.1080/13576500444000317.

emotions are okay and appropriate. It also seeks to grow and learn out of those hard times.

The way you perceive yourself and your life determines how you deal with it. When you perceive life with a self-compassionate attitude, you will more readily experience self-acceptance, consciously take care of your emotions and desires, and deal with the obstacles you face on a daily basis.

Physical and emotional well-being might seem so distinct as to each deserve their own domain, but actually, they are interrelated. Your physical conditions have an impact on your emotional well-being, and your emotional well-being has an impact on your body. For example, a physical injury can weigh on your nerves, causing emotional stress. But it also works the opposite way: stress can cause physical ailments, like psoriasis, weight loss or weight gain, neck injuries, and so on.

Consider how and to what extent you invest in emotional and physical well-being:

- How regularly do I invest time into my physical health, and do I make efforts to take care of my body in a positive way? (For example, getting physical exercise, sufficient sleep, eating a nutritional diet, practicing personal hygiene, avoiding habits of self-medicating, etc.)
- Do I have the tools and opportunities I need to work on my physical health?
- What is my internal dialogue like, particularly when things get hard?
- Do I allow myself to work through negative feelings with an attitude of self-compassion?

6. Economic and Material Well-Being

Making money: in a nutshell, that's what this domain is about. It's synonymous with financial well-being, economic well-being, and consumer well-being: essentially, this domain encompasses the physical comforts and safety afforded by wealth. Certainly, this domain impacts our quality of life. In order to feel safe, we need a secure living situation and material conditions that allow us to maintain our human dignity and function in a healthy way —that all requires some measure of financial stability. In fact, it's because of the importance of this domain that we don't argue for prioritizing quality of life *over* building wealth. Financial security, according to this research, can actually aid in quality of life—so long as profits are considered in balance with issues like sustainability.

However, it's worth noting that first-world Westerners often elevate this domain at the expense of all the others. And, interestingly, material well-being is not so much produced by the amount of money a person has in the bank, but by a person's *attitude* about the money that they have. Research has shown that the more someone is materialistic, the higher and more unrealistic their expectations for their standard of living, which leads to dissatisfaction.[31] This is another domain where we see objective circumstances and subjective perception both playing a part in a person's experience of quality of life.

Evaluate how and to what extent you experience material well-being or are progressing toward achieving a qualitatively sound living situation:

- To what degree do you feel safe, comfortable, and stable in your living situation?
- Are you consistently able to cover your expenses? Is money often a point of stress for you?
- Evaluate the degree to which you understand and practice wise strategies of personal finance.

7. Natural Living Environment

We had good reason for believing that the Experience Center's amazing natural grounds would have a positive effect on people. There's an amazing amount of research that attests to the benefits we experience when we get outside

---

[31] Sirgy, *The Psychology of Quality of Life.*

into nature. Even having plants in view within an urban setting can lower stress, frustration, and fatigue; it can also promote cognitive performance.[32] Some living and working environments can actually cause more stress if they are colorless, dark, and cramped. However, exposure to sunlight, growing things, and color can evoke positive moods and help people recover from fatigue.[33] Connection to nature can also help humans build resilience and experience better health.[34] It also—not surprisingly—causes people to take better care of the environment. Nature connectedness is associated with life satisfaction, vitality, and happiness.

However, "natural living environment" doesn't refer exclusively to nature—it simply refers to the environment in which you feel most natural. Many people feel most at home in a busy urban center, whereas other people prefer suburban life. Some people prefer to live alone, and others prefer a packed, lively household. Put simply, your environment has a significant impact on your experience of quality of life; ideally, your environment should help you feel rested, at home, and re-energized.

The domain of your living environment includes both your literal living environment (proximity to nature, rural versus urban context, housing situation, and so on) and the way in which you are able to interact with your environment. For example, if a city-dweller is suddenly unable to take advantage of all the social opportunities of living in a city—like many people experienced during the coronavirus pandemic, when businesses and event venues were shuttered—that will cause stress in this domain.

Consider how your environment impacts you and how you would like to invest in improving your natural living environment:

---

[32] Steven Kaplan, "The Restorative Benefits of Nature: Toward an Integrative Framework," *Journal of Environmental Psychology* 15 no. 3 (1995), DOI: 10.1016/0272-4944(95)90001-2.

[33] Rachel Kaplan and Steven Kaplan, *The Experience of Nature: A Psychological Perspective* (Cambridge: Cambridge University Press, 1989).

[34] Miles Richardson et al, "30 Day Wild: Development and Evaluation of a Large-Scale Nature Engagement Campaign to Improve Well-Being," *PLoS One* 11 no. 2 (February 2016), DOI: 10.1371/journal.pone.0149777.

- How often are you around growing things, like plants, trees, parks, and sunshine?
- Does your living and/or working environment promote a feeling of calm and focus, or does it cause you to feel stress?

8. General Life Satisfaction

This last domain puts the spotlight squarely on perspective: no one can experience abundant quality of life—regardless of how strong they are in the life domains—if they are determined to be dissatisfied with their lot. And conversely, if a person maintains a hopeful growth perspective that seeks to learn through challenges and practice gratitude, that person will most likely experience a high degree of life satisfaction, even if they have deficits in some of the life domains.

Self-awareness is a critical element of experiencing general life satisfaction. The extent to which people can connect to their feelings and accept them will have a large impact on how quickly they're able to process negative emotions, learn from them, and arrive at positive emotions. Inner dialogue and frame of mind are also important: if you constantly beat yourself up internally, you will struggle to enjoy life. However, the self-compassionate inner dialogue that we discussed in the "emotional well-being" domain can help you build resilience and greater satisfaction, especially during hard times.

General life satisfaction is improved by pursuing activities that feel meaningful, in accordance with your core purpose and core values. It's also impacted by efforts to govern your thought-life: by improving your affective well-being (moderating the frequency and intensity of positive and negative emotions and moods), emotional well-being as discussed earlier, and cognitive well-being (how people evaluate their lives overall, in terms of life satisfaction). Finally, it's informed by your experience in the specific life domains—for instance, your job satisfaction, marital happiness, and so on. These objective and subjective factors will all help contribute to your positive evaluation of your life, thus helping you to experience life satisfaction.

Consider in what way and to what extent you invest in increasing your self-awareness and self-acceptance and give meaning to your life.

- Can you easily identify your different emotions and explain why you're feeling them or how they came about?
- In your thought-life, do you tend to be hard on yourself or accept yourself for all your strengths and weaknesses?
- Do you spend time in activities that feel meaningful?

STEP 3: BUILDING SELF-AWARENESS ABOUT TENSIONS

As you read through the eight life domains, it's possible you were able to see that in some areas, you're experiencing robust quality of life. In other areas, you might see deficiencies. If you were able to recognize those differences, then you've gathered profoundly important information. We call these deficiencies "points of tension," and they describe any area of life that is not yet where you'd like it to be. These areas of tension can refer to a relationship, an aspect of your lifestyle, the way you spend your time, your living environment, and so on—basically, any part of life where things don't feel quite right.

By building awareness about these points of tension, you can be more successful wielding agency in moving toward improved quality of life in your own context. We had described these eight domains as the "necessary ingredients" for quality of life, so let's return to that metaphor. Imagine someone is getting ready to cook a great meal. Let's say, for the sake of the illustration, that this person has managed to collect all the necessary ingredients; all eight domains are represented.

However, that person must still cook their meal using the tools they have in their available context. A kitchen may be small, dark, and cramped or large, bright and spacious. There may be a wide array of tools to choose from or limited options for what's available. Neither context needs to prevent a person from enjoying the cooking process or producing something wonderful. However, the process may be easier or harder depending on the context. That's simply reality.

Still, if you're highly self-aware, you can make the best of even a hard context. Think of a cook in a small kitchen with only a few tools who has been cooking in that context for decades. That cook has most likely learned to optimize their tools and recipes to make fantastic meals, even within limitations; in other words, quality of life is possible, even within constraints. However, it's also likely the cook could give you a clear description of how they'd like the kitchen to change so that they could do more. In recognizing that deficiency—that tension—the cook has a clearer sense of purpose. They know where they would like to go to bring about desired change.

The third step in self-steering toward quality of life requires building self-awareness, particularly around points of tension. Points of tension can help us recognize where growth or change is needed. For instance, feelings of tension at work might help you recognize that you need to resolve an issue with a coworker. Feeling a sense of gloom when entering your dark apartment may help you recognize that this is not a space that is serving you. Feeling dissonance over your path in life might help spotlight that your current activity is not in line with your purpose and doesn't feel rewarding or meaningful. All those points of tension provide valuable information about where and how you might need to take agency in initiating positive change.

Points of tension can help us recognize where growth or change is needed.

In an ever-evolving world, it is important to recognize these dissatisfactions, shortages, or tensions and to consider them important sources of information: they are alerting you to an underlying wish for transformation. Try to translate the dissatisfactions, shortages, or tensions into desired changes that would better reflect your purpose and can contribute to its realization. Describe the future change opportunities you'd like to see and then break them down into specific steps that you want to realize, moving toward that desired future.

Think about where you might be experiencing points of tension in your own life, and consider how they might have useful information for you:

- What tensions can I register within myself? (i.e., Where do I feel dissatisfaction, shortages, or tensions in my life? How can these points of tension give me information about the changes I'd like to make? How might they inform my purpose of where I want to go?)
- What desired changes would I like to experience within myself and/or my circumstances? (e.g., "I want to work toward this goal.")
- What personal burdens, if any, keep me from working toward my purpose (e.g., "My kitchen is too small.")
- Where do I have capacity to strive for my purpose? (e.g., "But I can still try to make a great meal.")
- Where do I have strong capabilities? What are some of my personal limitations/weaknesses?

Having self-awareness about your capabilities and limitations will help shed light on where you can take action toward desired change and where you may need to accept your current reality. These personal facts will characterize your journey toward greater quality of life. You may find yourself beginning the journey with more obstacles than other people have, but it's important to note: no obstacle needs to impede your journey from happening.

"The journey of a thousand miles begins with a single step."

—Lao-tzu

Jake's Life Domains and Tensions

Let's return now to Jake. Where is he in the eight quality of life domains? What tensions, if any, does he feel in pursuing them?

- Jake's enrollment as a college student means he's encountering many opportunities for **learning and personal growth**. In addition to everything he's learning in his classes, he's engaging with cultures he's never encountered before, he's discovering new things about himself, and he's forming a clearer sense of what he believes in. This domain is a strong area for him.

- However, he feels some tension in the domain of **self-determination**: he knows what *he* wants to do with his life, but he constantly feels reminded of the potential obstacles that feel like they might impede him from achieving his goal, namely not having enough money and pressure from his parents.

- Jake is experiencing some deficiencies in his **productivity and activity**. Although he's doing schoolwork all the time, it doesn't feel productive in the same way that helping kids through the after-school program felt productive. He's also struggling to participate in the same activities that used to energize him, like games of pickup basketball. Between his classes, his Uber driving, and trying to connect socially at college, Jake hasn't found a new routine that includes hobbies or exercise.

- Regarding **leisure and social inclusion**, as a freshman at college, Jake experiences a great deal of new social opportunities. Although some of these feel shallow and unsatisfying, others feel exciting and meaningful—especially those with Lana, a young woman in his chemistry lab group and a romantic interest. He doesn't have much free time for leisure, though; he often feels stressed and hurried.

- Jake experiences a strong level of **emotional well-being**. From his time at the after-school program, Jake participated in a number of workshops and mentoring programs that helped him build a strong level of self-awareness and maturity; he brings a problem-solving approach to challenges. Jake experiences solid **physical well-being**, but to a lesser extent since he's moved to college. Although he's young and healthy, he's been getting less sleep, less exercise, and less healthy home-cooking since he moved from home.

- Jake feels deficiencies in **economic and material well-being**. He's scraping by on his earnings from Uber driving but constantly feels the burden of his loans and his relative poverty. Rarely can he afford to go out for meals or activities with friends. Still, he has housing, healthcare insurance, and a decent safety net should anything happen, so this is not truly a critical area for Jake—just a point of real tension.

- Jake's dorm room is dark and small; he finds it depressing. However, he's able to experience a positive **natural living environment** on his college campus, which has lots of trees, green grass, and beautiful landscaping.

- In terms of **general life satisfaction**, Jake would give himself a six out of ten. Although he's excited about his future, has a strong level of emotional well-being, and is regularly exposed to new social and learning opportunities, he also feels stressed and tired a lot. He senses that he'd feel a lot better with more sleep and more exercise—and more money in his bank account. He'd also like a girlfriend.

Someone like Jake is highly aware of their own possibilities and potential to achieve their goals—but they're also up against some obstacles and limitations. Are those obstacles insurmountable? Can Jake move beyond his limitations? Can he pursue greater quality of life, or is he at risk of apathy, complacency, and failure?

The question, in other words, is one of agency. Jake holds the steering wheel in his journey toward quality of life—but can he actually create momentum in that direction? In our next chapter, we want to begin to explore the ways in which limitations can be trespassed and obstacles overcome.

Perhaps Jake—and all of us—have greater agency to pursue quality of life than we realize.

EXPLORE FURTHER

If you'd like to learn more, discuss this content with others, or access tools for your own application, go to the interactive section of the book using this QR code.

CHAPTER TWO

PERSON TO PERSON

When conditions are so essential for humans,
let us make more human conditions.

—José Saramago, recipient of the 1998
Nobel Prize in Literature

Jake collapsed onto his dorm room bed and pushed his hair back. His room-mate, Leon, glanced over at him from his video game. "Ramirez. Why the long face?" he asked.

Jake sighed. "I don't know how I'm going to pay for school, man."

Leon's answer was easy. "Just take out loans. That's what I'd be doing if my dad wasn't footing the bill." He refocused his attention to the flashing images on his screen.

"I can't take out any more loans," Jake said. "My parents are on the hook for too much money already. They run a convenience store; they can't be responsible for all my debt."

"So get a job," Leon suggested. On his screen, something exploded.

"I'm already doing Uber driving," Jake said. "It's not enough. I can't pay for housing, and groceries, and school with just Uber. I don't have enough time. Plus, I've got to study."

Leon was not deterred. "So get a better job. My uncle works graveyard as a security guard. He makes $40 an hour. He could probably hook you up."

Jake thought about that. "Yeah, but…" He sighed again. "My mom would hate that. She told me to do whatever I needed to do to get good grades and make the family proud. How am I going to keep up my grades if I have to work nights?"

Leon pounded the keys on his keyboard, apparently finishing the level. He swiveled his desk chair around to look at his roommate. He was out of easy solutions. "Yeah, man. I don't know how you're going to pay for school either."

Jake sat up, his stress suddenly replaced by frustration. "This system sucks. In order to get a good job to make good money, I have to go into crazy debt. That's so stupid."

"What kind of job do you want to get?" Leon asked, his problem-solving wheels turning again. "If you get rich, you can pay off your loans later, no problem. What do you want to do?"

Jake looked at him grimly. "Be a science teacher."

Leon just laughed. "Oh man, good luck. You're going to be in debt forever if you want to be a teacher. Better to be a doctor or something. Or—I've got a better idea! Get really good at video games and livestream yourself. I know a guy who makes over six figures doing that. He plays video games for sixteen hours a day and makes buckets of cash. That's *my* backup plan." He turned back to his computer and reloaded his game. Within seconds, there were new explosions on the screen.

Jake just stared at his roommate. "I don't want to play video games for sixteen hours a day. And I don't want to be a doctor. I want to teach kids." Leon didn't respond. Looking for an excuse to leave his dorm room—and his overly helpful roommate—Jake grabbed his textbooks. "I'm going to the library," he said. "See you later."

On the walk to the library, Jake drank in the sight of the blooming trees and large green quads near the stately old brick buildings. What a contrast it was to the gray cement block where he'd grown up. He thought about his street—the blinking neon sign of his parents' bodega, which never seemed to have all the letters illuminated at the same time. The porn shop on the corner. The empty, weed-filled lot where he and his siblings used to play soccer. He wondered what kind of street Leon grew up on. Why did money feel like a nonissue to Leon, when it seemed to have all the power to make or break Jake's future?

All his life, Jake felt like he'd been running up against invisible boundaries. The financial system, education system, housing system, economic system—they all somehow seemed to favor the people who had grown up in nice neighborhoods and attended nice schools but seemed stacked against a kid like him. He wished people could just meet him—just talk to him, hear his story, hear his dreams and ambitions, learn about his skills—and then make a decision about whether or not he was worth a loan, or an apartment, or their investment. He wished things were different.

He wondered if they *could* be different.

THE CONSTRAINTS OF THE BOX

Jake's struggle is not unique. Many of us have felt boxed in at one point or another by crippling debt, or a toxic boss, or a bank that didn't endorse our business plan. In fact, there are many ways that a person's ability to pursue full quality of life runs up against constraints, thanks to various hindrances posed by the systems and hierarchies in our world. You might feel as though your possibilities in life are restricted to whatever you can experience within the confines of that box: a box with solid sides made up of inequitable systems, containing power plays, rules, roles, and limitations.

What is the point of all these organizational systems anyway? The organizations that run our world are generally there to ensure stuff is protected, people are organized, and no one takes advantage of the systems. For example, business hierarchies have evolved to supposedly maximize efficiency and profits. Militaries exist to protect a country's resources and citizens. Governments generate laws to mandate positive behavior and offer aid within a set of parameters.

So bureaucracies exist for a reason—the walls of the box are meant to offer security, structure, and protection. But so often, those tall, strong sides of the box hinder quality of life.

Here are examples of real people—either that we know personally or who have been documented in the news—that the current systems are failing:[35]

- Lori Creek works a nine-to-five job at a Fortune 500 company. After attending the annual company meeting, where she felt inspired by the discussion of the mission statement and avowed cultural practices, she pitched a great idea to her boss—but found that no one was actually interested in her contribution. She was given the advice to "just keep doing your job." She realized there was no room for real growth or contribution. Her life domains related to personal growth, self-determination, meaning, and productivity are all hindered in her workplace environment.

- Allison Gamba was an extremely successful stockbroker for Goldman Sachs in the early 2000s. After nine years working for the company, setting records for turning low-performing stocks into top earners, managing a team, and establishing herself as a top performer in the equities division, she was passed over for promotions.[36] She also earned roughly half of what some of her male counterparts made, issues that were made public in a class-action 2013 lawsuit

---

[35] We have changed the names of our personal acquaintances to protect their privacy.

[36] Alexia Fernández Campbell, "The Did Everything Right—and Still Hit the Glass Ceiling. Now, These Women Are Suing America's Top Companies for Equal Pay," *Vox*, December 3, 2019, https://www.vox.com/the-highlight/2019/12/3/20948425/equal-pay-lawsuits-pay-gap-glass-ceiling.

against Goldman Sachs. Racial and gender pay gaps are still a reality for people like Allison, who are unfairly denied abundance in their life domains related to economic well-being, pursuit of growth, and self-determination because of power plays related to advancement and pay gaps.

- Bob Phillips is an expert tiler who has been receiving disability payments while struggling with alcohol addiction, diabetes, and occasional homelessness. Bob knows that it would be good for him to start working again, which would build him up in the domains of personal growth, self-determination, productivity, and a stable living environment. However, if he starts working, he'll lose his safety net of the disability payments, and the rules don't allow him to try working for a limited time. He's afraid he'll fail to stay sober if he starts working. Ultimately, he concludes it would be better to coast on the disability and remain idle.

- Byron "Reckful" Bernstein was a famous video gamer with over 900,000 followers, reported by the Gazette Review in 2017 as one of the wealthiest gamers in the world.[37] In spite of that, he struggled with depression and mental health, and ultimately committed suicide in July of 2020.[38] Although he experienced abundance in the life domain of material comfort, there were tragic deficits in his physical and emotional well-being. This apparently is common among gamers, who may struggle with gaming addiction, a desire to escape, and poor self-care habits, like insufficient sleep, a sedentary lifestyle, and very little time spent outside.[39] There may

---

[37] Jessica Deml, "Top 10 Richest Gaming Streamers," *Gazette Review*, September 8, 2017, https://gazettereview.com/2017/09/top-10-richest-gaming-streamers.

[38] Jim Heath, "Top Gamer Byron 'Reckful' Bernstein Commits Suicide—Had Struggled with Depression," Jim Heath.TV, July 2, 2020, https://jimheath.tv/2020/07/top-gamer-byron-reckful-bernstein-commits-suicide-had-struggled-with-depression.

[39] Chris Foy, "How Healthygamer.gg Is Addressing Mental Health Stigmas," FHE Health, September 11, 2020, https://fherehab.com/learning/healthygamer-gg-mental-health.

also be deficits in the area of social interactions: popular gamers like Bernstein are "connected" to hundreds of thousands of followers but may experience few deep social connections in real life.

- Sara Maldova is a teacher who requested a more flexible part-time schedule when she became a mom. However, the district rules did not allow her to job-share or go down to part time. She was forced to choose to prioritize either her job and economic well-being or her social interaction with her family and general life satisfaction.

- The Seymour family owns a piece of beachfront property in a resort town. They decided they would love to open their beach to the public to enjoy but quickly learned that they would be held responsible if anyone got hurt or drowned while enjoying their beachfront. They decided to forgo their desire to contribute to the well-being of their community and help people experience health in their natural living environment domain so that they weren't at risk for being sued.

- Rachelle Faroul, a Black woman living in Philadelphia, sought to get a mortgage loan in 2017. The *Chicago Tribune* writes that, in spite of her large amount of savings, Faroul "was rejected twice by lenders when she tried to buy a brick row house close to Malcolm X Park in Philadelphia, where African-Americans were 2.7 times as likely as whites to be denied a conventional mortgage."[40] Because of power plays, discrimination, and rules, she was hindered in her pursuit of a natural living environment, in addition to economic and material well-being.

- Canadian music artist Kiesza (real name Kiesa Rae Ellestad) signed

---

[40] Aaron Glantz and Emmanuel Martinez, "Modern-Day Redlining: How Banks Block People of Color from Homeownership," *Chicago Tribune*, February 17, 2018, https://www.chicagotribune.com/business/ct-biz-modern-day-redlining-20180215-story.html.

with the major record label Island Records, but quickly began to feel trapped by the label's expectations and demands. She told the *New Statesman*, "It wasn't about growth and longevity. It was about: how much are we profiting right now? They weren't even really concerned about me as a person."[41] She even said she felt as though she lost her identify. The power plays of the label constrained her ability to grow as an artist and produce work that she believed in.

We could come up with thousands of examples where quality of life is constrained in some way by systematic red tape, power plays, fear, or greed. Some of us may have felt forced to choose between pursuing our passion versus pursuing a job that would pay better. Many older people may feel trapped by limited options heading into their retirement years. Many younger people may feel their opportunities are choked by red tape or the weight of debt.

Sometimes the constraints are overt, like when government agencies or workplace hierarchies deny a person's opportunities. Sometimes the constraints are more subtle, like in the case of Byron "Reckful" Bernstein, who may have felt so overwhelmed by social media pressure that he continued down an unhealthy path and neglected to take needed steps to prioritize his general well-being.

There are also innumerable examples of human connection being thwarted by current systems and cultural trends. Probably, most of us sense the growing polarities of our time. There is an increasing distance between how a product arrives in our hands versus where it began. There are disconnects created by social media, which promises to help us connect with others even as it proliferates harsh rhetoric and siloed viewpoints. There are more and more venomous exchanges between members of different political parties gathering their views from different sets of "facts."

---

[41] Ellen Peirson-Hagger, "'I Lost My identity': The Artists Who Left Major Record Deals to Form Their Own Indie Labels," *The New Statesman*, July 8, 2020, https://www.newstatesman.com/culture/music-theatre/2020/07/i-lost-my-identity-artists-who-left-major-record-deals-form-their-own.

We are not only constrained by systems; we are increasingly disconnected from each other. This is not a world that prioritizes quality of life. This is not a world that facilitates connections from person to person.

Often, we *think* we have power. We think we can steer our life's direction, but at some point, many of us realize that's not actually true. At that point, we realize that the box is not offering us protection so much as it is hindering our freedom. We might spot a crack in the wall—the recognition that, if things were different and we could just get beyond the constraints of the box, the possibility for greater quality of life exists. Our fictional character, Jake, spots this crack in the wall when he tells Leon that he feels frustrated with how his educational growth seems tied to financial instability and debt. He recognizes that—if things were different—he might have a chance at greater quality of life and financial freedom.

The crack in the wall: recognizing that the possibility for greater quality of life exists beyond the confines of the box.

But how do you squeeze through that crack? When you recognize that things *could* be better but feel powerless to do anything about it, feelings of frustration and emptiness can quickly follow. Maybe it would be better to ignore the cracks in the wall entirely and just make up your mind to live within the constraints that exist. Maybe it would be better to simply tell yourself, "For the next thirty years, until I retire, I'm just not going to think about how I could live differently." None of us can do anything about it anyway—can we?

Can we?

Uninventing Organizations

There's a well-known book called *Reinventing Organizations,* by Frédéric Laloux and Etienne Appert.[42] We like this book: it started an entire movement that led to holacracies and self-governance in the work place, which we think was positive in profound ways. However, perhaps things could be taken a step further. After all, reinventing organizations still maintains the "organization" element. It might be a better box—but it's still a box. Perhaps some organizational "uninventing" is in order.

We need organizations for two main reasons: first, they facilitate people working together toward a shared goal. And second, they provide a bank account and a tax number.

Well, what if people find new ways to work together toward a common goal? What if there is no board, no shareholders, and no boss, but instead, all of the value of the work is held by the people collaborating? What if there could be a way to store financial value apart from a bank account and tax number?

In the late 1800s, many manufacturers were looking for a way to make a better horse-drawn carriage. Inventor Karl Benz had a different idea: he decided to build an automobile. Perhaps *we* need to stop thinking about how to make better horse-drawn carriages; perhaps we should think of how to make something entirely new and find ways to live apart from organizations altogether.

We don't need organizations to actively organize ourselves in collaboration with others. We *do* need guidance, though. We need a vision for *how* a world might look that prioritizes quality of life and restores person to person connection.

---

[42] Frédéric Laloux and Etienne Appert, Reinventing Organizations: An Illustrated Invitation to Join the Conversation on Next-Stage Organizations (Brussels: Nelson Parker, 2016).

We don't need organizations to actively organize ourselves.

So—what might that look like? Here's an idea.

A PERSON TO PERSON SOCIETY

In our last chapter, we considered what humans need to thrive. Now we start to sketch out characteristics of a society that would prioritize those needs. In the coming chapters, we'll explore more deeply how to realize each of these characteristics.

The ingredients for robust quality of life:
a defined core purpose, core values, abundance in each of the
life domains, freedom to pursue one's goals, and personal
agency to "self-steer" toward those aims.

A Person to Person society seeks to provide an
environment that fosters all of the above.

An Environment, Not a System

A Person to Person society is not a thing. It is not an organization; it is not a system. It is an *environment* meant to facilitate people's unhindered pursuit of quality of life.

A system is a thing. It is a nonhuman entity that can work independently. Systems are not there to support individuals; an organization or system mainly exists to serve itself. An environment, on the other hand, invites engagement and exploration. It allows individuals to move and evolve within it—to engage with others and be seen without constraints.

The Person to Person environment is not a box or even a structure made from multiple boxes; it's more like a playground. All the subsequent descriptions describe this environment further.

Self-Aware People

A Person to Person environment pushes people to recognize their dreams and needs according to the quality of life domains. It encourages people to acknowledge their struggles and grow beyond them in an environment of support, safe communication, and transparency, as discussed in Chapters 3 and 4. And it's an environment that fosters real connection with other authentic people rather than their job title, or social currency, or political affiliation, or curated online persona.

No Invisible Barriers

A Person to Person environment allows people to do what they want to do, in the way they want to do it. It seeks to remove the invisible barriers that so often constrain our efforts—the clutter and complications of frameworks, power structures, and hierarchies. In the place of those entities, it seeks to connect people directly. You chart your *own* way on the map toward your vision of where you hope to go. Rather than forming your route based on the roads already there, you have the freedom to draw new ones. When natural obstacles present themselves—which they inevitably will—you have the freedom to be outspoken about what they are.

Personal Responsibility

For this reason, it's an environment that pushes people to take responsibility for their own well-being. Thriving requires effort. If you want to start a business, your ability to get a loan will depend on the quality of your business plan and idea—not by what you look like, bureaucratic politics, or formal requirements like a credit history. This removes the culture of blame: we sink or swim depending on the effort we put in. Because of this, each person needs to contribute and put in real work. That requires an intentional mindset and attitude, which we'll also discuss in Chapters 3 and 4.

Connections Happen Person to Person

It's an ecosystem where people rely on other people, rather than entities, to make something work. Loans are given person to person. Investments are made person to person. Collaboration occurs person to person. Needs are met person to person. Instead of starting with a framework and determining whether or not a person fits into that mold, we start with the person and consider what framework will best suit their ambitions. We ask: What are their needs? What are their capabilities? People discuss things with each other and make adjustments and modifications until they align toward what they want to achieve. When a mistake is made, people are honest about their role in that error and reflect on how they can do things differently next time. These dynamics can play out in a family, a workspace, or an entire movement.

Process, Not Product

A Person to Person ecosystem prioritizes process, not product. Putting all our efforts toward achieving an outcome or generating a *product* can often result in long working hours, friction toward competitors, and unhealthy personal habits. In other words, it can work against quality of life. By focusing our efforts toward optimizing a *process*, which aims toward a goal, we are freed to attend to the people we're working with and practice habits that aid in self-care. This ensures that the *how* of creating something is just as worthwhile as the end goal itself, which helps optimize quality of life from start to finish.

Global Network

It's an environment that is not limited by the stigmas and prejudices of a local place but—via modern technology—enables access to a global network of people using tools like the cloud, remote meeting tools, and cryptocurrency. Even if someone in your own zip code doesn't like your business idea, technology can enable you to pitch that idea to any number of collaborators all over the world. Provided it's a good enough idea, there will be plenty of people around the world who may say, "I like your idea, and I'd like to contribute. I could help you with money, or my time, or my network." Whether or not your idea goes forward will be determined by its merit, not by your personality or charisma, and not by boundaries imposed by banks, geographic region, race, religion, and so on. It will also be determined by your willingness to apply feedback. If you receive input on an idea—"I like your idea, but I see some ways it could improve"—you can apply that feedback, pitch the idea again, and find your collaborators.

Person to Person doesn't necessarily require that people physically engage *in person*. We believe it is possible to evolve toward worldwide "in-person" interactions without physical contact. To illustrate the contrast, consider the steps you would take if you wanted to get a bank loan in a traditional way. You would go to a bank, talk to a loan broker, fill out paperwork, and submit to a credit check; the loan would be handled by an unseen team of underwriters and most likely sold eventually to another lender. All of those interactions would be mostly unseen and deeply impersonal. In a Person to Person environment, one person engages directly with another. You have the opportunity to share your idea directly with a potential investor; you could talk with them personally, learn their name, see their face. A Person to Person society seeks to transform impersonal transactions into personal interactions.

Tools, Not Rules

A Person to Person society is built on tools, not rules. Rules are imposed on us, and they can squeeze the life out of the people they're imposed upon. Think of how insurance restrictions can prevent people from getting needed care or how corporate rules can restrict creativity. Tools are simply practical. Tools are invented and built by the people using them to fit their needs. They are dynamic and continually adapted to keep on supporting that need; when they no longer serve the people using them, they cease to exist. Whereas a rule is imposed upon us and can create restrictions, tools enable people to act and operate with greater ease.

No Hierarchies

A Person to Person environment does not have hierarchies. People come together around a common goal, which is determined by the pursuit of their own core purpose. They each freely commit to shared values and behavioral practices, which they will form together in a Collaborative Agreement (discussed in Chapter 5). No one can hire or fire anyone else; no one gives you your pay; no person's work is constrained to their job description. Instead, people identify needed areas for contribution and contribute according to their skillsets. That doesn't mean there aren't leaders; there will always be natural leaders in any group who use their gifts to help others define a direction. However, there is no formal leadership structure that gives any one person more power than another.

Power and Money Separated

But since people still need money to live and money is often attached to power, a Person to Person environment must therefore separate money from power. This is accomplished by attaching compensation to effort, which each person determines for themselves, as discussed in Chapter 6.

Value and Stuff Separated

A Person to Person ecosystem needs to find a way to avoid owning *stuff*, since the protection of *stuff* is largely what has led to wars, conflict, constraining rules, boundaries, and structures. So let's separate value from stuff. Let's find a way to hold the value of a house without actually owning the structure itself. Let's find a way to hold the value of company shares without actually being a shareholder. This can be accomplished through making assets sovereign—self-owned; not owned by people, but *used* by people. As people invest in a Sovereign Asset's value, they can hold that value for themselves. Sovereign Assets are discussed more in Chapters 7 and 9. When power is removed, and hierarchies are removed, and money tied to things is removed, then you have an open environment for people to work together.

In a nutshell, this kind of environment seeks to help people move beyond limiting power structures or systems that promote inequality and dissatisfaction, freeing people to experience greater quality of life. Also, a Person to Person community works by exchanging skills via collaboration, fostering authentic connection.

More quality of life; more human connection: that's where we're going.

e

A Person to Person environment seeks to create greater quality of life and more human connection.

QUESTIONS RAISED

This concept is deeply uncomfortable for some and seems totally unrealistic to others. It might feel like we're telling you to jump out of a plane without a parachute. If you're scratching your head with questions at this point, you wouldn't be the only one. So let's address a few.

What about the People Who Like Life in the Box?

Some people function best within structured systems with clear rules. Some people have been able to create a great life, in spite of the challenges posed by hierarchies and power plays. Our ideas for a Person to Person society do not require anyone to leave the box. We're not smashing the box; we're not seeking to destroy anything. It has never been our goal to be destructive in any way. Rather than dismantling anything, we're seeking to build something alongside preexisting systems.

In doing so, the Person to Person model attempts to provide an alternative to the status quo. It's meant to provide a way that things could be done differently within our present reality. That's why we call the Person to Person society a "heterotopia," "a different place." We're simply trying to widen the crack in the wall so that people have the freedom to explore a different world beyond it.

In describing an environment where people *could* live a life outside of current constraints, we're inviting you to try it. What people do with this freedom and this environment, well—that's up to you. That's not up to us to steer or decide or otherwise influence. Everyone will make their own version of how to apply (or reject) these ideas.

"You cannot swim for new horizons until you have courage to lose sight of the shore."

—William Faulkner, author

Don't Leadership Hierarchies Generally Work Best for Getting Things Done?

There's no problem with leadership in a Person to Person environment. There are still leaders, but they don't have the right to steer others without their permission. They don't have authority over others, but they do have influence. Organizations often create layers of inefficiency, which means you have people with great ideas who never are elevated high enough to make a difference. In a Person to Person environment, those people have opportunities to share their ideas in a meaningful way. That will be discussed more in Chapters 4 and 5.

A Person to Person environment *does* remove the competition element. When collaboration is allowed to occur in an environment that is not competitive, there is research that implies *more* can actually get done. Most people are familiar with Darwin's natural selection theory, which implies essentially that the strongest survive and the weak die out. However, there's another theory, known as multilevel selection theory, that suggests our survival depends less on individual prowess and more on the quality of an entire group.

In a famous experiment, evolutionary researcher William Muir set out to breed a top egg-laying henhouse, using evolutionary strategies.[43] He first put together a "dream team" group of high-egg-producing hens. However, the result of all these top egg producers being together was disastrous: they were prone to be far more competitive. Some hens pecked others to death;

---

[43] Tracy Ross and Melanie Davis-McAfee, "Scientists Use Chickens to Study New Theory of Multi-Level Evolution," in *All Things Considered*, produced by WKMS, October 8, 2018, https://www.wkms.org/science/2018-10-08/scientists-use-chickens-to-study-new-theory-of-multi-level-evolution.

others bullied each other to the point that the bullied hens stopped producing eggs. In this case, simply trying to breed the "strongest" individual hens actually led to lower egg-laying and violence—quite counterproductive for perpetuating the species.

A second henhouse was assembled. This one was a mixture of hens; some were top layers, and other hens in the group were less prolific in their laying but were used to sharing their space with the top-laying hens. The results of this group were profoundly different. Not only did every hen survive, but actually, their total egg production increased by 160 percent. The NPR program *All Things Considered* analyzed the study's conclusion:

> William Muir's experiment revealed the inaccuracies of thinking that creating a good society is merely a matter of picking the "best" individuals and breeding them for their hereditary traits. Rather, adaptive traits like cooperation, promoting harmony, and community building play a far larger role in evolutionary survival than Charles Darwin might have thought. In the case of the chicken experiment, laying more eggs was the end goal. By focusing only on the increased egg production, other tasks essential to the maintenance of the environment, often performed by weaker members, were ignored and the environment was damaged. The inclusion of individuals who contribute or promote cooperation and consensus building proved to be far more beneficial to the domain, regardless of the number of "top" genetic examples.[44]

In other words, multilevel selection theory posits that we will function at our best within an environment that promotes collaboration, not competition. A collaborative process can actually help people accomplish *more*, and at a higher quality. If that's the case, then removing workplace hierarchies could lead to us getting more done—not less.

---

[44] Ibid.

We function at our best within an environment that
promotes collaboration, not competition.

We also believe that traditional power hierarchies help foster a culture of blame. If something goes wrong at work, the blame lands on the manager, or project leader, or director. If you don't like your job, you blame your boss. In a Person to Person environment, people are equally responsible to participate and bring something to the table. That encourages people to take personal agency in helping to make something excellent.

How Will Anything Get Done If Fickle Followers Change Their Preference of Leader?

Wouldn't project momentum grind to a halt if people aren't obligated to stick with a specific leader who can help see it through? We think this can be largely resolved through a collaborative matrix, which we'll discuss in Chapter 3, which keeps everyone focused on achieving the goal of the collaborative. This tool asks people to identify where it is they want to go. They then find other people who care about that same goal and develop a shared commitment to seeing that endeavor through. This means each person is intrinsically motivated to work at their best and align their efforts in a series of decisions that serve their own interests—which, conveniently, will also serve the interests of the other people they're working alongside. Researcher Fischer noted that "the respect of others is crucial to subjective wellbeing."[45] The Person to Person environment, which encourages collaboration toward a shared goal, fosters this kind of mutual respect.

---

[45] Fischer, *The Good Life*.

How Can Any Society Operate without Rules and Laws?

By developing an environment in which people are incentivized to play fair, feel safe to be their authentic selves, have productive avenues in which to get their needs met, and are excited about working with others toward a shared goal, then many of the problems that laws seek to address become nonissues.

In William Golding's novel *Lord of the Flies*, a group of British schoolboys are marooned on a desert island after a plane crash. At first, the boys do their best to form a plan for rescue and a kind of governmental order for their discussions. Leaders emerge, and different boys agree to different responsibilities. But very quickly, the efforts at civility turn savage. By the end of the novel, the boys have seemingly devolved into beasts, prone to violence, bloodshed, and chaos. Golding's message seems to be that humanity is inherently evil. Only within the laws and rules imposed by higher authorities is civility possible.

We disagree with this, but our argument is not that humanity is inherently good. Rather, we believe that humanity is capable of real goodness within an environment that allows for and encourages it. Golding's desert island, for instance, was not such an environment. In the novel, the boys' survival is at risk and their rampant fears quickly translate into brutal power grabs. Many corporate environments, likewise, can foster fear and distrust. If we are to operate with thoughtfulness, rationality, and calm tempers, we need to feel safety and trust.

The Robbers Cave experiment, conducted by Muzafer Sherif in the 1950s, puts real data behind this point.[46] In this experiment, Sherif examined intergroup conflict by studying two groups of twelve-year-old, Caucasian, middle-class boys from a Protestant background in a summer-camp setting—not unlike Golding's British schoolboys. During the first week of the experiment, the two groups were isolated from each other and guided in bonding

---

[46] Saul McLeod, "Robbers Cave Experiment," Simply Psychology, published 2008, updated 2020, https://www.simplypsychology.org/robbers-cave.html.

activities to strengthen each group's shared identity. Each group organically formed group structure dynamics with leaders, inside jokes, and group norms. They even came up with team names: the Eagles and the Rattlers. During the second week, the two groups were introduced to each other and pitted against each other in competition. With each subsequent competition, tensions between the groups escalated, especially when "winning" was tied to a resource, like getting to eat first or getting a pocket knife as a reward when losers got "nothing." The competition-driven conflict became so intense that the researchers (posing as counselors) had to take steps to separate the groups and cool them down.

When the groups were reintroduced to each other, various unifying strategies were attempted, like doing a fireworks show with both groups in attendance. However, simply spending time together did nothing to ease the tensions. What *did* ultimately cause the two groups to begin mixing and bonding with one another was when they had a superordinate goal to accomplish, which required the effort of both groups. Again, this was particularly powerful when a shared resource was at stake. In one shared-goal scenario, the camp's water supply had been tampered with and cut off. The two groups worked together to identify the problem and figure out ways to unclog the water pipe. There were suggestions and collaboration across the two groups. When the water finally came back on, the Rattlers willingly let the Eagles drink first, since they didn't have canteens and were thirstier. After several experiences where the two groups were put in a position to collaborate on a shared goal, tensions noticeably eased. By the end of the conflict resolution week, the boys' seating arrangement in the cafeteria—with different group members sitting together—showed the power of the collaborative environment to heal tensions caused by the competitive atmosphere.

The environment that we will describe in greater depth in the subsequent chapters has the potential to allow people the safety and reassurance needed for productive collaboration to exist. When transparency is a given, when respect is afforded at all times, when tensions are regularly voiced and resolved, when groups can all align toward a common goal—an environment is created that allows for the kind of higher-level thinking required to productively work together toward a common purpose.

All of These Descriptions Sound Overly Vague

That's true: each of these aspects of a Person to Person environment would need quite a bit more explanation in order to explain how they could realistically work. In fact, they might each need their own chapter.

(That's why we will be giving them each their own chapter.)

This Still Feels like Jumping out of a Plane without a Parachute

We're not asking anyone to jump out of a plane. In fact, we're not asking anyone to even step off the ground. The steps described in the subsequent chapters are gradual and optional. In fact—they're ones we've tried out in our own life.

PERSON TO PERSON CAMPING

Our family tried out a Person to Person approach when we took a camping trip three years ago. Normally on a camping trip, the adults would do all the preparation, the kids would complain about tagging along, and by the time we got to the campsite, there would already be bitter feelings about the unequal distribution of work. Or if we had assigned the kids different chores to do, they would have done them—but reluctantly, since they had no ownership over the tasks. These roles have been easy to fall into in the past, but we knew they wouldn't serve our shared goal of having a fun camping trip together.

So, this time around, we recruited our four kids as collaborators. Before we ever left on the trip, we sat down together and talked about what kind of a holiday we wanted. We each shared what we hoped to experience and identified what we would need and how we should prepare to make those experiences happen. We also talked about each person's different skills and mapped out who should do what.

For example, we knew the campground had a pool, and we all liked the idea of swimming, but the pool would need to be cleaned out and filled. Maxime and Alexander were quick to announce they didn't want to clean out the pool. Pim said, "I *would* enjoy setting up the pool, but if I'm going to be doing that, someone else needs to do the cooking, and the dishes, and the garbage." She wrote down a list of all the chores that would need to be done in a day at the campsite, then announced, "All of these chores are for sale." Enrico offered to take out the garbage, and Maxime volunteered to do all the dishes. Lola and Alexander agreed to help with the cooking. Pim was able to focus her attention on cleaning out the pool, with Enrico and Lola's help. Joeri did all the technical aspects: installing the pumps and setting up the plumbing to direct water from the natural springs into the pool. We identified the needs by pointing out what we wanted to include in the holiday, and then each person took responsibility over making it happen with their own will and capacity.

The preparation for the camping trip felt easier, less stressful, and more fun than prior trips we'd taken. We also found ourselves doing tasks that we probably wouldn't have done if we had settled into our familiar roles—for instance, we would have made the two oldest boys clean out the pool, which they didn't want to do at all, and Pim would have likely done most of the cooking like she does at home, even though she was eager for a break in her routine. The discussion and collaboration meant we were all contributing in ways that we had chosen for ourselves. Our camping experience got off to an enjoyable start—then took an unexpected turn. Two hitchhikers showed up. They also had a need: they wanted a place to sleep for the night and asked if they could stay on our campsite.

We said, "No problem! But we are doing collaborative camping. If you want to stay here, we'd like you to join in. And please give us feedback on our experiment." After a brief explanation, the hitchhikers quickly signed up for a few of their own chores and started pitching in. Later, they told us that the experience made them feel very quickly included. They had the sense that they could actively participate and contribute to the shared holiday, which made them feel less like we were giving them charity and more like we were all exchanging skills and contributions.

The effort had been to set aside all of the usual roles and "job descriptions" and to ask each unique person, with all their unique skills, to take agency in contributing toward a shared goal. That was how we began to shape a Person to Person environment in our own lives. By the end of the weekend, we all felt like our collaborative camping experiment had been a great success—and made for a fun holiday.

The Person to Person environment starts small. For our family, it started with a camping trip. For a family like Jake's, their "Person to Person" inter-play might mean he discusses his dreams with his mom and dad. Rather than demanding that he pursue a lucrative career, they might consider Jake's teaching gifts, seen in the after-school program where he volunteers, and voice their support. They set aside their frameworks of expectations of what he *should* be, and instead, consider how to support who he *is*.

It starts small, but it scales up. On a much broader level, a Person to Person environment might mean you have the freedom to start up a business with the support of many small "grassroots" investors who believe in your idea, instead of getting a bank loan. Or rather than "flushing" your money away via rental payments, you recruit a team of people to invest in a house with you, where your monthly payments reimburse and reward each investor, enabling you to earn something equivalent to equity. Opportunities are made when one person or many lend their gifts, resources, or skills to another person, to build up *their* gifts, resources, and skills.

WHERE WE BEGIN

So how can we begin to create a different sort of place without completely removing ourselves from our current context? We start with our behavior, our choices, our attitudes, and our mindsets. Since a major element of quality of life is subjective, we begin the journey with the elements of perception that are within our control, considering our own individual needs and our responsibility in relating positively to others.

In our last chapter, we identified the objective and subjective domains of quality of life and pointed readers to our website to access processing tools that can help you begin your own "self-steering" journey. Our character Jake is going to start in the same place. By intentionally building self-awareness about his own needs, he's going to find that he's begun a journey toward creating an entirely different "place" for himself—one that will foster greater quality of life and stronger human connection.

Connection

Jake arrived at the library and pulled out his textbooks. He stared at them, feeling completely uninspired to study. His brain still churned over the conversation he'd had with Leon. Finally, he pulled out a blank notebook and wrote down, *What is my purpose? What am I here for?*

For about three minutes, he sat and stared at the words. Finally, he leaned forward and started scribbling quickly.

I want to help people learn and create. I want to make a living by helping people. I want to help people discover their own potential and what they're good at.

He stared at those words. Then, he wrote, *What am I good at? I'm good at teaching and connecting with others. I can go deep with people about big ideas. I know who I am and where I come from and what I want. I'm a good problem solver. I can think of innovative solutions when resources are short.*

Feeling compelled to balance his self-assessment, Jake continued: *What are my weaknesses?* His first thought was cynical: *Making money.* He sighed. He thought for a while and continued writing: *Trusting in my own dreams. Overthinking things. Prioritizing idealism over pragmatics. Being too serious. Assuming people will judge me because of my background.* He paused. Were those personality traits or weaknesses? He rubbed his eyes, registering how tired he was. Then he added, *Getting enough sleep.*

Suddenly, Jake heard a familiar voice. "Hey, stranger. What are you working on?" He looked up. It was Lana, from his chemistry lab group. His stomach flipped.

"Hey Lana. I'm just... processing." He looked at her, wondering if they had gotten to know each other well enough yet for him to confide in her. He decided to risk it. "I had a weird conversation with my roommate."

She sat down across from him. "Oh yeah? What about?"

Jake sighed. "Basically, I need to make more money. But I feel like there's no good way for me to do that without sacrificing my schoolwork. My roommate, Leon, was trying to help me but not actually being very helpful. It almost felt like he was trying to impose his solutions on me, but without trying to fully understand the situation, you know? So it ended up just feeling invalidating." He paused, wondering if he'd shared too much. "So, right now I'm just trying to..." He paused. What *was* he trying to do? "Sort out my priorities, I guess."

"Huh." She looked at him thoughtfully. "Well, according to my Psychology of Leadership prof, you're doing the best thing you could be doing."

"What? Why?" Jake asked.

"This class is super interesting," Lana said. "It's all about how to lead others well and establish healthy groups and stuff, but supposedly effective leadership has to start with you. You have to 'know thyself' if you want others to follow your lead—and for that matter, relate productively to people in any relational context. So if you want Leon to really understand how best to help you, he needs to know who you are and what really matters to you. And you need to know that about him. Which means..." She tapped his notebook. "Start with processing." She smiled. "Anyway. I think it's cool you're digging into your priorities. It's going to give you so much clarity. And maybe it will help you if you and Leon revisit the conversation."

Jake smiled, nodding. "Thanks, yeah. I think it will." He turned over Lana's words in his head, mentally patting himself on the back for opening up to her. He stood up, suddenly feeling a new wave of inspiration.

"Are you taking off?" Lana asked.

"Yeah," Jake told her. "I think I'm ready to go revisit that conversation with Leon. But..." he paused. "It would be awesome to hear more about that class. Would you want to talk about it sometime? Like, over coffee or something?"

She blushed. "Yeah, sure."

Jake deeply inhaled as he walked out of the library into the spring air. He wasn't sure exactly what he would say to Leon or how he would solve his immediate problem of being broke, but something inside him had shifted. He didn't know what, but it made him feel good.

EXPLORE FURTHER

If you'd like to learn more, discuss this content with others, or access tools for your own application, go to the interactive section of the book using this QR code.

CHAPTER THREE

MINDSET

Building Awareness, Growing Alignment,
and Forming a Healthy Team

A mind is like a parachute, it doesn't work if it is not open.

—Frank Zappa

When Jake unlocked his dorm room door, he found Leon lacing up his running shoes, dressed in athletic clothes.

"Hey! That was a quick study session," Leon commented.

"Yeah, I got distracted about other things and decided to just roll with it," Jake responded. "You going for a run?"

Leon nodded. "Decided to take a break and stretch my legs. I was getting destroyed by that last level. Is it pretty nice out there?"

"Yeah, it's gorgeous out." Jake paused. "You mind if I join you?"

"Sure, come! So long as you can keep up," Leon grinned.

Jake smiled. "You're going to be eating my dust, amigo." Leon headed outside to stretch, and Jake quickly changed before joining his roommate.

For the first ten minutes of their run, Leon talked about his video game: the hidden traps, the other players, the solutions he *thought* he'd discovered, the brutal smackdown that immediately followed, and on and on. Jake listened with growing irritation. This was not what he wanted to talk about.

"So *then*," Leon continued, "I tried watching some tutorials on YouTube to figure it out, but none of them were very good. It was either just a video of someone playing, without any commentary on what to actually do, or it was a super annoying person just talking, without any footage from the actual game. But then—this is crazy—I started Googling, and I found a massive report with interviews from all the game's beta testers—like, with *thousands* of conversation transcripts from the early testers, giving feedback on what they did, how they did it—everything. I made a copy of it because I'm sure the game company is going to take it down as soon as they realize it was leaked. If someone combed through that report, there would be so many strategies to unlock. Can you imagine the market there would be for something like that?"

He looked at Jake and laughed. "Never mind. I know you're not the type to watch video game tutorials." Jake shook his head wryly. "But maybe you should be," Leon said. "So you can get really good and then get reeeeally rich."

Jake saw his window. "Yeah, Leon—about that. Look, I know that you were trying to be helpful before with making those suggestions. And I really appreciate you trying to help . . . But . . ." He paused, trying to think of where to go next. They turned a bend and began heading downhill toward Frosh Pond, their shoes slapping the pavement.

Leon glanced over at him. "But?"

"But," Jake continued, "it honestly wasn't that helpful. Look, Leon," he said, "I think you and I grew up in pretty different contexts. Your suggestions probably make sense for your context, but not mine." Before he could lose his nerve, Jake began to describe more of his own story—the block he lived on, his parents' store, the monthly struggle to pay the bills, the after-school program. "I *loved* teaching those kids, Leon. Honestly, that program is probably the thing about home that I miss the most. Well, that and my mom's cooking." The two young men laughed. "So," Jake continued, "it's easy enough for you to say that it's a terrible idea to go into a job that won't pay much, but teaching is what I love. It's what I'm good at. That's where I want to make a difference. That doesn't change the fact that I still need to make money, but...I want to do it the right way, is all I'm saying."

Leon nodded soberly. They reached the pond. "Want to take a breather for a sec?" he said. He sat down on the stone wall bordering the water.

Jake laughed. "Ha! You *are* eating my dust."

Leon scoffed. "No way. I could see that *you* needed a break." Jake began stretching beside him. There was a pause. Leon said, "My life hasn't been easy either, you know. Just because my family has money doesn't mean it was a great time growing up."

Jake looked at Leon. "Yeah?" He paused, waiting for Leon to continue. When he didn't, Jake risked prompting his friend. "What was it like?"

Leon waved his hand dismissively. "Nothing crazy. Dad was always at the office or gone on business. Mom's best friend was her wine bottle." He shrugged, letting out a dry laugh. "I just did my own thing." He looked at Jake. "Anyway—it's cool you know what you want to do. You've got a passion. I envy that. All I know is that I want to find a job that will let me be around for my family. I mean, assuming I get a family, eventually."

Jake stood, looking at his roommate. There was a lot about Leon that was starting to make sense. "Sounds tough, man. You're right—my parents didn't have any money, but they were around."

Leon shrugged. "It is what it is." They paused, waiting until two professors had passed them by on their walk up the hill. He groaned and gestured at the hill. "I just realized we've got to run back *up* that thing." Jake laughed and nodded.

"Hey," Leon said, suddenly inspired. "I have another idea." Jake raised his eyebrows. "Don't look so skeptical," Leon said, "I think you're going to like this one. What if we make video tutorials together? For my game?"

Jake shook his head and started to respond, but Leon interrupted. "No, listen—this could work! I'll use that open-source document to decipher the code and figure out the strategies needed for each level. I can tell you what to communicate and get the snippets of the actual game playing. Then you figure out a way to teach it in a way that's interesting and quick."

Jake was still skeptical. "Leon, in order to make money on YouTube, you need a following. It takes a long time to get enough viewers to actually make anything."

Leon was not deterred. "Do you know how many views there were on the last crappy video I watched to try to figure out how to beat that last level? Over a million! Besides, I have a following. I'm crazycricket. I already have, like, twenty videos online about other stuff. I have 476 followers! And I know the levers you need to push to get your video to the top of the search results."

Jake laughed. "Crazy cricket? Levers to push?"

Leon said, "Well, people to pay, that is. Come on, man. We could do this." Jake looked at him, starting to feel intrigued. Leon continued. "Look—*you* would be teaching. Making a difference in so many young gamers' lives..." Jake laughed. Leon continued. "It's better than Ubering, right?"

Jake said, "This could actually be cool if we could get it to work." They started the jog back up the hill. Jake asked, "Down the road, if we really did get a following, could we make videos about other stuff? Like, how-to videos about life skills or something inspirational?"

Leon clapped him on the back. "Now you're talking! Yes. We start with the game and go on to world peace. It's brilliant." They both laughed. For the rest of the run home, they began planning—Leon agreed to mine all the data he could about the game to gather the tips they needed, and Jake agreed to find popular tutorial videos to get ideas about the best ways to teach content online. Leon said, "I know a guy, Tommy, who has tons of videography equipment. I'll see if he can help us."

Jake said, "Yeah, my friend Lana might be able to help us too. She has a lot of great ideas about how groups can function well." He glanced at Leon, self-consciously. "You'd like her."

Leon gave him a good-natured grin. "I think *you* like her." Jake laughed and shrugged. When they got home, they both pulled up their laptops and started doing their respective research.

Jake quipped, "Leon, you should take a shower. You smell."

"You're smelling yourself. *You* should take a shower."

For the first time since moving in, Jake felt like he and his roommate were authentically connecting. A collaboration had begun.

THE IMPORTANCE OF MINDSET

Jake's and Leon's efforts to identify their purposes and capabilities illustrate the first crucial step in building healthy Person to Person interactions: developing an intentional mindset. There's a quote credited to Buddha that explains how mindset leads to behavior:

The thought manifests as the word,

The word manifests as the deed,

The deed develops into habit,

And the habit hardens into character.

If this notion of thoughts becoming actions and then habits is true, then taking the time to intentionally examine your *beliefs and thoughts* is imperative if you want your *actions* to be productive, helpful, meaningful, and considerate of others.

How does a mindset work, anyway? Are we dealing with Freud's ego, superego, and id? The conscious, subconscious, and unconscious? Growth mindset or fixed mindset? Although there are many ways to understand the facets of how our minds work, we think Marsha Linehan's identification of the **rational mind**, **emotional mind**, and **wise mind** is the most helpful in building quality of life and healthy collaboration.[47]

The **rational mind** is anchored in facts, reason, logic, and pragmatics. It is cool, allowing you to put things in perspective and seek objectivity. It is also task-focused, enabling you to structure plans and think logically. The rational mind enables analytical thought and goal setting, informing you about which steps to take to execute a plan. It's your rational mind that determines which food is healthiest to eat, which train will get you there fastest, what career path will make the most sense for your future goals, and so on. However, by itself, your rational mind doesn't consider your personal needs or feelings. In Jake's scenario, the rational mind would tell him to get a job—*any* job, at any time of night or day—that will get him the most money, seeing that as the solution to his problem. By itself, therefore, the rational mind is limited.

The **emotional mind** is the source of passion, creativity, and love, along with "negative" emotions like anger, sadness, and fear. In fact, it's largely your emotional mind that helps determine your core purpose because it's your emotions that tell you what you feel strongly about, what matters to you, and what you love. Your emotions are wonderfully informative teachers; they help highlight your passions and giftings. Your emotional mind can also signal triggers to be aware of, which have the potential to trip you up. By paying attention to your emotional sensitivities, you develop an increased ability to govern them.

However, just as the rational mind can pose a danger when operating alone, the emotional mind by itself can be volatile. Emotions are mainly impulsive, and if emotions are given free reign, you can easily become deregulated and lose self-control. Therefore, either the rational or emotional mind, taken by itself, can threaten quality of life. They must be balanced and mediated.

---

[47] Marsha Linehan, "Dr. Marsha Linehan Teaches Wise Mind," Psychwire, October 13, 2019, video, 1:14, https://www.youtube.com/watch?v=X_BmPxd0Eiw.

This is accomplished through the **wise mind**, which is essentially the collaboration between the rational and emotional mind. Your wise mind helps you determine that something not only *is* right, but also *feels* right. It's your inner wisdom that allows you to connect with your purpose (informed by the emotional mind) and make plans about how best to pursue it (informed by the rational mind). For instance, Jake's *rational* mind understood that he needed to make more money, but his *emotional* mind—informed by love for his parents and his respect of their wishes—knew that working the graveyard shift didn't feel like the right thing to do. His conclusion to seek out another alternative was determined by his *wise mind*, which balanced his objective needs with his emotional intuition. The wise mind enables you to express yourself in a helpful way and understand how to balance practical rational considerations with your emotions.

When you build self-awareness about your rational mind, emotional mind, and wise mind, you are actively shaping your identity, in the same way a potter presses clay to bring it into a desired shape. If a potter has a clear sense of what she wants to create, then every decision she makes can help shape the piece of pottery that emerges. Her rational mind gives her clarity about which movements have the potential to ruin the piece and which actions will best serve it. Her emotions can spark her creativity and inform her ideas about how best to finish the piece. Her wisdom about her intended purpose guides creation. Likewise, in combining your emotional output with your rational output, you are able to more readily structure your thoughts and feelings, choose helpful strategies, and employ behaviors that can help you move toward your purpose.

Collectively, our mindset is enormously powerful in determining our behavior and, therefore, our future path. In fact, Mahatma Gandhi's paraphrase of Buddha's quote emphasizes this link: "Your thoughts become your actions; your actions become your habits; your habits become your values; and *your values become your destiny*." Your mindset, in other words, helps chart your course for the rest of your life. When you craft your mindset deliberately, you not only chart a deliberate course; you become capable of expressing yourself to others on your life's journey. With awareness about your purpose, thoughts, and emotions, you can be strategic and joyful in your decision-making.

Joy—and all its influence on quality of life—is a key goal in your mindset shaping. Consider mindset as it informs the eight domains of quality of life. If you want to enhance your learning opportunities, you need to *know* what you want to learn about. If you want to increase your self-governance, you need to be *aware* of your core purpose. If you want to optimize your living environment, you must *understand* the environments in which you thrive. In every area, your cognitive mind plays a part in helping lead you to greater joy. Mindset also directly impacts the way we interact with other people: our social relationships, emotional well-being, and general life satisfaction can only be optimized if we have a healthy level of self-awareness that enables us to interact positively with others.

So not only does this intentional shaping of your mindset help you to productively manifest your own identity and quality of life; it also strengthens your participation in a group. When you have equipped yourself with necessary knowledge about who you are, you can stand by your vision, stay true to yourself, recognize people with similar values, pursue your goals, and experience comfort in relationships. The better you know yourself and learn to express yourself to others, the more frequently others will have the opportunity to fully know and understand you.

Mindset is so important, in fact, that it has the power to either promote or destroy healthy collaboration, as illustrated powerfully in the tragedy of the commons.

Mindset can either promote or destroy
healthy collaboration.

PERSON TO PERSON

The Problem with Self-Serving Behavior

The tragedy of the commons is a well-known phenomenon first explored by William Forster Lloyd in 1833 when he noticed that cows grazing on private property seemed to be thriving, whereas the cows that grazed on the common fields, available to anyone, were thin and small.[48] Moreover, the private fields looked lush and green, as opposed to the brown, overgrazed common fields. Garrett Hardin reflected on Lloyd's observations in his seminal 1968 work titled "The Tragedy of the Commons," observing that when a resource is made common to all, the most frequent tendency is for people to abuse that resource, fail to maintain it, and tax it beyond its useful sustainability. He wrote, "Ruin is the destination toward which all men rush, each pursuing *his own best interest* in a society that believes in the freedom of the commons. Freedom in a commons brings ruin to all."[49]

When each person pursues their own best interest at the expense of the whole, we rush toward ruin.

The challenge presented by the tragedy of the commons is self-serving behavior. Take, for example, the problem presented by overfishing on the high seas. Each individual fishing crew is likely aware that if changes aren't made to the fishing industry, the oceans will be overfished to the point of unsustainability, which would mean ruin for all. However, if one fishing crew considered limiting their catch to help sustain the fish population, they might

[48] William Forster Llyod, *Two Lectures on the Checks to Population: Delivered Before the University of Oxford, in Michaelmas Term 1832* (Oxford: Oxford University Press, 1833), reprinted in part in *Population, Evolution, and Birth Control: A Collage of Controversial Readings*, ed. Garrett Hardin (San Francisco: W.H. Freeman, 1964).

[49] Garrett, Hardin," The Tragedy of the Commons," *Science* 162 no. 3859 (1968). DOI: 10.1126/science.162.3859.1243.

reason that another fishing crew would overfish that area in their absence. Their logical conclusion: "We may as well overfish it first and reap a profit." When everyone comes to that same self-serving conclusion, the common resource is destroyed for all.

Hardin suggested that the only two ways to avoid the tragedy of the commons were to turn all common resources into private property or to create top-down regulations to control who had access to the common resource. Most Western countries favor the private property approach. However, that doesn't ultimately solve the problem of the limited resource; it only means wealthy people have access to it and poor people don't. Private property lends itself to inequality and, ultimately, war. When there is too little of a resource, people fight over it. Top-down regulations are not an ideal solution either, since they limit personal freedom.

However, the Nobel laureate economist Elinor Ostrom generated a different solution—one that related to mindset.

A Solution to the Tragedy of the Commons

Elinor Ostrom rejected the notion that all people were condemned to experience the tragedy of the commons as a matter of course.[50] She put forward eight principles that could help establish collaborative boundaries and agreements that could lead to proper stewardship of the common resource. Her theories were written primarily from an economist's perspective, and her work was hailed as groundbreaking.

A commitment to collaborative principles and boundaries can lead to proper stewardship of a common resource.

---

[50] Flavio Felice, and Massimiliano Vatiero, "Elinor Ostrom and the Solution to the Tragedy of the Commons," American Enterprise Institute, June 27, 2012, https://www.aei.org/articles/elinor-ostrom-and-the-solution-to-the-tragedy-of-the-commons.

From there, the Australian organizational psychologist and leadership professor Paul Atkins set about making Ostrom's eight principles prescriptive.[51] He wanted to identify behaviors and actions that could help make Ostrom's descriptive principles actionable. Using his expertise as a behavioral therapist, Atkins began to develop a number of tools that could provide people with the resources they needed to act on Ostrom's recommendations. We'll say more on this in a moment.

There were many reasons why Atkins believed his prescription could effectively "cure" people from experiencing the tragedy of the commons. Although a self-serving mindset may *seem* instinctive, he and others pushed back against the foregone conclusion that humans were biologically incapable of true, sustained collaboration. Rather, a great deal of evolutionary research shows that humans are hardwired for "prosocial" behavior.

Take, for example, the fact that human beings experience such a prolonged stage of helplessness in their early years, compared to all other animals. From our earliest days and for many years, we require help in order to survive. What's more, the majority of infants find a plethora of humans willing to make sacrifices in order to help them. These nurturing instincts, which are innate to us as humans, are the *opposite* of self-serving behavior. Humans have a long-term cooperative upbringing, and as a result, natural selection has endowed us with many prosocial instincts.

Furthermore, the act of helping people turns out to have many biological, social, and cognitive benefits. For instance, grandparents who help out in the raising of their grandchildren remain more active, cognitively sharp, and socially fulfilled.[52] Additionally, research shows that specific "reward centers" in the human brain (posterior superior temporal sulcus) are activated when

[51] Paul W. B. Atkins, David Sloan Wilson, and Steven C. Hayes, *Prosocial: Using Evolutionary Science to Build Productive, Equitable, and Collaborative Groups*, (Oakland, CA: Context Press/New Harbinger Publications, 2019).

[52] Ian McKay and Danielle K. Nadorff, "The Impact of Custodial Grandparenting on Cognitive Performance in a Longitudinal Sample of Grandparents Raising Grandchildren," *Journal of Family Issues* 42 (2020), DOI: 10.1177/0192513X20976729.

humans collaborate.[53] What does that mean? It means our brains are wired to *enjoy* working productively with other people. When we can share in good work with others, recognize improvement, and track progress toward a worthwhile goal, we experience real pleasure. There's additional research that shows we experience increased well-being both when we receive help and when we give help.[54] To put this simply: we *are* prosocial creatures.

Humans have successfully evolved due to their prosocial collaborative tendencies. Furthermore, humans experience pleasure and fulfillment when they work collaboratively with others.

But, clearly, we don't always act like prosocial creatures, as the tragedy of the commons illustrates. Both Ostrom and Atkins believed that boundaries, agreement, commitment, and clear guidelines were needed if our better angels were to prevail against our darker impulses. To help those angels, Atkins and his team built the Prosocial ARC Process, a method for helping any group, anywhere in the world, work better together. It's a method that combines Ostrom's research with biological science, evolutionary science, and contextual behavioral science.

Essentially, Atkins's Prosocial Core Design Principles characterize healthy collaboration. And what do they all have in common? They start as a mindset.

[53] David Sloan Wilson, Mark Van Vugt, and Rick O'Gorman, "Multilevel Selection Theory and Major Evolutionary Transitions," *Current Directions in Psychological Science* 17, no. 1 (2008), DOI: 10.1111/j.1467-8721.2008.00538.x.

[54] Elizabeth Dunn, Lara Aknin, and Michael Norton, "Spending Money on Others Promotes Happiness," *Science* 319 no. 5870 (March 2008), DOI: 10.1126/science.1150952.

PROSOCIAL CORE DESIGN PRINCIPLES

Let's review: if we want more quality of life, we need an environment that is free of hierarchies, power plays, fear, and greed. We also need one that gives us greater personal agency to pursue our purpose and abundance in each of the life domains. Additionally, we need opportunities to form authentic connections to other people.

All this means we need strategies to collaborate harmoniously—ones that we freely choose and commit to of our own accord. These eight research-based Core Design Principles enable us to do exactly that.

1. Strong Identity and Understanding of Purpose

A commons fails for several reasons, but one is because people don't feel any ownership of it. Atkins's first principle seeks to correct that. **For everyone in the group to feel a sense of shared ownership and belonging, they need to come together around a common purpose.** When there's no shared understanding of purpose, people will be less committed to a group and feel less connected to its endeavors. This first principle, therefore, is key for motivation and commitment. People will be inclined to work at their best, *contributing* to the commons, when they believe in the purpose of what they're doing. We intentionally highlighted purpose as an essential element of quality of life in Chapter 1: it is essential not only for individual well-being, but also for a successful collaboration.

A shared sense of purpose is also important for coordinating action: if everyone knows what they're working toward, it's much easier to see what needs to happen and when. Atkins stresses that, to do this well, purpose needs to constantly be in group members' minds: "talk about purpose, remind people of it in meetings . . . debate it, evolve it at annual retreats."[55] There are many ways to do this well: groups can form a vision or a mission statement,

---

[55] Atkins, *Prosocial.*

draft their values, consider where they want to be in five years, and so on. What's most important, Atkins notes, is that there's a "continual reflection on 'toward.'" In other words, team members must constantly know where they're going, why they want to get there, how they're planning to accomplish that, and ways they can manage to stick with it.

2. Equitable Distribution of Costs and Benefits

Equity is also key if group members are to feel fully committed to the group and work at their best. Any perception of inequity tends to lead to disillusionment and disengagement. **Therefore, if you want your collaborating team members to contribute their best, there should be an equitable distribution of costs and benefits.** The financial strategies that we'll discuss starting in Chapter 6 aim to accomplish this principle.

Creating true equity can be challenging, and it's not an easy topic to discuss. It's also true that certain roles require longer hours, just by virtue of their nature. For example, a video editor may spend four hours editing a video, whereas the on-screen talent may have only needed to work for an hour to record their segment. The best way to create a balance among team members' workload and rewards is by focusing on how to create "win-win" outcomes. You can do that using some or all of the following tools:

- Clarify team members' roles. Be transparent about the expectations and requirements of those roles and discuss what team members might need in order to fully commit to those requirements.
- After identifying each person's needs, consider how to best meet those needs within the context of the group. Work together to pursue an outcome that works for everyone.
- Focus on creating equity in the *process* of the collaboration, not just at the end.
- Transparent surveys can be a helpful tool to gather needed data about needs or feelings regarding equity.

- Be transparent about allocation of rewards and benefits.
- Try to make conversations about needs, not comparisons. Comparisons can easily create divisions of "us" versus "them," whereas acknowledgment of each member's needs invites connection and clarifies practical next steps. Pursue unity by discussing how the group can work together to help meet each other's needs while pursuing their common goal.
- Avoid creating policies that do not acknowledge differences in effort or contribution. Giving everyone the same rewards and benefits, regardless of their effort, can actually sap motivation.

Once all group members are aligned and committed to a common purpose, ask the question "How can we ensure that everyone gets their needs met while working toward this goal? What would a win-win situation look like? How can we ensure fairness in working toward that win-win scenario?"

3. Fair and Inclusive Decision-Making

In order to maintain strong commitment and investment among your team members, they each need to feel like they have a place at the table. Collaboration, by definition, means working with other people. For frictionless collaboration to happen, **each group member needs to feel confident that they have a voice in the decision-making process**, particularly in those decisions that directly affect them. Not only does this help maintain motivation; it also will improve your decision-making as a group.

In small groups, this will be relatively straightforward. In larger groups, the decision-making process may involve consulting with a representative or designated leader of a set of group members, voting, or providing opportunities to voice dissent or concern. The meetings that we'll discuss in Chapter 4 seek to promote this inclusive process. In any context, consider what method of decision-making will efficiently and inclusively involve the people affected by the decision.

4. Peer-Based Monitoring of Agreed-Upon Behaviors

Let's go back to the tragedy of the commons: imagine that all cattle farmers agree that they will only allow five of their cows to graze on the common fields—but then one farmer slyly brings in a sixth cow, hoping the others won't notice. Not only would this breach of the agreement threaten the sustainability of the common resource; it would also threaten the unity of the group. Other farmers might follow suit, and any farmers still abiding by the agreement would naturally feel angry. Everyone would walk away feeling that the agreement itself was useless.

For that reason, a solution to the tragedy of the commons requires accountability. **Peers should be allowed and expected to monitor the behaviors that all group members agreed on.** As Atkins states, "Self-serving behaviors increase when there is a lack of transparency."[56] For this reason, transparency is a major element of a Person to Person environment, in everything from open dialogue to blockchain technology, as we'll discuss in later chapters.

The best form of monitoring within a collaboration will not be sneaky or coercive; it can be a simple check-in with a colleague or a meeting where everyone reports what they're working on. The goal is for other team members to have the opportunity to notice what their group members are doing. These opportunities should happen on a consistent basis. This not only will strengthen the sense of collaboration, but it can provide opportunities for encouragement and troubleshooting as challenges arise. It also helps foster needed transparency to ensure agreed-upon behaviors are maintained.

5. Increase Helpful and Decrease Unhelpful Behaviors

Imagine that one group member consistently shows up late to the group's meetings. A different colleague often "goes dark" and won't respond to emails or texts when she's in a bad mood. Another group member tends to have a

---

[56] Ibid.

short fuse and sometimes yells at other teammates. These would be examples of *unhelpful* behaviors: any behavior that threatens productive and healthy collaboration. In contrast, *helpful* behavior aids the collaborative process. Sometimes increasing helpful behavior will require intentional effort, like if one group member makes great contributions whenever she's asked but tends not to share unless prompted.

People are complex beings, and every collaborating group will find their own unique set of challenges and giftings represented by their group members. **In order for collaboration to thrive, each member must commit to increase their helpful behaviors and decrease their unhelpful behaviors.** The chronically late person should commit to improving their punctuality. The colleague who goes dark needs to commit to responding, even briefly, when others reach out to her. The hothead should commit to learning strategies for self-control. The quiet group member should make a point to contribute her ideas more often.

These discussions and commitments occur during Commitment Sessions, which we'll discuss in greater length in Chapter 4. During Commitment Sessions, group members embrace their responsibility to voice their own challenges and to explore how to overcome them. They also are able to consult their colleagues for expertise so they can learn from one another. No one is expected to be perfect, but there should be transparency about what's working and what's not working and a collective effort to constantly be strengthening your own contribution toward enabling sustainable collaboration.

For the sake of consistency and helping people stay motivated, consequences may be in order when people commit unhelpful behaviors. Atkins notes, "Research shows trust increases in groups when graduated sanctioning occurs for unhelpful behaviors... Effective groups have in place responses to transgressions ranging from open, compassionate conversation to find out what happened, to sanctions or even, ultimately, exclusion from the group."[57]

---

[57] Ibid.

Although we agree with Atkins that unhelpful behaviors need to be addressed, we differ with him on the right way to do that. Sanctions and exclusion from the group can easily be viewed as power plays, which have no place in a Person to Person environment. We believe the Troubleshooting tool discussed in Chapter 4 is a more effective way of handling unhelpful behaviors, one that still maintains personal agency. Commitment Sessions are also a safe place to work on unhelpful behaviors. As long as people are willing to participate in those sessions—actively reflect, participate, and share—the collaboration can continue and obstacles can be overcome. But if a group member repeatedly doesn't show up to Commitment Sessions to engage with a Troubleshooting tool, they effectively remove themselves from the collaboration. In that case, that's a choice they make, not one that's imposed upon them.

Still, we agree with Atkins on the goal of any form of accountability: to always move toward productive change: "How can we (you) do things differently next time?" Some of the tools we'll discuss in our next chapter will help group members identify the reasons behind their unhelpful behavior, along with positive next steps to help address them. It's important not to ignore unhelpful behaviors because—just as in the cattle-grazing example—that will demoralize other team members and erode the group's trust.

At the same time, helpful behaviors should be explicitly celebrated and encouraged. These affirmations not only spotlight and encourage behaviors that will aid the rest of the group; they also validate a person's hard work. This can occur via a formal system of recognition or through more organic expressions of thanks. Affirmation could also come via development opportunities or an increase in earnings. When looking to show gratitude to someone, consider that person's unique values and personality. Someone may appreciate a privately given gift, whereas someone else may feel most affirmed with a public shout-out. In any case, the praise communicated should be genuine.

6. Fast and Fair Conflict Resolution

Even in the best collaborative environments, conflict is still inevitable. When different people with different gifts come together, it follows that differences will need to be worked out. In fact, in a truly authentic and safe environment, conflict may come up with greater frequency than in a traditional working environment. This happens because people feel safe to share what they really think and will advocate for their ideas rather than suppressing their opinions out of fear they'll be judged or penalized. Therefore, **it is essential to commit as a group to a healthy conflict resolution process and corresponding principles.**

Conflict is something that many of us would rather avoid. It's uncomfortable and it can lead to negative feelings. However, this essential element enables groups to maintain authentic, transparent communication. Conflict also has the ability to hone the group's direction and even strengthen their shared commitment. To do it well, however, people need to develop the emotional and communicative skills to handle it. It's also key to set aside assumptions about what other group members may think and instead practice reflective listening, which will allow you to listen and then confirm your understanding of the other person's perspective.

The strategies to address conflict would be generated when groups develop a Collaborative Agreement in their early days. We'll discuss the Collaborative Agreement more in a moment, and in much greater depth in Chapter 5. Part of this group agreement involves coping and remediation strategies. Essentially, group members do the hard work to brainstorm any and every conflict scenario they could envision themselves running into and then are challenged to develop solutions and strategies to deal with those potential conflicts. In order to stay true to their commitment to work toward a successful collaboration, this foresight is necessary. It will help them build awareness about supportive strategies and conflict mediation tools and stay mindful of other possible resources.

What sort of strategies might be included? Atkins recommends some of the following conflict resolution methods:

- Practice active listening and respectful, assertive communication.
- Create a role for a trusted, impartial mediator.
- Alternately, create a judicial committee with rotating membership.
- Use an escalation process: conflict is first addressed in a one-to-one conversation; if not resolved, then it would go to a mediated conversation, and so on.

A healthy conflict resolution plan for any group will identify both *principles* of conflict resolution and a *plan* for steps about how conflicts should be resolved. For instance, the New Zealand nonhierarchical organization Loomio—referenced by Atkins as a model for conflict resolution—recommends principles like, "We have mutual responsibility and care for each other. We act in good faith and work to be constructive, empathetic, and honest. We resolve conflicts with both our individual needs and the needs of the cooperative in mind...Resolution means the parties involved feel heard."[58] They also have published a clear process for conflict resolution, identifying each step of escalation with an emphasis on trying to get conflict resolved at the lowest possible level.

A conflict resolution plan that prioritizes speedy resolution, fairness, respectful and honest communication, good listening, and empathy can ultimately strengthen a group's harmony as they collaborate together.

7. Authority to Self-Govern (According to Principles 1 through 6)

Let's say that you're a middle manager in a large corporation. You embrace all of the above principles, and you want to move your team toward a healthier collaborative environment. However, your HR governing body won't allow

---

[58] "Conflict Resolution Process," *Loomio Cooperative Handbook*, Accessed September 6, 2021, https://www.loomio.coop/looking_after_people/conflict_resolution.

you to make cultural changes. They mandate conflict resolution according to a specific set of rules. The hierarchy is enforced regardless of its impact on your team's cultural health. You want to make changes—but you're stuck.

This points to the problem of an inability to self-govern. **In order for groups to truly organize themselves according to these Core Design Principles, they must have sufficient autonomy to do so.** In some contexts with rigid expectations or rules, this may be a significant challenge. However, in many contexts, the authoritative body may be inclined to allow for more freedom when they are presented with research about the efficacy of the Core Design Principles. Teams may experience more autonomy if they clarify how their purpose is aligned with the greater organizational purpose or pursue training in areas like cultural change, transformational leadership, or sociocracy.

The first step in moving toward self-governance is simply awareness. If you are in an environment that operates via the exertion of top-down force, then recognize that paradigm of force. Begin with your mindset and attitude. Grow awareness of your position, the areas where you do have agency, and the force that's being exerted upon you. Then find the crack in the walls. Acknowledge the confinement of the box so that you can seek out a solution. Remember the power we wield with our mindset: even if the positive change is only allowed to start internally, that can still make a powerful difference in how we engage with our environment and other colleagues.

Ultimately, true self-governance can only exist in an environment that is free from hindrances and hierarchies. That is why we have devoted a great deal of time and energy toward envisioning a Person to Person environment that would allow for this freedom.

8. Collaborative Relations with Other Groups

Imagine that you're in a collaborative group that has the shared purpose to build community gardens in economically depressed neighborhoods. Your own group might do a great job getting itself off the ground, knitting itself into the fabric of the community, and operating according to the Core Design Principles. It's beautiful: there's a flourishing community garden in the empty lot between the hair salon and the smoke shop. But then what? What about all the other neighborhoods that your own collaborative group isn't big enough to reach? Can this model scale up?

It can, and in fact, it has. Some of the world's most recognizable large companies, such as Microsoft and Spotify, have adapted a management strategy called Agile, which essentially relies on a large number of small teams to get their work done.[59] Large teams can't operate with speed or agility, but small teams can, making them more innovative and dynamic—provided they collaborate effectively with one another.

The eighth core design principle acknowledges the importance of combining efforts with other groups in order to get big things done. Atkins writes, "Just as individuals need shared purpose, so do groups of groups. Just as there should be equity between individuals, there needs to be equity between groups and so on."[60] This means that **the first seven Core Design Principles must also apply to interactions between other groups**. All coordinating groups must have a strong conflict resolution process; all groups must have a strong understanding of their shared purpose; all groups should prioritize fair and inclusive decision-making and so on.

Atkins recommends a polycentric governance to accomplish this sort of intergroup collaboration, a recommendation once again based on the work of Elinor Ostrom. A polycentric governance has multiple centers of semi-autonomous decision-making leadership.[61] Essentially, all groups get a voice, but they also operate with independence. There are other resources as well, offering strategies to form collaborative relations between groups. Literature

---

[59] Steve Denning,. "Can Big Organizations Be Agile?" *Forbes*, November 29, 2016, https://www.forbes.com/sites/stevedenning/2016/11/26/can-big-organizations-be-agile/?sh=541501b838e7.

[60] Atkins, *Prosocial*.

[61] Keith Carlisle and Rebecca L. Gruby, "Polycentric Systems of Governance: A Theoretical Model for the Commons," *Policy Studies Journal* 47 no. 4, DOI: 10.1111/psj.12212.

written on sociocracy can be helpful in arranging this kind of intergroup collaboration. Another helpful resource is Stanford's Collective Impact approach, which was created to enhance collaboration between groups and has been studied for its effectiveness.[62]

You'll know that groups are working well together if they operate with consistent alignment with their shared purpose, with fairness and inclusivity, with transparency, and ultimately with efficacy in their work. The groups should not primarily serve their own interests, but those of the larger context. For instance, the first community garden collaborators should not focus on making their own particular garden "the best" by hoarding resources, but instead should focus on the larger goal of uplifting depressed communities by sharing resources and starting community gardens in a number of different neighborhoods.

Core Design Principles in Brief

CDP1: Establish a common purpose so that everyone in the group experiences a sense of shared ownership and belonging. This shared purpose should be frequently revisited.

CDP 2: Ensure that everyone gets their needs met while working toward the shared purpose in a fair and equitable way.

CDP 3: Each group member needs to feel confident that they have a voice in the decision-making process.

CDP 4: Encourage transparency; peers should be allowed and expected to monitor the behaviors that all group members agreed on.

CDP 5: Each member must commit to increase their helpful behaviors and decrease their unhelpful behaviors.

---

[62] Sarah Stachowiak and Lauren Gase, "Does Collective Impact Really Make an Impact?" *Stanford Social Innovation Review*, August 9, 2018, https://ssir.org/articles/entry/does_collective_impact_really_make _an_impact.

CDP 6: Commit as a group to a healthy conflict resolution process and corresponding principles.

CDP 7: Establish sufficient autonomy to self-govern.

CDP 8: Collaborate with other groups according to principles 1 through 7.

Groups form healthy collaboration toward a shared aim when each individual is free to pursue their own purpose in line with their values and when *each person* commits to these Core Design Principles. The efficacy of a group's inner workings begins with the potency and power of each individual's mindset.

So how would this commitment begin? What would it look like, practically, for each person in a collaboration to commit to these Core Design Principles?

We will be discussing practical tools over the next two chapters to help individuals and groups put these Core Design Principles into action. The first tool, the individual matrix, calls upon individuals to employ their rational minds, emotional minds, and wise minds as they consider how to move toward a desired purpose.

Individual ACT Matrix: A Prosocial Tool

In several chapters of this book, we'll be referencing the ACT matrix, a tool developed by Atkins's partner, Steven C. Hayes, that can help build self-awareness, both for individuals and for a collective group.[63] ACT stands for Acceptance and Commitment Training, which is an indication of how it helps its users to both *accept* the helpful and unhelpful behaviors they bring to the group and *commit* to strengthening their contribution. The

---

[63] Steven C. Hayes, "Acceptance & Commitment Therapy (ACT)," Association for Contextual Behavioral Science, accessed September 9, 2021, https://contextualscience.org/act.

ACT matrix should first be filled out individually and then as a group. The self-awareness generated by this tool will help groups anticipate potential conflict, consider values and motivations, and identify strengths. (We've provided a blank ACT matrix on our website for readers to engage with; please see this chapter's QR code.)

The matrix begins with four quadrants arranged along two perpendicular axes. The vertical axis is labeled "Inner" (at the top) and "Outer" at the bottom. It acknowledges that for every person who shows up to the table, that person brings both an inner world of thoughts, feelings, and motivations as well as an outer collection of observable behaviors.

The horizontal axis is labeled "Away" (on the left side) and "Toward" on the right side. This axis recognizes the universal human behavior that moves *toward* activities we enjoy and find pleasurable and *away* from activities we find painful or uncomfortable.

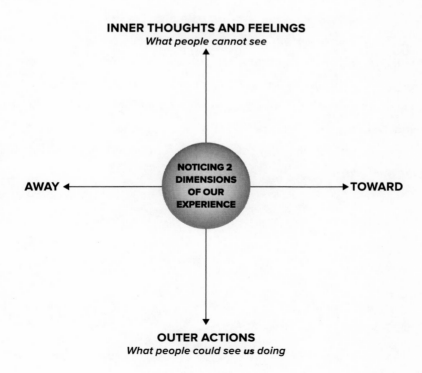

Now, there are four quadrants represented in the matrix; each of those quadrants can be understood to encompass a different area of our mindset and subsequent behaviors, based on the combinations of the two axes.

For instance, the top-right quadrant can be labeled "Motivation." When you combine the *inner* thoughts and feelings that cause a person to move *toward* something they enjoy, that's essentially what you get: a person's intrinsic motivation. If our character Jake were to be filling out this matrix, he would write down the things that motivate him: his values, his beliefs, his goals—essentially, the things that matter most to him. We saw him consider this earlier, in an informal way, when he was journaling in the library.

The lower-right quadrant can be named "Engagement." When a person's *outer* actions reflect what they most enjoy moving *toward*, you tend to see the areas of life where they are productively working toward their purpose. Engagement refers to the observable behaviors that indicate what a person values—essentially, everything described in the "Motivation" quadrant. Mainly, it encompasses their positive, helpful behaviors. Jake might write down in this quadrant things like, "I treat everyone like an equal by not judging anyone. I try to build others up by validating their choices and behaviors. I try to help people discover new ideas and share knowledge by engaging in discussions and asking sincere questions." The entries in this quadrant should name behaviors that someone could see and observe. People should not only become aware of *what* they find important to do, but also figure out *how* they can do or express it.

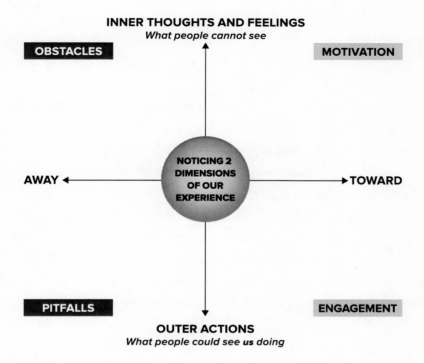

INNER THOUGHTS AND FEELINGS
What people cannot see

OBSTACLES

MOTIVATION

NOTICING 2 DIMENSIONS OF OUR EXPERIENCE

AWAY

TOWARD

PITFALLS

ENGAGEMENT

OUTER ACTIONS
What people could see us doing

The top-left quadrant, where a person's *inner* thoughts coincide with the activities they would prefer to move *away* from, can be labeled "Obstacles." These can be understood as a person's inner hang-ups, insecurities, and/or triggers. In other words, they are any thought or feeling that would prevent a person from moving *toward* their source of motivation and preferred behaviors for engagement. In Jake's case, he might write down something like, "I'm afraid I'll be judged on my background, not as an individual. I sometimes feel insecure about my dreams and can easily second-guess them."

The fourth, lower-left quadrant can be labeled "Pitfalls." This area encompasses our *outer* behaviors that take us *away* from our desired behaviors and purpose—in other words, our vulnerabilities. This area helps to identify those unhelpful behaviors that could easily lead us to disrupt the flow of a group's work. In Jake's case, he might write down, "I can shut down fast when people challenge my ideas. I lose confidence in them, even when I know they could actually be a good solution. I also hesitate before taking action—I want to analyze everything to death, which means I sometimes can drag down a project's momentum."

When participating in a self-governing group that wants to collaborate in a healthy way, you should first complete this matrix individually. After completing it, each colleague will share the information they learned with one another. The exercise will help you gather clarity about your pitfalls, vulnerabilities, and desired behaviors—just as we saw Jake get clarity for himself after journaling in the library. Armed with that clarity, he was able to explain his values and purpose more effectively to Leon, which enabled them to arrive at an idea for a collaboration that suited both of their inner motivations. One of the tools we'll describe in Chapter 4, the Behavior Chain Analysis, can help with building self-awareness in these areas.

After each group member fills out their own personal matrix, the group should come together and fill out the matrix as a shared group. But before it does, each group member might want to analyze the group's potential matrix on their own first. You would do this to preserve the authenticity of each group member's response, which could otherwise be influenced by a loud voice in the group. For instance, if Jake knows that he gets triggered when people raise their voices, and Leon often raises his voice, it will feel safer for him to fill out the group's "Obstacles" quadrant on his own first: "I tend to shut down when people yell. Leon sometimes yells, which gets to me." When the group comes together, Jake's consideration of the group's motivation, engagement, obstacles, and pitfalls are already preserved. There will be more honesty and safety in discussing the group's matrix when each group member has thoughtfully filled it out with the group in mind.

When doing the group matrix, you're considering the *group's* shared purpose in the "Motivation" section, the *group's* shared values, and so on. In the "Obstacles" quadrant, you're thinking of thoughts or feelings from yourself or other group members that could interfere with working toward the shared goal. In the "Pitfalls" section, you're thinking of interfering behaviors from yourself or other group members.

Finally, the group would gather together and fill out the matrix collectively, considering the group's shared motivation, engagement, obstacles, and potential pitfalls. The point of all this is to maximize everyone's awareness of why you want to collaborate and how you want to get there, while being aware of all the ways things *could* go wrong, with the express purpose of strategizing so that things go right.

Here is how a completed matrix might look, considering the group's shared purpose. Note that the quadrants are numbered in the same order we discussed them: top right first, then lower right; then top left, then lower left:

INNER THOUGHTS AND FEELINGS
What people cannot see

OBSTACLES

[3] What thoughts and feelings might hook me or others and get in the way of moving toward [1] and [2]?

Feelings: nervousness about making a mistake.

Thoughts: "What I've got to share isn't interesting; I'd better shut up."

AWAY

[4] What might people see us doing when we are hooked by the thoughts or feelings in [3]?

Unhelpful behaviors: Not speaking up, taking too much space and therefore silencing others.

PITFALLS

NOTICING 2 DIMENSIONS OF OUR EXPERIENCE

MOTIVATION

[1] What matters most to US as a group? What shared values and aims should we hold to?

Values, beliefs: respect, dignity.

Outcomes: forming working relationships, creating a helping culture in the group.

Processes: everybody gets to speak and share; we'll speak up if group process is unhelpful.

[2] If we were really living in line with the values In [1] what would we be doing more of or less of?

Helpful behaviors: giving everyone a voice, being nonjudgmental.

TOWARD

ENGAGEMENT

OUTER ACTIONS
What people could see us doing

[5] Given all of this, what else do we need to do to remain compassionate and effective?

Group culture: listen carefully to one another, be compassionate toward others with different interests and styles, risk speaking openly, be kind to ourselves if we make a mistake.

The final step in completing this matrix is step 5: drawing conclusions. After gathering self-awareness in the four quadrants, individuals and groups should consider what steps should be taken to ensure the group remains on track toward helpful behaviors that will help them move toward their purpose. In this spot, portrayed on the graphic's right side, the group should brainstorm aspects of their desired group culture.

These cultural commitments will be ironed out and crystallized later when a group forms a Collaborative Agreement; we'll discuss that more in a moment, and in much greater depth in Chapter 5. However—especially for people who are not prone to be self-aware or are conflict-averse—this first step is critical for laying an early foundation of understanding. Once again, we return to the importance of mindset. Only when each group member understands their own strengths and vulnerabilities, their own motivations and values, and their own potential for disruptive behaviors can a group self-govern effectively. It's these principles, and the *practice* of these principles, that will help people engage in truly prosocial behavior and move away from the self-serving habits that can so easily disrupt collaborative work.

Groups will only self-govern effectively when each group member understands their own strengths and vulnerabilities, their own motivations and values, and their own potential for disruptive behaviors.

If you're thinking that this seems like a lot of effort right out of the gate—you're right. Collaborating well, in a way that will set a group up for long-term health and sustainability, *does* require a lot of effort at the start. You're trying to ensure alignment from the very beginning, considering what the group really wants to do. You're ironing out: Why are we collaborating? What's the purpose, and why does it matter to us? What will each of us contribute to get there? What behaviors might interfere with our ability to move forward?

Think of this as building a foundation. When a builder builds a house, the most interesting part of the build involves getting the walls up, putting in the windows, and putting on the siding and paint. But, actually, these steps in the process are far less important than laying a strong foundation. The process of digging, leveling, pouring concrete, setting rebar, and so on is laborious. It takes a long time, and it doesn't look like much is happening from a distance. But each one of those steps is crucial if you are to build a structure with the potential to last. The same is true when working with others in a sustainable collaboration.

Begin Building a Collaborative Agreement

In Chapter 5, we'll discuss the process of building a Collaborative Agreement with a group. This agreement—essentially, a group covenant, promise, or commitment—helps codify some of the desired behaviors the group will identify after these early brainstorming sessions and also clarify what processes will exist to help resolve conflict and tensions.

One key part of the process asks for each person's commitment in the area of mindset. Each person is asked to build real self-awareness about their personal essence, core purpose, values, helpful and unhelpful thoughts, and helpful and unhelpful behaviors. Essentially, they are asked to bring their full authentic self to the group. We've discussed this self-awareness process in our previous chapter and in the previous sections.

Out of that process of self-awareness, each group member should commit to a mindset of personal agency. In other words, each person says, "I have power to act, and I am responsible to act in helpful ways." Many people have had experiences where they sought to avoid conflict, shut themselves down in a hard conversation, or were passive instead of active in their communication. Unhelpful behaviors might feel instinctive—but they are behaviors that we choose nevertheless. This commitment affirms the fact that we can choose different behaviors—helpful behaviors, behaviors that will better help us move toward our desired direction.

Marsha Linehan, who we discussed in Chapter 1 as a pioneer of dialectical behavioral therapy (DBT), built her therapeutic approach around this concept that people possess the ability to "self-steer" and be their own case managers. She strongly believed in the capabilities of people to take positive action in their lives. Yes, circumstances can often be difficult—but we still have the ability to do something about it. After helping her clients identify what a life worth living would look like, Linehan reminded each client of their task as humans: to collaborate in the business of their life's improvement. She asserted that if they wanted to get better, they had the responsibility to participate, ask for support when needed, and ultimately take action. Every one of us, in fact, has that responsibility: to chart a pathway toward greater quality of life.

With that agency in mind, here's an example of a commitment that a person might initial, affirming their *power* to act:

A COMMITMENT:
I HAVE POWER TO ACT

1. I have power to act autonomously without oversight or control.
2. I have power to seek the materials and information I need.
3. I have power to ask others to treat me with honesty and respect.
4. I have power to ask others to honor their commitments.
5. I have power to identify internal and external tensions and to work to address them along with my colleagues.
6. I have power to be myself and to show my true self to others.
7. I have power to seek advice and make considered decisions.

---

8. I have power to discuss and address inadequate strategies and behaviors that interfere with making our collective impact.
9. I have power to find solutions to issues that I identify.
10. I have power to focus on my personal growth.
11. I have power to look for a shared truth and look at where opposites meet.

The list could go on—we are powerful in many ways! Affirming a commitment to statements like these takes away a person's ability to blame others in their group when things go wrong. It reminds each person what they are capable of doing.

Out of that power flows responsibility. A Collaborative Agreement would also ask each person to commit to a mindset that affirms they are responsible:

A COMMITMENT: I AM RESPONSIBLE TO ACT

1. I am responsible for being self-motivated and bringing my whole potential.
2. I am responsible to provide the materials and information I have.
3. I am responsible for treating others with honesty and respect.
4. I am responsible for honoring my commitments.
5. I am responsible to collaborate with my colleagues and address their internal and external tensions.
6. I am responsible for providing colleagues a safe space to show their true selves by not judging them.
7. I am responsible for offering advice and respecting others' decisions if they don't cause harm.

8. I am responsible for being approachable by my colleagues.

9. I am responsible for addressing issues that I come across.

10. I am responsible for collaborating with others for their personal growth.

11. I am responsible for expressing my views while listening to those of others, even if they are opposed to mine.

Once again, groups will likely be able to brainstorm a long list of areas where each person can affirm their full responsibility.

Let's go back for a moment and think about the original context that inspired the observation of the tragedy of the commons. Imagine that you have a group of medieval farmers who all rely on a common field to graze their cattle. The farmers have various core purposes—one wants to provide for their family; another wants to secure recognition and importance in the town by expanding his farm. However, all their purposes intersect when it comes to their need to sustain the shared common field. No one's cows will get any fatter if that field gets overgrazed; therefore, they have a shared purpose of maintaining the field.

Now let's imagine that all of these farmers sit down together, each with a mug of coffee and some buttered bread. They share a bit about their backgrounds and what each of them really wants out of life. They admit to some of their vulnerabilities; they vouch for their different strengths. They start to map out an agreement of what it might look like to support one another in their shared goal of maintaining their common resource of the field. Questions are raised: What if someone starts taking more than their share? How should we handle it? They identify a conflict resolution process that is respectful and firm and upholds each farmer's dignity. They agree to hold each other accountable if a farmer starts practicing the unhelpful behaviors he admitted to sometimes engaging in; they will talk through those behaviors with him. They each agree that they have power and responsibility to uphold their agreement. When they finally leave their campfire to head home to their wives and their suppers, the farmers feel as though they've left the company of friends. They feel safe, they feel known, and they feel reassured that they are among colleagues who will protect their interests, even as they protect the interests of others.

That is a context for productive collaboration. *That* is a setting that can empower each person to work, unhindered, toward their dreams. *That* is armor against the tragedy of the commons. And *that* is a Person to Person environment.

TESTING SHARED VALUES

Jake's phone vibrated on the library table. He glanced at it: the text was from Leon. *Where r u?* it read.

Glancing at Lana, who sat across from him, Jake quickly texted back the name of the library where they were studying: *Bernard. What's up?*

Several minutes passed. His phone remained silent. It occurred to Jake that Leon might be coming to see him, which—in his mind—was not ideal, given his company. He texted Leon: *I'm w Lana. Can we talk later?*

Before he could press send, Leon was there, dropping his backpack with a thud onto the table. Lana sat back, surprised. "Hey," Leon said, his voice too loud. "Bad news." Several other students looked up sharply with cross expressions. One of them put a finger to her lips: "Sh!"

Leon rolled his eyes at the silent rebukes and sat down next to Lana, across from Jake. Lana made eye contact with Jake and raised an eyebrow. "My roommate," he whispered. "Lana, Leon. Leon, Lana."

"Good to meet you," she whispered.

"Ah, so you're the famous Lana!" Leon said.

"I'm famous?" She turned to Jake and smiled. He blushed and darted Leon a warning look.

"Bad news," Leon hissed in a whisper to Jake. "Tommy's not going to work with us."

"What? Why not?" Jake whispered.

"Well, mainly because it turns out that he's an asshole," Leon said. "I just met with him after our Digital Systems course. I told him the whole plan—I figure out the content, you write the script and present it, he films it and edits the video. And immediately he was asking about how much he was going to get paid. I told him, 'That comes later; we've got to get something off the ground first. We'll figure out how to split it once we get some revenue.' But he wouldn't even agree to start unless I could guarantee him a hundred bucks per video. Are you kidding me?"

"Dang," Jake said. "Yeah, that's not going to work."

"He was trying to throw his weight around and was getting all pushy with me. I was all, 'Correct me if I'm wrong, but are you or are you not a fricking *college freshman*?' Anyway. It was clear to both of us pretty fast that it wasn't going to work. So we need to find someone else."

"Well, the more I think about it, the more I think we need someone who can do more than just film and edit," Jake said. "Most of the best YouTube teaching videos have animation. We need a graphics person, someone who could also film and edit."

Lana spoke quietly. "I might know someone."

The two young men turned to her. "Who?" they asked simultaneously. Leon's voice was once again too loud. The shushing girl turned around in her chair and looked at him angrily. He gave her a goofy grin and waved back. Whispering now to the others, he asked again, "Who?"

"Alex. She's in my Psychology of Leadership class. She did a presentation recently that blew everyone away. The content was honestly pretty thin, but she had put together this incredible video—with graphics and animations, like you said, Jake. It was so well done."

"Do you think she'd be up for working with us?" Jake asked.

"I can ask her. Or—actually . . ." Lana paused, thoughtfully. "It may not be 'her.' It may be 'them.' I think Alex is gender-neutral."

"You're kidding me," Leon said flatly. "Gender-*neutral*?" Both Jake and Lana turned to him. Lana raised a single eyebrow—Jake was beginning to learn how powerful Lana's eyebrows could be. Leon rolled his eyes at their admonishing looks. "Oh, come on. Can we all agree that gender bending is a little ridiculous?"

There was a pause. "No. We cannot all agree on that," Lana said coolly.

"A girl is a girl; a guy is a guy," Leon said. "End of story."

"Not the end of the story, dude," Jake said. "Look: you and I did some good bonding during that run, right? We're friends—right?"

"Right," Leon said, as though that were obvious.

"Well—the bonding happened because you actually cared about where I was coming from. You listened to my story and heard about my family, and the bodega, and all that. And I heard a little about *your* story, which helped me better understand what you're all about. Don't you think it's likely that Alex has a story to share too? And maybe it's worth learning more about her— I mean, *them*," he corrected himself, "before writing them off completely? Sounds like Alex could have something major to contribute to our team."

"Leon," Lana said. She looked at him with a probing gaze. "Does vulnerability make you uncomfortable?"

"What?!" he laughed nervously, then looked at Jake in appeal. "What kind of a question is that?"

Jake shrugged. "It's a legitimate question, Leon."

Lana followed with another. "Do you talk about your feelings very often? Do you ever admit to making mistakes?"

"Ummm . . ." Leon laughed nervously. "No. Because . . . I'm perfect."

Lana was not deterred by his sarcasm. "You and Jake and Alex are not going to have much of a collaboration if you're unable to be your authentic self or let others be their authentic selves." Leon just stared at Lana, his forehead knit together in confusion.

"Her parents are both therapists," Jake explained helpfully.

"In order to be your authentic self," Lana said patiently, "You need to be willing to be vulnerable. Otherwise, this happens." She gestured to him. He looked at her with a confused expression. "You exchange productivity for name calling. You don't understand something, so you disparage it."

Leon whispered to Jake, "She uses big words."

Lana spoke slightly louder: "In other words, you start acting like an asshole." The shushing girl looked at Lana and huffed loudly at her nearby table. She slapped her textbook shut with a bang, then began to make a show of packing her books into her bag.

"I'm the asshole?" Leon asked, weakly.

"Only when you refuse to see someone's whole self and treat them with dignity and respect," Lana said. She put her hand on Leon's shoulder. "Leon. *Your* whole self is worthy of dignity and respect. Even the parts of you that you don't like. It's all worthy. And so are others."

Leon looked back to Jake. "She's doing Jedi mind tricks on me."

The shushing girl pushed past them, indignantly. "Wait!" Leon called after her. The girl turned around and looked at him with a cross expression. Awkwardly, Leon whispered, "I'm sorry I was loud." He paused, then whispered again, as if in clarification: "I'm not an asshole." The girl's expression changed to one of mild annoyance. She mouthed, "Thanks." Then she put her finger up to her lips again—"*Sh!*"—and walked away.

Leon turned back to Jake and Lana. "I'll be nice to Alex. I'll be good," he said.

Lana smiled at him warmly and took his hand. "You *are* good. That's why you can be good to others."

Feeling a touch jealous of the warm fuzzies he was witnessing, Jake decided it was time to get back to business. He stood up. "Cool. Lana—can you text Alex for us? Leon, you and I can get cracking on our stuff." To his relief, Lana and Leon dropped their handhold and began to pack up their bags. Enough studying; it was time to get to work.

EXPLORE FURTHER

If you'd like to learn more, discuss this content with others, or access tools for your own application, go to the interactive section of the book using this QR code.

PART TWO

COMMUNITY
COLLABORATION

*Men build too many walls and
not enough bridges.*

–Joseph Fort Newton

CHAPTER FOUR

TOOLS FOR COLLABORATION

*How to Cultivate Healthy Attitudes toward
Frictionless Collaboration*

Be the change you wish to see in the world.

—Anonymous

When Jake and Lana entered the dorm room, they found Leon reclined in his desk chair, tossing a tennis ball up in the air and catching it again. He was wearing a bright-red shirt emblazoned with the words "MAKE AMERICA GREAT AGAIN."

"Seriously?" Jake asked him. "*That's* what you're going to wear to meet Alex?"

"What?" Leon asked, feigning innocence with a goofy grin. "It's a comfortable T-shirt. It's clean."

"So why haven't I seen you wear it once since we've been living together?" Jake demanded.

Leon caught the tennis ball and leaned forward. His goofy expression changed to a scowl. "You said everyone gets to be their authentic selves. Well, this is part of my authentic self. If I have to respect Alex's gender bending, she should have to respect my MAGA shirt."

"Alex is not 'she,'" Lana corrected, with an edge in her voice. "Pronouns are they, them, and their."

Leon scoffed. "That doesn't even make grammatical sense," he muttered.

Lana sat down. "Leon," she said with a note of sternness. "We want this to work out, which means—"

She was interrupted by a loud buzzing sound. Jake rubbed his eyes. "Shit. She's here. *They're* here," he quickly corrected. Leon grinned in triumph at his roommate's verbal slip and threw the tennis ball at him. The ball hit Jake in the stomach and he winced. "Dude!" he said to Leon. Lana shook her head at both of them. She walked over to the buzzer and pressed the button to let Alex in.

"Well, they're on their way up," she said, resigned. "So. This should be interesting." Jake picked up the tennis ball and threw it back at Leon, hard. Leon caught it with one hand and grinned. There was a knock.

Jake opened the door and smiled nervously. "Alex!" he said in greeting. "I'm Jake. You know Lana. This..." he paused. "This is Leon, my roommate."

"Hey," Alex greeted them collectively and entered the room. Alex was tall, brown-skinned, and dressed all in black, wearing a tight, dark shirt with baggy, ripped black jeans and combat boots. Their long dark hair was coiled in a bun on top of their head, set off by large, bright-red gauges worn in their ears. Tattoos wrapped down both of Alex's arms where the skin was exposed. In spite of himself, Leon straightened up a little.

"Hey," he said back to Alex, with a jerk of his chin. Alex stared at the words on Leon's T-shirt, then met Leon's eyes with a probing stare. After he finally dropped his gaze, Alex turned to the rest of them. "So, who's going to fill me in on this project?"

"Yes, of course—here, sit down," Jake said, and offered Alex his desk chair. He and Lana sat down on the bed, a fact that made him blush in spite of his determination to stay cool. He began explaining the vision for the YouTube videos that he and Leon had discussed, both the short-term goal of making money and building a following, then the long-term goal of using their platform for positive messaging. He explained each of their roles: "So, Leon is going to figure out the content we share; I'm going to teach it and assemble the information in an accessible, interesting way. Ideally, you would contribute as a video editor and possible animator."

Lana spoke up. "And I'm the group therapist, slash leadership consultant." This was met by a grin from Jake and an eye roll from Leon. Lana continued. "We'd love to know more about you, Alex," she said. "I've seen some of your work in class, but it would be great for Jake and Leon to know more about your design work and your experience and everything. Your interests. You know, just—more of who you are."

"Sure," Alex said. Leon was surprised by how feminine Alex's voice sounded. They weren't fitting his expectations of what he'd imagined a "gender-neutral" person to be. "Well, I'm good at art. I'm good at design. That stuff has always felt really easy to me. I started doing videography and filmmaking in high school when they recruited me for the student journalism team. We won some awards. Umm..." They paused, thinking. "I don't think in words; I think in pictures, so all my notes in class are illustrations."

"I've seen them," Lana said appreciatively. "They're amazing."

"But that's not what I'm actually interested in. My real passion is black holes."

"I'm sorry, what?" Leon asked, leaning forward.

"Black holes," Alex said matter-of-factly. "Holographic worlds, the gravitational leviathans of the universe that twist space and time, you know. So I'm pursuing a dual degree: a BA in graphic design and a Bachelor of Science in physics and astronomy. The graphic design is my way of paying the bills until I'm done with my post-doc research in astrophysics."

"Dang," Jake said, impressed.

"Also, I'm Samoan. Not that I'm big on checking demographic boxes or anything, but it tells you something about my background."

"Yeah, what demographic boxes *do* you check?" Leon asked. Lana and Jake both shot him a warning look.

Alex looked at him with a steady gaze. "Very few," they answered. "'I am large. I contain multitudes.'"

Leon looked shocked. "I know that quote. I love that quote. That's Bob Dylan, right?"

"Walt Whitman," Alex corrected.

"I almost had that tattooed on my body when I turned eighteen," he said.

"I *have* that tattooed on my body," Alex said coolly. Leon opened his mouth but Alex spoke first. "You can't see it." They stared at Leon. "So, what about you?" Alex said. "What's your story?"

Leon straightened up. Jake noticed that his roommate's neck had started to flush. He cleared his throat. "Yeah, well—my thing is coding and software engineering. I'm into video games. I'm politically conservative—I'm guessing *you're* pretty liberal," he said.

"*I'm* liberal," Lana said. "Is that a problem for you, Leon?"

Alex ignored Lana's comment and calmly responded to Leon. "I don't consider myself politically anything. I subscribe to a lot of libertarian principles. I'm socially liberal and fiscally conservative. I read Karl Marx and Adam Smith. I'm an anarchist at heart but a capitalist in practice." Alex paused. "Like I said, I don't like boxes."

"Leon, tell us about your family," Jake said gently.

Leon shot him a look of surprise. "What does that have to do with anything?" he asked.

Jake shrugged. "It's part of who you are."

Leon sighed and scowled. "Well, I'm Irish-German. My dad is a super successful workaholic who has crazy-high expectations. No one can please him, least of all himself. My mom is…whatever. I have a half-sister who's way older than me." He shrugged. "We're an 'all-American' family," he said sarcastically.

"You seem tense," Lana observed to Leon. "What's up?"

"Look, there's a definite three-versus-one vibe right now," Leon said, throwing up his arms. "If you can't be cool with my asshole self, then maybe we should just quit before we get started."

"Leon, no one is ganging up on you—" Lana tried to interject.

"No offense, Lana, but why are you even here?" Leon shot at her. "You're not involved with this YouTube project. You're not filming, or performing, or generating content, so why are you here? As far as I'm concerned, you're mostly just distracting my roommate from doing his work on the project. And your therapist act is getting old."

Jake stood up, furious. "Look man, I don't know what's going on with you right now, but you really are acting like an asshole. We're going to talk about this later. But I think this meeting has gone about as far as it can productively go." He grabbed his coat and his book bag. "Alex, it was awesome meeting you. Lana, I'm sorry—I have to get out of this room. I'll call you."

"I'm leaving too," she said. She grabbed her bag and avoided looking at Leon as she followed Jake out. "Alex—see you in class." The door shut loudly.

There was a long pause. Finally, Alex picked up their satchel and walked over to Leon, who still sat in his desk chair, his face flushed all over. Silently, Alex held out a closed fist. Confused, Leon looked up. Alex held his gaze. Finally, awkwardly, Leon made a fist and bumped Alex's hand. Then Alex turned and walked out of the dorm room, leaving Leon alone.

MINDSET LEADS TO ATTITUDE

In our previous chapter, we discussed the fact that productive collaboration must start with an intentional mindset. If we are to avoid the tragedy of the commons, we need to deliberately set aside self-serving behavior and instead adopt the prosocial principles that can help us embrace the nurturing, collaborative instincts that are part of our biological wiring. Many of Atkins's prosocial principles relate to an internal mindset—principles like developing a strong identity and understanding of your purpose. Other prosocial principles describe behaviors that are directly *informed* by our mindsets, like the decision to increase your helpful behavior and decrease your unhelpful behavior; another one would be the commitment to fast and fair conflict resolution. Particularly when it comes to these mindset-informed behaviors, attitude has the power to make or break successful collaboration.

Take our illustration of Jake and Leon's group, for instance. At this point in the narrative, each person has identified key aspects of their identity, and they've formed a shared purpose. The group members have started to identify their different roles and responsibilities. They've shown a willingness to share and collaborate with decisions. In other words, they're doing a lot right. However, even with a healthy beginning, there's still enormous potential for conflict and friction. In this case, the friction comes about largely as a result of attitude.

Attitude can be defined as the *manner* in which mindset translates to behavior. Mindset relates to our thoughts, feelings, and internal decisions; behavior relates to our actions, external decisions, and observable movements. Attitude serves as the bridge between the two. It's *the way* in which we express behaviors, and it will color the tone of the collaborative process. You can express a helpful attitude, a cheerful attitude, a sullen attitude, a deferential attitude, an introverted or extroverted attitude, and so on.

~ ల ~

Attitude can be defined as the manner in which mindset translates to behavior.

Leon's attitude in our opening illustration was obviously very negative. He was combative, defensive, and sarcastic. Although his mindset was still aligned with the project's purpose and his actions were still serving the project, his *attitude* created significant friction in his collaboration with the others. In fact, because of that negative attitude, he indicated a readiness to drop the project entirely.

Conflict and tension are inevitable when collaborating with other people because we all come to the table with different experiences, different skills, and different personalities. A diversity in these areas can lead to a richness of ideas, but it can also pose myriad challenges. Something as seemingly insignificant as a T-shirt or a pronoun can have the potential to be misconstrued by team members with different preferences and turn into a source of conflict. Different work preferences, styles of communication, and personalities can turn into even bigger clashes.

However, successful collaboration requires that people commit to pursuing a positive attitude. Granted, it is difficult to simply force yourself to adopt a different attitude when you're stuck in a negative mood, like Leon was. Frictionless collaboration doesn't mean you always need to *feel* positive, but it does require that you *commit* yourself to using resources that will help move your attitude in a productive direction. For instance, rather than choosing to stew in bitterness, you would commit to the process of airing your feelings of tension aloud so that a conflict-solving process could begin with other team members. That's why the two commitments we discussed in our previous chapter, about each group member's *power* to act and *responsibility* to act, are key.

Frictionless collaboration requires that you commit yourself to using resources that will help move your attitude in a productive direction.

In this chapter, we're going to describe a number of collaborative tools that can help groups rise above these challenging moments, shape a productive attitude, and pursue positive interactions with other group members. There are certainly other tools out there that can help groups work together effectively, but these are the ones that we've experienced to be most effective. We encourage groups to avail themselves of any and all resources that will optimize their collaboration; each person and each group will need to determine which tools best serve their purpose.

COLLABORATIVE TOOLS

These tools acknowledge two important realities, true of every person:

1. **We all bring both helpful and unhelpful behaviors to any setting.** We are each shaped by our past experiences and our future desires. We are human beings, each possessing our own set of strengths, weaknesses, skills, and hang-ups. For all these reasons, we cannot and will not be perfect.

2. However, **we also have the capacity to grow**. We can commit to behaviors that will help us move in a healthy direction. We can take personal responsibility to pursue development in key areas that will enable us to make a greater contribution to the people around us.

By openly acknowledging our flaws, we can choose transparency. By committing to learn, we can choose growth. When we come to a collaborative process with both transparency and a commitment to grow, we not only become better collaborators—we become better human beings.

Each of these tools is meant to fuel healthy collaboration, but on a broader scale, they each help fuel greater quality of life. These resources will help us engage more fully and authentically with one another, enabling genuine connections from person to person. Each tool is also made available for your own personal reflection on our website; please see this chapter's QR code.

When we choose to be transparent
and commit to growth, we not only become
better collaborators—we become
better human beings.

Troubleshooting: Building Awareness

This first tool is one that pessimists and worst-case-scenario thinkers can embrace: you troubleshoot by building awareness about all the potential pitfalls that may come. Another way to describe this first tool is "foreseeing an unwanted future." By imagining all the ways that potential pitfalls could lead to an unwanted future, you and your team can take steps to prevent that unwanted future from happening. We discussed this activity briefly in our previous chapter when we discussed the ACT matrix, but we're going to explore it more thoroughly here.

For this troubleshooting exercise, you make efforts to grow awareness about yourself, your team, and everyone's preferred styles of collaboration. Your awareness about yourself will primarily come through introspective reflection; that process could have started with the ACT matrix. This Troubleshooting tool is one that's employed mainly at the beginning of the collaboration's work,[64] and each colleague engages with the self-awareness they have at the start of the process. So, for instance, Alex may know that they sometimes lose interest on a project if it starts to become boring and will move on to a different project that seems more interesting, leaving the first one undone. That's a tendency that could threaten the productive work of the collaboration, and it's important for Alex to communicate that tendency to the group.

---

[64] Done as a preliminary step in creating the Collaborative Agreement, discussed further in Chapter 5.

After identifying potential trouble spots, it's each colleague's responsibility to then identify strategies that will help them overcome that pitfall. Alex, for example, might decide to proactively communicate when they can sense growing boredom and come to the group for accountability and help—either in shifting responsibilities or motivation to finish the project. Group members can also help each other brainstorm these solutions.

Each colleague should do this troubleshooting process for themselves and also listen to their teammates' troubleshooting processes, weighing in as appropriate during the brainstorming process. Finally, the group looks at the body of potential pitfalls they've identified and tries to generate as many ideas as possible about how the group might falter in their work together. We saw an example in the opening illustration about how Jake's group was vulnerable to falling apart, as a result of several combustive pitfalls colliding: Leon's defensiveness, Jake's tendency to escape during conflict, and Lana's reactiveness as a result of pride. Only Alex managed to keep a cool head—perhaps because Alex is used to people reacting against their differences and has learned productive strategies to cope with other people's rudeness.

The troubleshooting exercise would prompt colleagues to consider how their own tendencies could cause trouble, along with how their interactions could spark new conflicts. In considering all these ahead of time, colleagues can make a plan out of their "wise minds" to mitigate the trouble when it comes.

In short, the Troubleshooting tool looks to build awareness in three key areas:

1. Your own potential pitfalls and strategies to overcome them.
2. Your teammates' potential pitfalls and strategies to overcome them.
3. Your team's collective potential pitfalls and strategies to overcome them.

The troubleshooting process is firstly a way to become more aware of those feelings that might "hook" you, those thoughts that might keep you from pursuing your goals or dreams, and/or any behaviors that might interfere with your ability to experience frictionless collaboration with others. But secondly, it also requires that you envision helpful actions or resources that will support you as you pursue growth toward effective collaboration. So, while building awareness about pitfalls helps you become more aware of what *isn't* helping you, the Troubleshooting tool simultaneously invites you to reflect on what *will* actually help you to overcome these difficulties. That combined knowledge will increase the probability that you and your group will be able to build the future that you actually want.

The Troubleshooting tool invites you to consider what strategies will help you to overcome your hang-ups, obstacles, and difficulties.

Let's consider the example of Leon. For whatever reason, Alex's addition to the group seems to rattle Leon; he also seems alternately drawn to and repelled by Lana and Jake's invitations to be vulnerable. His reaction to circumstances that make him uncomfortable is to get aggressive and hostile and blame others. In order to move forward in a productive way in this collaboration, Leon needs to commit to pursuing self-awareness about why he becomes so combative in situations that make him feel insecure. Once he builds this self-awareness, he should share his discoveries with the group—which might be something like this: "If I think there's a chance people won't approve of me, I tend to deliberately push them away. I just want to clarify that I genuinely want to be in a healthy relationship with each of you. If I start acting defensive or combative, that says more about my fear of being rejected than my lack of faith in you. I'm open to feedback if—and when—you see that happen. Just let me know that you can see I'm struggling with the aggressive thing, and I'll work on it." Leon doesn't have this self-awareness yet—but by the end of the chapter, he'll be getting there.

By identifying and then communicating your potential pitfalls to the group, you grow everyone's awareness—particularly your own. Everyone on the team will be more attentive in dealing with this interfering behavior. Your group members are also likely to have more patience and compassion with you as you display interfering behaviors because they will understand the fears that are behind those unhelpful actions; they'll also appreciate the fact that *you* know it's a problem and are working on it. Altogether, your team will experience greater ease in communicating about interfering behaviors and will increase its collaborative skills.

If anyone struggles to engage with the troubleshooting process because they lack self-awareness, several questions can get the ball rolling. The first two questions help people identify their pitfalls; the third asks them to identify solutions to overcome those pitfalls, and those solutions can be brainstormed as a group:

- **Do I ever experience tensions or feelings that steer my behavior in such a way that I create obstacles for myself in achieving my long-term goals?**
- **Do I ever get feedback from others who say that I behave inadequately or do something unhelpful?**
- **Is there anything I can do to mitigate my unhelpful behaviors and overcome them, for the sake of our collaboration?**

If Leon were to engage with these troubleshooting questions, he would have a hard time not owning his unhelpful behavior. Here's how he might respond to each one:

- Do I ever experience tensions or feelings that steer my behavior in such way that I create obstacles for myself in achieving my long-term goals?
  - » Leon's response: *Um, yes. I want to do this project with Jake, but I keep acting like an asshole. I intentionally do rude things, and I'm mean to*

> *Lana when she tries to help. It's like I'm sabotaging myself, not to mention the work we're trying to do.*

- Do I ever get feedback from others who say that I behave inadequately or do something unhelpful?
  - » Leon's response: *Lana says I'm uncomfortable being vulnerable. She said— what was it? I exchange productivity for name calling. When I don't understand something, I disparage it. Jake says I'm unhelpful and called me an asshole.*
- Is there anything I can do to mitigate my unhelpful behaviors and overcome them, for the sake of our collaboration?
  - » Leon's response: *I can take a pause. Sometimes if I just have some time to cool down, I realize that I'm self-sabotaging and get my head on straight again. I can also write down the reasons why I want to stick with this group and make it work.*

How should people engage with this Troubleshooting tool if they hate the idea of voicing tension aloud? Communicating about tension with your group is a key part of this troubleshooting process—both owning your own pitfalls and providing feedback that alerts others to their own unhelpful behaviors. (Note: there's a productive and an unproductive way to communicate feedback to others, which we'll discuss in greater depth later in this chapter.) However, for some people, communicating openly about tension feels deeply uncomfortable.

When people experience trouble communicating about pitfalls, that trouble largely occurs on a mindset level. But mindsets can be changed under the right conditions. When everyone in a group decides to operate according to the same guidelines, then safety can be afforded to the person who dreads conflict. Ideally, each team member will agree not to judge each other; they will all commit to communicate respectfully, listen, and contribute in a constructive way. These shared commitments can make transparency feel safe for everyone.

In traditional hierarchical organizations, people often depend on their bosses to call out areas of dysfunction or tension; if and when the boss doesn't, the employees may be reluctant to initiate a problem-solving process because they don't feel ownership over the workplace environment. However, in a true collaboration, when everyone is on the same level, everyone is responsible for maintaining the group's collaborative health.

When each person in a group builds awareness about the ways they could potentially go off course, they're all motivated and alert about how best to stay *on* course. They learn how to mitigate and manage their potential pitfalls; they also gain the information they need to pursue targeted development in key skill areas. When everyone seeks to increase their personal skills and build up the collective skills of the group, the collaboration will richly benefit. The more we become familiar with our own needs, tendencies, pitfalls, and abilities, the better we can learn how to take care of them and make the best use of them.

The Troubleshooting tool is where self-awareness begins. It's done at the start of the collaborative process so that inevitable conflict can be planned for, and it should be engaged during a time of calm, when everyone is functioning out of their "wise minds." In doing so, colleagues optimize the chances that they will be able to manage that conflict productively when it comes, building resilience against challenges and sustaining their collaboration.

However, the self-awareness process shouldn't *end* with the troubleshooting process. Most of us may have some limited self-awareness that is informed by the experiences we've already had. But when we get into new experiences— for instance, Leon working with Alex, a person far different compared to most of the people in Leon's demographic bubble—we discover new triggers and pitfalls. For that reason, an additional self-awareness tool is required, one that can be implemented even in the midst of strong emotions and done at any time during the collaborative process. That's what the Behavior Chain Analysis tool is for.

Behavior Chain Analysis

The Behavior Chain Analysis is a behavioral therapy tool that provides a way to analyze all the elements that influence your behavior. This tool will draw your attention not only to the circumstances that might trigger you, but also the thoughts that hook you, like interpretations and judgments. Often, an unhelpful (and frequently emotionally clouded) thought can escalate your feelings, driving you to do things that feel right in the moment, but that interfere with your long-term goals. For example, in our narrative, Leon said that he perceived a "three-versus-one vibe." Actually, all three group members were eager to support Leon and better understand him. His incorrect interpretation that they were ganging up on him led to his angry response and unhelpful behavior. The Behavior Chain Analysis helps a person break down all their behavioral components so they can actively intervene and change their behavior.

The ability to analyze our own behavior allows us to determine what causes it and what maintains it. In other words, you're asking yourself, "What are my triggers and what *keeps* me in that negative headspace?" Knowing this information is important for any of us if we want to change our own behavior.

Here's how it works. Any behavior can be understood as a series of linked components. These links are "chained" together because they follow in succession, one after the other; one link in the chain leads to another. For behaviors that are well rehearsed—that is, responses that we have often—a reactive behavior may appear instantaneous. It might seem the flow between thought and action cannot be broken down into steps. A "chain analysis" provides a series of questions for unlocking these links that sometimes feel stuck together:

BEHAVIOR CHAIN ANALYSIS QUESTIONS

These questions are also provided on our website, for personal reflection.

1. What is the problematic behavior?
2. What prompts that behavior? (circumstances, thoughts, feelings, etc.)
3. What is its function? That is, what am I getting out of behaving like this?
4. What interferes with resolving this behavior? In other words, why do I keep doing the unhelpful behavior rather than changing it?
5. What aids are available to help solve the problem?
6. What is the consequence of this behavior?

By working through each of these questions, you will build a better understanding of *why* you behave the way you do and how that behavior functions and continues, and build clarity about whether or not this behavior serves your purpose. It gives you more information about how you can decrease your unhelpful behaviors and ultimately increase your ability to self-govern.

Let's consider how Leon might respond to each of these questions. If he struggles to do this process on his own, he might be helped by the counsel of an empathetic, emotionally intelligent person, like either Jake or Lana:

1. What is the problem?

   I get angry and lash out at my group members.

2. What is prompting it?

   When I sense that people disapprove of me somehow. That pisses me off.

3. What is its function? That is, what am I getting out of behaving like this?

   If I push people away, then I'm in control of the situation. They're not rejecting me because of me; they're rejecting me because I intentionally pushed them away. That makes me feel less exposed.

4. What interferes with resolving this behavior?

   I'm afraid that if I show people my whole self, they'll hate me and won't want to be around me. That's basically the message I got from my dad growing up.

5. What aids are available to help solve the problem?

   I can choose to trust that my group members actually want to know who I am and won't reject me when they learn more about me. I can try to stop myself from letting those thoughts run away with me by doing deep breathing and taking a break to calm down. I can journal about the things that are good about me so that I am more confident I have something good to offer.

6. What is the consequence of this behavior?

   When I intentionally push people away, then the result I fear actually comes true. It's a self-fulfilling prophecy: people don't want to be around me anymore because I won't let them. If I actually want people to stick with me, I need to do something different.

When a person walks through each of these steps, they get the opportunity to go back and examine where in the chain they might have the ability to change something. Leon might conclude, "Next time I start to assume that people disapprove of me, I'm actually going to question that thought. Maybe I can even ask my group members to tell me what they think about me in that moment and just dialogue about it. At least then I'd be dealing with factual information, not my fears and assumptions."

These helpful conclusions will ideally be supported and encouraged by your group members. Each of them will also be owning their unhelpful behaviors and doing their own Behavior Chain Analysis. If Jake owns his tendency to shut down when he feels attacked, if Lana admits to trying to control others when she feels anxious, if Alex acknowledges that they tend to leave projects unfinished when something new and interesting comes up—then Leon might very well feel more safety in working through his own challenges. A collaborative team supports one another; they walk alongside each other during the messy process of trying to improve behavior, failing, and trying again.

Sometimes, a person might say, "When you do [this thing], I just can't help reacting." But when you engage in blaming others for your behavior, you put yourself in a victim's position and deny the fact that you have real power over your actions. In fact, you do have power over how you respond to other people. You had a thought, which prompted a feeling, which triggered a behavior. By analyzing *what* thoughts, feelings, and behaviors are linked together, you can identify the different steps between a trigger and response and learn to interrupt them. Eventually, you can "unlearn" that unhelpful reaction and learn to adopt a new one. This exercise builds on the discoveries that would have been first generated during the ACT matrix work: you're tracking the *inward* thoughts that manifest in *outward* behaviors and figuring out how you can move *toward* the engaging behaviors that will move you toward your purpose.

Each person is responsible for initiating the Behavior Chain Analysis; most likely, this initiation will be prompted when a person experiences the consequence of their unhelpful behavior. Leon, for instance—when left alone in his dorm room—will realize that his outburst has jeopardized the entire group's ability to move forward on the project, exactly the result that he's afraid of and one that threatens his purpose. If and when he makes this realization, it is his choice to engage in this analytical activity. Likely, a person will also be prompted by their commitment to recognize they have power and responsibility over their actions, as discussed in the previous chapter. Some people will prefer to do this analysis independently; others will be helped the most by talking through it with their group members during a Commitment Session, which we'll discuss at the end of this chapter. People can even try to engage a Behavior Chain Analysis in the heat of the moment, if they're willing to work through the questions.

That doesn't mean group members don't have the opportunity to address another group member's interfering behavior. However, this should not be done via accusation. Instead, group members should own their *own* interfering behaviors, which may have been triggered by another person's actions. For instance, the next time Jake, Lana, Alex, and Leon are gathered, Jake might say, "I've realized that I tend to shut down and escape when I feel attacked. It's 'flight mode'—I want to get out of conflict by escaping it. But I recognize that running away isn't ultimately helping our collaboration. Instead, I need to find a way to stay engaged, stay calm, and talk through a conflict in a productive way."

It doesn't work to push someone to talk about a feeling that they're not willing to talk about. That will only cause someone to get defensive. However, if group members are *invited* to process about a behavior that impacts the rest of the group's ability to collaborate, in the context of a safe space where other group members are sharing about their own struggles, they'll typically feel more inclined to self-reflect. We'll discuss this more in our section on Commitment Sessions.

Development Objectives: Personal Goal Setting

Once people have built awareness about the ways they could potentially disrupt the productive collaboration of the group, they can identify areas for personal development. Essentially, this is personal goal setting. You identify an objective in terms of how you want to develop yourself to grow as a collaborator, and that may relate to your collaborative skills, your interpersonal abilities, working through some personal struggles, or strengthening your technical skills. This process of identifying Development Objectives can be done on your own or in a group Commitment Session, which we'll discuss in a moment. Regardless of where or how you form these objectives, this tool is primarily one for personal use.

The Development Objectives process is not focused on a specific outcome; it's not about a target to hit. Rather, it's a *process* that you identify wanting to take yourself through. When thinking of goal setting as a process, a collaborative group becomes a safe place to learn. Each colleague can learn through trial and error—what works and what doesn't? What's helpful and what isn't?

For example, Leon might set as a personal goal, "I want to stop picking fights with my group members." Using the information he's gathered from the Behavior Chain Analysis tool, he would work with his group members to develop strategies to help mitigate that unhelpful behavior. Some strategies will likely work better than others, but there's freedom for trial and error. For instance, Leon might initially agree to try to engage with Lana's questions in a heated moment but find that—when he's emotionally flooded with adrenaline, in "fight mode"—he's not able to engage those questions productively. He might try a different strategy: taking time away from the group to cool off. The safe, transparent learning-process environment created by the group would allow for this experimentation.

If Leon made his Development Objectives about an outcome instead of a process, he might easily get discouraged. Focusing on a specific result can cause obstacles to rise immediately: "I won't succeed. This won't work. I'm going to fail, and my group will hate me." Those unhelpful thoughts will block anyone quickly. But by focusing on a process instead of a result, group members are given permission to try, struggle, and try again, gradually giving themselves practice in behavior that will eventually help them move forward.

Forming Development Objectives is about identifying a process that you want to pursue, not a result that you want to achieve. This allows for safety in trial and error.

With this tool we also acknowledge what is already working and going well. That means we're actively encouraging ourselves, cheering ourselves on, and learning how to practice self-validation. The Commitment Sessions, discussed more in a moment, would be the ideal place to provide this encouragement. During a session, a group can provide a safe space to cheer for their own helpful behaviors or those of others. By sharing information with your group about your own personal Development Objectives, you can highlight your helpful behaviors, skills, and expertise. A facilitator can actively encourage group members to cheer for themselves by asking them to explicitly share one of their personal evolutions or a gratifying moment at the start of a Commitment Session, for example. Alternately, they each might start the session by naming one of the qualities they appreciate about another group member.

This affirming process will not only help us to build more self-esteem and experience more comfort during collaboration, but it will also make us more resilient for feedback as well. When you become more aware of your variety of skills and less focused on your shortcomings alone, your urge to defend yourself will decrease. This can increase your willingness to learn from feedback and will help you evolve. For someone like Leon, whose struggles largely arise out of a fear of rejection, this affirming process can be especially powerful in helping to overcome personal hang-ups.

FORMING DEVELOPMENT OBJECTIVES: KEY CONSIDERATIONS

These questions are also provided on our website, for personal reflection.

- What is my objective for development? In other words, in what areas do I want to pursue growth?
- What tools and/or strategies do I want to try out, to grow in this area?
- What process will I use to evaluate my progress and reflect on how it's going?
- What strategies/tools are helping me engage productively with my group? What behaviors can I be proud of?

Strengthen Interpersonal Skills

The *Troubleshooting* tool starts the process of building awareness about personal hindrances and interfering behaviors, along with how to prevent interfering behaviors from happening; the *Behavior Chain Analysis* goes deeper in generating self-awareness; and the *Development Objectives* are about setting a process goal for growth and development. Now we get to some specific tools that can help people implement that growth for the benefit of their collaboration (and, in fact, all their relationships) through using interpersonal skills. Interpersonal skills are helpful behaviors to achieve effective collaboration with others, but they can also be useful to anyone pursuing an effective relationship.

Collaboration and interpersonal relationships give you benefits (shared responsibility, support, dialogue) but can also induce difficulties (conflict, disagreement, micromanagement). For example, some people are inclined to be very accommodating to the will of the other group members and don't acknowledge themselves. Over time, they lose their self-esteem and feel less and less confident in their own ideas. Other people might be overly focused on their own goals, pushing to have things their way and seeking acknowledgment for their contribution. That can cause difficulties in relationships because other people will feel dominated and frustrated to not have a voice.

Part of forming a healthy collaboration involves each group member committing to working on these interpersonal skills, a commitment that would be crystallized in the Collaborative Agreement, which we'll discuss in our next chapter. These interpersonal skills provide tools that help people work toward effective collaboration.

These interpersonal skills can help group members act effectively in three areas:

- Achieving a specific objective
- Maintaining healthy relationships and ending unhealthy relationships
- Maintaining your self-esteem

While working on these interpersonal skills, it's worth staying mindful of the difficulties identified during the troubleshooting exercise. Those various hindrances that can prevent you from being effective might be insecurity over your lack of skills, worrying thoughts, emotional reactions, indecision, environmental factors, myths, or a combination of different factors. Being able to adequately anticipate the occurrence of and triggers for these difficulties will help you to remain effective in the collaboration while working to build up these skills. Once again, you're invited to engage in your own reflection about these interpersonal skills by referencing the associated content on our website, accessible via this chapter's QR code.

Skill 1: Self-Advocacy to Reach Your Goals

Let's say that your neighbor wants to borrow your car. They're not insured to drive your car, and their own cars have plenty of dents on them. You want to say no, but you don't want to make the relationship awkward. So instead, you say yes and then experience stress, frustration, and worry until the car is returned. If something does happen to the car, you might feel excessive anger both at your neighbor and yourself for not saying no in the first place.

This illustration points to the importance of self-advocacy to reach your goals. In order to disengage from the culture of blame that characterizes so many interactions in today's world, you need to self-advocate for the things that matter to you. Self-advocacy enables you to reach your goals and increase the chances that people will take you seriously.

This is likely an interpersonal skill that Jake, who has the tendency to flee from conflict, would struggle with; we've provided examples of how Jake could commit to practicing each skill.

- **Describe what you mean: provide clear information and explanations.**
  - » Jake might clearly state his goal: "I want us to move forward with this YouTube project, and I want each person to follow through with their roles and responsibilities."

- **Show your feelings and express your opinion to clarify why something is important to you.**
    - » Jake might tell his other group members, "I feel bummed that we're struggling to get this collaboration off the ground. I think it's an awesome idea, and I really want to see if it has the potential to generate some extra income for us. That would help me a ton, and I'm also really excited about the idea of using a YouTube platform to spread positive messages."
- **Stand up for yourself, allowing yourself to have a voice and be encouraged.**
    - » Jake's words here might be, "I know I'm an engaging teacher, and I think I can make content that people will want to watch."
- **Strengthen your position by explaining the mutual benefits of reaching your goals.**
    - » Jake might remind the other group members, "All of us have a reason to do this. Leon, you're going to take a deep dive into content that you already care about and could start making money in an area where you're a true entrepreneur, where you have control over how much time you invest. Alex, you're going to be able to get valuable experience, which is going to make you more marketable as a designer and videographer. Lana, this is an opportunity for you to try out some of the leadership principles that you're so excited about and see if they work. This project benefits all of us."
- **Stay alert and mindful if you believe your point is worth making and ignore attacks.**
    - » Jake might say, "I don't believe any of us actually wants to quit. I think we've just hit a speed bump and we need to work through it."
- **Negotiate, reverse roles, explain the problem to others, and ask them for solutions.**
    - » Jake might focus on Leon here: "Leon, this project was your idea. Do you really want to quit, truly? Or do we just need to brainstorm some strategies to get past this?"

- **Radiate self-confidence.**
  - » In order for Jake—or anyone—to radiate self-confidence, he needs to remember why his stance has merit and why his ideas have worth.

These skills are meant to give you more than one opportunity to continue the conversation in an adequate way while trying to reach your goal. They're tips and tricks for anyone who wants to grow in the area of self-advocacy to increase their abilities to effectively communicate.

Skill 2: Affirm Others to Maintain Healthy Relationships

One important way to build unity and trust among group members is to communicate your approval of other group members and your interest in them, and affirm who they are. Skill 2 is especially relevant to people who might struggle at times to affirm other people's ideas. This might be a challenge for Alex, who doesn't personally experience gratification from verbal affirmation. Alex has learned to pursue their own agenda as an artist, apart from what people think or say about it; generally, Alex expects other people to do their assignments in a group, whether or not there are verbal warm fuzzies exchanged. However, this attitude can come across as aloof or disinterested, even though that may not be an accurate reflection of how Alex really feels about the other group members.

Lana might also struggle with this skill at times. She can be so confident in her own ideas that she sometimes forgets to consider where other people are coming from. However, both Lana and Alex want to help the group thrive as a united whole, making this interpersonal skill an important one for them to lean into.

When your aim is to maintain healthy relationships, your interpersonal skills will help you to maintain or improve your collaborative relationships. This skill of affirming other group members can help you work together to achieve your common goals.

In order for the collaborative relationship to remain healthy, group members could commit to the following affirming practices:

- **Be friendly: don't attack, threaten, or make judgments.**
  - » When Lana sees Leon again, she could open the conversation with a friendly greeting, a joke about how they left things, or even a hug. This disarming greeting would help communicate she wants to continue to work together in the collaboration, even though their last interaction ended on a bad note.
- **Show your interest.**
  - » Alex could demonstrate this by asking questions about Leon's discoveries in gaming or Jake's history with teaching.
- **Validate others by being attentive and recognizing and supporting them.**
  - » Alex could grow beyond their attitude of apparent aloofness by complimenting the other group members when they do something well and being specific about what they liked.
- **Behave in a relaxed manner using humor and diplomacy.**
  - » Lana can get so passionate about her ideas that her intensity leads in any conversation. She can help put her group members at ease by leading instead with humor. She can still pursue her ideas but may decide her group members are most likely to go with her if she asks them questions that build her understanding of where they're coming from and affirming their ideas.

Skill 3: Respect Yourself to Maintain Your Self-Esteem

When your aim is to sustain your self-esteem, it is important to act with respect for yourself. Acting with dignity is essential. Self-esteem helps you to feel good about yourself and be confident in your ideas, and allows you to have more harmonious interactions with others. The combined effect promotes collaboration.

This is an area Leon will want to grow in. His veneer of brash arrogance masks his inward insecurity. He can easily slip into mental thoughts of self-loathing, convincing himself that people disapprove of him and will reject him if they see his true self. That mindset will disable Leon from productive collaboration, but he can pursue progress in his area by working on Skill 3.

To make sure you respect yourself while trying to achieve your cooperative goals, you commit to:

- **Be honest with yourself and others**
  - » Leon can choose to be honest with his other group members when he's struggling with a negative mindset. He can also recruit them as truth-tellers, checking his perception of what he assumes they think with their actual thoughts.
- **Not apologize for valid actions**
  - » Leon might be embarrassed of emotions like sadness and fear; if he were to share those sorts of feelings with his group members, he might feel compelled to apologize for them. However, he can demonstrate respect for himself by recognizing that these emotions are valid.
- **Hold on to your values**
  - » Leon's insecure emotional reactions are not consistent with his values to promote collaboration in the group. Until he is able to experience greater self-governance in that area, he can hold on to his values by apologizing to his group members when he lashes out and continuing to work on his reactiveness.
- **Be truthful, not lie**
  - » Leon should check his assumptions and seek to be transparent with his group.
- **Not act helpless if you're not**
  - » Leon shouldn't play the victim; instead, he can respect himself by owning his power and responsibility to grow in areas where he struggles.

- **Not exaggerate**
  - » Exaggerating can be a technique that blame-casters use, inflating a wrong done to them to manipulate others. However, Leon could respect himself and achieve greater clarity about perceived slights if he simply focuses on the facts of what happened.

Each person will have areas where they are naturally strong interpersonally, and other areas where they are naturally weak. For instance, Lana is exceptional at perceiving the emotional state of other people but may need to shelve her own ambitious agenda sometimes to honor other people's ideas. Alex has commendable self-control but could show more warmth.

By learning where you are most effective in your interpersonal skills, you can lean into those strengths. Other group members may be able to benefit from your wisdom in a certain area of interpersonal skills, helping them grow. It's also important to recognize that certain factors can reduce your interpersonal effectiveness; for instance, Jake balks and runs when he senses conflict. In building self-awareness about your interpersonal effectiveness and challenges, you can better facilitate collaboration with your colleagues.

By taking yourself through these collaborative tools—both individually and as a group—you'll be better equipped to return to the ACT matrix and fill it out with your entire group in mind. You'll now have a much clearer idea of what troubles have the potential to arise, what behaviors you'd like to commit to, and what skills and strategies can help you to do that.

Here's what Jake, Alex, Lana, and Leon might come up with after working through some of these tools. They're now highly aware of ways their group could possibly struggle and have made a plan for ways they can push through those struggles and maintain their commitment to the collaboration:

INNER THOUGHTS AND FEELINGS
What people cannot see

OBSTACLES

What thoughts or feelings might hook us from moving toward our motivation and positive engagement?

Thoughts: I can't do this; I suck; my group members suck; maybe this isn't worthwhile; this sloppy quality is good enough.

Feelings: Insecurity, distrust, anger, apathy, uninspired, laziness, discouragement, losing faith.

MOTIVATION

What matters to the group?

Values, beliefs: educate, inspire, artistic excellence, belonging, healthy collaboration, respect, self-advocacy, commitment; we have the power to make this work.

Outcomes: creating excellent video content that educates and eventually inspires, making some money.

Processes: want to have fun.

AWAY ◄————— **NOTICING 2 DIMENSIONS OF OUR EXPERIENCE** —————► TOWARD

What might people see us doing when we're hooked by interfering thoughts/feelings

Unhelpful behaviors: micromanagment, disengagement, "tantrums," running away, procrastination, in-fighting, condescension, impulsive when investing $.

How will we make this work?

Observable behaviors: make great videos; speak our truth; listen to what others try to tell us; tacos should be available at every meeting (lol); budget $; show up to Commitment Sessions and work on our stuff; take agency and get our tasks done; address tensions; our video content will be grounded in what is meaningful to us (arts, music, positive messaging, etc.).

PITFALLS

ENGAGEMENT

OUTER ACTIONS
*What people could see **us** doing*

These tools, and particularly the interpersonal skills, will play a particularly important role in Commitment Sessions, where tensions are aired and addressed. Conflicts arise when underlying tensions are not addressed. In order to make sure collaborative tensions *are* addressed and resolved on a regular basis, collaborating groups should check in regularly via Commitment Sessions.

COMMITMENT SESSIONS

Given that a Person to Person environment deliberately does away with organizational structures and hierarchies, the only thing that ensures groups will function in a productive, healthy way is each group member's *commitment*, made at the beginning of the entire process.

We've discussed how a person's commitment to their group can be manifested by pursuing growth in the interpersonal skills. It also comes out in a commitment to your Development Objectives and to building awareness using the Troubleshooting tool and Behavior Chain Analysis. But one of the most important ways you commit to your group involves simply showing up.

Specifically, showing up to your group's Commitment Sessions.

Commitment Sessions are an important tool to enable personal and collective development and also to encourage effectiveness when things get tough or challenging. What happens at these group meetings? They can function in a number of different ways, but they mainly serve to provide a safe environment in which to address tension and check in with each group member about their progress toward their Development Objectives. By meeting in this way, team members will grow in their motivation to give their best, increase their capability in the interpersonal skills, generate more self-awareness about their hang-ups, and increase the group's effectiveness—both their own and their group members'. The meetings also provide a platform to monitor the behaviors that the group members have agreed on, allowing for accountability. They allow for an exchange of feedback and expertise, as each group member supports the others.

So how do they work? Here's how we structure our Commitment Sessions.

We begin with a five-minute exercise that helps everyone bring their attention into the room so we all start on the same page. For instance, we might do a mindfulness exercise or some calming physical movements.

Different group members take turns as that session's facilitator, so whoever is in charge of facilitating that session will ask something like, "Who has a topic we should discuss?" The other colleagues indicate if they have something they want to talk about; then time is evenly allotted to each topic and someone volunteers to monitor the time.

For instance, if we've budgeted two hours for the meeting and there are five topics, each topic might be allotted twenty minutes. If there's only an hour available, the topics will need to be touched on more rapidly, perhaps five or ten minutes each. In these cases, colleagues will often offer to take turns: "Ashley's topic is more important to address today. Mine can wait until the next meeting." Also, since people will be training themselves to speak up about tensions, some issues may be productively addressed outside a formal Commitment Session. The Commitment Session Hierarchy of Priorities can help clarify which topics are most pressing.

COMMITMENT SESSION
HIERARCHY OF PRIORITIES

(This will be the only hierarchy endorsed in this book!)

1. Address those things that might destroy the collaboration
2. Address those things that interfere with the effectiveness of the collaboration
3. Address those things that might contribute to increasing the experienced quality of life of yourself and your team members.
4. Celebrate growth and progress.
5. Address other things that matter to you whilst collaborating with your team.

Once the topics have been identified and budgeted time, the facilitator will prompt someone with a topic to share.

The person sharing will start by expressing their hindering feeling, that is, the tension or difficulty they're experiencing. Often, the tension may be associated with their ability to carry out their responsibilities. The group can support the person sharing to explore that tension by asking clarifying questions, such as:

- Do you have any idea what is causing this hindrance?
- Have you ever dealt with a similar tension, and if so, how did you deal with it back then? Could that same strategy serve you now?
- Which of your strengths could serve you here?
- Did you take a look at your initial troubleshooting work to remember which prevention strategies you might have to put in place?
- Which strategies did you try already, and how did or didn't they help you?
- What exactly do you think you need in order to be able to deal with this?

After identifying the tension, the focus turns to seeking a solution. The group member would ask their teammates for advice in figuring out a strategy to address the tension. Other team members offer their experience in dealing with similar difficulties or tensions. By sharing their expertise, they offer strategies that might also serve their colleague. Then that person identifies which strategy they want to try for next time. This might begin with a statement like, "I've been experiencing tension during my meetings with Jerry. I usually have a lot of points I want to address in those meetings, but Jerry always has a lot to say and doesn't typically pause or ask me questions. I start to feel worried as I see the time ticking by because I sense there won't be time left for me to discuss the things I need to talk about. It would be helpful for me if I had a realistic idea of how long Jerry needed to share his points so that I could budget time accordingly, or maybe I could start the meeting with my agenda points and we tackle those first, and then Jerry talks. What do you all think? Can the rest of you help me figure out the best solution for this?"

Another topic might be, "I'm feeling tension with Angela because she hasn't been showing up to our appointments to work on our part of the project. That's preventing me from completing my responsibility for the collaborative. I'm wondering if we should change the responsibility assignments? Or maybe, Angela, you can help me understand what's going on that's preventing you from coming to our appointments."

Someone else might acknowledge their own struggle, recognizing that their contribution to the group has been compromised: "I'm having a really hard time at home right now, and the personal struggles are taking up so much of my energy. I'm not concentrating well on work right now, and I know I've been late more than once. I also know I'm not responding soon enough to emails. I want to share with you all how I'm coping with the situation at home. I'd also love your tips and advice on how to stay better organized within the personal chaos."

Together, the group tackles each topic with a focus on learning and rebuilding trust. Everyone understands this is not an opportunity to complain or vent; instead, we are solution-focused. Before feedback is offered to any team member, we make a point to mention something that we appreciate in that team member—something affirming about how they are helpful; then the constructive feedback follows. It's not a complaining session; it's a Commitment Session. We are committed to the health of the collaboration and the well-being of each group member.

We also take time to celebrate growth. Time is allotted for people to point out specific instances where they have observed growth in other group members toward their Development Objectives. Someone might say, "Alex—I know you've been working on verbally affirming others more often. When you told me how much you liked my work the other day, that really made me feel seen and appreciated. I can see real growth in how you're pushing yourself in that area, and it's making a difference, at least in my life!" The sessions usually feel energizing and encouraging.

We end the meetings by figuring out who will come up with the opening exercise for the next meeting and assigning a new facilitator. Finally, we try to wrap up with a simple ritual: each person shares a "one-word reflection" to conclude the meeting. Then we shift gears and resume our normal activity. A group's choice for how to end their Commitment Sessions might depend on how much time they want to dedicate to the meeting. If you only have one hour, you might choose to devote most of your time to the topics.

There is no talk about agendas. There is no discussion of who is going to do what assignment and how. There is no talk about future goals or trajectories—all of that information is discussed in different meetings, which we'll discuss in a moment. The Commitment Sessions are entirely focused on personal growth and resolving tensions for the health of the group.

The frequency of how often a Commitment Session occurs can change depending on the environment; for instance, a new collaborative group might want to do them once a week, whereas a group that's been working together for some time may not need to meet more than once a month. There's no rule on how often these Commitment Sessions occur, but regularity is key; otherwise, those points of tension find other ways to leak out in unproductive ways.

Here are some other characteristics of Commitment Sessions:

- **Everyone shows up as a human.** We are not "human resources"; we are human beings, and everyone is in a state of process. Whereas a typical organization has a myopic focus on operations, outcomes, and *stuff*, these sessions put the spotlight on process: on the *people* doing all the stuff. The sessions may be awkward; they may be difficult at times. However, they provide a place to acknowledge that things are not always easy and allow other people to breathe new ideas and energy into an area where you might feel exhausted.

By giving this process a place inside a collaboration, we are given the opportunity to be our true selves and to learn more about our fellow humans.

- **You come together around a shared goal.** Everyone has the shared commitment to support one another, push one another toward the goals each person has identified for themselves, and encourage each other. Recognize that everyone in the group wants to keep working in a healthy way and do their jobs productively and professionally. When those common denominators are in place, individuals who are vastly different people can be brought together.

- **Progress takes time.** That's allowed: it can take a long time for someone to "unlearn" a destructive habit or to start practicing a new strategy. Growth can be hard and slow. The Commitment Sessions aren't always easy, and they don't guarantee a fix. However, they provide a helpful, safe way to build a healthy collaboration with others toward a common objective. These sessions can help families, groups of friends, sports teams, and so on—any group of people who want to grow and work together harmoniously. And over time, everyone will get better at engaging in a productive way.

- **Emotions are part of it.** Choosing to express your emotions in a caring and constructive way enables you to be authentic and process your feelings toward a productive end. This, again, benefits the collaboration. It's possible to communicate your emotions constructively, even when heated, provided you respect the agreement to be willing to learn and to do your best to stay collaborative. If you become unregulated in your emotions and can no longer communicate productively (as Leon experienced), the most helpful thing might be to choose to leave the meeting to calm down, then return when you feel more balanced. If you know that you have a tendency to fly off the handle, this would be an area where your group members could help you come up with helpful strategies to cope with it.

- **Members agree to be responsible for the team's outcomes.** A group will succeed or fail based on the contribution of its members, which means the team's outcome is tied to each group member's effort. Because of this, colleagues are responsible to address the other group members on the commitments they made. If you witness something going wrong, you are obligated to address it. If you don't, and a problem escalates because you failed to mention your concerns or objections, you are partially responsible for the situation that unfolds. When each person takes responsibility to be mindful of any interfering aspect—any bad decision, unhelpful behavior, or sloppy work—then the entire collaboration will benefit, especially as the team works together to explore helpful solutions.

- **A professional facilitator might be helpful for the first few sessions.** Most people will not be used to functioning in an environment like a Commitment Session. It might be helpful to enlist the guidance of a professional mediator, facilitator, or coun-selor to help the group establish the safe environment required for a Commitment Session and monitor helpful versus unhelpful behaviors. Once the group has a sense of how they should be run, they can each start taking turns as facilitator.

- **Come prepared.** Participating in a Commitment Session always has the intent to increase the group's skills. Everyone should come prepared with their Development Objectives and/or ACT matrix. If someone shows behavior that is ineffective, the facilitator might recommend the person use the Behavior Chain Analysis to explore which behaviors would help them to be more effective next time. Coming adequately prepared will help you to balance your mindset in advance and react out of your wise mind. You'll feel more comfortable participating and more collaborative toward your team members.

- **Remember that you are a team and you can choose to collaborate well.** Holding on to a negative behavior or negative emotion is something that you choose to do. However, each person has the ability and the opportunity to choose to engage in helpful behaviors that will serve the collaboration. Assume that everyone in your group wants the collaboration to be successful, and share honestly in that spirit of good faith.
- **Attendance is mandatory.** This may sound like a "rule," but actually, a Commitment Session is simply the main way each person demonstrates their commitment to the collaboration. It's where colleagues actively pursue the personal growth we've discussed in the rest of this chapter, and it's where they actively engage with their other group members. They are what *makes* a collaboration. To skip a Commitment Session or consistently show up late means that you are actively withdrawing yourself as a participant in the collaboration. Your other group members will take the hint, and the collaboration will move forward without your involvement.

COMMITMENTS FOR COMMITMENT SESSIONS: AN EXAMPLE

- We agree to always be present at Commitment Sessions on time and stay until the end; we agree to keep phones out of sight and off or, if necessary, on silent.
- We agree to participate actively and constructively, remaining compassionate, mindful, and dialectical.
- We agree to take responsibility for voicing our concerns and triggers and to come adequately prepared.

- We agree to share what strategies work for us and what makes them work.
- We agree to not tell our colleagues what to do.
- We agree to take turns as facilitator.
- We agree to repair with the team in some way when we're unable to attend a session; for example, I will tell my colleagues about the holiday that kept me from attending the last session and how it energized me and increased my ability to contribute to the group.
- We agree to exchange information in order to better understand each other.
- We agree to stay focused on our common identity.
- We agree to stay focused on our shared values and common goals.
- We agree to expose and discuss tensions in a nonjudgmental way (use feelings statements; do not treat thoughts and assumptions as facts) and be willing to call out the "elephant in the room" when others are ignoring or not seeing the elephant.
- We agree to find and learn to apply solutions to conflicts after we properly assess the problem.
- We agree to seek support and encouragement.
- We agree to share our own expertise and offer and select helpful advice.
- We agree to have the humility to admit our mistakes/difficulties and the willingness to have the group help us solve them.
- We agree to be willing to go through a Behavior Chain Analysis as a way to explore and facilitate behavioral change.
- If we feel that the Commitment Session is not being useful or we don't like the way it is being run, we agree to say something about it rather than silently stewing in frustration.
- We agree to carry on even when feeling burnt out, frustrated, tired, overworked, underappreciated, hopeless, or ineffective. (Granted, that is easier committed to than done.)

Are Commitment Sessions truly necessary? Are the benefits worth the time and investment of putting them together? We say yes.

Communication and transparency are essential to our ability to collaborate. The Commitment Sessions tool helps us maintain clear and consistent channels of communication so that tensions and conflicts can be addressed as they emerge, and everyone has a chance to offer help to their team members when they ask for support. It is true that these Commitment Sessions ask for an investment of time and energy, but they also offer incredibly rewarding change opportunities. They also increase the sustainability of the collaboration. If a team of collaborators wishes to operate in an environment where there are no hierarchies or power plays, there is wholehearted effort, and there is a sense of being seen, known, and valued—then Commitment Sessions are essential.

Commitment Sessions are essential for groups to operate in an environment where there are no hierarchies or power plays, there is wholehearted effort, and there is a sense of being seen, known, and valued.

Other Meetings

Granted: the work still must get done. There will always be day-to-day tasks that need to be taken care of, along with big-picture questions that need to be considered and decided upon. Essentially, there are three other types of meetings that any collaborative group will find necessary:

- Strategy: meetings to define vision and approach
- Governance: meetings to define responsibilities and accountabilities
- Tactical: meetings to organize day-to-day work

There is no shortage of excellent material available for anyone who wants to research ways to conduct those meetings, so we will refrain from diving too deeply here. Generally, we find certain approaches to be more conducive to a Person to Person environment than others. Some of our favorites are the Holacracy© method, the sociocracy approach, and the Agile method. All of those can be further explored with a quick Google search. However, these are not the only methodologies that can work. Far more important than the method is the mindset with which you approach these sorts of meetings. Any method chosen for organizing should allow people the responsibility to self-steer: to do whatever is in their power to act on their chosen responsibilities, to involve other team members when their support is needed, and to communicate transparently in order for the other team members to stay informed of the progress. All this is based on everyone's shared wish to accomplish the project. Essentially, you trust people to do what they need to do.

COFFEE AND COMMITMENT

Jake stayed out late, coming back to the dorm only after he knew Leon would be asleep. He'd talked with Lana about the Leon situation and had some good ideas about how to broach the subject with him in their next conversation... But he wanted them both to do it after a good night's sleep.

But after Jake's late night, Leon ended up being the first to rise—and he was ready to do penance.

After the meeting had ended so disastrously the day before, Leon had initially distracted himself by smashing cars and blowing people up in his video games. Eventually, though, he shut the game down—and then he did the wise thing of sitting with himself in silence. Leon lacked Lana's therapeutic insight and was nowhere near as self-aware as Jake, but he knew he felt badly about the way the interaction with the rest of the group had gone.

He also felt ashamed—his blowup had led to the exact opposite result he'd wanted. He began beating himself up about the T-shirt ("Why did I wear that?") and his instigating comments. Finally, miserable and full of self-loathing, he'd gone to bed.

But the new morning made Leon decide things were perhaps not beyond hope. Maybe—if he apologized and promised not to do it again—the group would give him another chance. He still wanted to do this collaboration, but not so much because of the money it might make him or to take a deep dive into his video game anymore. It was the fellowship he wanted. He'd loved the initial collaboration experience with Jake—the bonding, the discoveries, the meaningful conversations about something real. He liked that Lana had said that he was good and worthy. He liked Alex's fist bump. He wanted these people in his life. Leon didn't assume they would like him—he usually assumed people would dislike him. But perhaps they would find him useful and allow him to stick around.

Quietly, he left the dorm room and headed to the student cafeteria to pick up a few donuts and coffee.

When Jake finally woke, it was to the sight of Leon sitting across from him on his own dorm bed, staring at him earnestly and holding out a maple bar. "Hungry?"

"Wha...?" Jake asked.

"I have the jelly kind too. And an apple fritter. I wasn't sure what you liked. Here's coffee."

Jake slowly sat up, sleepily trying to remember Lana's advice from the night before. He couldn't. "Lemme go to the bathroom, Leon."

After a pee, and some stretches, and splashing water on his face, Jake returned to Leon. "Alright—I'll take the coffee now. Thanks for..." he gestured to the donuts and coffee.

"I'm sorry, man," Leon said. "I don't know why I do that. Act like an asshole, I mean. I feel really bad about what I said to Lana. And I'm positive Alex hates me." He paused. "Guessing you all hate me."

Jake took a big bite out of the maple bar. "We don't hate you, man," he said, his mouth full. "We wanna make it work." He swallowed. "But it's not going to work if there's a repeat of last night—I mean, like—a repeated repeat. Repeatedly happening." He took a gulp of coffee.

"I know. Shit, I know," Leon said apologetically. He paused. "Do you think Lana can fix me?"

"No," Jake said, shaking his head adamantly. "I don't think anyone can 'fix' anyone else. We're not robots with wires loose. We're humans. But I think you can grow, if you try. And I think we can help you grow. And you can help us grow too."

"Okay," Leon said nodding. "So—I'm still in this?"

"Yeah, man," Jake responded. "If you're not quitting on us, then we're not quitting on you."

"Alex too?" Leon asked.

Jake nodded. "Alex said they find you 'intriguing,' and apparently that's a good thing in Alex's book." His conversation with Lana was finally coming back to mind. "But—we want to talk about a few things. We think we should form a group agreement. Like—ways we agree to behave and things we should all try to avoid so that we can ideally avoid a repeat of last night."

"Especially a repeated repeat," Leon said, with a faint teasing smile.

Jake grinned. "Exactly. And Lana's got some tools for self-awareness that she says you should try. I mean, if you're willing."

Leon nodded. "I'm willing."

Jake nodded. "Well, then. That's a pretty good start."

EXPLORE FURTHER

If you'd like to learn more, discuss this content with others, or access tools for your own application, go to the interactive section of the book using this QR code.

CHAPTER FIVE

THE COLLABORATIVE AGREEMENT

How to Build a Contract to Enable Sustainable Collaboration

*A group becomes a team when
each member is sure enough of himself and his
contribution to praise the skills of others.*

—Norman Shidle, author of *The Art of Successful Communication*

It had been two weeks since Jake and Leon had reconciled over donuts. Since then, the group had produced two YouTube videos, the second with Alex's help and polish. They'd also each done a fair bit of what Leon liked to call "navel-gazing": building up their self-awareness; completing the ACT matrix tool, which Lana had found in her Psychology of Leadership textbook; and even holding their first Commitment Session. (Lana, Alex, and Jake all loved it; Leon's review was, "Excruciating but helpful.") Now they were ready to codify their group agreements.

"Remind me why we're turning this session into a party vibe again?" Jake asked Leon. He was stringing up white twinkle lights around the ceiling. Leon was busy setting up dartboards.

"Because if I'm going to sit around and talk about the rules that we all need to follow in this collaborative group, I want to be drinking beer while doing it." Leon began hammering nails into the wall.

Jake shouted above the noise. "They're *tools*, not rules, Leon." Leon grinned in response and raised his hammer. Jake continued. "The whole point is that we set this up so that we can live outside the rules. You know—we each do our own thing but still contribute to the whole and make sure no one acts like a jerk."

"I know, I know; you've told me the spiel. It's cool! I'm game. And frankly, I probably need it." Leon turned on some techno music with a bumping bass line. "But like I said—I want to have some fun while we all get super deep and theoretical. In fact, I wouldn't mind if we played drinking games at the Commitment Sessions too. Would definitely help me with the navel-gazing."

Jake turned to Leon soberly. "No, man, we've got to be totally lucid in those meetings. That's where we need to show up as our truest selves."

"I'm *kidding*," Leon protested. "Here." He handed Jake a Corona. "*You* need to loosen up a little." There was a knock on the door. Leon swung it open to greet Lana and Alex. "Perfect timing!"

"Have you guys seen the views on the first two videos?" Lana asked excitedly. "There's more than a thousand for the first one, and the one that Alex helped with already has *seven hundred*, even though we just posted it two days ago! I had no idea this game was as popular as it is."

"AAA-LEEEX," Jake cheered, giving Alex a fist bump.

Alex grinned. "That's right. Enough of amateur hour. So, what is this thing all about? I thought we were forming a group agreement tonight, but you guys look like you're throwing a party."

"That's right! It's a Collaborative Agreement party," Leon said, raising his beer. "We're going to have fun while we're getting serious."

"I like it," Lana said approvingly. "Do you have vino?"

"Of course we have vino; I knew you would want vino." He turned conspiratorially to Jake. "We *knew* Lana would want vino." He pulled a bottle out of their mini fridge. "If Lana approves, then everyone approves." Leon clapped Jake on the back, and Jake grinned with obvious relief. It *did* help that Lana liked it.

The four helped themselves to drinks and then sat down at a card table the two men had set up. Lana got out her laptop. "Alright, I'm taking notes."

Alex got out their digital sketchbook. "And I'm doing pictures." Jake and Leon looked at Alex quizzically. "Remember?" Alex asked. They pointed to their head. "This noggin doesn't do words. Only pictures."

"That's cool," Jake said. "I'm more of a visual learner too, actually. Okay, team. It's pep talk time. We want to do this thing together. But we want to do it without any hierarchy bullshit. We want to show up, as our whole selves, work our butts off to create amazing stuff, hopefully make some cash, and treat each other with respect."

"That's right," Lana said, typing. "These are the '*tools* of engagement'—"

"Not rules," both Jake and Leon said in unison.

She grinned. "Exactly! Oh, and before I forget…" She reached into her backpack and pulled out some papers. "I did research. I pulled some stuff about forming group covenants, agreements, et cetera. This material is interesting on Conscious Contracts—it reads informally but can actually be a legal document." She laid down a stapled packet. "And *this* is also worth looking at…these Core Design Principles. Apparently, these are the principles that guide seamless collaboration."

"Where did you get all that?" Leon asked. "Your parents?"

"I don't remember that stuff from Psych of Leadership," Alex remarked.

Lana cocked her head and smiled, pleased. "I found this on my own, thank you very much. You all thought I was kidding about serving as the leadership consultant, but I take my position very seriously."

Alex began paging through the documents. "You found all this by Googling? Dang."

Lana leaned over to Alex and muttered, "I may have also gotten a tip or two from Prof Harrison. So—" Lana picked up the pages on the Core Design Principles and studied them. "I'm thinking we should write out our purpose, our shared values, the ways we agree to treat each other..." She began typing. "Okay, what else should be included?"

Leon piped up. "I think we should talk about what we each bring to the table. Like strengths and weaknesses. And it *probably* would be a good idea to include emotional triggers. Mainly for my buddy Jake here, quick to fly off the handle." Jake gave him a playful shove. Leon made eye contact with Jake and Lana. "See? I'm learning!"

Lana grinned. "Yes, you are!"

Alex spoke up. "We should make a plan for how we're going to resolve arguments, like the other night. And everyone should commit to doing their part in getting their shit done. I've been in way too many group projects where I've had to carry the whole thing. If something comes up that prevents you from finishing something, that's fine—communicate with the rest of the group. But don't just slack off."

"Yes—" Lana said, typing furiously. "And on the same note, I think we should all consider ourselves responsible for calling out relational tension, or anything that's preventing us from being fully engaged." She paused and thought. "I feel like it would be helpful to have some positive reinforcement in place. Like how to encourage helpful, productive behavior that helps everyone in the group."

"Should we punish negative behaviors too?" Jake asked. They all thought about that. Alex tapped their pen on the sketch pad to the beat of the techno.

"My hunch is no," Lana said. "My parents have always said that negative reinforcement works in the short term but usually doesn't help anybody in the long term. But if we all full-on commit to this agreement, then it's more about holding each other accountable to *keeping* the agreement. Like we're regulating, not policing. And that way, hopefully someone will recognize for themselves if they've broken the agreement." Jokingly, Leon raised his hand.

"You and me both, Leon," Jake said. "We're all going to have to work at it." He held out his beer bottle to "cheers" with his roommate: *clink.*

Lana paused and began typing again. "But maybe we should write up something about how specifically we're going to monitor behaviors and keep that accountability."

"Good call," Jake said. "I think we should get some logistical frameworks in there too. Like how we're going to make decisions—you know, are we voting? Is there a main point person on different parts of the project that gets to make unilateral decisions?"

"Let's figure out money," Leon commented. "Who gets how much, how much we want to invest in the project itself, that kind of thing."

"Can I just say how cool I think it is that we're doing this?" Alex asked. "At my last job, the manager was a total SOB. He treated everyone like we were his personal slaves and expected us to answer his emails and texts literally at any time of day or night. And I worked my ass off but never felt like I was doing anything meaningful. It was so toxic."

Lana pointed at Alex. "*That* is exactly why we're going to put some thought into this. Even when you take the boss element out of it, I feel like group projects are just often a terrible experience. We should be fully committed to making this thing work as best as we possibly can."

"We're all committed," Leon said. "*I'm* committed."

"Yes," Lana said. "That's why we're making a big deal about it and writing this down."

Alex held up their sketch pad, showing a toolbox with several tools beside it. "And drawing it down."

Jake said, "Okay, crew. That's a pretty sizable list. Let's start talking about purpose. What do we want this group to be all about? Yes, we're going to make videos. But long term, deep down—why is this important?"

"Wait!" Leon said. He handed everyone a dart and gestured to the dartboard. "We're getting serious and deep again, which means that your boy Leon is feeling compelled to lighten things up. Lowest score has to answer first."

WHAT IS A COLLABORATIVE AGREEMENT?

By now, we've talked about the mindsets needed for healthy collaboration and the attitudes that will help foster helpful behavior. A Collaborative Agreement is simply the formalization and articulation of those helpful discoveries. It enables a group of collaborators to assemble a set of agreements to commit to, meant to facilitate frictionless collaboration. The agreement provides a place to help team members define their shared values, their common purpose and goal, and their commitment to positive behaviors that will serve the rest of their collaboration. The formalization of these values, goals, and helpful behaviors makes the agreement unambiguous. It creates transparency. It creates trust.

A Collaborative Agreement makes the group's shared commitments unambiguous, creating transparency and trust.

These agreements can be legally binding documents; however, unlike a typical legal contract, they should not present as opaque, nearly incomprehensible fine print. They're meant to be usable, engaging, and interesting; in fact, Alex's sketches illustrate an important element of a Collaborative Agreement, which is visuals.

Another phrase used to describe these Collaborative Agreements is

"Conscious Contract," a term coined and trademarked by our friend Kim Wright.[65] Here is how she defines it:

> The Conscious Contracts® model is a proprietary process for creating sustainable, values-based agreements. The process provides a framework for authentic communication, discussions, and relationship design. It builds on best practices of modern contracts like plain language, design thinking, and using visuals. It is also influenced by restorative justice, collaboration, and conscious business practices.
>
> A key principle is that contracts do not belong to the lawyers or the court. They are living documents which reflect the parties' desires to come together for a shared purpose. Participants in the process find that they are inspired and even have fun in the process. They discover a new level of trust, clarity, and empowerment—or they quickly realize that alignment is not possible and part as friends.
>
> The Conscious Contracts® process can be used to create many types of contracts where a good relationship is important to the fulfillment of the agreement. They can be especially useful between co-founders, impact investors, companies and vendors, landlords and tenants, publishers and authors, employee-employer, or even for intra-family agreements.

Although a Collaborative Agreement would be built via a slightly different process than a Conscious Contract, the two types of agreements are similar: they both seek to create sustainable, relational, and values-based agreements. In the same spirit as Kim's description of a Conscious Contract, the Collaborative Agreement is meant to help establish transparent, authentic connection and provide opportunities for each group member to do their best work in pursuit of a greater goal. Each group member is encouraged to show up as their authentic self, with all their gifts and all their mess. The

---

[65] More information can be found at https://consciouscontracts.com.

agreement prompts each group member to own their strengths and acknowledge their weaknesses. It identifies opportunities like the Commitment Sessions, where each person will be prompted to learn and grow; it will also spell out a description of how the group intends to run their operations and decision-making/governance processes, and define their strategy. For all these reasons, the Collaborative Agreement has a large emphasis on personal responsibility: the only thing holding each group member to this agreement is their own personal commitment; therefore, each person is expected to do the individual work that will help them contribute their best. But the agreement also emphasizes collaboration. Finding alignment is key; identifying shared values is crucial.

This might sound like a strange process to some; it's certainly not a commonplace practice in most businesses. So, before discussing how to form a Collaborative Agreement, it might be worth considering some of the typical ways new employees are initiated into their workplace's "collaborations." This will help us evaluate if the typical approach in most corporations is effective—and if not, how we can improve upon it to enhance quality of life and person to person connections.

Not "Business as Usual"

Most typical corporate workplaces function with a top-down approach. Employees don't join a business of their own accord; they are hired by a person with seniority in the organization. Rather than offering their strengths and skills to contribute to a group, employees are brought in through the conditions spelled out in a job description. Once hired, the employees are usually trained on what their "function" will be, what is expected of them, whom they will report to, who they need to be at the job, which extra benefits they can enjoy, and, if relevant, the duration of their contract.

The emphasis on job descriptions can create problems. For instance, if a person finds that she's expected to do a job that is different than the job description she was hired for, she'll feel confused and frustrated. Alternately, even if the job description is consistent with what an employer expects an employee to do, an employee may settle into the complacent confines of that job. They may not look to grow beyond it because that's not in their job description. Instead of utilizing the full scope of their creativity and skills, corporate employees often do what's expected of them and call it a day; if they don't, some form of sanctions may result.

The hierarchical structures of most organizations can also sap an employee's sense of personal responsibility. If there's dysfunction in a neighboring department, you might say, "I don't care. I'm getting my paycheck; I'm doing what I'm supposed to do. What do I care if that other department is falling apart?" Hierarchies provide us with easy opportunities to cast blame elsewhere—"It's my boss creating the toxic atmosphere, not me"—and disengage. In larger groups, when an assignment falls through the cracks, there are plenty of opportunities for finger pointing: "So-and-so is the marketing person; they should have done that." "Well, no one communicated to me that I was supposed to do that..." The easy blame-shifting provided by the hierarchical structure means that people rarely are prompted to pursue personal growth or address their unique challenges.

Personal responsibility isn't the only area that may potentially take a hit; trust may also be compromised in a typical hierarchical organization. Transparency may be lacking in corporate businesses, meaning that employees may doubt the true equity of pay and promotional opportunities. It's not unusual for there to be rules and codes of conduct spelled out on a corporate level, but the actual company culture may flout those. The inconsistency between values espoused and values in practice can result in many employees feeling jaded and distrustful. Rather than rules *regulating* human interaction, they actually undermine it. And any arbitrary change in those rules can cause employees to feel like they've gotten the rug pulled out from beneath them.

That was the case when corporate leaders at the company Basecamp were forced to deal with the turnover of roughly a third of their employees after making sweeping cultural changes. In the announcement that detailed the changes, the Basecamp leaders said that anyone who didn't like the changes was welcome to quit and take six months' pay as severance.[66] A significant portion of their staff did just that, citing the new changes as their reason for leaving.[67] The company lost: they were forced to scramble to rebuild their staff. But the exiting employees also lost: their years of work in building Basecamp from a tiny startup to a multimillion-dollar company were rewarded with a scant six months' salary—hardly a fair representation of their effort. This case study points to the fact that a "company" itself should not be treated as a living thing, where the "company's" needs take priority. Actually, a company is made up of living human beings, doing the work. When the leaders of Basecamp changed the rules and forced a power play, they were unapologetic about making themselves "winners" and the minority dissenters "losers." But the result wasn't good for anyone.

This example of Basecamp is particularly noteworthy because it was, in many ways, the "ideal" corporate culture. It was a "friendly" company with strong ethics; the leaders solicited feedback from their people; they offered amazing benefits and boasted a thriving company culture. Their message to employees was something akin to "Now that you have all these benefits and perks and good pay—go be your authentic self!" However, people can't be genuinely authentic unless they feel truly safe. In any organization with a hierarchy, if someone has power over you, there is not true safety. You'll always be looking over your shoulder, and at any point, your boss could change everything—which is exactly what happened at Basecamp. Even an "ideal" company can't solve the problems posed by organizational hierarchies, which inevitably lead to power plays. The only way to organize people effectively

---

[66] Jason Fried, "Changes at Basecamp," world.hey.com, April 26, 2021, https://world.hey.com/jason/changes-at-basecamp-7f32afc5.

[67] Kim Lyons, "Basecamp Implodes as Employees Flee Company, Including Senior Staff," *The Verge*, April 30, 2021, https://www.theverge.com/2021/4/30/22412714/basecamp-employees-memo-policy-hansson-fried-controversy.

without that possibility is through a Collaborative Agreement.

As we portrayed in our previous chapter, disagreements will often occur in a group, and even a "split" of a collaboration is definitely possible in a Person to Person environment. However, the Basecamp debacle helps confirm that *distributed* management—where people work together to arrange assignments and responsibilities—is better to help people grow, take ownership of their lives, and set themselves free to live out their potential. But it shouldn't stop there. If you also want to get rewarded for your effort, you need *distributed ownership* of the value you contributed to create. We'll discuss this more in our next chapters.

A Collaborative Agreement process attempts to resolve many of the problems caused by hierarchical structures, limiting job descriptions, rules, and unequal compensation. When each member of a collaborative group comes to the drawing board, they participate in crafting the culture they want to create. Each person commits to a high level of responsibility in terms of their contribution. The joint formalization of the agreement provides transparency. It eliminates power plays; no one is ordering the others to "toe the line." Instead, the group collectively draws the line together, and each person agrees to uphold the agreements formed. Accountability is maintained through regular Commitment Sessions, which help address friction, facilitate individual and collective growth, and clarify next steps. No one can get away with being a jerk for very long if they're still showing up to those Commitment Sessions, engaging with their group members' feedback, and working on their interfering behaviors.

A Collaborative Agreement not only formalizes the operational agreements, but also all "soft" agreements: Who am I, and how will I contribute? What are my commitments? Why does this collaboration matter to me? Both the operational agreements and the soft agreements contribute to a communication-oriented and human-centric environment. Rather than starting with assumptions, judgments, or ideas, the Collaborative Agreement process offers a clear understanding of who the group is as a team—honoring all the different and unique team personalities—and how the team will agree to operate, deal with each other, and manage the projects of the collaboration.

By formalizing the agreement early on in the collaborative process, group members are able to identify their shared commitments when everything is still blue skies. Later on in the collaborative experience, as challenges pop up and the weather gets stormy, the Collaborative Agreement serves as an anchor in those rougher waters. The shared commitments then provide the group with direction as to how best to move forward.

These sorts of agreements not only ensure more effective collaboration; they also clarify *how* to collaborate and ensure transparency amongst collaborators.

So how does one go about doing it?

THE HOW: PHASES FOR BUILDING A COLLABORATIVE AGREEMENT

First, there's the need to ***explore* and get more insights** about who we are as individuals, why we meet up, and why we want to collaborate. This first phase involves forming a shared identity, articulating the purpose of the collaboration, identifying who's bringing which talents to the table, naming the vulnerabilities and pitfalls we might meet in the process of collaborating, and finally, determining which helpful resources we might need to overcome them. More broadly, this first phase seeks to answer: what makes us a team?

After communicating and aligning on our insights, the second phase is to ***identify* the tools and agreements** that will help bring those insights into productive fruition. This phase would name many of the tools discussed in the previous chapter—the Troubleshooting tool, the Development Objectives, Commitment Sessions, the ACT matrix, and so on. It would also describe the plan for how to run meetings related to operations, governance, and strategy. This phase mainly identifies strategies and resources to ensure everyone is functioning at their best. It also lays out certain operational plans to help the work go smoothly.

And last but not least, we *commit* **to the process of working toward our shared purpose**. Group members initial each page and sign at the end. Phase 3 solidifies each person's affirmation that they will take agency in giving the collaboration their best.

On our website, we have provided a complete outline of a Collaborative Agreement, broken into these three phases, along with their related components. (Please see this chapter's QR code.)

Phase 1: Exploration
Establishes what makes the group a team

Phase 2: Identifying Strategies and Tools
Ensures everyone can function at their best and that the work operates efficiently

Phase 3: Commitment
Solidifies each person's affirmation of personal agency to give the collaboration their best

---

It's important to note the *process* element that the group commits to. A Collaborative Agreement is not a onetime document that gets signed, then shut away in a file drawer. It is an ongoing, evolutionary process. As the collaboration evolves, we will encounter obstacles on the way and will be invited over and over again to find ways to overcome them. In our narrative, for instance, Jake's group is dealing with a relatively small operation at this point in their work. But down the road, they may become more successful and want to expand their collaboration—Alex and Leon might continue to make videos focused on the video game while Jake and Lana make videos that are more focused on positive life skills. A change like this will force the group to grow and evolve; they might need to bring in more people to help execute their new vision. The Collaborative Agreement would need to be revisited, rediscussed, and recommitted to.

It was no accident that Lana pulled out a copy of Atkins's Prosocial Core Design Principles when the group sat down to form their agreement. Substantively, our recommendations for a Collaborative Agreement cover seven of the eight themes from the Core Design Principles (CDPs) that are fundamentally important in achieving frictionless collaboration. Building the Collaborative Agreement therefore also requires reflection on the eight CDPs and the team's interpretation on how to fulfill those CDPs in their unique collaboration.

As Jake, Leon, Lana, and Alex illustrated, there are different ways to build a Collaborative Agreement, which can be adapted to a person's preferred learning style. Those who prefer the seriousness of verbal communication can build it like Jake and Lana are—referencing research and writing it down. Visual learners like Alex might prefer incorporating pictures and images. Those who like a more playful approach, like Leon, can turn it into a game. In fact, we've provided a description of a "Collaborative Agreement" game on our website, for those who like the sound of this approach, which guides groups in building the agreement by going through the different game challenges, as both individuals as well as a team. And yes—it involves darts and a dartboard.

Since colleagues take agency, they have the ability to introduce the approaches that suit them and their team the best. A robust Collaborative Agreement will ensure certain fundamental elements are hit so that the CDPs are addressed directly in the group's shared agreements.

ELEMENTS CONTAINED IN A COLLABORATIVE AGREEMENT

Phase 1: Exploration

In order for group members to feel intrinsically motivated to work together and give their best to a collaboration, the work at hand needs to be connected to what they genuinely care about. That's why we began our book with a focus on personal essence, and this first phase prompts group members to share that essence with the rest of the group via the **personal introduction**. This phase also identifies the group's shared **purpose** and notes **strengths and pitfalls**, both as individuals and as a group.

Personal Introduction

The personal introduction component of the Collaborative Agreement is meant to facilitate introduction and alignment between group members.

This phase begins with **each member committing to be their true self** throughout the Collaborative Agreement process. There will be no posturing, no pretense, no attempts to impress—just real, true humans willing to be transparent about what motivates them and what sometimes holds them back. When we first met Jake back in Chapter 1, he was gathering this necessary information about himself. We further explored tools to build self-awareness in Chapters 3 and 4. Likewise, it would be appropriate for group members to use tools like the personal ACT matrix ahead of the Collaborative Agreement meeting so that, in this first introduction phase, they are equipped to express key aspects of themselves to the group, such as their purpose, motivation, values, skills, and hang-ups. However, that certainly isn't mandatory. You can also choose to do the exercises as a group, exploring both the individual and group elements in each other's company.

Why do we begin with a commitment to authenticity? Knowing who you are and your purpose is the starting point to being a colleague in an effective collaborative. If you're going to work productively alongside other people toward a goal you feel deeply invested in, you need to actually *know* what you're deeply invested in. You also need to be able to acquaint your group members with your skills and hang-ups. Additionally, it's important for you to be able to communicate your values so that the group can help develop shared principles. You can't help your group effectively collaborate if you're pretending to care about things you don't actually care about or suggesting you have skills in areas you actually don't.

So we begin with a commitment along these lines: "I will show my true self and be authentic throughout this process."

Now the group takes the opportunity to form **aligning statements about what mindsets and attitudes will guide their collaboration**. Each colleague should express the values that guide them while they live their lives and pursue their purposes. From that bank of values and principles, the group can begin to form statements about the values that will guide them collectively. For example:

- Although we're not perfect, we will continuously make an effort to collaborate.
- We can risk making mistakes: trial and error help us evolve.

These statements will set the base-level attitude for the group's successful collaboration. They will allow group members to make decisions on how to collaborate effectively and can help dictate the choices that are made at any given moment. Those shared values will then help guide the group as they work through the rest of the Collaborative Agreement and throughout their collaboration.

Next, each group member **affirms their personal agency**. They acknowledge what their abilities are and name what responsibilities they want to choose to commit to. They might initial their agreement to the personal commitment lists that were discussed in Chapter 3:

Personal Power and Responsibility

Tapping our personal power unleashes great potential and great responsibility:

I HAVE THE POWER TO:

- Act autonomously without oversight or control

- Seek the materials and information I need

- Ask others to treat me with honesty and respect

- Ask others to honor their commitments

- Identify internal and external tensions and work to address them along with my colleagues

- Be myself and show my true self to others

- Seek advice and make considered decisions

- Discuss and address inadequate strategies and behaviors that interfere with making our collective impact

- Find solutions to issues I identify

- Focus on my personal growth

- Look for a shared truth

- Look at where opposites meet

I AM RESPONSIBLE FOR:

- Being self-motivated and bringing my whole potential

- Providing the materials and information I have

- Treating others with honesty and respect

- Honoring my commitments

- Collaborating with my colleagues as they address their internal and external tensions

- Providing colleagues with a safe space to show their true selves by not judging them

- Offering advice and respecting others' decisions if they don't cause harm

- Being approachable

- Addressing issues that I come across

- Collaborating with others for their personal growth

- Expressing my views while listening to those of others, even if they are opposed to mine

Next, each group member provides their own **personal essence** profile, answering the following questions. We've provided sample answers from Lana.

1. What is meaningful to me?

    a. *Making a positive impact in the world, using my gifts as a leader and calling upon my knowledge of therapeutic tools. Mainly, I just want to make the world a better place and feel like I'm contributing. I'm open to different ways of doing that.*

2. What do I most wish to change in the world? (What is most valuable to me?)

    a. *People's self-awareness. I want to help people feel safe in being real—fully acknowledge what they're about, what they're good at, what they believe in, etc. That way, every person can give their very best to the world. If everyone is doing that—how could the world NOT become a better place?!*

3. What impact am I most invested in? (What concrete action do I intend to do to bring about change?)[68]

    a. *Within this little group, I will alert my team when I see tensions so that we can address them. I will model and encourage patience and understanding. I will be a sounding board for group members so they can reflect and grow. And more broadly, I'll try to do that in every context I'm in and maybe find a profession that gives me a broader platform for impact.*

---

[68] Although each group member might be inclined to share their "life's purpose" in this question—in Lana's case, "[I want to find] a profession that gives me a broader platform for impact"—the focus here should remain on how they intend to make an impact through the *group's work*. The goal with the personal essence profile is to clarify *what* and *how* they, as their true selves, will commit toward the collaborative's impact for change. In other words, where their personal investment will intersect with the group's impact. The reason that the focus remains on the group is so that a colleague's personal goals don't hijack the group's work. For instance, if Lana is more focused on her own efforts to make broad impact than what's best for the group, she might push them to hurry along to making the quality of life videos before they've developed a stable following for their video game tutorials. That could end up threatening the sustainability of their collaboration. However, if she is committed to supporting and prioritizing the group's impact (*supported* by her own goals, but not *driven* by her own goals), she will be more objective about the proper timing and process for their work.

PERSON TO PERSON

4. What gives me the greatest sense of belonging?
   a. *When people allow me to be fully me and trust me with their whole selves.*
5. What sense of growth am I seeking?
   a. *I want to grow as a leader, listener, and practitioner of the tools I discover.*

Now it's time for each group member to consider their **reasons for sticking with the collaboration**, even when things get hard. This would help someone like Leon push through moments like what was depicted in the last chapter. Rather than quit in an emotional outburst, Leon would be steadied in his commitment by considering his answers to these questions. Or in Jake's case, there might be days when he gets tired of teaching about video games, but these considerations would help him stay motivated to get the work done.

Here are Jake's answers to the "stick with it" questions, which should describe as concretely as possible:

1. Why being part of this collaborative is important to me?
   a. *I'm going to be able to make some extra money, which I definitely need. I'll get experience teaching and hopefully build an influential online profile, which could help me get a teaching job down the road. I get to hang out with some pretty cool people.*
2. What personal benefit I will get from this collaboration?
   a. *Money, teaching experience (maybe a girlfriend???)*
3. What strategies I can use to help myself hold on to my commitments in difficult times?
   a. *I will push myself to create excellent content, which will help me stay interested in the work, even though I'm not really into the game. I will remind myself that engaging in conflict can actually help our collaboration strengthen and grow, and that's actually healthier than sweeping it under the rug. I can invest in my friendship with each group member.*

These considerations will serve as a handle during rough patches. In Jake's case, making money to pay for college might not be his highest personal aspiration, but it will still be something that he can remind himself of to overcome difficult times and stick with the collaboration.

After the personal essence profile and the "stick with it" rationale, individuals name their **coping and remediation strategies**. In our previous chapter, we explored how Leon would develop these strategies to help him overcome his knee-jerk defensive reactions when he feels insecure; each colleague will need to develop their own plan to overcome their own struggles.

Here are Leon's answers to the coping and remediation strategy questions:

1. What possible problems do I foresee in collaboration? (Speak only for yourself.)

   a. *I will be an asshole sometimes. I hate to be micromanaged, and that makes me rebellious. I get annoyed when people act like know-it-alls. If I think people disapprove of me or are going to "quit" on me somehow, I blow up and try to push them away.*

2. How will I consciously deal with my personal vulnerabilities and/or obstacles in order to promote collaboration?

   a. *Step 1: take a break; do deep breathing. Step 2: journal about why I'm so pissed off and try to remember why I'm good / what I have to offer. Step 3: return to group; submit to Lana's questions; get advice from group. ← SO SELF AWARE! PS Deal with dad issues, eventually.*

3. How will constructive collaboration benefit me personally?

   a. *I will have friends. (← IRL) I will make some money. Maybe this will be the start of a brilliant entrepreneurship that will give me the life I want???!*

By forming a personal introduction that recognizes each colleague's power and responsibility to act; their personal essence, which gets at the crux of their motivation; and their coping and remediation strategies, which identify how they will move past their pitfalls to be a stellar contributor, each group member is able to be fully authentic—empowered to work at their best.

PERSONAL INTRODUCTION COMPONENTS

1. Each person's commitment to being their authentic self throughout the Collaborative Agreement building process
2. Aligning statements about what mindsets and attitudes will guide the collaboration
3. Affirmation of personal power and responsibility
4. Personal essence profile
5. "Stick with It" rationale
6. Coping and remediation strategies for each individual

Purpose

CDP 1: Establish a common purpose so that everyone in the group experiences a sense of shared ownership and belonging. This shared purpose should be revisited when a group member signals that they are experiencing a decreased sense of shared ownership and/or belonging.

The next component of the exploration phase is to identify the group's shared purpose, which incorporates CDP 1: ensuring that everyone experiences shared ownership and belonging. This involves recording the reason for the group's work. It identifies the *why*, the *what*, and the *how*—similar to a strategic vision-casting meeting.

This element of the Collaborative Agreement would not be something that changes without a great deal of thought and work; it might be revisited yearly, but likely not more often than that. This, of course, depends on the overall scope of the purpose of the collaboration. You can imagine there is a difference of scope between Jake and his team (creating video-game instructions) and the Quality of Life World Foundation (increasing people's resilience in dealing with the challenges of life). The scope of the purpose will help determine how often this should be revisited.

Without a board of directors or a CEO, colleagues need guidance in a new form of leadership, one that they form themselves. One way of approaching the purpose component is to consider **motivation** (the *why*), **impact** (the *what*), and **approach** (the *how*). These three considerations can help serve as a compass for the group, helping identify the reason for the colleagues to come together and clarifying their direction as they grow and evolve.

The **motivation** is the *why* and addresses the reason for the colleagues to come together. The motivation should identify what the colleagues find important as a group, such as values, beliefs, motivation, desired outcomes, and so on, and provides the vision of a desired future. (This information would show up in the top-right quadrant of the ACT matrix.) The collaboration should not simply exist to make money, as that will provide limited incentive for colleagues. Instead, group members should think further and deeper than that, considering how the group's shared motivation connects with their own personal essence.

For example, we contributed to creating an open-source Collaborative Agreement online that's already being used by different collaborators around the world as an example and inspiration for their own Collaborative Agreements.[69] The motivation statement written there, based on a fictional band of musician collaborators, is:

- We want to create a collaborative environment that allows us to embrace our true selves and passions to replace the current dysfunctional systems.

---

[69] It can be found at https://QOL.to/CollaborativeAgreement.

- This organization is our way of breaking free of the box that we find ourselves in. The intent is not to build a traditional institution that can wield power over us as individuals. Instead, we wish to come together to create an emergent Collaborative, a joint effort that binds us to one another and brings about the potential with each of us.

A shared motivation statement could also be simpler. For example, here's what Jake, Lana, Leon, and Alex might come up with:

- We will create high-quality instructional YouTube content about Leon's video game, and eventually content that more broadly shares messaging about quality of life (desired outcome). This will help us make some money, give us needed experience in areas that matter to us (desired outcomes), and help us spread positive messaging about quality of life to a broad audience (vision). We believe the world needs more positive messaging about how to create more quality of life (belief). It will also help people have more fun, us included (values).

The **impact** statement guides the concrete steps toward change. In other words, it provides an idea of what specific things you can do to impact the world so that it becomes a better place in the future, if the purpose is successfully executed. Leon, Alex, Lana, and Jake might write this for their impact statement:

- We will include slow-motion clips of certain key moves of the video game (Leon's playing); Jake will provide catchy intros, teaching, and narration; Jake will also find music; Alex will film, create graphics to highlight key elements, and do the editing.
- We will gradually start to discuss quality of life concepts in the videos so that gamers can think about self-care and well-being. Lana will research and generate.

Finally, the **approach** spells out *how* group members will act while they pursue their shared purpose. The detailed description for approach would cover observable behaviors that will enable group members to be successful in pursuing the impact action steps and work toward their shared group purpose. Here's an example of what Jake and his group might come up with:

- We will listen to each other, be supportive, be helpful, and show empathy at Commitment Sessions.
- We will get our work done according to the timelines we've agreed to, and if we can't, we'll communicate with each other.
- We, as a group, will use tools like the ACT matrix and Behavior Chain Analysis to help us optimize our collaboration.
- We will align ourselves with the Core Design Principles so that our collaboration will help us all maintain strong quality of life and good working relationships.

Using motivation, impact, and approach as the guiding compass, each colleague is able to participate freely, strategically, and productively within the collaborative.

MOTIVATION, IMPACT, APPROACH

These three elements should characterize the group's write-up about purpose in the Collaborative Agreement. They should also be addressed in any proposal a group member puts forward to make a change in the collaboration.

Motivation: the *why*. A purpose statement represents the things we find important as a group (values, beliefs, motivation, processes, desired outcomes); it is the vision of a desired future. (This information would show up in the top-right quadrant of the ACT matrix, under "Motivation.") Motivation answers the question: why are we working together?

Impact: the *what*. A description of the action steps we can concretely take to impact the desired future. (This information would show up in the bottom-right quadrant of the ACT matrix, as specific actions.) Impact answers the question: what specific steps and actions do we plan to take?

Approach: the *how*. A detailed description of our desired behaviors: the ways in which we can act and behave that will increase our ability to successfully impact change and work toward our purpose. (This information might also show up in the bottom-right quadrant of the ACT matrix as the values-based behaviors. It would show up in step 5 of the ACT matrix, under "Group Culture.") Approach answers the question: how do we want to behave while working toward our purpose?

The discussion of purpose helps a group define the rosy picture of what their purpose is, what they want to do to work toward that purpose, and how they want to go about it. However, in our last chapter, we acknowledged that sometimes people's personal pitfalls can "hook them" and prevent them from working productively. Each colleague must be responsible for identifying their own issues that could impede the collaboration. They are also responsible for calling out opportunities, propose actions, and use tools to improve the collaborative process—which leads us into our next component of exploration.

Strengths and Pitfalls

CDP 2: Ensure that everyone gets their needs met while working toward the shared purpose in a fair and equitable way.

This section would include content from the **individual ACT matrices** that we've discussed in previous chapters. By mapping out each colleague's strengths, the group has a better sense of who should take on what responsibility. For example, Leon has strengths in software coding, game expertise, and finance. It would make sense for him to take on responsibilities related to those areas. However, Leon should not sign up as the creative director for the YouTube videos because creative art direction is not in his wheelhouse; that role should probably fall to either Jake or Alex.

Discussing strengths and pitfalls also prompts group members to consider their **available resources, capabilities, and needs**. For instance, let's say that—next quarter—Alex signs up for a demanding class load and simply has less time to devote to the collaborative group. Alex would then be much more limited in their resource of time and should communicate that limitation to the group. Or if Leon recognizes that he needs additional tools to complete his analysis of the video game, he'll need to voice that need to the rest of the group. The goal here is to ensure that everyone is fully capable of executing their different responsibilities; that way, there's no reason for excuses or blame-shifting. Group members should help each other figure out the best ways to get their needs met.

Not everything is doable. It's a fallacy to say, "I can do anything. If I want something bad enough, I can do it." That's simply not true. Your circumstances play a huge role in determining if you can do something or not. For instance, if Jake has to take on another part-time job to pay his bills, he will simply not have as much time to contribute to the group. Limitations should be acknowledged and play a factor in determining who does what. Each person should estimate the time, habits, effort, and skills that will be required, then ask themselves, "Can I realistically put in that time and action?" The collaboration will fail if people don't calculate their expectations in balance with their abilities.

Each time a new collaborator joins the collaborative, they will be invited to work through the process of building the agreement so that they have the opportunity to fully align with it. The dynamic, evolutionary aspect of the Collaborative Agreement offers every participant the opportunity to contribute.

The last step in the exploration phase involves naming the group. Let's return to the party in Jake and Leon's dorm room and see what they come up with.

Picking a Name

"What should we call ourselves?" Jake asked.

Lana had stuffed her cheeks with marshmallows that she had pulled from the young men's snack cupboard. "Fluffy Bunny!" she said, which came out hopelessly garbled. She proceeded to crack herself up. Drool dribbled from her mouth.

"That's…cute…" Leon said, with minor alarm. He looked at Jake and raised his eyebrows. Jake covered his eyes and shook his head, laughing.

"What about Schwarzschild Radius?" Alex asked.

"What is *that*?" Leon asked.

"It's the radius of the event horizon surrounding a nonrotating black hole," Alex explained glibly. "I just think it sounds badass."

"I'm not sure we want to imply anything on YouTube is similar to a black hole," Jake contended. "We're going for greater quality of life for viewers, not interminable screen time."

"Fair enough," Alex said. "Why not just use our initials then?"

"L, J, L, A?" Lana said, having swallowed her marshmallows. "That's a bit pedantic, don't you think?"

"It's basic, but clear," Jake said. "I'm fine with that. How should we line them up?"

"Ladies first!" Lana crowed, sipping her wine. "LALA."

"Um, that leaves out Jake entirely," Leon corrected. "You need a 'J' in there."

"Whoops! Sorry, Jakey," Lana said, taking another slurp.

"JALL makes the most sense," Alex said. "Any other combination of letters just doesn't sound good."

"Boo, 'L's are last?" Lana pouted. "I'd rather be up front, next to Big J." She ruffled Jake's hair. Both Jake and Leon raised their eyebrows at each other.

"Well, I'm glad that's how you feel," Jake said, and gently took Lana's empty wine glass. "Maybe we do water in this next glass... and I'm going to make you some toast," Jake said.

"Peanut butter!" Lana crowed.

"JALL it is, then," Leon agreed. "The JALL Collaborative."

Phase 2: Identifying Strategies and Tools

Phase 2 seeks to address the needs and resources identified during the strengths and pitfalls discussion during the exploration of Phase 1. This section will also map out plans for how the group will operate, run meetings, make decisions, and so on.

How to Make Decisions

> CDP 3: Each group member needs to feel confident that they have a voice in the decision-making process.

In our previous chapter, we mentioned that—in addition to Commitment Sessions—any group of collaborators will need a plan for how they're going to conduct **strategy** sessions (how to determine and evolve purpose, impact, and approach), **governance** meetings (who is accountable for what and who takes responsibility for what), and **tactical** (operations—i.e., what needs to happen to get the work done) meetings.

For example, we know the JALL collaborators want to eventually expand the focus of their YouTube videos from just gaming content to positive messaging about quality of life.

- At a **strategy meeting**, they might determine it's time to move in that new direction, and they'll discuss the best way to approach it.

- At a **governance meeting**, they'll determine what new responsibilities are required to carry out this new project and assign who will take on those different responsibilities. For instance, Lana might be responsible for developing the content for the new quality of life videos; Leon might take on the job of recruiting new advertisers; Alex might make a new graphic to use for these videos to help distinguish them from the others, and Jake might write a new intro script.
- At a **tactical meeting**, they'll exchange relevant information to keep the project moving forward. For instance, Jake would get Alex the new graphic to use for the thumbnail picture of the quality of life videos.

In our next chapter, we'll also discuss how to run **Contribution Sessions**, when colleagues determine who gets compensated, and for how much, and in what way.

In this section of the Collaborative Agreement, group members should identify the plan for those meetings: will they be using a Holacracy© approach? An Agile approach? A sociocracy approach? The plan for these meetings should be spelled out, with a focus on how each group member will be ensured a voice in the decision-making process (CDP 3).

Each group will also decide on a **meeting schedule** for their team. Considerations surrounding team meetings might include:

- How team meetings are called, scheduled, facilitated (rotated roles) and documented (meeting minutes).
- Who can call a meeting; for instance, any colleague can convene a team meeting if one other colleague agrees.
- How and where they should be held. For instance, team meetings should be held in person or via video conference as often as possible.
- Other details: for instance, email or chat message may be used to arrange and document meetings, but should not be used for decision-making.

Consider how your group will make decisions in a fair and equitable way. For instance, you might decide that a decision like updating or **changing the Collaborative Agreement** requires a 75 percent majority. In our next chapter, we'll discuss ways to ensure that the weight of each group member's vote is an accurate reflection of the amount of effort they have devoted to the collaboration. For instance, group members that have put in the most effort will have a larger percentage of the vote than other group members who have put in less time and effort; this voting evaluation also considers experience and the value of a person's contribution. That way, the weightiest votes are cast by the people who are chiefly affected by the outcome of the decision. This ensures a fair decision-making process that honors the people who have put in the greatest effort, while still giving everyone a voice. We'll say much more about this in Chapter 6.

The agreement might also detail the **process for proposing changes**, something that would likely happen at a governance meeting. We recommend that any change start with a proposal presented with the group, naming the purpose, impact, and approach of the suggested change. This proposal shouldn't just issue complaints—it's not a question of saying you want something changed because you don't like it. It's a question of proposing *how* you would like to change it; the solution should be embedded into the proposal. The proposal will be evaluated by the other colleagues, based on the merit of the idea, its consequences, its application, and the people who will be affected by it. Then the group discusses if it's a wise change or not and implements the decision-making process they've agreed on, making sure the new change upholds the group's purpose.

> ## PLAN FOR MEETINGS AND
> ## DECISION-MAKING
>
> 1. A plan for how groups will address strategic, tactical, and governance issues.
> 2. Details about how and when meetings should be called.
> 3. A plan for how decisions will be conducted in a fair and equitable way.
> 4. Recommendations on how changes should be proposed and decided on.

These agreements and plans will simply help iron out the group's operational processes, ensuring greater efficacy. The plans will also help ensure that each group member gets a voice in the decision-making process.

Plan to Increase Helpful Behaviors and Decrease Unhelpful Behaviors

> CDP 4: Encourage transparency: peers should be allowed and expected to monitor the behaviors that all group members agreed on.
>
> CDP 5: Each member must commit to increase their helpful behaviors and decrease their unhelpful behaviors. Unhelpful behaviors will be addressed and tackled, working toward desired change; helpful behaviors should be acknowledged and celebrated.

This is where many of the tools we discussed in the previous chapter would be named—the Troubleshooting tool, the Behavior Chain Analysis, Development Objectives, and interpersonal skills. The plan to optimize behaviors should articulate a plan for how colleagues should hold each other accountable to their agreement toward personal growth (CDP 4). It should also include a commitment from each person to work on their struggles and lean into their strengths (CDP 5).

This kind of agreement not only ensures more authentic collaboration; it also clarifies *how* the group will collaborate and ensures transparency amongst collaborators. These plans help colleagues refrain from starting with assumptions, judgments, or ideas, but instead work with a clear understanding on who they are as a team. They acknowledge all the unique team personalities and spell out how the team will deal with each other.

Since there's no top-down punishment or sanction enforced on anyone in a Person to Person environment, everything depends on a person's commitment to follow through in the areas we've already addressed. The expectation is that they *will* take agency, that they will pursue personal growth, and that they will show up and work at the group's shared collaboration—as they agreed to. If a person fails to follow through on their commitment(s), this would be addressed, discussed, and managed during the Commitment Sessions. If a person fails to show up and engage during the Commitment Sessions, then the person essentially removes themselves from the collaboration.

Commitment Sessions, then, are the next logical component in the second phase of the Collaborative Agreement.

Resolving Conflicts via Commitment Sessions

CDP 6: Commit as a group to a healthy conflict resolution process and corresponding principles.

Commitment Sessions ensure CDP 6 is achieved within a Person to Person environment. This section of the Collaborative Agreement will describe the Commitment Sessions and answer questions such as, "What do we do when we feel tension?" "How am I feeling about my impact?" "How am I feeling about others' impact?" "Is everyone, including me, holding up our commitments?"

Objectives and Commitments

The monthly Commitment Session is our way of making sure we remain in sync and transparent. This is not about operations, but about us. Communication is essential for interpersonal processes to be effective.

Session objectives

- Exchange information in order to better understand each other
- Stay focused on our common identity
- Stay focused on our values and common goals
- Expose and discuss tensions
- Find and learn to apply solutions to conflicts
- Seek support and encouragement
- Get advice

I commit to

- Always be present at Commitment Sessions
- Participate actively and constructively
- Take responsibility for voicing my concerns and triggers
- Share what works for me and what makes it work
- Not tell my colleagues what to do
- Take turns as facilitator
- Make up for my absence if I am unable to attend a session

Colleagues can commit to a healthy environment in Commitment Sessions by affirming some of the example statements:

- **My commitment**: I choose to work with my colleagues to maintain the spirit of belonging by showing up to Commitment Sessions.
- **My commitment**: I commit to constructively use emotions. When I face tension, I consciously commit to reflect on:
  » What I am feeling
  » What I am thinking
  » What I am doing
  » What my emotion tells me
  » Remembering my goal is to "collaborate successfully."
- **My commitment**: I choose to deal with my feelings and emotions in a caring and constructive way, trying out some of the tools and strategies I come up with at Commitment Sessions, with the input of my colleagues.
- **My commitment**: I choose to look for and to practice helpful interpersonal skills to facilitate effective collaboration, such as self-advocacy, affirming others, and respecting myself.

As discussed in our previous chapter, Commitment Sessions are a powerful tool to optimize collaboration and allow each person to be seen, valued, and supported.

Phase 3: Commitment to the Collaborative Agreement

CDP 7: Establish sufficient autonomy to self-govern.

Finally, it's time for everyone to affirm their commitment to all of the above. Colleagues can initial their commitment as they go through each element of the Collaborative Agreement or wait until the end of the process to do so.

A collaborative process won't always be easy, but it offers a constant challenge with thousands of opportunities for team members to evolve and grow. Therefore, it requires dedication, courage, and **commitment as an anchor for balance or stability** when things get tough. The commitments made as part of a Collaborative Agreement will always point back to your initial intent to make things work effectively. The agreement stands for a balanced choice, safeguarded from emotional impediments.

In some ways, a Collaborative Agreement is similar to wedding vows. It's a commitment made when everything is going well, which people agree to abide by when things inevitably get hard. It's not about expectations, remunerations, or sanctions. Instead, it's about **commitment**, **contribution**, **validation**, **equity**, and **agency**. Like a bride and groom affirm their intent to work at their marriage, to love and honor their spouse, and to care for their union throughout life, this agreement expresses similar commitments for as long as people contribute to a collaboration.

We have used commitment statements to help illustrate what collaborators are agreeing to, when discussing each different section of the agreement. Here's a short list of some of the agreements colleagues would ultimately commit to abiding by:

COLLABORATIVE AGREEMENT:
EXAMPLE LIST OF COMMITMENTS

- I choose to wholeheartedly commit my effort to this collaboration and will hold to that commitment in spite of my changing moods.
- I commit to bringing my authentic self to the collaboration.
- I commit to owning my personal power and responsibility to act.
- I commit to using coping and remediation strategies to develop my unhelpful behaviors, in the interest of effective collaboration.

- I choose to show up to Commitment Sessions and work with my colleagues to maintain the spirit of belonging.
- I commit to working at dealing with my emotions in a caring and constructive way.
- I choose to practice helpful interpersonal skills, such as self-advocacy, affirming others, and respecting myself, for the sake of facilitating effective collaboration.

Group members might also want to consider what it practically looks like to remain in a collaborative team—and what actions would indicate that a person is removing themselves. In the example Collaborative Agreement available online, the fictional group commits to a series of statements that affirm what behaviors will indicate a wish to remain in the collaborative:

Remaining in the Collaborative

Each colleague is and remains a member of the collaborative of their own volition. A colleague can never be dismissed by their colleagues.

- If I default on my commitments in this agreement or to my colleagues, they can challenge me in our Commitment Session to help me figure out what's holding me back and to look for skills and strategies that will help me live up to my commitment.

- If I show insufficient progress toward living up to my commitments, I will resign from the collaborative.

- I commit to attending the Commitment Sessions as they are essential to effective collaboration. When, by exception, I cannot attend, I will make up for my absence by restating my commitment to my colleagues in the first Commitment Session following my absence.

- I acknowledge that by being absent four consecutive Commitment Sessions without prior coordination with my colleagues, I will have resigned from the collaborative.

- I can also choose to resign from the collaborative on my own initiative after informing my colleagues in writing 30 days in advance.

Even with a commitment like the one above, though, it's important to remember that a collaborative is not a "thing." It's not an entity like a company, or small business, or organization. It's simply a group of people working together toward a common goal, and when the goal is achieved, they move on. People may come and go; there is no specific term required. A collaborative exists while there are multiple people putting effort toward a shared aim, and for as long as that's occurring, the tools and agreements we've described thus far will help them optimize their experience working together.

Ultimately, the commitments affirmed by each group member help them achieve the Core Design Principle 7: the authority to self-govern. These agreements are living proof that colleagues have the autonomy to make decisions and act on issues or opportunities that fall within their current area of responsibility. They have the ability and authority to coordinate efforts through teams and maintain transparency through tools and practices. In other words, they have the self-steering power to engage productively with others, Person to Person, so that they can do meaningful work in a positive environment, therefore achieving greater quality of life.

We are capable of being our own case managers. We don't need to depend on anyone else to tell us what to do. We can take agency to create the lives we want, in the company of others who know us and respect us.

All of that can be accomplished by a person's own willing commitment to say, "Yes, I am able to do this, I want to do this, and I commit to doing this." That's what comes together in a Collaborative Agreement. It serves as a collective repository of a group's commitments, agreements, and tools for maintaining an optimal collaborative environment. The agreement can be formed in a number of ways and in a number of processes. Not only is this experience deeply meaningful; it can also be fun!

A COLLABORATIVE
AGREEMENT CASE STUDY

So, what does this look like when it actually plays out in real life?

Our colleague, Fernanda Guerra, was able to supply us with a beautiful description. We became acquainted with Fernanda Guerra through Kim Wright's training on Conscious Contracts. Fernanda is an attorney in Rio de Janeiro, and her company, SER Consultoria,[70] helps people form legal documents in the form of Conscious Contracts—essentially, a Collaborative Agreement.

Fernanda told us about a startup company she worked with, called Troca, which had experienced a good deal of success in their early days. Troca is run by a husband-and-wife team, Mayara Paes and Tarso Oliveira. At face value, Troca is a headhunting company: they recruit job candidates for companies looking to hire new talent. However, Troca's mission is more about social transformation than basic headhunting. They specifically focus on recruiting people in vulnerable conditions—those who are particularly economically depressed or have been historically marginalized, for instance. They get to know each potential worker, form a professional diagnosis, assess their talents, and then—with the help of other NGOs and social assistance institutions—they connect those people with companies looking for new talent and diversity. They seek to unite people, enterprises, and causes in the interest of building greater social equity—a Person to Person endeavor, if there ever was one.

Troca's efforts in the struggle against social inequality had received nationally renowned awards, such as the FIS Transforma Award 2019, and recognition in the German-Brazilian Chamber of Commerce and Industry Program (AHK Rio) and Think Big Incubation from Fundação Telefônica 2019. As a result, they were expanding their business and were preparing to receive capital contribution from investors. For that reason, a social contract had to be formally and legally registered with the government.

However, Mayara and Tarso wanted something more for their company than just a basic legal registration with facts like their address and the list of partners. They wanted a social contract that could carry their company's very DNA—their purpose, values, and nature. Also, as husband and wife, Mayara and Tarso felt strongly that in addition to encompassing Troca's characteristics,

---

[70] SER Consultoria's website is: https://sustentandoeloseloreais.com/.

the social contract should also help foster harmonious relationships, from both professional and personal perspectives. In other words, they wanted to run a successful business—but they also wanted to maintain a happy home life! Seeking a more connected and customizable legal experience, they were able to work with Fernanda to draft a formal document that was nevertheless focused on relationships and shared values.

They wrote their social contract with the following goals:

- Sustain the business.
- Sustain the interpersonal relationships.
- Help create an environment of trust, transparency, and commitment.

The partners worked with Fernanda over a series of meetings to craft this contract; later, it was formalized by Fernanda's firm—but not in "legalese." The language and design were made to be accessible, while still ensuring judicial validity; that way, the document could be used and referenced often by Troca's team.

Tarso later reported, "As we formalized the contract, we created a conscious relationship, both as a couple and as partners. SER played a fundamental role in the facilitation process, focusing on relationship details and asking questions that we would probably never ask." The contract now impacts approximately fifteen people—including partners, employees, and investors. Mayara and Tarso have said that the agreement has played a significant role in informing the daily interactions and cultural environment of their company. The processes developed for facilitating dialogue continue to be applied in everyday work, especially regarding empathy, respect for limits, making demands in an ideal way, and dealing with conflicts and solving them. Tarso reported to Fernanda that although "the object built was the contract . . . the conscious process [goes] far beyond the paper. It has not been created to be in some drawer, but to be internalized." The contract not only helped capture the company's DNA; it plays a direct role in helping maintain the life and health of the company.

Troca is thriving, both as a company and as a group of collaborators. You can read more about them at their website: https://sejatroca.com/.

And speaking of collaborators forming their own Collaborative Agreements, it's time to return to the dorm room and check in on our fictional colleagues.

THE NEXT CONUNDRUM

Around 2:00 a.m., the group wrapped up the strategies and tools phase. Beer bottles filled the room's recycling bin, and an empty wine bottle perched on top. Alex had changed the techno music to an Icelandic folk singer. The party vibe had decidedly cooled.

That is, for everyone except Leon.

"Boom!" Leon said. "Phase 2 is DONE!" He struck a superhero's pose, tossing a cape he had found somewhere and put on. "Alright, on to the commitment phase. Lana, can you send the document to our printer so we can all sign?"

Lana, who had spent the last hour Googling about Holacracy© meetings and typing up the agreement, sleepily passed her laptop to Jake. "You take it from here," she told him. She flopped down onto Jake's pillow and closed her eyes. Jake stared at the laptop, drunk and uncomprehending.

"Here, I'll print it out," Leon said impatiently, and took Lana's computer from Jake. He tapped Lana's foot. "Lana, wake up; we're gonna keep the party going and do the commitment phase next. I'll pour you more vino!"

"Dude, we should be sober for the commitment phase," Jake observed sleepily.

"I've never felt so intelligible!" Leon crowed. He grabbed one of the darts and twirled around three times so his cape swirled. "Up! Up! And AWAY!!" He threw the dart violently at the dartboard. It bounced off the metal rim and fell to the ground. "Damn it."

Alex murmured quietly while doodling on their digital sketchbook, "Intelligible . . . belligible . . . bellabul. Baby bull. Baby bell." They sighed. "Oooh, I could go for some Babybel cheese."

Leon picked up the dart and turned around to face the others. Jake looked half asleep, leaning against the wall next to Lana's sleeping figure. "Okay, fine. We'll wait to do the commitment phase until morning. But we still need to talk finance! We've got to figure out who gets paid what, and what money we want to invest, and all of that *biz-nass*." He held out the darts. "Lowest score has to answer first. Who's up? Alex?"

"Do you have Baby Bell cheese?" Alex asked in a singsongy voice, not looking up from the sketch pad.

Leon swooped over to the mini fridge, opened it briefly, then slammed the door shut. "I do not have this cheese you speak of," he announced.

"Then . . . I pass," Alex mused from the beanbag.

Leon sighed in frustration. "Jake?" he asked. "Come on, buddy; your turn for darts!" Jake's eyes were closed. Leon leaned forward and shook him by the shoulders. "RAMIIIIREEZZZ! Wake up!"

Jake roused abruptly and rubbed his eyes. "Leon. Buddy. We should stop. This has been a great Collaborative Agreement party. But we're tired. And we're also pretty sauced."

"But we're already getting ad offers! The money is gonna start coming in; I need to know what to do with it!" Leon said.

"Put it in your piggy bank," Jake said, and slowly began cracking up. Alex looked over at him and started silently laughing.

"The three little pigs," Alex gasped through silent laughter, pointing to the three others. "I'm the Big Bad Wolf!" Tears of mirth began streaming down their cheeks.

Leon studied the three. Finally, with an attitude of resignation, he removed his cape. "Okay," he said. "Maybe we pick this up tomorrow."

EXPLORE FURTHER

If you'd like to learn more, discuss this content with others, or access tools for your own application, go to the interactive section of the book using this QR code.

PART THREE

ECONOMIC ENVIRONMENT

Change is the essential process of all existence.
You must challenge your preconceptions,
or they will most certainly challenge you.

–Sarek, *Star Trek: Discovery*

CHAPTER SIX

COLLABORATIVE FINANCE

Human nature demands recognition.
Without it, people lose their sense of purpose
and become dissatisfied, restless,
and unproductive.

—Ricardo Semler, Semco CEO and corporate innovator

A month after posting their first videos, Leon was ready to make an exciting announcement. He sent out a text to the group: *It's payday, gang. Meet at our dorm tonight and we'll divvy up the $.*

Jake and Lana arrived together, followed shortly after by Alex. As Jake and Leon greeted each other with a fist bump, Jake said, "Man, this couldn't have come at a better time. My cell bill is due tomorrow, and I do *not* have the cash for it."

"So we've actually made some money off these videos?" Alex asked. "How much?"

"After subtracting the money I paid to publicize the videos, our ad revenue made us just over a thousand!" Leon said exultantly. "And if we can keep up the momentum, it's just going to keep on coming in!"

"So how does that shake out?" Lana asked. "Split it four ways, $250 each?"

"Yeah, we never did figure out the finance plan after *some people* got too sleepy to finish talking about it during our Collaborative Agreement party..." Leon cleared his throat loudly and looked pointedly at Jake and Lana.

"Whatever, dude, you plied me with vino," Lana said.

"So I guess we're doing it now," Leon continued. "I was thinking like thirty, thirty," he said, gesturing to himself and Jake, "and twenty, twenty," he finished, gesturing to Lana and Alex.

"Three hundred dollars for me?" Jake said. "Even bett—"

"I'm sorry, *what?*" Lana said, folding her arms. She narrowed her eyes and looked at Leon and Jake. "Thirty percent for you two? Twenty percent for us? Is that because you're... *the men?*" she asked, her voice dripping with sarcasm.

"Or do I get a smaller share because I'm *black* and *queer* and *nonbinary?*" Alex said, equally as dangerously.

"Uh oh," Jake said.

Leon quickly protested. "No, it has nothing to do with that. We've done more work; that's all."

"And our work is *naturally* less valuable," Lana continued, her voice still sharp as a razor. "I mean, I'm such a little woman, what could *I* offer that has any real value? Forget about the fact that the kind of leadership consulting I have been providing our group is worth hundreds of dollars per hour!"

Alex spoke up. "This feels like serious patriarchy bullshit."

Carefully, Jake tried to intervene. "Lana, Alex, I don't think Leon is trying to be sexist—or racist, or... anything else. He's just put in a lot of hours, and so I have I... I mean, Alex, you didn't even help on the first video—"

"*I've* put in a lot of hours," Alex contended. "Do you know how much it would cost to rent the camera I've been using by the hour? It's not cheap."

"I think we need to do a Commitment Session," Leon croaked out weakly. "I have a tension."

Lana ignored him and turned her gaze on Jake. "Just because I'm your girlfriend now doesn't mean you get a pass on this one, Jake. This is bullshit."

Leon interrupted. "Wait, 'girlfriend'?!" he asked incredulously. He looked at Jake. "Dude! When did that happen? You've been holding out on me!" He slapped Jake on the back.

Jake looked at Lana with a loopy, happy grin. "I know," he said to Leon. "I kind of can't believe it."

Lana softened momentarily, grinning at Jake in spite of herself. Then she stiffened again. "Hang on. Do you see this face?" she pointed to herself. "This is not the face of happily ever after. We need to work this out."

Jake sighed. "Guys, I hate this. We're breaking everything we agreed to, in terms of how we would treat each other. We can do better than this." He sat down. Slowly, the others sat as well.

Leon spoke up. "I did not, in any way, mean to come across as sexist or patriarchal. I'm really sorry if that's what I communicated."

After a pause, Lana spoke. "I'm sorry for reacting so strongly. Money is a loaded topic for me. It feels associated with respect. And I am not cool with being disrespected. But . . ." she looked at Leon. "Maybe that's not what you were implying."

Leon shook his head, then reached over to Lana for a fist bump. She grudgingly bumped him back.

"And I'm sorry I let my stress about money cloud my objectivity," Jake said. He thought for a moment. "Okay. It seems to me like we're looking at a few different things. We know how much money we have. That's easy: $1,000. So it seems like we need to discuss numero uno: how much effort we put in. Dos: how much our different contributions are worth. And tres: how much money we actually need."

Leon added, "Don't forget about, four: how we're going to invest in the project itself. And five: how we're going to distribute future funds. We should make a plan for that."

Lana spoke up. "But Jake—reimbursement, effort, the value of your contribution—don't those all boil down to money? Basically?"

"No, I don't think so," Jake said. "At least, they don't need to. Look, money is clearly a loaded topic. At least for me—"

"And me," Lana said.

"So," Jake continued, "Let's separate them out and talk through each one, independent of the other. Hopefully, that will help us answer some of these questions of effort and contribution with a clearer head."

SEPARATING MONEY FROM POWER

Money *is* a loaded topic, and it's been the source of inequity for much of history. Not only does money often lead to workplace tensions and perceived unfairness; it also is heavily associated with power. Those people and organizations with the money have the power; people without significant financial assets, privilege, or material advantages lack power, and they're often hindered from pursuing their goals as a result. In some countries, for instance, it's almost impossible to rent an apartment unless you have proof of a permanent work permit and steady income. A student like Jake, with an unsteady flow of income, wouldn't have the ability to even rent an apartment. The stress of insecure housing might lead him to take a job working nights, leading to poor performance in school, which could have a negative impact on his future career. It's easy to see how financial inequities can perpetuate systems that make the rich richer and the poor poorer.

The connection between money and power has led to many "gatekeeping" organizations, like banks, credit bureaus, mortgage lenders, investment firms, and so on. Even governments can play gatekeeper. For example, the

SEC (US Securities and Exchange Commission) claims to "protect investors, [promote] fairness in the securities markets, and shares information about companies and investment professionals."[71] But they've essentially created a class of people called "accredited investors," and only that elite class has access to the regulated financial instruments that are required for every good investment deal. Their stated mission is noble—but the way it plays out perpetuates inequity. The only thing a person needs to become an accredited investor is money, implying that poor people are incapable of understanding the financial market and therefore prohibited access to equal opportunities.

These gatekeeping organizations concern themselves with security, protecting assets, determining who is "good" for loans, who should be privy to certain information, and so on—but if you don't meet their certain criteria, you're out of luck. You might try to get a loan for your new entrepreneurial endeavor from a bank that advertises itself as "small-business friendly," only to have your hopes crushed by an impersonal institution telling you that your plan isn't good enough.

But what if there was a way to separate money from power? What if there was a way to recognize effort and contribution as having their own inherent value, apart from money? What if our financial dealings could be done person to person—in an authentic, efficient way, without the red tape or stringent requirements of the financial gatekeeper organizations? Instead of organizations with concentrated power proactively blocking new financial initiatives and increasing inequity, what if people could operate with real agency of their own to obtain what was best for them? What if you had the opportunity to pitch a business idea to a global collection of investors, not just the financial backers available to you within your own town? Or turn everyone benefiting from your work into micro-investors?

---

[71] What We Do," U.S. Securities and Exchange Commission, modified November 22, 2021, https://www.sec.gov/about/what-we-do.

The collaborative financial environment, with its accompanying tools, seeks to provide these opportunities in the following ways:

- It affirms contribution and effort as possessing their own inherent worth, separate from money.
- It seeks to expand access to funds for investment and opportunity.
- It looks to build a global community of investors who will have the chance to invest in an idea based on its merit, not on a stringent list of requirements.
- In doing so, it seeks to enhance person to person connections. The chance to partner with someone across the globe gives us the chance to build relationships with diverse people, acquainting us with different perspectives, values, and experiences; this can heighten our authentic connections with other people.
- The collaborative finance environment aims to increase efficiency in the exchange of funds, doing away with the paper shuffling and red tape of traditional financial intermediaries.

Collaborative finance affirms contribution and effort as having their own inherent worth, seeks to expand access and equity, and looks to build person to person connections across the globe to increase the efficiency and personability of financial transactions.

Here's an example. Let's say that a woman named Maggie lives in Portland and goes to the same artisan café every morning for an espresso. She always gets the Colombian roast, and one day, the barista mentions that that particular roaster in Colombia wants to move part of his production from washed beans to natural dry. "Apparently," the barista reports, "it's better for the environment, and it's a way to get a sweeter and more authentic flavor."

"That's amazing!" Maggie says. "When will it be available?"

The barista isn't sure; he explains to Maggie that the farmer is still trying to recruit investors to build out the necessary facility he needs. In a Person to Person financial environment, Maggie would be able to participate in the investment directly by contributing to the farmer's new facility, or she could contribute a small extra amount of money with each cup of coffee she buys. She would receive information about the farmer along with the financial details of his new investment, allowing her to follow him on his journey. (In Chapter 9, we'll explore more fully an online cloud community that facilitates this connection more easily.)

When Maggie drinks her cup of coffee, she would know the name and location of the farmer who grew and roasted it, allowing her to feel a personal connection with him; she would understand that she is part of the collaboration that brought this coffee into existence, giving her a sense of satisfaction and purpose; she has greater quality of life knowing that she's contributing to a better environment; and finally, she may get a financial return because of the investment. That's a person to person connection; that's a way to provide increased access to financial funds, increase efficiency in lending, and allow for collaborations to occur across the globe.

But we're starting to get ahead of ourselves. The collaborative financial environment has many elements, and each one builds on the others. Because these tools can be complex, we're going to provide a brief narrative illustration for each tool, sticking with our same characters, in order to help readers comprehend the tools' usefulness.

It's important to note: these tools are meant to be established upon the foundation we've established in our previous chapters. Take the illustration of Jake's group, for instance: their emotional talks on money only became grounded when they returned to the agreement they had forged as a group already. The Core Design Principles and a group's Collaborative Agreement should guide the collaborative finance process in order to ensure the value of authentic connection is upheld.

So where does collaborative finance begin? We start where Jake and his friends left off: separating monetary rewards from effort with Collaborative Points.

1. COLLABORATIVE POINTS: MEASURING EFFORT

"Okay—let's get an idea of our comparative effort first," Jake said. "We're going to set money aside for a second." He grabbed a box of poker chips off of Leon's bookshelf and dumped the chips onto the bed. "Let's describe our effort with a point value. So here's what I did: I researched the best YouTube teachers, translated Leon's tips into catchy instruction videos, wrote the narration, recorded the videos with Alex, and then worked with Alex during editing to determine the videos' final editing cut. I'm going to give myself 10,000 points for effort." He took ten blue poker chips.

"The blue ones are only worth $10 apiece," Leon said wryly.

"Whatever, man. I'm making this up as I go," Jake said. "Can we make them worth 1,000 points each?"

"Well—sure, but hang on," Leon said. "What metric are we using to evaluate these points? Is this just random, or are you basing your value on something in particular?"

"Good question," Jake said. "Let's come up with a rubric of sorts. Categories of assessment. How about: one, how hard we worked—as in, how many hours. Two, how useful was our contribution toward the final product? Three, the relative talent required to do whatever we did." He pretended to toss long hair over his shoulder for a moment. "I mean, I *was* the on-screen talent." Lana rolled her eyes good-naturedly. "And also, the scarcity of that talent. Some skills are rarer than others, and we should take that into account."

Alex nodded. "Those categories make sense to me," they said. "So if you're at 10,000, then I'm probably around 8,000 or 9,000—but only because I did one less video," Alex said to Jake. "Other than that, I feel like our time, effort, and contribution is pretty much equal. I did the filming with you and all the follow-up editing. I also developed some graphics, which is similar to you spending time doing research. I would say our skills—or *talents*, as you say—are pretty comparable. No one else in our group is a natural teacher like you, but no one else does filmmaking like me. And we were both pretty integral to the videos getting produced."

"And don't forget," Leon said, "the videos you helped with got way more views, which indicates how valuable your contribution is."

"Okay, so maybe I go with 9,000." Alex said. They turned to Jake. "I would think that next month, our points would basically be the same, since we're doing all the videos together now. Or, actually, I might get *more* points, since you won't need to be spending as much time doing research, but I'll still be spending a lot of time developing graphics, editing, et cetera."

"And making our videos look boss," Jake said. "Yeah, that all makes total sense. Are you sure you feel good about 9,000 for this month?" Jake asked.

Alex gave him a steely, pondering look. "Yes," they finally said slowly. "I think I probably put in slightly less time than you this month. So that feels fair."

Lana made a *tsk-tsk* sound. "Not great optics, gents," she said. "Paying the LGBTQIA BIPOC person less than the white boy."

"Okay, I'm Hispanic, first of all," Jake said. "And we are not talking about payment yet; this is only about effort. *And*—Alex was the one who chose 9,000, not us!"

"Gadzooks, I know! I was just teasing," Lana said.

Leon looked at Alex, "But you do have an *amazing* number of initials to work with, don't you? LGBTQIA BIPOC?"

"It's all part of my plan to take over the world," Alex said smoothly.

"Okay, here are nine poker chips for you," Jake said to Alex. "Leon? What about you, buddy?"

"Well..." Leon looked carefully over at Lana and Alex. "I did all the research for the gaming tips to give you. I rebranded my YouTube channel and figured out how to get our videos featured on some other key channels. I also spent a lot of time promoting our videos on social media and made all the arrangements for the ads on our videos. I invested about $500 to make our videos more visible, which was a big risk—although I've paid myself back for that. Still, I think I probably spent the most hours of anyone. I also think my skills are pretty unique—there was some programming and networking that I did that I don't think anyone else in our group knows how to do. All of that was definitely useful and necessary for the videos to get posted and make us money."

"Wow. I didn't realize you did all that," Lana said. "So...what would that make you? Like—13,000?"

"Really?" Leon said. "I was going to say my total would probably be higher than Jake's, but I was nervous to say anything higher than 12,000..."

Jake said, "It seems like the main distinguishing factor for us at this point comes down to hours. We're each bringing unique skills to the table, and all of our contributions have been integral to the final product. And I think you spent the most hours of all of us. So 13,000 sounds fair to me, amigo." He turned tentatively to Alex and Lana. "What about you two?"

Lana and Alex gave each other a long, considering stare and seemed to come to an agreement. Alex spoke. "Agreed." Jake handed Leon thirteen of the poker chips.

Lana sighed. "Okay, my turn. So...I *do* feel like what I brought to the table was valuable," she began.

The others agreed vocally. "But..." Lana continued, "if I'm being honest, it didn't actually take a ton of my *effort*. I did do about an hour's worth of online research to find the Core Design Principles and the stuff about Conscious Contracts. I was Googling a lot during our Collaborative Agreement party, and I typed all that up. But all the therapy stuff I brought to the table was informed by growing up with my therapist parents. And the leadership material is all stuff that I'm learning in my class, which I would be taking anyway."

"Don't undervalue that," Alex said to Lana.

"Yeah, as you said—leadership consulting and therapy are super valuable skills," Leon agreed. "And you've basically led our whole group in forming this weird, cool collaboration we've got going on."

"Thank you for saying that," Lana responded. "I do believe I've done a lot to help our group gel and orient itself in a healthy direction. But I also see that everyone else's contributions have been important. So, given that our group is mainly distinguishing our contributions based on the hours we contributed... maybe 7,000?" She looked at the others. "Is that fair?"

"Does that seem fair to you?" Jake said.

She thought about it. "Yes. It feels like a fair assessment of my effort," she said. "Especially because I know you all respect and value what I contributed."

Leon brought up a calculator on his phone. "Okay, so we're dealing with a total point value of 39,000," he said. "That means I produced 33% of the effort, Jake did 26% of the effort, Alex did 23% of the effort, and Lana did 18% of the effort." He studied the figures. "That seems about right, yeah?" The others nodded their agreement.

"Can I make a suggestion?" Jake said. "Remember how we were trying to figure out a good voting system during our Collaborative Agreement process and we realized that, with a group of four people, we were probably going to end up having voting ties a lot? Well, what if we attach our votes to these percentages? That way, whoever is doing the most work also gets the biggest vote on where the work goes."

"That's a cool idea," Alex said.

Lana and Leon agreed. "Although it makes me want to go out and do a bunch of work for our group right now so I can get a bigger vote," Lana said. She looked at the others and sheepishly acknowledged, "I tend to think I ought to have one of the biggest votes in any context."

How Collaborative Points Work

The effort of someone contributing to a collaborative is measured in Collaborative Points. As Lana illustrates, each colleague wants to be respected and recognized for their efforts and contribution. The most effective way to do that is not via money—which can easily become an inaccurate or skewed portrayal of someone's effort. Contribution can be most objectively assessed via a calculation that begins *distinct* from money.

To keep emotions neutral, we use an arbitrary unit of account that we call Collaborative Points. The points represent the "weight" of each colleague's effort and the value of their contribution. As Jake's group illustrates, groups can come up with a way to evaluate their contribution and effort, such as considering the rarity of each person's skill, how integral their contribution was for the final product's fruition, the hours devoted to the collaboration, and so on. Effort can also include anything that helps the collaborative achieve its goals (time, money, network, commission, material, etc.) and will always be translated into points. What matters most in the points evaluation is the *comparative* evaluation. In a collaborative, the effort provided by a colleague is always represented *relative* to the effort provided by other colleagues; as we illustrated, Jake provided a baseline point value that the others used to comparatively assess their own point value.

At first, people will likely use mechanisms to anchor the discussion of points to something familiar and quantifiable, like hours spent or the standard monetary value for a given contribution. For example, one hour of accounting yields 50 points; using your personal car yields 10 points per mile; a onetime sale yields 1 point per $100 of turnover; providing an office space yields 500 points per month, and so on. This is similar to the "Slicing Pie" method invented by entrepreneur Mike Moyer, which guides startups in how to split startup equity in a fair way.[72] It explains in detail how to anchor points to real-world measurables and helps groups start with a known frame of reference while learning to let go of that anchoring data.

One benefit to rewarding group members with points is that points can represent a wide range of rewards. While points *can* translate into a monetary payout, as we'll see with Jake's group in a moment, they can also represent other things. For instance, Collaborative Points also represent the weight of a colleague's vote. When a group of collaborators needs to make a decision about strategy, each group member's vote will be weighted according to their Collaborative Point percentage. The person with the most points will also have the "heaviest" vote. That way, the people putting in the most work will also have the largest say over the group's direction.

It's vital to remember that, when discussing each member's points, colleagues should do their best to maintain the helpful mindsets and attitudes we've discussed in our previous chapters. These discussions should occur during Contribution Sessions, which are essentially illustrated in this chapter. The description of how those sessions should proceed should be added to the Collaborative Agreement. (The JALL group might have managed to hammer this out in the previous chapter, had they not gotten so tired and drunk.)

---

[72] To dive deeper into the Slicing Pie method, check out: https://slicingpie.com/.

Contribution Sessions are meetings where colleagues determine
each individual's relative effort and financial earnings
in a helpful, equitable, and respectful way.

Forming a plan for level-headed and respectful Contribution Sessions is important: as our fictional group illustrates, conversations about money and/or contribution can easily go sideways. However, when each group member comes with an intentional mindset and engages in an environment that allows for safety, trust, and transparency, the conversations are given a chance to be helpful and productive.

The group Radical, which focuses on helping people co-manage and co-own with attention to our innate human needs, has a method to help group members engage in a helpful way with each other when assigning points.[73] Each group member is given an allotment of points that they must give to their group members—they're not allowed to keep it for themselves. The exercise gives them a chance to consider each group member's contribution and affirm the effort of others, while also helping them consider the group members' relative contributions more objectively than if they were only thinking about their own points. We'll illustrate this method in our next section about quality of life. This is one more example of the flexibility allowed by the Collaborative Points and the opportunities they provided for experimentation.

Collaborative Points should also be recalculated on a regular basis. Group members' contributions will not remain static month to month. Alex hinted at this when they speculated that next month their total would be larger than Jake's. One way that this collaborative financial environment prevents

---

[73] More information about Radical Purpose can be found in the book *RADICAL Companies*. See Matt Perez, Adrian Perez and Jose Leal, *RADICAL Companies: Organized for Success without Bosses or Employees* (Pradera Media, 2021). See also https://www.radicalpurpose.org.

power plays and hierarchies from forming is that points are not accrued over years and generations, the way that money or shares sometimes are. Points should be an accurate reflection of the group's *current* distribution of effort. They should be reevaluated on a regular schedule—that could be month to month, quarter to quarter, or project to project: whatever makes sense for the nature of each group's work.

Collaborative Points should be an accurate reflection of the group members' current distribution of effort and reevaluated on a regular schedule. This prevents hierarchies and power plays from forming.

So how would a person keep track of their Collaborative Points? Similar to how an hourly employee would keep a daily record of their time contribution, colleagues in a collaborative would each keep track of what they've contributed on any given day. For instance, Leon might note that he worked from 10:00 p.m. to midnight, or Alex might note the market value of the graphic that they created over the weekend; those notes could be called their "effort log." Although an hourly employee would only keep track of time, colleagues in a Person to Person financial environment keep track of other forms of contribution as well—effort, the comparative value of a person's work, and so on.[74]

This might seem more complicated than business as usual, but it also allows for greater accuracy. Most people who have worked in a group can attest that one person's hour is not equal to another person's hour. During Joe's "work hour," he might get coffee, chat with a coworker, check in on Facebook, and get

---

[74] The Slicing Pie method mentioned earlier creates a helpful day-to-day model that translates various forms of effort into points and ensures that different categories like hours are quantified in the same way.

some work done. During Tracy's hour, she might have her nose to the grind-stone the entire time. If Joe and Tracy were to evaluate their effort in terms of Collaborative Points, where 100 points equals 100% effort, Tracy might say she deserves 99 for that hour, while Joe would admit he deserves somewhere around 60. That difference in effort will be more accurately depicted in points related to effort than a blanket hourly wage. The level of transparency and trust required to do this effectively will only be possible in the kind of Person to Person environment we've taken care to describe in the previous chapters.

After colleagues have maintained their "effort logs," those logs would be referenced during a Contribution Session to inform each person's Collaborative Point total. For instance, let's say that next month, Leon, Jake, Alex, and Lana come to their Contribution Session, notes in hand. Alex begins: "In the last thirty days, I've done X, Y, and Z. I estimate that I deserve 10,000 points this month." Each colleague shares their accounts of their effort since the last Contribution Session, and then the group assigns points for that most recent period of time. If they do monthly Contribution Sessions, they would be assigning points for the effort of the last thirty days, but these sessions could also be held every two weeks, every quarter, or after every completed project—whatever works best for the group.

This means that the Collaborative Points that colleagues are working with—which inform their distribution of funds and voting weight—are recalculated at every Contribution Session. The point totals determined at the session function as a snapshot of the effort each colleague put in over the period of time since the last Contribution Session.

And then what? Let's say that Alex gets a point total of 9,000 during April, and 10,000 next month in May, but then gets ill during June and has to seriously scale back their work, only earning 3,000 points. However, during June, the group has a big decision to make, and Alex is entitled to a vote. Should Alex have a tiny vote, simply because they got sick? Should Alex's pay drop to an unsustainable amount, threatening their ability to pay rent and their bills? The answer, of course, is no.

So how should we calculate Collaborative Points in a way that prevents anyone from amassing points and asserting power plays, but also in a way that prevents volatility as circumstances change month to month?

We recommend that Collaborative Points be calculated as a running sum. For example, in a group like the JALL Collaborative, it would make sense to average together the past three months of points for a fairer representation of their comprehensive effort. So Alex's Collaborative Point total going into the month of July would be 7,333—the average of April, May, and June. Alex would be entitled to withdraw 7,333 points' worth of cash and would still have 7,333 points' worth of a vote—even after being so sick during June. At the next Contribution Session at the end of July, Alex's points from April would "expire," and the new three-month total would be the average of May, June, and July.

The "averaging" period will change, group to group, depending on the work that is done. For instance, a building architect might put in a massive amount of time and effort at the start of a construction project, detailing how a building should be designed. However, it might take months or even years before that building has been completed and is fully paid for. For work like that, it would make sense to calculate Collaborative Points across a project's duration rather than every three months. Ultimately, each group will need to decide the most logical way to calculate and average Collaborative Points to appropriately and equitably suit the nature of their work.

Calculating points as a running sum means they don't accumulate like shares; they are constantly reassessed. That means that Collaborative Points will fairly and consistently reflect a colleague's contribution, and no one person has the ability to amass power.

By discussing effort on a consistent basis during the Contribution Sessions, colleagues have regular opportunities to address tension, ensure that people are compensated equitably, and reassess who has done the most work and therefore deserves the loudest voting voice. Not only does this system allow for greater accuracy and equity; it also helps groups avoid power-play scenarios.

2. CONSIDERING QUALITY OF LIFE: RECOGNIZING "WORTH"

"Hang on," Leon said, scrutinizing the numbers he'd typed into his Excel spreadsheet. "Something's not sitting right." He tapped his finger on Lana's column. "I don't like this."

"Why not? What's wrong with my column?" Lana asked.

Leon swiveled his chair around to face the rest of the group. "I've got the most points right now."

"That's fair," Jake said. "You've done the most work at this point."

"Yeah, but listen," Leon said. "I would have quit this group entirely if not for Lana. She walked me through all that navel-gazing. The main reason I stayed committed to the group and put in all the time I did was because of how our group worked through all those self-awareness conversations, and did the Collaborative Agreement, and all that. Most of that came as a result of Lana."

"Awww!" Lana said, pleased.

"It doesn't feel right to me that I have the most points and she has the fewest. Maybe it's a fair reflection of effort, but...I don't know. It doesn't feel like the whole picture."

Alex held up their digital sketch pad. In one corner was a dollar sign. In another corner was a bucket marked "Effort." In between, Alex had sketched a host of other images—a person on a mountain top, another person guiding a trio of blindfolded people, someone working at a computer, people laughing together, books, hearts. "The bigger picture," Alex said. Alex began pointing to the different images. "Achievement. Personal growth. Productivity. Friendship. Learning." Alex looked at the others. "There's more here—" Alex made an inclusive gesture, implying all of them. "—than just money and effort."

"Quality of life," Lana mused, looking at the sketch pad.

"Wow—true," Jake said, studying the images. "Okay. Good," he said. "Let's evaluate what we've each contributed in quality of life."

"You mean how much we've contributed to one another? Like—in this group?" Lana asked. "Or to the world at large?"

"Um, let's talk both," Leon said. He turned to Jake. "Any ideas about how to divvy this up?"

"Yes..." Jake grabbed the poker chips again and pulled out a stack of red ones. "Okay—let's first talk about the quality of life we created through making the videos themselves."

"You mean for gamers?" Leon asked. "I mean...we helped people play the video games better."

"There are a lot of comments that talk about how badass the videos are," Lana said. "People like them, so they're obviously having some sort of impact on people's life satisfaction."

"True," Jake said. "Although I'm thinking that making video games more fun isn't going to have a *huge* comprehensive impact on people's quality of life. You know—on their friendships, physical health, et cetera." He looked at Leon. "Is that fair?" Leon shrugged and nodded. "So..." Jake looked down at the poker chips. He counted out twenty. "Each of these chips is worth 100. I'm going to say we get a score of 2,000 for quality of life."

"What is that based on?" Alex asked.

"No idea. It's a completely arbitrary number. But we can use it as a base for comparison in future months," Jake said. "Okay—*now*..." He passed out the poker chips like a card dealer, giving each person five. "You are not allowed to keep your quality of life poker chips. You have to distribute them to each other, based on the quality of life you experienced from each colleague during our collaboration. That's how we're going to measure our internal quality of life contribution."

Immediately, Jake and Alex passed three of their chips to Lana. Leon gave her four. "What?!" Lana said. "I'm so delighted!" She picked up the ten poker chips and then let them fall in a stream back onto the bed where she was sitting. "I never expected red poker chips to give me so many warm fuzzies," she said, beaming.

Jake gave one of his poker chips to Leon. "For your amazing entrepreneurial vision," he said. Then he gave one to Alex, "For your excellence in quality."

Alex grinned. "Yeah, you definitely sound like a future teacher," Alex said to Jake. They gave one back to him. "For your leadership. And for being a fun collaborator on the videos." Alex passed their last chip to Leon. "For growing." Leon furrowed his eyebrows in confusion. Alex shrugged. "You started with the MAGA shirt. Now we're actual friends. I see your skills and talents; you're seeing my skills and talents..." They paused. "It's good to be viewed as a whole person."

Leon smiled, touched, and nodded in agreement. "That might be the coolest poker chip I've ever gotten. Thanks, Alex." He looked at his last poker chip. "Dang it—I was planning to give this to Jake since he was the one to start this whole thing, but now I want to give it to Alex too..."

"Give it to Jake, and I'll give Alex an extra one of mine," Lana said. She turned to Alex and passed them two poker chips. "For being brilliant and for making it safe for all of us to be as weird as we authentically are." Alex grinned. Lana passed two to Jake. "For your courageous vulnerability and self-awareness. Also, for being a good kisser," she grinned. Jake blushed.

"Woah, woah!" Leon said. "*Okay* now, kids..."

"Hang on, sparky; I haven't forgotten about you," Lana said. She gave him her last poker chip. "Because I'm so damn proud of you for navel-gazing." Leon grinned and accepted the chip.

They all sat there for a moment, feeling happy and loved.

"So, what do we do with these?" Leon asked Jake.

"I don't know!" he responded. "But that was awesome."

Leon turned to his computer. "Okay, I'll record our scores, and we'll figure out how to reward our quality of life contributions down the road."

Quantifying Quality of Life

Remember: economic value only represents one of the eight life domains. Although money might *enable* some other domains, it remains a very narrow representation of someone's contributions. Therefore, a collaborative financial environment should consider quality of life as a key value component as well. The flexibility of the points and discussions of value would lend themselves to that consideration.

As a collaborative group matures, they are able to consider other less tangible forms of contribution—and that's when we return to considering the value of quality of life. For instance, in Lana's case, her contribution to the group's formation was harder to quantify in terms of money or time, yet the group could all recognize the tremendous value her counsel had brought to their quality of life as a functioning group. As another example, consider a food bank. A food bank does not usually produce an economic return, but they provide people with a great deal of quality of life. We tend to label organizations like these "nonprofits," but we don't actually consider the quality of life they create, nor do we try to assign a value to it. Those sorts of less quantifiable contributions deserve to be considered with equal weight as something more easily quantified, like equipment rental costs.

So how should something as abstract as quality of life be quantified? As the JALL colleagues illustrated, quality of life should first be measured in terms of how a collaboration's contribution has affected the world around them. They gave themselves a score of 2,000 for their videos; a food bank, in comparison, might earn a score of 30,000. Although Jake admitted that his initial declaration of 2,000 points was arbitrary, quality of life could be more objectively quantified in terms of the life domains discussed in Chapter 1. For instance, how many domains did the contribution impact, and to what degree? For the JALL Collaborative, their overall produced quality of life might increase when they start doing videos that address aspects of well-being—for instance, making a video for gamers about the importance of sleep. Since that would impact the domain of physical well-being *and* general life satisfaction, their quality of life score would increase.

Once a group has determined a score for their *external* quality of life contribution, they could divide up that score among their colleagues, based on how each person has impacted the group's *internal* experience of quality of life, as we illustrated. In its early phases, this process would largely function as a celebration. Each person has the chance to receive recognition for their efforts, which creates the added bonus of strengthening connections between team members. It's also an opportunity for colleagues to affirm one another for all the ways they have each worked to live up to the helpful behaviors outlined in the Collaborative Agreement—basically, for making it more fun to work together.

An arbitrary score may seem like an insufficient form of reward for generating quality of life. During the COVID-19 pandemic, there were paltry attempts to recognize frontline healthcare workers' Herculean efforts to care for people amidst the health crisis. These reward attempts were well intended but deemed largely insufficient: can tiny bonuses and 8:00 p.m. cheers really compensate for the exhausting ordeal those frontline workers endured? Surely not. However, we think that a celebration like the one we just depicted among the JALL members might be more rewarding if it were to take place within the actual working team. For instance, if doctors and nurses made a point to share individual recognition amongst their teams for amazing contributions during the pandemic, that might have felt more meaningful than a government authority issuing them a minor tax credit.

Still, it's worth pointing out that there *should* be a tangible way to reward quality of life contributions. If quality of life became a community-wide recognized asset, colleagues could be rewarded in any number of ways: extra vacation days, a larger vote when making group decisions, getting access to better deals, like Yelp points; receiving discounts; private admission to special places, like national parks or Disneyland. In whatever form, the rewards for quality of life should help the recipient increase their own quality of life. The vision outlined in the chapters that follow would help foster the kind of environment that could generate quality of life rewards on a community scale.

But wait—there's still some money to deal with. Considering effort and quality of life contribution is valuable, but these colleagues are still living in the real world and have financial needs. Let's get back to the JALL group's efforts to divvy up their $1,000 fairly.

3. THE DRAW: FUNDS DISTRIBUTION

"So we've figured out effort. We've discussed quality of life," Leon said. "Now what? Are we ready to deal with cash?"

"Yes," Jake said. "I think we should divide up the cash based on the Collaborative Points."

"And leave the quality of life score aside?" Lana asked. "Rats."

"That makes the most sense," Leon said. "Not to discount your quality of life score in any way, Lana—but since the *money* was made mainly through the effort we produced, I think it's probably most logical to use our Collaborative Point percentages to split up that pot of $1,000."

"That's pretty straightforward, then," Alex said. "I have 23% of our points, so I get $230."

"And I have 26%, so I get $260," Jake said. He grinned. "That's a relief. I'll be able to pay my cell bill and still have a little extra."

"Wait, guys—hang on," Leon said. "That doesn't leave us with any money to invest in growth, or for our day-to-day operations. I need to submit some payments to the lever vehicles that are pushing our videos to the top of the search lists. And if we want to grow this effort—which I think we should—we should operate ourselves as a responsible startup. No startup is going to distribute 100% of their profits in salaries. We can't consume it *all*. We need to think long term and budget something for the actual business."

Jake looked at him. "How much are we talking, amigo?"

Leon shrugged. "Well... I need to pay $100 to the service that's promoting our videos. And I think we should put some money toward a bigger advertising campaign in the future. There's an amazing service that would seriously launch us, but we'd need to have about $10,000."

Jake let out a low whistle. "How the hell are we going to come up with $10,000?" he asked. Leon started to answer, but Jake interrupted. "Are you wanting to keep this entire $1,000 to put toward that future goal?"

"No, I'm not," Leon said. "I'd like to put *something* aside, though."

"Like... half?" Lana ventured.

"How do you guys feel about budgeting 40% for the business and 60% for us?" Leon asked. "That's $100 for our operation costs and $300 for long-term growth. And then $600 for us to split."

"So we're only going to have $600 to split?" Jake asked bleakly.

"I'm fine with setting $400 aside out of the pot," Alex said. "Because this is going to help us grow, right? It's going to help us make more money down the road."

"Exactly," Leon said. "Thinking about the long-term health of what we're doing actually serves all of our self-interests. We need to think about sustainability. There's no point putting in all the work that we are if we don't leave ourselves enough money to operate and survive. The same rationale goes for growth. We can't get any bigger unless we invest money in growth."

"That all makes sense to me," Lana said. "So how does that shake out?"

JALL'S DISTRIBUTION:
PERSONAL MAX FOR IMMEDIATE WITHDRAWAL

- After setting aside $400 from the original $1,000 they made, the group has $600 left. They split that according to the percentages they figured out earlier when calculating Collaborative Points. Here is what each group member could potentially withdraw.
- Jake: 26% of $600 = $153.85
- Alex: 23% of $600 = $138.46
- Lana: 18% of $600 = $107.69
- Leon: 33% of $600 = $200.00

Trading Options Enabled by Points

Jake looked at his assigned number bleakly. "Okay—I get the long-term budgeting thing. I support it, in theory. But Leon, I'm sorry, man, I need more than $153 to get through the end of the month."

"How much do you need?" Leon asked.

"I mean..." Jake sighed and stared down at his hands. "Two hundred dollars, at least, would be great." He looked at Lana sheepishly. "Are you disappointed that your new boyfriend is totally broke?"

She laced her fingers through his. "I like *you*, not your debit card," she said. Then she grinned. "Besides, I don't see you as broke. I see you as richly aiding my quality of life."

Jake laughed. Feeling a bit better, he turned back to Leon. "Are you sure we need to save all that money for the future?"

"I don't want to touch that $400 right now. It's an investment in ourselves," Leon said. "But if you need more in the short term, I can fund you. Just sell me some of your Collaborative Points."

"What do you mean?" Jake asked. "How would that work?"

"Look—our group's point total is 39,000. And we made $1,000 total. That means each point is worth..." He pulled out his phone calculator and did some quick math. "...0.0256 cents. So sell me some of your points, and I'll give you some of my cash."

"Wait...what?" Jake rubbed his hair. "My head is hurting again."

Leon said, "You need an extra $47 to get you up to $200. So if I spot you $50, that works out to..." He did some math. "To 1,953 points. Sell me that many points and I'll give you an extra $50."

"Why would you do that?" Jake asked. "The Collaborative Points aren't worth anything beyond helping us figure out how much cash we get in the short term." He picked up a handful of poker chips and let them drop back onto his bed. "You don't want to trade real cash for poker chips, man."

"I disagree," Leon said. "I actually think the Collaborative Points are going to be pretty valuable one day. And I would be very happy to buy some of yours."

Alex leaned forward. "Why?" they asked. "Are you equating points to shares? Like, the points we create now could be worth a lot in the future if our project starts making more money?"

"Not exactly," Leon responded. "Although, Alex, you can see where I'm going." He took a deep breath. "Look, we're functioning like a startup, right?" The others nodded. "Well, in typical startups, people usually put in a ton of time and effort, and it ends up being a long time before the company becomes lucrative."

"Kind of like us," Lana observed.

"Right," Leon agreed. "So the way startups usually try to compensate people for all the time they put in is by giving out shares. And then, if the company *does* become successful eventually, those shares end up being worth a lot of money. But I don't like shares because they lead to power plays and hierarchical bullshit." He scoffed. "Basically every dinner conversation I had with my dad growing up was him complaining about how the shareholders were being idiots. And that system also tends to be pretty unfair. Usually the founders get a bunch of shares, but all the other people who contributed a ton of work in the beginning get left out in the cold. I mean—they get their paychecks, but hardly any of that long-term value represented in the shares."

"You think our points system is going to work better?" Jake asked.

"I do," Leon said. "Because we're planning to recalculate them every month, which means our record of points will be an accurate representation of the effort each of us put in. If we were doing shares, that wouldn't necessarily be the case—the founders would get a bunch, and then they'd *keep* a bunch, regardless of how their hours changed later on. But with these Collaborative Points, we're keeping track of our genuine effort. That means if we connect the points with future money—like, our someday, *maybe* money—we could be sure that they were a fair representation of the work we put in."

"Dang," Jake said, amazed. "I can't believe my little poker-chip inspiration managed to accomplish all that."

"So—back to your $50," Leon said. "If you're willing to sell me..." he checked the number on his phone again. "... 1,953 points, then I will trade you $50 of my short-term cash."

"So that would mean I have less points, so... less future money, I guess?" Jake asked.

"Right," Leon said. "It's kind of a gamble. We might not ever get that future money if this collaboration ends up dying out, so it might be my loss. But if we *do* become really successful, the points you trade me would probably eventually be worth more than $50. And then it would be your loss. So—it's your call."

"Don't forget about the voting mechanism," Lana said to Jake. "Remember? We decided that our points percentages would impact the weight of our votes when we make future decisions."

Jake thought about that. "Well—I legitimately need an extra $50 if I'm going to be able to pay my bills this month without taking out more loans. So...let's do it. Let's trade."

Jake and Leon's Trade

	Entitled Cash/Points	Short-Term Requirement	Gap	Trade	Points Traded	New Entitled Cash, Post-trade	New Point Total
Jake	$153.85 / 10,000 points	$200.00	($50.00)	$50.00	-1,953	$203.85	8,047
Leon	$200.00 / 13,000 points	$0.00	$0.00	($-50.00)	1,953	$150.00	14,953

"Okay," Leon said to Jake. "I am sending $200 to your Venmo account...and..." He set down his phone and turned back to his computer. "Updating your Collaborative Point total. Great." He turned to Alex and Lana. "Your turns. Let's take a look at your totals."

Alex and Lana's Draw

	Collaborative Points	Share	Entitled Cash (CP% * $600)	Short-Term Requirement
Alex	9,000 points	23%	$138.46	$100.00
Lana	5,000 points	18%	$107.69	$50.00

"How much do you two want to withdraw?" Leon said.

"How much do I have again?" Lana asked. "I'll just take the full amount."

"You're entitled to 18% of $600, which works out to $107.69." Leon said. "But you don't have to take out the whole thing."

"Why wouldn't I take out the whole thing?" Lana asked.

"Because of the someday maybe money," Leon said. "Any money that we don't withdraw today has the potential to grow down the road, if we become more successful. It's the same as with the Collaborative Points."[75]

"Huh," Lana said. "Interesting."

"I'm entitled to $138, but I don't need my whole thing. I'll take $100 out," Alex said. "And I'll leave $38 in for potential future growth." Alex looked at Leon. "I can see where this is going. I like your ambition."

Leon grinned. "I love that you get this too, Alex. And yes—come on! Let's build, let's grow, let's *do* it." He began typing into his phone, sending $100 to Alex's Venmo account. "So—the remaining $38 is going to still be in my account for now, but I'm not going to touch it. I'll keep it earmarked as your long-term investment money. And I'm going to start looking hard for some sort of app or vehicle that can help us make this whole process easier." He looked up from his phone. "Okay, Lana. You're up."

"Well…" Lana considered. "I'm honestly doing okay on cash right now too, but I did have my eye on these concert tickets for Initial Revolution…"

"What?!" Jake said. "Initial Revolution is playing here? When?!"

"I know!" Lana said. "I was going to take you." She grinned. "It's on campus, so tickets are cheap: $25 each." She looked at Leon. "So I'll take out $50. And leave $57.69 in."

The group sat down around Leon's computer as he typed new figures into the Excel spreadsheet. They each chimed in with their different numbers as they calculated the short-term cash each of them was entitled to, their new totals after withdrawing the short-term cash they needed, and their current points. Finally, they all recorded the new totals, with Jake's and Leon's new "balances," post-trade, reflected.

"Okay," Leon announced. "So each of us has a little money left that we're saving for the future."

"What money do I have left?" Jake asked. "I thought I withdrew all of mine."

"Not so, mon frère," Leon replied. "You have $3.85 left."

---

[75] We will explore this concept more in future chapters.

"Ha!" Jake laughed. "And our Collaborative Point totals have changed, right? My percentage dropped, and yours went up a little."

New Totals, Post-draw

	Actual Withdrawal	Remaining Balance / Remaining Points	Relative Share, Post-draw
Jake	$200	$3.85 / 8,047 points	21%
Alex	$100	$38.46 / 9,000 points	23%
Lana	$50	$57.69 / 7,000 points	18%
Leon	$0	$150 / 14,953 points	38%

Analyzing the Draw and Collaborative Points

Note how Leon's totals now look different from the others. Leon decided not to withdraw any of his entitled cash, and his trade with Jake meant he increased his points. As a result, Leon clearly has the biggest relative share, with 38%, compared to the next largest total: Alex's, at 23%. However, once they reevaluate Collaborative Points next month, those totals are likely to change.

This is especially noteworthy because if and when the group has a major decision to make, Leon's relative share would be by far the most weighty. Here is where we see the other main function of Collaborative Points: as a voting mechanism. Although the points help determine each group member's monetary draw, as illustrated, that function of the points would only occur on one day. Every day during the rest of the month, the Collaborative Points would fill their other function: determining voting weight when the group makes a decision.

COLLABORATIVE POINTS HAVE FOUR MAIN FUNCTIONS:

1. They determine, affirm, and validate each colleague's effort, to effectively separate money from contribution.
2. They are used to determine each colleague's draw and can be traded.
3. They are a voting mechanism, where each colleague's percentage of points determines the weight of their vote.
4. They help determine each colleague's Future Value (soon to be discussed).

In our previous chapter, we mentioned that a group might spell out the following process for making decisions in their Collaborative Agreement: we need a 75% majority for a decision to go forward. The Collaborative Points help ensure that the decision-making process is fair because they put the weightiest votes in the hands of the colleagues putting in the most effort. Any outcome of a decision will naturally have the biggest impact on the people doing the most work; therefore, the people who are doing the most work should have the biggest say.

However, points have a very limited existence. As discussed, Collaborative Points are calculated as a running sum. That means every time Collaborative Points are calculated, the colleagues have a new number, reflecting the average of their points over the past period of time (for example, three months), a period determined by each collaborative group. But that total will be periodically revised, which means that a person's voting weight is also consistently updated. When you've put in a lot of energy in a given month, your point value will increase, as will your voting voice. This helps incentivize everyone to contribute their best while also helping to ensure that no one person in the group amasses power over the others.

The last function of Collaborative Points is in their impact on each group member's Future Value, a consideration that would mainly be relevant for startup scenarios.

4. ECONOMIC AND FUTURE VALUE

"Hey, can we go back to this idea of 'someday maybe money' before we wrap this up?" Leon asked the others. "I think I have an idea about how we could estimate how much our Collaborative Points could be worth eventually, if our project gets more lucrative."

"You mean, like, assign them a monetary value? For the future?" Lana asked. "How would we do that?"

"We figure out how much we *should* have made for the work that we did," Leon said. He stood up and stretched. "Hang on. I think I need to put on my superhero cape to figure this out."

As Leon went to his closet to fetch his cape, Jake called after him. "What do you mean, Leon? How are we supposed to figure out how much our contributions are worth if we're not basing it on the $1,000?"

Leon came back. "Well, look. We made a thousand bucks because we're just starting out. But—as Lana pointed out—leadership consultants typically make crazy money per hour. Or look at Alex—the videography and editing they're doing, not to mention the graphics... That all would cost a pretty penny."

"I can tell you exactly how many pretty pennies," Alex said. They stood up and walked over to the mini fridge. "Freelance videographers get paid somewhere between $75 and $150 per hour. Since I'm still building my experience, I would probably be on the lower end, but I'm also bringing my own equipment, which should boost my value because it would be expensive to rent." Alex rummaged through the fridge. "I'm helping myself to a snack, by the way."

"Feel free," Jake said.

"So," Alex continued, "if I were working for a typical business, I could claim an hourly rate of $100." Alex pulled out a string cheese and peeled off the wrapper. "That's about ten thousand pretty pennies per hour."

"Okay—and how many hours do you think you logged total, Alex?" Leon asked.

"I probably put in about twenty hours. Maybe more." Alex bit the top off the cheese. "So—that's $2,000 I gave our little group for free. You're welcome," they finished, mouth full.

"You don't pull down the strings?" Lana asked Alex. "Why eat a string cheese if you don't engage the stringiness?" Alex shrugged. Lana asked, "Can you get me one too?" Alex opened the fridge again and tossed her one.

"Try to focus, everyone," Leon said. "Alex contributed about $2,000 worth of value to our group."

"I'm focused now," Lana said, dexterously peeling off a strip of string cheese. "And I'm amazed, Alex—$2,000!" Lana said. "That's double what we actually made."

"That's right—that's why we should figure out what we *deserved* to make," Leon said.

"Why?" Jake asked, going to the fridge and getting himself a string cheese. "So we can feel grumpy about all the work we're doing and not getting compensated for?"

"No," Leon said. "So that we *can* compensate ourselves in the future, if we make good. So here's what I propose. We should all figure out approximately how much each of us contributed in value through our work. It's hypothetical. But we should still be realistic. Then I'm going to figure out how we can connect that value to our Collaborative Point totals."

Each group member began working out what each of their contributions would be worth, often turning to Google for help. They considered their equipment costs, the going rate for their various skills, and the range of contract payments for a project like theirs. Finally, they came up with the following designations.

DETERMINING JALL'S ECONOMIC VALUE

- Teaching and content production from Jake: worth around $1,400
- Videography and editing from Alex: worth around $2,000
- Leadership consulting and administration from Lana: worth around $2,100
- Gaming and overall IT skills from Leon: worth around $3,500
- The group also made $1,000 in revenue, which is added to their total.
- Total economic value of the project = $10,000
- 100% of the Collaborative Points are therefore worth $10,000.

How to Determine Economic Value

This discussion occurs to assess a fair, realistic economic value for the group's activity. For groups like Jake's, who are just starting out, the discussion would be hypothetical but still realistic; for instance, Alex's videography is worth $100 an hour, even though the group can't afford to pay that amount yet. The group logs the contribution, with the intention of distributing value to Alex eventually, once the collaboration makes more money. (We'll discuss more how this would work in Chapter 9, when we discuss Value Cards.)

A few brief notes to help clarify how group members can determine their economic value, as a basis for determining their Future Value:

- Even though our narrative characters helped determine their Future Value via each person's contribution, it's important to note that the economic value of a collaboration is calculated as a sum total. We'll explain why in our next section of narration.
- The discussion about points and economic value should not be aligned at all. Points represent effort; economic value relates to money—and remember, we want to keep those two things separate

initially. Points relate to each group member's personal contribution. The economic value will apply to the monetary value generated by the group *as a whole*. Although each group member's skillful contributions will have helped produce that value, the economic value is not an individual calculation; it's a group calculation. In JALL's situation, the group as a whole created $10,000 of value.

- For Jake's group, the total economic value they produced was the sum of the different skill contributions plus the ad revenue from the videos. For different types of collaboratives, the economic value might represent additional categories—a truck rental cost, for instance, or the sale of a product.
- Economic value can be determined by assessing market data about what that skill, product, asset, and so on would cost if someone were to pay for it. Any revenues made by the collaborative group would be added to the total of those other assessed values.

Now let's get back to the collaborators in the dorm room.

JALL's Discussion of Future Value

"Okay, so basically—all the work we put into making these videos is worth about $10,000. That's what our contributions might be worth collectively if we weren't working for ourselves as entrepreneurs," Leon said. "Like—that's what someone else would have had to pay us to do this work for them."

"I would be very happy if I got paid $2,000 for the work I did," Alex said.

"We're rich! Hypothetically speaking, that is," Lana said with a grin.

"So—this $1,400 that I contributed—is that what I'm entitled to down the road, if we start making more money?" Jake asked. He crumpled up his cheese wrapper and tossed it into the bin. "And by the way, don't you think it's funny that teachers are *still* ridiculously underpaid, even when it's hypothetical?"

"Don't sell yourself short, Ramirez," Leon said. "That $1,400 isn't your someday maybe money. I was thinking we would figure out totals referencing our Collaborative Points, based on that $10,000."

"Really? Why?" Jake asked.

Leon shrugged. "Number one, because it will be simpler down the road once we're dealing with other forms of revenue that aren't directly related to our own contributions. Like—let's say in a year, an old video that none of us have touched in a year suddenly gets super popular and makes us $2,000. Who gets that $2,000?"

"Um..." Jake studied the latest columns in the Excel spreadsheet. "Well...Yeah, I don't know."

"Okay, now what if I said we're going to divvy up that $2,000 according to our Collaborative Point percentages? Now do you know how much everyone gets?"

"Oh—yeah," Jake said. "I get 21%."

"There you go. So if we attach our someday maybe money to our Collaborative Points, this is going to be way easier to scale. But also, teacher man, it's going to help us be more equitable. The people who put in the most effort get the most someday maybe money. You're not going to get shafted just because teachers don't make a ton of money in the real world. You'd be fairly compensated for your *effort*. So—here—let's figure out what everyone would have if we attached Collaborative Points to the someday maybe money."

"I'm sorry," Lana said. "Can we please choose a different name than someday maybe money? I don't know why I find that so annoying, but I do."

Leon walked over to the mini fridge. "What do you suggest, then?"

"How about 'unrealized potential'?" Lana suggested.

Jake grinned. "That's so Lana."

Leon stared into the mini fridge. "Did you schmucks eat the rest of the string cheese?" He looked at them all. Lana raised a feeble hand. Jake grinned at him guiltily.

Alex looked Leon in the eye. "Yes, my friend. We have consumed your cheese."

"Well, damn it." He looked at them all and then zeroed in on Lana. "I don't like unrealized potential," he said. "It's too flowery and abstract."

"That's why I like it," she said.

"How about 'Future Value'?" Jake suggested. "It allows for slightly more abstraction but still communicates the point."

"Bingo," Leon said. "Let's go with Future Value."

"I think I will continue to call it 'unrealized potential,' if you don't mind," Lana said. She looked at her column with pleasure. "I have so much unrealized potential. In fact, I want more unrealized potential. I want to figure out other things I can do for our little group project."

"Really? It's the *unrealized* potential that gets you motivated?" Jake asked incredulously.

"I resent your use of the word 'little,'" Leon said to Lana. "I have no intention of keeping this project little. We're going places, lady."

Lana turned to Jake with a smile and raised her eyebrows. "Which is exactly why I want more unrealized potential, thank you very much."

JALL's Future Value

	New Point Total (Post-trade)	Collaborative Point Percentage (CP%)	Future Value (CP% * $10,000)
Jake	8,047	21%	$2,100
Alex	9,000	23%	$2,300
Lana	7,000	18%	$1,800
Leon	14,953	38%	$3,800
Totals:	39,000	100%	$10,000

Where each point is worth $0.256

Determining Future Value

As illustrated, Future Value is determined by the economic value of the group's work, then divvied up between the group members via their percentages of effort determined by their Collaborative Points.

So, for example, the JALL Collaborative determined the economic value of their efforts was $10,000. Since Jake has 21% of the group's Collaborative Points, he has $2,100 in Future Value. That's different from the $1,400 in economic value that he estimated contributing with his teaching skills, but—given that the group determined collectively that Jake had done 21% of the work, he still gets 21% of the Future Value. Again, at this point, all the Future Value calculations are hypothetical. But maybe they won't *always* be hypothetical. If and when the money starts coming in, the group members will be ready to fairly distribute the value.

It's worth returning here to the "gamble" that Leon and Jake made when Jake traded some of his Collaborative Points for $50 in short-term cash. When Jake made that trade, his Collaborative Points dropped, and so did his percentage—from 26% to 21%. If Jake's Collaborative Points hadn't dropped as a result of that trade, he would have approximately $2,600 in his Future Value ledger—a difference of *$500* from what he has now. Leon had told Jake that the points might be worth much more than $50 in the future—*if* the group should experience future success. The Future Value column indicates just how much more those points would be worth. In this way, the collaborative finance system incentivizes long-term investment—strategies that could ultimately help someone like Jake get out of the cyclical poverty he's grown up in. We'll explore this more in future chapters.

Why else might a group go through the trouble of calculating their Future Value? We can think of several other key reasons.

First, considering the full economic value of a group's collective effort helps lead to more quality of life than measuring the worth through the actual revenue. Remember some of the eight domains of quality of life:

self-realization, productivity and activity, social inclusion, emotional well-being, and so on. If we say that *all* the effort and time that Jake's group members devoted to their endeavor is only worth $1,000, their contribution is demeaned. However, when the full economic value is calculated, group members are affirmed in many of these quality of life domains: their efforts and productivity are valued in the real world, increasing their sense of *self-realization*. Feeling validated for their effort strengthens their role in the group (*social inclusion*) and leads to more work satisfaction and overall enthusiasm among group members (*emotional well-being*).

Second, keeping track of the Future Value is a practical way to ensure group members are rewarded in the future for the effort they're putting in today. As Leon discussed, some companies assign founding members shares when the company is just starting out; the value of those shares increases as the company becomes more profitable, and eventually the shareholders can cash out. The collaborative finance environment does not have shares, but calculating the Future Value serves a similar purpose—it allows groups the possibility of assigning Future Value. However, whereas shareholders can ultimately use their shares to make power plays, the Future Value and point system do not allow for that. As discussed, points are recalculated regularly, and Future Value doesn't come with any voting rights.

Although Collaborative Points disappear and are recalculated on a regular basis, the ledger of Future Value does not disappear; the colleagues continue adding to it, month by month. If their collaboration fizzles out, those numbers will never be realized beyond nice figures in an Excel spreadsheet. However, if the entrepreneurial venture thrives and succeeds, those numbers will allow for equitable rewards for all contributors down the road.

For groups that are already well established, there's no need to calculate the economic and Future Value of their work because the cash would be regularly flowing in and effort could be sufficiently rewarded in the present. However, for a startup situation like the JALL Collaborative—where there's lots of effort up front without much cash flow to begin with—the Future

Value calculations help ensure that colleagues will be fairly rewarded for their effort eventually, if the collaboration starts making more money.

❧

Future Value should only be calculated when the amount of actual money earned is much different than the amount of time, effort, and money that is put in, as in a startup scenario. Future Value provides validation for creating something out of nothing and ensures that group members will be compensated later if the collaboration becomes more profitable.

HOW TO CONDUCT A CONTRIBUTION SESSION

To replicate the JALL group's process, these are the steps that a group of colleagues would take in administering their own draw. This process succeeds in hitting all the points that Jake and Leon identified needing to work through at the start of this chapter: how much effort colleagues put in; how much the different contributions are worth (both in terms of quality of life and economic value); how much money each person is entitled to and needs; how the group will invest in itself; and finally, how group members will distribute future funds.[76]

1. Figure out each colleague's **Collaborative Points**, relative to their other group members. Convert those points to a percentage value.
2. Discuss the group's **quality of life** contributions, both externally and internally, and assign QOL scores. Collaborators should allow this score to inform their own system of rewards related to quality of life.

---

[76] This material is also provided on our website for the reader's convenient reference; please see this chapter's QR code.

3. **Distribute funds** via the draw.

    a. Assess how much money is available to distribute; the JALL group had $1,000 total.

    b. Determine how much money should be taken out of the group's allotment of real cash to invest in the asset. (In the JALL group, this was the $400 they set aside to run day-to-day operations and invest in promoting their brand.) The money required for daily operations is put in a checking account, and the investment money will be set aside in a long-term investment account.[77] We'll explain more about this investment account in our next chapters.

    c. Determine how much money is left to be distributed to the colleagues. (In the JALL group, they had $600 left.)

    d. Determine what short-term cash each colleague is entitled to by multiplying their Collaborative Point percentages with the available cash (i.e., 25% of $600 is $150).

    e. Each colleague determines how much of their entitled cash they want to withdraw for their short-term needs and how much they want to keep in their own long-term investment account.[78] If one colleague does not have enough money for their short-term needs, they can trade Collaborative Points for extra cash. (You can assign a monetary value to points by dividing the total cash earned by the total points. For JALL, this would be $1,000 divided by 36,000 points.)

---

[77] In fact, the $400 will be distributed to each colleague's individual investment accounts, according to their Collaborative Point percentages. This money cannot be withdrawn as cash but can only be invested in long term asset vehicles. Each colleague has the freedom and autonomy to determine if their allotment of investment money should go toward their own collaborative endeavor or go toward another investment vehicle of their choosing. We will explore this further in our future chapters.

[78] Short term needs must always be balanced with the sustainability of the collaborative and a person's own long-term interests. This is especially important as money increases—just because the group makes $15,000 one month doesn't mean that each person *should* each take a huge sum for themselves. It's also important to remember that any money *withdrawn* via the draw is taxable. However, any money put into the long-term investment account can be used as collateral for loans or investments; since it's not withdrawn, it's not taxable. This enables people to build long term financial security, a point we'll explore more in the next chapter.

f. New totals should be calculated. Based on each colleague's remaining Collaborative Points, new percentages should be determined.

4. Determine **economic and Future Value**. If groups are in a startup situation, where their effort far outstrips their revenue, they should calculate their **economic value** by assessing the market value of their contributions and assets, and add that to their revenue. Then the group should use that total and distribute it among the colleagues, based on their Collaborative Points. So, in JALL's case, Jake was assigned 21% (his Collaborative Point total) of $10,000 (the economic value), resulting in $2,100. Those numbers will be recorded as **Future Value**.

COLLABORATIVE FINANCE:
TYPES OF ACCOUNTS[79]

- **Collaborative Checking Account**: This account is used for day-to-day operations. It should be small—only containing the minimum money required to cover the collaborative's operational needs. In our narrative, Leon needed to pay a marketing vendor $100 to promote their video; this $100 would be deposited in the Collaborative Checking Account.

- **Collaborative Points Account**: This point value represents each individual's effort and contribution and will be recalculated on a regular basis. It would be represented as both a point value and a percentage.

- **Quality of life score**: This number would be tracked and added to each month. These points do not disappear like the Collaborative Points do. Each collaborative group can discuss ways to practically reward one another for their quality of life score.

---

[79] This material is also provided on our website for the reader's convenient reference; please see this chapter's QR code.

- **Investment Account**: This is like a savings account, and each individual colleague has one.[80] This account is connected to real cash made by the asset endeavor, which has been distributed to the colleagues via their Collaborative Point percentages. All of the money that the colleagues decided *not* to withdraw for their short-term needs would be shown in their Investment Accounts.[81]
- **Future Value Account**: Relevant only for startups, this account holds hypothetical money that will be realized if the collaboration becomes more profitable in the future. Each colleague has their own Future Value Account, and their hypothetical cash totals would be determined by their Collaborative Point percentage totals, post-draw.

IS THIS REALISTIC?

Can we really believe that people would discuss money and relative effort in such a peaceable way? Won't people always push for more money for themselves? Shouldn't people be expected to fight over who has done the most work? Let's take a moment to consider briefly whether or not human beings are capable of these rational, cool-headed discussions.

First of all, let's remember the care we've taken to create an environment in which people feel safe, have a voice, and feel recognized and affirmed for

---

[80] One major difference between an Investment Account and a typical savings account is that the money deposited into an Investment Account cannot be withdrawn. It can only be used to invest. This incentivizes long term financial planning and allows people to use their invested money as collateral for loans; also, since the money is not withdrawn and therefore not considered income, money in an Investment Account is tax-free. We will discuss this further in Chapter 8.

[81] These Investment Accounts would also hold each colleague's distribution of the money which the group has elected to invest in the asset; in the JALL group, this would be the $300 they want to devote toward building their brand. In our next chapter, we will explain how the Collaborative Cloud environment enables this mechanism and explain the reasoning behind it.

their contribution. The Core Design Principles, which have been woven into the environment created thus far and established via the Collaborative Agreement, help to ensure frictionless collaboration. The CDPs correct the tragedy of the commons and ensure each person can operate from a place of rational stability, not fear. Within such an environment, these kinds of talks *are* realistic—and, in fact, they're happening.

There are real companies that have given their employees the freedom to identify their own contribution. The Brazilian company Semco is a well-known pioneer in this area.[82] Under the leadership of Ricardo Semler, the company decided to institute a radical form of institutional democracy and allow their employees to name their own salaries. Although many leaders and shareholders expressed skepticism and dismay at the prospect, the experiment was successful. Semler provided employees with a range of salary data for their respective positions and allowed employees to name what they believed they should be paid. The employees chose salaries that were consistent with market standards and their own experience. One employee even turned down a recommended pay raise because he claimed he was content with his current pay. Under Semler's leadership, the company experienced an annual growth of 40 percent per year, and he was named Brazilian Businessman of the Year and one of the Global Leaders of Tomorrow by the World Economic Forum.[83]

Semco's radical industrial democracy mainly corresponded to what they paid their employees. We think people are capable of taking these sorts of equitable discussions further, considering a wide range of forms of contribution, such as a quality of life score, in addition to a range of rewards like numbers of days off, and so on.

However, it stands to reason that some sort of apparatus would be needed to keep track of all these numbers and accounts. And surely modern

---

[82] "What Happens When Employees Choose Their Own Salaries," Semco Style Institute, accessed May 24, 2021, https://semcostyle.com/what-happens-when-employees-choose-their-own-salaries.

[83] "Ricardo Semler," accessed September 27, 2021, https://ricardosemler.com.

technology can come up with a method of tracking them all beyond the JALL group's clumsy Excel spreadsheet records and phone calculators.

So that's where our Person to Person environment is heading next.

NEW NEEDS

After Lana and Alex had left to go home to their own dorms, Leon and Jake looked at the spreadsheet totals they had created, talking back and forth, making sure the numbers were correct.

"Dude. I think what we just did was pretty rad," Jake said. "How cool would it be if every business turned into a collaborative like ours? People wouldn't just be employees waiting around for their paycheck. They'd actually be rewarding themselves for how much effort they were putting in! If that's how everyone showed up to work, can you imagine how much more engaged people would be? It would pretty much change the world."

"I know, right?!" Leon said. "I might pass on these ideas to my dad." He gave a short laugh. "But knowing Dad, he'd hate it. Guys like Dad don't get rich using systems like this. Still, he might find it interesting." He looked back at the computer and absentmindedly tapped the keys. "I don't think this could scale, though. You'd need an app. Or some sort of an online banking system that wasn't an actual bank. Something that just kept all the information organized and allowed people to have access to their money, but without any institutional arm controlling the money."

Jake looked at his roommate and gave him a friendly slap on the back. "There's your next project, my friend." He stood up and stretched. "And *my* next project is to figure out how I can do more for the group next month. Maybe I should see if Alex can teach me how to do some of the editing. Or I can start generating new video ideas."

Leon looked over at him. "Why do you want to do more? You're doing good already."

"Gotta impress my new girlfriend with more unrealized potential," Jake said and flexed.

CHAPTER SEVEN

THE REINVENTION OF PRIVATE PROPERTY

The first man who, having enclosed a piece of ground,
bethought himself of saying "This is mine," and found people simple
enough to believe him, was the real founder of civil society.
From how many crimes, wars and murders, from how many horrors
and misfortunes might not any one have saved mankind,
by pulling up the stakes, or filling up the ditch, and crying to
his fellows, "Beware of listening to this impostor; you are undone
if you once forget that the fruits of the earth belong
to us all, and the earth itself to nobody."

—Jean-Jacques Rousseau, *Discourse on the Origin*
and Basis of Inequality among Men

Leon's phone buzzed with a text from Alex. It read simply, *We need to talk.*

"Oh shit," Leon said to Jake in their dorm. "Have I said anything to Alex to offend them that you can think of?" Jake looked thoughtfully at

Leon and shrugged. The phone buzzed again. *Meet me in the art building, room C105.*

Leon texted back, *Now?*

His phone buzzed again: a thumbs up. He sighed nervously and grabbed his jacket. "Guess I'm meeting Alex. Wish me luck, amigo."

Jake called after him. "I'm sure it will be fine!"

When Leon arrived at room C105, he peered through the window that ran alongside the door. Alex stood in front of a massive floor-to-ceiling whiteboard. They were resting their chin on a dry-erase pen and staring at the floor thoughtfully. On the board behind Alex, they had drawn a house.

Tentatively, Leon poked his head inside. "Hey Alex . . . Everything okay?"

Alex looked up sharply. "Good! You're here. I'm stuck, and I need you to help me get unstuck."

"You need my help?" Leon asked. "I thought you were pissed at me."

Alex didn't even acknowledge this remark. "You know how we separated money from effort when we did the draw?" Leon nodded. "That was pretty cool," Alex said.

Leon wanted to sit down, but there was nowhere to sit. "Yeah, I thought so too. I'm trying to find a way to make the whole process smoother and easier but haven't found anything yet, so—"

Alex held up a hand and he stopped. "Pause, please. Is there a way . . ." Alex hesitated. "Is there a way to separate other things? Like, for instance . . . a way to make private property public but still let people retain the value of private property? Maybe . . . separate value and usage rights, somehow?"

Leon furrowed his brow. "What do you mean?"

Alex sighed heavily and sank down to the floor in a cross-legged position. Leon took this as a cue and followed suit. "Look," Alex spoke. "My older sister, Elisa, lives in San Jose. It's one of the most expensive cities in America. She's trying to buy a house with her husband, and they both make good money, but they still can't afford anything. All these private companies are buying up the properties for cash and using them to secure their pension funds.[84] And I feel like that's happening everywhere. There are so many people getting priced out of the housing market."

Leon nodded, concerned. "I know. My family has a vacation home in Malibu, but it just sits empty most of the year. Dad doesn't even want to Airbnb it. And I know a ton of wealthy families like that—they just sit on these properties and don't do anything with them, but they're gaining value by just sitting there empty, so people hang on to them. And the corporations you mentioned are making the problem worse."

"That's exactly right!" Alex said, stabbing the whiteboard pen in his direction. "I remember going to Malibu once on a road trip with my high school friends. We were trying to find a beach to sit on for a while, but everywhere we went was marked 'Private. Private. Private.' I didn't see a single person using those beaches. And there were tons of fences. Soooo many fences. I was like, 'Um—who gave you ownership over the frickin' shore?!' That seemed like total bullshit to me."

"So, what is your suggestion?" Leon asked. "You want to make private property public?"

"Not exactly," Alex said. "I'm not totally sure how to go about this." They paused, then sprang up, turned around, and began drawing furiously on the whiteboard, speaking as they drew. "It feels like all the kids in the preschool have each grabbed a toy for themselves, and everyone is just sitting in their own little corner, saying 'Mine, mine, mine.'" Alex began drawing chubby, angry toddlers clutching teddy bears and brandishing lollipops. "And that's stupid because (a) no one's having fun, (b) some kids have four or five or six toys, while other kids have none, and (c) the toys shouldn't even belong

---

[84] Adam Schrader, "US House Prices Are Being Pushed up by Pension Funds That Are Outbidding Middle Class Families," *Daily Mail Online*, June 12, 2021, https://www.dailymail.co.uk/news/article-9678943/US-house-prices-pushed-pension-funds-outbidding-middle-class-families.html; Ryan Dezember, "If You Sell a House These Days, the Buyer Might Be a Pension Fund," *The Wall Street Journal*, April 4, 2021, https://www.wsj.com/articles/if-you-sell-a-house-these-days-the-buyer-might-be-a-pension-fund-11617544801.

to the kids anyway; they should belong to the preschool. And the preschool teachers should encourage the kids to effing *share*."

Alex spun around to look at Leon, still sitting crisscross applesauce. He nodded, trying to look serious. "Everyone would have more fun if they started sharing," he observed. "Sharing is caring."

"That's right!" Alex said. "So this is what I mean. Look—the toddlers in the preschool should *all* get to play with the toys. The preschool teachers should say, 'These toys belong to the school, and we can all take turns.' And then all the kids get to use them and swap them around. So—is there a way to do that for adults, with private property? That way, people like my sister could find a toy to play with. Or rather, a house to live in."

"You mean you want all the grown-ups to share their lollipops and teddy bears and swanky beachfront mansions?" Leon asked.

Alex guffawed. "Yes! I'm not talking communism, though—like, I don't think the state should confiscate the properties or anything. This is something that people should get to choose for themselves."

"Good luck getting toddlers or Wall Street pension fund managers to willingly share their toys," Leon said.

"Well, but what if people could still keep the *value* of their private property? They share the usage...but keep the value. Is there a way to do that?"

Leon stared hard at Alex. "I don't know...But maybe we can come up with some ideas." He stood thoughtfully and walked to the whiteboard. Then he looked at Alex. "Why did you just ask me to come? Why not Jake and Lana too?"

Alex sighed. "I didn't want to scare the little lambs. I figured you were the only one that could roll with my anarchy and start to figure out how to implement it."

"Huh," Leon said. He looked back at the whiteboard. Then, inspired, he took a marker and began drawing a grid over the house, dissecting it into roughly one hundred small squares. "I might have an idea."

The Painful History of Private Property

Alex's concerns for their sister are not unique, nor is the housing crisis a new crisis. In the 1880s, the famous economist and reformer Henry George erected a giant billboard in the middle of a vacant lot in New York City. The billboard read:

> EVERYBODY WORKS BUT THE VACANT LOT. I paid $3,600 for this lot and will hold 'till I get $6,000. The profit is unearned increment made possible by the presence of this community and enterprise of its people. I take the profit without earning it.[85]

George's billboard was both a protest and a political campaign stunt: its message pointed out the irrational injustice of a vacant lot earning money simply by being privately owned—being effectively wasted by the rich, at the expense of people who could use and benefit from it. Leon and Alex made similar complaints when they considered the empty fenced beaches and unused mansions. As the world's wealthy have gotten richer, their abundance of privately held assets have gobbled up a disproportionate percentage of the world's goods. That means less for everyone else, at much steeper prices.

Now the housing crisis has been made worse by private corporations buying up family homes.[86] Anonymous shell companies, Wall Street hedge funds, and other corporations looking to secure their employees' pensions are all competing with individual buyers—who, of course, pose no real competition at all. Although Henry George's billboard was posted ironically,

---

[85] Science, Industry and Business Library: General Collection, The New York Public Library, "'Everybody works but the vacant lot', Henry George," New York Public Library Digital Collections, accessed October 24, 2021, https://digitalcollections.nypl.org/items/510d47de-036a-a3d9-e040-e00a18064a99.

[86] Hannah Ziady, "Wall Street Is Buying up Family Homes. The Rent Checks Are Too Juicy to Ignore," *The Mercury News*, August 2, 2021, https://www.mercurynews.com/2021/08/02/wall-street-is-buying-up-family-homes-the-rent-checks-are-too-juicy-to-ignore.

these corporations are using the same inequitable strategy it boasted about, at the expense of the middle class.

But it's not just the housing market that is straining under the pressure of privately held property—although that strain is felt all over the world. The challenges created by private property have opened a Pandora's box and have led to inequality, wars, exhaustion of resources, violence, power plays, and all sorts of other devils.

We have managed these problems for centuries, with the wealthy and powerful pulling us forward through history, dragging the have-nots along behind. However, at this point in time, we find that these clumsy management strategies are no longer working. The world is too small for us to all have our fences. There are simply too many of us. We are rapidly exhausting the world's resources, yet because of varied political interests and countries' power-mongering, environmental sustainability takes a distant back seat to economic concerns and power plays.

Nonetheless, private property has also driven much of the world's innovation and evolution. So how can we keep the good while eliminating some of the bad aspects of private property? How can we keep the baby but throw out the bathwater?

To answer this question, it's worth taking a look at what history looked like before private property was invented. And to do that, we have to go back—*way* back. Specifically, we have to look at life before the agricultural revolution began, around 10,000 BCE, when people began opting for a farming lifestyle instead of hunting and gathering, and began building fences around their fields.

So imagine you're wandering the earth with just a few tools hewn out of stone. Your possessions are what you can carry—typically what is necessary to catch and keep food. Life is lived hand to mouth, moving with the seasons in the company of a small group of close companions. Consumption is based on need, not greed. Because humans do not consume more than they need, the earth and animal populations maintain relative equilibrium with humans. Resources that exist are available to anyone who cares to access them: there is no problem showing someone the way to a clean water well or tipping off your neighbor to a herd of bison.

In this era, people rely on their fellow tribesmen to survive: more than one spear is required to take down a buffalo, and there is safety in numbers. Generally, people are collaborating instead of competing. In his book *The Sovereign Individual: Mastering the Transition to the Information Age*, investment writer James Dale Davidson points to the hunter-gatherer epoch in history, suggesting that this was the last time humans were truly free individuals.[87] The plus side: collaboration, freedom, and environmental sustainability. However, people's survival was also constantly at risk—a serious drawback.

The agricultural revolution changed things. People started to settle down, producing and storing food from their own cultivated gardens and fields. No longer were they wandering the earth, trying to avoid starvation or death from exposure. This produced an enormous burst in innovation: people had time to think about creating new methods, tools, and inventions because they had the stability to do so.

During this time of the agricultural revolution, humans also began producing more than they could consume, resulting in an economic surplus. This led to the invention of "saving." Humans began to actually accumulate wealth—and society began to stratify itself into various levels of "haves" and "have-nots."

Now imagine you're a hunter-gatherer who is late to the farming party. You happen across a small gathering of huts and farms. You're starving, a "have-not"—the bison have eluded you. And there, in this stranger's garden, are all sorts of tasty bites that you don't even need to run after and catch. So why not? You help yourself.

Obviously, this would not have sat well with the settlers who had put in effort all year long to grow their food—even if they did have more than

---

[87] James Dale Davidson and William Rees-Mogg, *The Sovereign Individual: Mastering the Transition to the Information Age* (New York: Simon & Schuster, 1999).

enough. These inequities led to plundering and stealing, which in turn led to owners inventing ways to protect their goods—that is, their assets and private property.

This led to fences and private security forces—soldiers, mercenaries, guards, armies, strongmen—all engaged in the business of force to protect this newfangled notion of private property. The business of force was a game where the winner took all. The dominant forces wiped out their competitors and eventually became kingdoms.

The private security forces morphed into public security forces, called governments. Government systems emerged in order to secure the protection of goods and maintain production. This, naturally, made investments in weaponry lucrative and helped spur on wars and rivalries between tribes, groups, and nations. The collaborative spirit that previously defined humanity was exchanged for one in which it was *us* versus *them*. Humans became defined not by our common shared experience, but by who our enemies were. We have been exploring and refining this model for roughly the past twelve thousand years, and in many ways, this polarizing spirit still defines us today.

So, How Do We Get Out of This?

Over the last century, we've seen various initiatives to try to "fix" the system, such as co-ops, nonprofits, and so on. However, these well-meaning organization efforts are still ultimately guided by the same rulebook of hierarchical institutions: they operate with shares and shareholders, they use company accounts, they function with boards, and they lend themselves to politics and power plays. Larger-scale efforts to rewrite a country's economic approach have usually been initiated by the powers that we ourselves have put in place—and there was no incentive for those powers to completely divest their authority. Not surprisingly, none of the initiatives put forward by various leaders or governmental powers has made any real dent in the inequality, unsustainability, and territorial violence created by the private-property problem. As the saying goes, "We cannot solve our problems with the same thinking that created them."[88] You could also argue that there has not been sufficient technology to enable security, financial stability, and freedom to coexist—until now.

So our question becomes: is it possible to get rid of the fences and all the problems posed by private property, yet still enable people to engage with their finances in a way that allows for personal freedom, a collaborative spirit, environmental sustainability, and financial stability? And if so, what *would* be some of the defining aspects of a Person to Person financial environment?

A Person to Person Financial Environment

Here are some ideas:

- **People need a way to hold on to the value of their assets.** No one wants the insecurity of the hunter-gatherer days. Given that one of the quality of life domains is economic and material well-being, this aspect of private property is one we want to hang on to. People should have a way to save their resources and invest them to generate new capital.
- **Innovation should remain a priority.** Probably the greatest gift private property has given us is that it has massively spurred innovation and evolution. Any successful new financial environment must reward entrepreneurism and innovation.
- **Assets should be shared.** Like the toys in the preschool classroom are meant to be shared, a truly equitable financial environment should take the "private" away from "property." When assets become shared, there is a greater incentive to steward them for the greater good, not selfishly. This not only allows for greater equality, but it

---

[88] This quote is usually attributed to Albert Einstein.

allows for more peace and fewer wars. It also means we are more incentivized to consider how an asset should be used in the context of our greatest asset—the earth. There is a finite amount of resources on Earth; hoarding by some will always happen at the expense of others, thereby hindering frictionless collaboration in a Person to Person world. Finally, if assets are shared, we are not burdened by them and can therefore move around the world with greater flexibility. Again, consider the preschoolers in the classroom. If they trust that the toys will still be there in the classroom tomorrow, they can leave for the day with nothing on their backs. If they try to keep all the toys to themselves, however, they must carry the burden of those toys to and from school every day. In today's world of remote workers and global connections, it is an advantage to have greater freedom of movement than today's private property practices allow. Therefore, we must seek to enable the *shared use* of assets while still allowing people to hold on to the *value* of their assets.

- **Assets should *not* be taken coercively.** No form of force has a place in a Person to Person environment. If private property is to become shared, that must be a decision that property owners make of their own accord because they recognize the benefits made possible by doing so.

- **The competitive open and free market should play a role.** The market is the fairest and most equitable way to exchange goods; we can let that play out more than we do now. Whereas fiat currencies' values are determined by political machinations that have everything to do with power yet very little to do with quality of life, the market's values are determined by real-world influences that directly impact the people engaging with the market. Although it's true that the free market is not invulnerable to manipulation, technology like blockchain can at least ensure that all transactions are transparent, making manipulation visible to those who care to look for it.

- **The world needs a seat at the table.** As we speed toward the cliff of a global climate catastrophe, we need to give the planet a louder voice at the negotiating table. Until now, financial progress has often been viewed as a competitor with environmental sustainability—and financial progress almost always wins. As a result, we are on a climate precipice graver than ever before in human history. Somehow, environmental sustainability must be incentivized as *part* of our financial environment.

- **We need incentives for fair play.** We know ourselves too well to deny the instinctive sharp edges in humans that drive us to take advantage of others; we've seen these instincts drive us for most of human history. As the saying goes, "Absolute power corrupts absolutely." Therefore, a Person to Person financial environment must incentivize fair play and be resilient against corruption. We know that humans act out of self-interest—so let's make a financial environment in which it is in a person's best interest to collaborate and play fair. It is no good to tell an organization to behave like a good citizen if there are no meaningful incentives to motivate good citizenship. Rather than appealing to people as Google's unofficial motto, "Don't be evil," did, we should seek an environment in which people *"can't* be evil." This can only be achieved by removing any possibility of a power play. When there is no power to be seized, there is no reason to fight. What remains are incentives to collaborate.

- **Let's not smash anything.** A Person to Person financial environment should exist as an option alongside the present system and be one that people choose to join voluntarily. Ideally, it will grow until everyone has joined and there is nothing left in the old system; however, any evolution takes considerable time.

- **There needs to be legal and technical support for this kind of environment.** Daydreams are all well and good, but if a new financial environment is to exist, it needs to be legal, sustainable, secure, and user-friendly.

So how do we bring this about? Alex and Leon have the same question.

REDEFINING PRIVATE PROPERTY

Alex and Leon studied the grid Leon had drawn on top of Alex's house.

"I think the fundamental question we should start with," he told Alex, "is: what is private property? Like, what are its basic elements?"

Alex stared back at him. They lifted up a finger. "One: you have the right to use it. It belongs to you legally. You've got to take care of it, and you get to decide what to do with it."

"Yup," Leon said. "And you have the right to its value. That's what you were talking about earlier. So...how do we split those two things up? Do they *have* to go together, or could we make those two things distinct?"

"Are they split up with renters and landlords?" Alex asked. They mused, "On the one hand, renters get to use a property," Alex pointed out. "And the owners still get the value."

"Yeah, but that's not what we're talking about," Leon said. "Renters are not incentivized to take care of it, and they don't get to decide what to do with it. They live in a property, sure, but they're throwing their money away."

They both turned back to the board and studied it. Alex pointed to the grid. "What is this business here?"

Leon shrugged and scratched his head. "I don't know...I was thinking, like...ownership shares? Like, maybe...someone could own 80% of the house but sell the extra 20% to other people?"

"You're talking about micro-investing," Alex said. "That's the new cool thing for investors to do, apparently.[89] A startup company buys the house

---

[89] Sarah Paynter, "Startups Bring Micro Investing to Real Estate." *Yahoo! Finance*, February 18, 2020, https://www.yahoo.com/now/startups-bring-micro-investing-to-real-estate-212726244.html.

and then sells it in pieces to a lot of micro-investors. But then you're still dealing with renters and landlords—albeit a lot of landlords. The renters throw their money away while the investors get to pocket it. That's fine for the landlords, I guess, but it doesn't help my sister own her own home. And what happens to the property when the investors are all paid off and the debt is gone? The company owns it, and the rich get richer. You still end up with the haves and the have-nots." Alex walked over to the whiteboard drawing of the angry toddlers and tapped them with the plastic pen. "That's still some preschoolers holding on to toys and not sharing them."

Leon walked over to the angry toddlers and studied them. "The reason the toddlers can share is because none of the toys belong to them. They belong to the preschool." He looked at Alex, quizzically. "Is there a way to put all the assets into a giant preschool? Like—a giant entity that owns them all but lets the kids have all the benefits of the toys?"

Alex's eyes grew big. "Now you're talking. Go down that road further."

The Universal Ownership Vault

The world has tried this strategy before: putting all the toys in a single preschool (metaphorically speaking). The experiment was called Fort Knox, and it didn't work out very well. But the story of Fort Knox can still help instruct us as we go down this road.

After the World War I, several battered European nations were forced to sell much of their gold to rebuild. The US—looking to stabilize its economy after the stock market crash of 1929—was a good buyer, paying $35 per gold ounce. *History of the London Good Delivery List 1750–2010* notes:

> "A flow gold commenced...which quickly reached flood proportions," Samuel Montagu's Annual Bullion letter commented. "Never before has such a huge movement of gold taken place in so short a time...Accommodation

of all mail steamers was booked well ahead and many other vessels than the regular liners were pressed into service as bullion carriers."[90]

Fort Knox was quickly built in Kentucky to accommodate the United States' new treasury. Then, during World War II, there seemed to be a very real threat that Hitler might pillage all the European countries of their remaining gold. Since the US had most of Europe's gold anyway, the Allied countries decided that the safest place to keep their treasuries of gold was in the United States. They shipped more of their gold to the US and put it under lock and key in the heavily guarded Fort Knox. In the agreement of Bretton Woods in 1944, the allied world leaders—gathered in Bretton Woods, New Hampshire—agreed to attach the dollar to the gold standard and thereby *replace* the gold standard with the US dollar as the global standard of exchange.[91] Financial analyst and author "Adam Smith" notes of this Bretton Woods Agreement:

> The dollar met all the criteria of a key currency. The United States honored its obligations. It had military and political power. Its institutions were stable. It had every opportunity for economic growth and price stability.[92]

Tying the dollar to the gold standard helped secure the US as the world's new dominant superpower, guaranteeing the rest of the world's currency and making itself the only country on Earth with the ability to simply print dollars.

Initially, this seemed like a good plan. Under the leadership of Roosevelt, Truman, Eisenhower, and Kennedy, the world's storage of gold, and therefore the US dollar, seemed secure: one ounce of gold was still reliably equal to

---

[90] Koos Jansen, "Where Did the Gold in Fort Knox Come from? Part One," *BullionStar*, March 3, 2015, https://www.bullionstar.com/blogs/koos-jansen/gold-fort-knox-come-part-one.

[91] Kimberly Amadeo, "How a 1944 Agreement Created a New World Order," The Balance, updated September 3, 2020, https://www.thebalance.com/bretton-woods-system-and-1944-agreement-3306133.

[92] Adam Smith [pseud.], *Paper Money*, (Summit Books, 1981), excerpted in "Commanding Heights: When Currencies Began to Float," Public Broadcasting Service, accessed November 6, 2021, https://www.pbs.org/wgbh/commandingheights/shared/minitext/ess_currenciesfloat.html?utm_source=pocket_mylist.

$35, as spelled out in the Bretton Woods Agreement. However, the United States' entrance into the Vietnam War under Johnson and Nixon made the US a much shakier steward. As the rest of the world nervously looked on, America seemed to be burning a hole in its pocket, spending its money on infrastructure and wars. There was no way to know if the number of dollars being printed and circulated by the US was still consistent with the bars safely stored. How could the other countries know that Nixon wasn't simply spending their gold on war?

This uncertainty was too much. Finally, French President Charles de Gaulle took action, sending a warship to the US. He sent a message to Nixon that he was coming to collect France's gold and demanded that containers be prepared to ship it back to Europe. The UK followed suit. In 1971, Nixon responded to their demands by announcing that the world would no longer operate according to the gold standard. (In fact, the US had printed far more dollars than it had gold to guarantee them. "Adam Smith" writes, "Everyone could see that if the Euro holders all cashed in their dollars, Fort Knox would be bare in a day."[93]) America had effectively broken the peg that they had promised would hold up the rest of the world's currencies.

The result was global instability and a massive fall in the dollar's worth, leading to soaring inflation. However, Nixon scrambled—proving himself worthy of the nickname "Tricky Dick." Nixon went to the Saudis in 1974 and arranged to tie the worth of the dollar to the price of oil, thereby creating the petrodollar.[94] From that point onward, any country that wished to buy oil had to purchase it in dollars. As a result, the US once again reestablished the dollar as essential to the world market, secured its value to the price of oil through the control of the monopoly on oil exchange, and reasserted itself as the dominant global superpower. This allowed the dollar to remain the world's reserve currency while granting the US the continued exclusive

---

[93] Smith, *Paper Money*.

[94] Zaw Thiha Tun, "How Petrodollars Affect the U.S. Dollar," Investopedia, September 13, 2021, https://www.investopedia.com/articles/forex/072915/how-petrodollars-affect-us-dollar.asp.

ability to print it. This decision transformed the world's currency and has played a massive role in influencing political decisions ever since.

We should take a number of lessons from the Fort Knox/Bretton Woods debacle, especially if we are to repeat any semblance of the experiment.

First of all, let's take note of the problems with Fort Knox.

1. **Fort Knox was not transparent; it was completely closed.** No other governments had the ability to verify that the number of dollars in circulation was still in accordance with the amount of gold stored. They had to trust the US government to be truthful about the world's storage of gold, but it wasn't, and there was no system of accountability to check up on it.

2. **The lack of accountability led to corruption.** We cited the phrase "Absolute power corrupts absolutely" earlier, and that was certainly the case. People are people, and vices like fear, greed, and power hunger are all real factors that impact behavior. The kid who holds the cookie jar, to some extent, should be expected to help himself. In the case of Fort Knox, too much power was given to too few people—namely US leadership. There was no public debate over how the US intended to fund the printing of billions of dollars (and now trillions of dollars); all of those decisions happened behind closed doors.

Going back to Alex's preschool illustration, we can imagine that the teachers of Smallville Preschool have amassed the world's storage of toys and made the spiteful decision to keep them all to themselves. In that case, the world's preschoolers would not have a better time of it. Sure, the Smallville preschoolers might have plenty of toys when they show up at the school, but they're unwittingly helping to deprive the rest of the world's toddlers of those toys. No solution to the problem of private property can have a human being at the helm. It is simply too much to ask any group of humans to wield absolute power with perfect benevolence.

But what if a world vault could be made transparent? For instance, perhaps if there had been webcams in Fort Knox and the "dollar-printing room," President Charles de Gaulle could have seen that Nixon was printing far more dollars than there was gold and would have said, "Hey! Stop that!" before Nixon blew up the gold standard. What if there were systems of accountability in place that would impede corruption? What if trust in the ethics of humans wasn't a requirement because technology was in place to guarantee the veracity and implementation of an agreement?

Let's entertain this with the idea of creating a Universal Ownership Vault. We can imagine that this vault is able to hold the world's assets in storage. This vault is fully transparent and fully secure: no one is able to enter this vault and remove the gold. In fact, this vault holds not only gold, but also the deeds to houses, cars, boats, and property; it holds patents, brands, and so on. People own the *value* of the assets held in the vault, but not the assets themselves; therefore, there is shared stewardship of the assets' usage. And rather than one country or one group guarding it, the vault is secured by people the world over, through the use of blockchain-enabled technology.

Could that enable us to share more effectively and promote greater equality? Could that allow for the kind of freedom we enjoyed in the hunter-gatherer epoch, while still giving us the ability to maintain personal financial security and build wealth? Could this give the world a seat at the negotiation table and help us avoid human corruption? Could it serve a Person to Person environment and help promote a Quality of Life World?

Well, yes. It could.

IS SUCH AN EVOLUTION NECESSARY?

Before we take Alex and Leon's thought experiment any further, it's worth calling out the elephant in the room: this seems like a proposal to reinvent the global economy. How did we get from Jake's library journaling about his purpose, to a group of four students discussing healthy collaboration, to *this*—coming up with some sort of Universal Ownership Vault that would permanently alter the notion of private property as we know it?

Let's address this question practically, theoretically, personally, and pragmatically.

First, a practical note: as noted before, the Person to Person recommendations are optional. The recommendations proposed do not require a sweeping alteration of all world economies. This is an environment that is set up *alongside* what already exists, building off of current legal structures and requirements, using cutting-edge technology. It is there for whoever wants it—with a little legwork, as the following chapters will describe.

Now let's address the theoretical aspect: is it actually necessary to reinvent private property in order to achieve a Quality of Life World? Do we have to wade into such technical, economic, and legal complexities, beyond the warm and fuzzy atmosphere that the JALL college students have created in their collaboration? The answer is yes. You can be beautifully arranged in a collaboration, but if you don't take away the boss aspect or remove hierarchies, you don't solve for equality. Additionally, personal finance and economics affect every aspect of the life domains we discussed in our earlier chapters:

- Finances impact where we can afford to live, which affects our physical well-being, our natural living environment, and our economic and material well-being.
- Finances also largely impact the opportunities available to people to learn and grow, such as the ability to attend an institution for higher learning, pursue training, or travel.
- The world's political and economic machinations impact the stability or instability of a country, the taxes required of its people, and the worth of its currency, which all have a direct impact on the opportunities available to a country's citizens.
- Private property creates wealth and poverty, and therefore inequality.

- Wars are fought and violence is perpetuated because of fights over private property.
- Economic concerns have largely competed with the efforts to curb climate change. If natural disasters continue to increase in frequency and severity because of a delay in addressing climate change, a huge percentage of the world's people will be confronted with a life-altering crisis.

It would be easy to go on. Simply put: we can't pursue a Quality of Life World without addressing private property and its fundamental impact on so many of the power structures in our world and their related hierarchies. If we're serious about creating a world that prioritizes quality of life, we have to strongly consider the financial arena, particularly this area of private property.

Now let's think personally: who would possibly go for this? What kind of person would actually be willing to risk giving up their private property for the greater good? First of all, as the following chapters will explain, this kind of reinvention of private property would be accomplished securely and legally, and would offer many advantages. There are extensive mechanisms in place to lower risk and amplify the benefits. Still, it's worth acknowledging that this "alternative" economic option is not for everyone.

Who is it *not* for? This Person to Person financial environment would not interest anyone who is solely interested in personal enrichment. For all the people out there who are mainly interested in acquiring private property for themselves and don't especially care about the global impact of their decisions—you just keep doing your thing.

Who *is* it for? This financial environment is for people who have resonated with the Person to Person message up to this point. It's for people who care about creating a positive legacy that still allows for financial security and investment opportunities—like MacKenzie Scott or Charles "Chuck" Feeney, who choose to use their wealth to craft a legacy of helping others climb out of poverty. It's for people who want to move the world toward environmental sustainability sooner rather than later—and for people who believe collective benefit *can* be a by-product of everyone's self-interest. In short, this financial environment is for people who want to invest in a better world, exchanging private ownership for greater good and serving themselves in the process.

This financial environment allows people all the same benefits of private property—namely the usage rights and the value of their assets—but puts the *ownership* of assets in a Universal Ownership Vault, meaning that private property becomes held in a public trust, owned by everyone and therefore no one. The collected body of assets can then be tied to a form of currency, just like the dollar was tied to gold to guarantee its worth in the Fort Knox days. However, unlike Fort Knox, this vault would be made transparent, stewarded, and governed by all its users, through technology. (More on that soon.)

We're getting into the pragmatic element, so let's address this fourth consideration. What would need to happen to bring about an optional, effective, secure financial environment that would allow for person to person connections and ensure that people could hold on to the value of their assets, but would allow the assets themselves to be held in some sort of Universal Ownership Vault?

- There would need to be a **legal structure** to build this financial environment on top of preexisting legal requirements surrounding private property. No one wants to break any laws. This legal structure can be created (and has already been) through a foundation for the public good and through stewardship companies. We'll explain this in the second half of the chapter.
- There would need to be a **technical structure** that would allow for a fully transparent vault, easy communication between users, efficient financial transactions, and heightened security to protect the assets. This can be accomplished through technical tools like blockchain and smart contracts, and taking the form of a

decentralized autonomous organization (DAO); these are tools that will be described in a concise and simple way in our next chapter.

- Then there's the practical question of how assets would be used once they were in the vault. And how would they get into the vault in the first place? And who would manage them and steward them? And how would those assets inform the financial transactions needed to live life and prosper? These questions are addressed through the concept of **Sovereign Assets**, introduced in this chapter and explained in much further detail in Chapter 9.

Alex and Leon are going to stumble their way into these needs as they continue to brainstorm their epic ideas in the art room.

The Need for a Foundation

"Okay…" Alex said. "So, we want to try to come up with some sort of majestic, massive, epic preschool that holds all the world's toys and lets all the world's children play with them. Like a vault. A huge toy vault."

"Yeah, but Alex, who is going to voluntarily put their toys in the vault? My dad isn't going to donate his Malibu mansion to charity anytime soon," Leon scoffed.

Alex looked probingly at Leon. "What is this business?" Alex asked, swirling a hand in Leon's direction. "With your dad? What's the deal there?"

"What?" Leon asked defensively.

Alex turned to the whiteboard and began to draw a young man facing an older man with a tie and suit jacket. In between them, Alex drew a heart, then colored it black. Alex turned back to Leon, raising an eyebrow.

Leon's face clouded. "I mean, don't most adolescents have bad relationships with their parents?" he said sarcastically. Alex folded their arms, looked at Leon, and waited. He sighed. "I've just…I mean, basically, I don't feel like I matter to him." His face flushed and he coughed. "Wow, I can't believe I just said that out loud."

Alex sat down on the floor across from Leon, who followed suit. Leon paused for a long time before he continued. "I can probably count on one hand the number of times Dad looked me in the eye and asked me a meaningful question about my life. To Dad, money isn't a *means* to quality of life—it *is* life. Even when we would do so-called family vacations, Dad would be on his phone with business partners. I remember tugging on his arm when I was eight years old because I saw Captain Jack Sparrow while we were at Disneyland. He snapped at me to let him talk and then went back to his cell phone."

Alex stayed quiet, looking deeply at Leon. He shrugged awkwardly. "I guess that's why I've been so eager to find a way to manage our group's finances that doesn't have me at the helm of it all. I *hate* being in charge of it—I almost feel allergic to it. I hate that our group money is sitting in my bank account. It makes me feel like I'm becoming my dad rather than carving my own way." He paused and looked down in his lap. "Anyway . . . I'm still trying to find an app that could help us keep track of all the different numbers."

Alex took Leon's hand and squeezed it. After a pause, Alex said, "I know what it is to hear the message that you don't matter." Leon looked up sharply. Alex smiled ruefully. "L-G-B-T-Q-I-A, B-I-P-O-C. That's a lot of material for haters to work with." They paused. "There's a reason I've got thick skin."

Chastened, Leon looked down at his lap again. "I guess I sound pretty white-boy-privilegy. Talking about trips to Disneyland, and my wealthy dad, and not wanting to be in charge of our group's money . . ."

Alex shrugged and grinned teasingly. "I mean, you *are* a privileged white boy. But I don't think feeling valued is a privilege thing. I think it's a human thing. We all want to be seen. We all want to be known. We all want to be worthy." Alex paused again, looking right at Leon. "I see you." They held out a fist.

Leon grinned, relieved, and bumped Alex's fist. "I see you."

After another moment of quiet, Leon coughed again and rubbed his belly. "Hey—are there any snacks in this building? I'm hungry."

"*Gosh*, me too," Alex said. "Yes, let's go to the lounge." The two left C-105 and headed to the art students' lounge. Three of the room's walls were covered with murals. The fourth was painted with chalkboard paint and covered in chalk doodles, poems, and messages from the art students. There were toys and board games on most of the table surfaces. In the middle of the lounge was a massive table covered in Legos. Alex headed to the kitchen area in one end of the room and got busy making toast.

"Dang, this is awesome," Leon said, staring at everything. "How do you guys get anything done when you have all these distractions?"

"Au contraire," Alex responded. "An artist's work is creativity. Distractions feed creativity, which feeds the work." They opened the fridge. "What do you want on your toast? Peanut butter or jam?"

"Is there Nutella?" Leon asked.

Alex gave him another piercing look. "I have a very, very secret stash of Nutella." They paused, then finally said, "Which I will share with you. Close your eyes. I don't want you to see my hiding spot." Obligingly, Leon did. He heard Alex rummaging through cupboards.

"I hope you can enjoy the irony of this moment," Leon commented, eyes closed. "You want to put all the world's toys in a universal preschool and get rid of private property, but you don't want to share your Nutella. In fact, you're *hiding* your Nutella."

"Do I contradict myself? Very well, then, I contradict myself. I am large. I contain multitudes," Alex quoted. Finally, they said, "Okay. You can open." They were spreading Nutella on two pieces of toast. "And I concede your point. Humans are all a bunch of selfish SOBs. That's why we need a way to make sharing a little easier, right?"

Leon shrugged good-naturedly. "We could say that consumption goods are different than assets—I mean, not *every* item of private property should be universal. Like underwear. No one wants to share my boxer shorts."

Alex let out a great guffaw again, a blast of belly laughter that filled the art lounge. Leon grinned. "But you should know that Nutella *is* the devil," he said. "They burn down the Amazon rainforests to get their palm oil."

Alex turned to him, aghast, their mouth full of chocolate spread. "Ah' you fugging w' me?" they asked. Leon shook his head. Alex swallowed the bite. "Well *damn it*." They looked gloomily at the jar of Nutella. "It's such a drag to be principled sometimes."

"It's true," Leon agreed. "I generally try to avoid being principled, if I can help it. Although my friends are trying to change that."

"Well..." Alex looked at their toast and then over at Leon's. "This is the last supper then. Eat up."

Leon took his toast over to the Lego table and sat down. He began picking up the pieces and assembling them. "Okay, confession: I am a huge Lego geek. Like—I was as a kid, but secretly, I still am."

Alex grinned and looked over at him. "*There's* a little weirdness! I knew you had it in you. What are you building?"

"A house for your sister," Leon said. Alex let out another loud guffaw and brought the toast over, sitting down across from Leon. They studied Leon building the Lego house and munched the toast thoughtfully.

"Your dad wouldn't donate to charity..." Alex mused quietly. "Charity... Hey!" Alex spoke more loudly. "Can we go back to that micro-investing idea you had earlier?"

Leon looked up briefly, then returned his focus to the Legos. "Why? I thought you said that was no good. The renters throw their money away and the landlords benefit, and the company benefits most. The haves and the have-nots, et cetera."

"Okay but... what if there were no *company* at the top? What if there was a charity or a nonprofit at the top? Like, a foundation for the public good? Something that wasn't in it for profit?"

Leon looked up thoughtfully. "An entity that couldn't legally profit? Huh. Well, yeah, that would be better than a *for*-profit company."

"And the only thing the foundation does is just *hold* the assets. Like—it's just an epic warehouse. They don't profit from the assets; they just hold them and deal with the taxes. Like the preschool just holds the toys. Get rid of the power-hungry teachers, and just let the kids show up to the toy warehouse and check out the toys. Like a public library!"

"Wait, we've got too many metaphors going," Leon said. "Let's just be literal for a second. You've got a foundation for the public good that simply holds the assets. No one can profit off the asset holdings or use them for their own purposes."

"Because if they did, they'd go to jail," Alex supplied.

"Okay—good," Leon continued. "And this epic warehouse somehow holds assets like houses."

"Or the deeds, I guess," Alex said. "It holds all the proofs of ownership. So the foundation gets to hold the assets, like the preschool holds all the toys."

"Be literal, please," Leon interjected.

"But then people like my sister get usage rights of the assets, that is, the houses. The *literal* houses." Alex took a big bite of toast and licked Nutella off their fingers.

"So...who *would* get the value of the real estate? And all the profit from the increasing equity?" Leon asked.

"Maybe the renters," Alex mused. "Like—they could rent to own, from the foundation," Alex continued. "And we could try to really limit what the foundation is responsible for so that they can't amass power or influence. Like—we could say that basically the only employee the foundation needs is a guard to keep all the assets safe inside the vault."

"But then who would be in charge of actually dealing with all the legal and administration stuff of buying houses, et cetera? There's a lot to do in real estate beyond just holding the assets," Leon pointed out.

Alex shrugged. "I don't know. Maybe little baby companies? I'm just shooting in the dark right now. Would your dad donate the Malibu house to charity?"

"I have already said explicitly and literally that he would not," Leon said dryly.

"Hang on; he'd get a massive tax advantage if he donated that beach house to charity. Especially if he could still *hang on to the value*." Alex wiggled their eyebrows. "Okay, get this: your dad donates his beach house to the foundation. How much is it worth, do you think?"

Leon blew out his lips and shook his head. "I don't know, a beach house in Malibu? Five million, easy."

"Good glassy-eyed gorillas," Alex exclaimed. "That is insane!" Leon shrugged. "Okay, well let's say he donates this five-million-dollar mansion to the foundation and then gets the receipt." As Alex spoke, they climbed onto the couch and stood, bouncing as they spoke. "He gets a massive tax *credit* and no longer has to pay property taxes or worry about upkeep—"

Leon interjected. "He also wouldn't have to pay capital gains, which is the main thing holding him back from selling it right now."

"Okay, *yes*," Alex continued, still bouncing. "And *then*, the foundation lets a nice little family like my sister's start renting to own, and *that* makes your dad feel like a hero...and *plus*!...Your dad still somehow gets to use all that value to invest in other things!"

"How would that happen?" Leon asked. "How would he still get to use the value to invest in other things?"

Alex stopped bouncing and looked at Leon, stumped. "I don't know. I was hoping you would figure out that part."

Leon nodded and continued building his Lego house. "Alright. I'm intrigued. I think my dad would be intrigued. Let's explore the idea."

The QOL World Foundation and the SASTOs

The Person to Person financial environment starts with one leg in the real world and plants another leg in a virtual world, where value has been tokenized and made digital. The foundation—what Alex refers to as a charity—and the

Sovereign Asset Stewardship Organizations (SASTO)—what Alex calls little baby companies—help bridge the gap from one to the other.

Because we're starting in the real world, we have to use some "necessary evils," namely companies, shares, and shareholders. However, these are set up in such a way that power plays and hierarchies are impossible. Ultimately, these necessary evils enable us to get to a place where the people actually using and profiting from the assets are free of all the negative elements of private property we've already described.

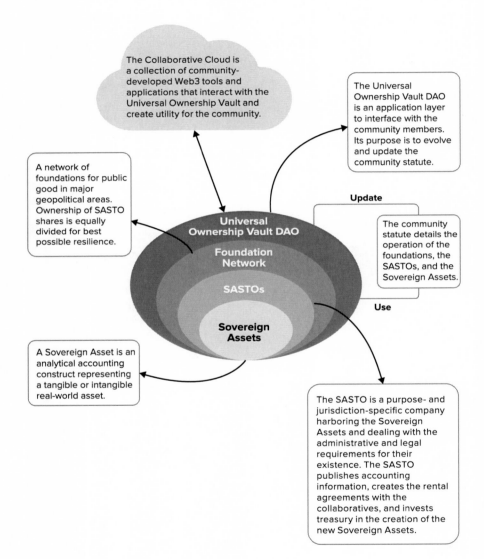

The Collaborative Cloud is a collection of community-developed Web3 tools and applications that interact with the Universal Ownership Vault and create utility for the community.

The Universal Ownership Vault DAO is an application layer to interface with the community members. Its purpose is to evolve and update the community statute.

A network of foundations for public good in major geopolitical areas. Ownership of SASTO shares is equally divided for best possible resilience.

Update

The community statute details the operation of the foundations, the SASTOs, and the Sovereign Assets.

Universal Ownership Vault DAO

Foundation Network

SASTOs

Sovereign Assets

Use

A Sovereign Asset is an analytical accounting construct representing a tangible or intangible real-world asset.

The SASTO is a purpose- and jurisdiction-specific company harboring the Sovereign Assets and dealing with the administrative and legal requirements for their existence. The SASTO publishes accounting information, creates the rental agreements with the collaboratives, and invests treasury in the creation of the new Sovereign Assets.

The Assets

Let's start in the real world. Imagine you have an asset—like Leon's father's Malibu beach house. And let's imagine that Leon's father decided he actually *did* want to put his beach house into this Universal Ownership Vault. He donates the deed of ownership into a foundation, which would then assign it to a Sovereign Asset Stewardship Organization—a.k.a. a SASTO. Because the foundation is essentially a nonprofit organization, Leon's father gets all the benefits of donating his asset to charity.

The SASTOs: Sovereign Asset Stewardship Organizations

The ownership deed of this asset is held and stewarded by a SASTO. A SASTO is a small company—like an LLC or Ltd—and operates within a local jurisdiction. For example, the deed of this Malibu mansion would likely be held in a Malibu-based stewardship organization. The company is in charge of dealing with the administrative, accounting, and legal requirements of the assets it holds. It also arranges contracts with the people who will use the asset; so the SASTO would contract with a family who would move into the Malibu house and live there.

There is no "business plan" in a SASTO; there is no money to be made and no employees. The only reason for a SASTO's existence is to legally represent the asset. In fact, a SASTO is even assigned a cryptic name, like Fv8h13x, so that it won't lend itself to branding. There is no business identity in a SASTO, no strategy or opportunities for growth. It is solely a legal vehicle. Although it is called a company, it is a company in name and legal status only.

This company runs on a very small operating budget. Everything that has to be done is mainly procedural and executed by community volunteers as a "shared duty" that serves their and everyone else's interest.[95] No one is on the payroll of a SASTO; if a SASTO ever needed work done that went beyond the legal representation that volunteers could provide, like accountancy, for instance, it would contract an accountant who is paid out of an operation fund.

If you want to avoid power plays, you need to avoid putting people in places of power. The limitations of a SASTO are deliberately in place to prevent a hierarchical structure that would lead to power plays. This is true even in the instance of shares. Each SASTO has shares, but the *only* shareholder for that company is the foundation, which holds all the SASTOs.

So how does the foundation work?

The Foundation

The foundation holding the SASTOs must exclusively function for public good. For instance, in Belgium, there is a Quality of Life World Foundation, which holds the SASTOs in that region. As different regions of the world choose to participate in this Person to Person financial environment, there would ideally be a foundation on each continent. A network of foundations would help protect this novel environment from external government interference. We can see this through the example of China's decision in 2021 to ban all cryptocurrencies.[96] All cryptocurrency mining had to cease in China, but because of the distributed character of the blockchain technology, the activity required for the networks to continue functioning was redistributed to different parts of the world as participants in those areas stepped up to fill

---

[95] How would that work? This volunteer participation is made possible by a Decentralized Autonomous Organization (DAO), which will be discussed more in depth in the next chapter. Let's say a form needed to be signed in one of the SASTOs. The DAO would select a random person in the community who was plugged into the network and notify them, "You're the designated person to sign this document." That person would certify the monthly VAT (value-added-taxes), annual report, etc. Essentially, that person would be like the Manager of the Day. Through the DAO people **receive rewards** for their participation and effort and are also incentivized to participate because they hold value in the system.

[96] Reuters, "China Declares All Crypto-Currency Transactions Illegal," *BBC News*, September 24, 2021, https://www.bbc.com/news/technology-58678907.

the gaps.[97] Likewise, a Person to Person network of foundations would split the equity of the SASTOs, which hold the real assets. Even if one foundation were to become a target of a government's censorship, the assets could be split up to the others and therefore remain secure.

The foundation has very strict constitutional bylaws that forbid the foundation from doing anything to profit off those ownership shares. It cannot collateralize them or sell them; all it can do is possess them. As Alex said, it functions more like a charity for the public good. It has a limited treasury and operates with a minimal amount of money; there is no way for any person affiliated with the foundation to profit from the value of the assets it holds. So no person can pretend to be Richard Nixon and steal a gold bar out of the vault. The foundation is simply responsible to ensure that the assets are there, that they stay there, and that they're legally allowed to be there.

However, whereas the foundation's *constitutional* statute describing what the foundation can and can't do is not evolutionary or debatable, there is a community statute, which *is* evolutionary. The community statute would describe everything else that would be relevant for safeguarding, appraising, and managing the assets, for example, how much money should be in a sustainability fund for a house in San Diego. The community statute is an evolutionary document, determined and maintained by—you guessed it—the local community and shared across all foundations in the network.

Together, the SASTOs and foundation(s) make up the Universal Ownership Vault. With all these assets in the vault, it now becomes possible to publish the *value* of the assets. When the value of an asset is publicly available, new possibilities arise via the decentralized web to tokenize the value of those assets. For example, if the UOV determines that the Malibu beach house has a value of $5 million, tokens of value can be generated that represent the value of that beach house in the vault. Then someone like Leon's father

97 Sissi Cao, "Bitcoin Miners Are Migrating en Masse during the Global Energy Crisis," *Observer*, October 18, 2021, https://observer.com/2021/10/bitcoin-miner-relocation-china-to-us-global-energy-crisis.

could use those tokens as a form of currency on the decentralized web. This "tokenization" process is similar to how the gold bars in Fort Knox were attached to the dollar and guaranteed its value. However, unlike Fort Knox, the Universal Ownership Vault will operate with total transparency, enabled by some of the technological tools we'll explore in Chapter 8.

The Universal Ownership Vault safely stores assets and publishes their data in a transparent way. But how and where does all that information get published?

DAO

The specific technology that hosts the Universal Ownership Vault is called a DAO: a decentralized autonomous organization. The main benefit a DAO allows is transparency: anyone can see into the vault at any time, and the value of each of its assets is regularly audited and published for all to see. It also allows participants to steer the operation of the vault—engaging in governance and operations—by defining procedures, valuation methods, and so on. In other words: everything is visible and everyone who is on the DAO is able to participate in how it runs.

But then *how* and *where* do people actually transact with this value? That's something we'll explore in our next chapters, as we dive deeper into the possibilities made available through the decentralized web, where people are able to interact with the published value provided by the Universal Ownership Vault. The tools made available on the decentralized web allow people like Leon's father to donate their assets to the Universal Ownership Vault but still retain and use the value. (If some of those technical concepts are unfamiliar, we'll explain them all simply in our next chapter.)

Before we head there, though, there's one more element to explore: how could someone like Alex's sister benefit from these constructs?

Let's return to Alex and Leon as they explore the final element of this redefinition of private property: the practical usage of these donated assets, known as Sovereign Assets.

Sovereign Assets

Leon looked up at Alex, puzzled. He took a bite of his Nutella toast and considered. "So...a foundation buys the house...And then what? You had mentioned micro-investors earlier—you think micro-investors could work if the assets were held by a foundation?"

"Maybe," Alex said. "But I can't talk my way through my idea unless I can visualize it. Umm...here," Alex said. They grabbed several Lego people: a knight, a firefighter, Luke Skywalker, Princess Leia, and Minnie Mouse. "Okay, I'm going to make my sister Elisa be Princess Leia." They grabbed another Lego person—a pirate. "And this can be her husband, Wes." They lifted up the pirate and Princess Leia and wiggled them. "Weee neeeed a house! Weee are sick of paying rent!"

"Why do they sound like rodents?" Leon asked.

"They've been turned into Lego people," Alex said. They put Princess Leia and the pirate aside and lifted up Luke Skywalker. Alex made him talk: "Sister! I want to help you buy this house. I have gathered some friends, and we've all chipped in to buy it. You can pay us back with your rent and gain equity!"

"I'm sorry, are *you* Luke Skywalker?" Leon asked.

"Sure," Alex said. "The force is strong with me, so that makes sense."

"Okay, so—Luke Skywalker—you're going to help your sister buy the house via crowdfunding?" Leon asked. "Is that it?"

"Right, we're micro-investors. We all own little, tiny pieces of the house. Little Lego bricks!" Alex crowed. They grabbed a Lego brick and put it into Luke Skywalker's tiny Lego hands.

"Then who actually holds the deed?" Leon said. "Oooh," he said, it suddenly dawning on him. "The foundation holds the deed! Right?"

"Yes. The foundation owns the house. It's like the preschool that owns the toys. And look...when all of the investors pool their money to buy the house, then they all get to hold some of the value." Alex started taking Leon's

Lego house apart and putting chunks of it in front of Luke Skywalker, the firefighter, the knight, and Minnie Mouse.

"Hey, that's my house!" Leon protested. He began taking the chunks back and reconstructing it.

"Okay, fine, you can keep the house assembled. But each of them gets a Lego block—that represents their investment in the house. So—rather than a single person having to pay outright for the whole thing, they've split the investment among them. And now Elisa and Wes start to gradually pay the investors back via monthly payments."

"Like rental payments?" Leon asked.

"Well—sort of, but they're not just throwing the money away. They're actually slowly building equity. Here, watch."

Alex made Princess Leia pick up a green Lego block and hop over to Luke Skywalker. In a high voice, Alex said, "'Here, dear sibling! This is my December payment. Now I believe I have paid you back for the money you used to purchase your part of the house! So—this is the money." Princess Leia set the green Lego block down at Luke Skywalker's feet. "And I will take the equity!" Princess Leia picked up the yellow Lego block that had been in front of Luke Skywalker. Princess Leia hopped back over the pirate, and Alex said in the same high voice, "Look, babe! We own the value of one-fourth of our house now!"

"Why are you saying it like that?" Leon asked. "'Own the value?' Why not just say 'own the house'?"

"Because we're getting rid of private property, remember? The foundation owns the house. The Lego people hold the *value* of the house. My sister and Wes are using it and slowly earning the value."

"Huh," Leon said. He studied the Lego people. "So—the foundation holds all the assets, like a house."

"Right," Alex confirmed again.

"And since it's a foundation for the public good, it can't profit off of its asset holdings. Which means renters can actually rent to own. Although it's not rent to 'own' since no one owns it, but they're essentially building equity."

"Correct," Alex said. They had found a Yoda figure and wiggled it. In a Yoda voice, Alex said, "Wise, you are."

"But then who takes care of the house? If Elisa and Wes aren't the actual owners, why would they be incentivized to actually care for it? Renters are notorious for trashing houses," Leon pointed out.

Alex made Princess Leia gasp. "I beg to differ!" They set Princess Leia down and considered Leon's question. "They're incentivized to take care of it because they hold part of the value. If they trash the house, the house is worth less, and their Lego blocks are worth less money. If they improve the house, the house is worth more, and their Lego blocks are worth *more* money."

"Aaah, I get it," Leon said. "So..." he leaned down and studied his Lego house. "Okay, let's say I used about a thousand Legos to build this house. I mean, obviously I didn't; I've only been working on it for like thirty minutes. But let's say when it was done, there were a thousand blocks there. And we could guess that a modest home in San Jose would cost about $1 million. So each of those Lego blocks would be worth $1,000." He looked over at Princess Leia and the pirate, who had four blocks in front of them. "And right now, Elisa and Wes are standing in front of four of them. So they've earned $4,000 back in equity."

"*If* they keep the house nice," Alex said. "If they improve the house and get the value up to $1.2 million, then those blocks are worth more. If they trash the house and its value falls, the blocks would be worth less."

"Okay, I'm following." Leon studied the Lego creation. "So—are Elisa and Wes stuck there until they finish paying off all the investors?"

Alex shrugged. "No, I don't think so. Look—if they move out, they still have their blocks. And then, when someone new moves in, the new renters' monthly rent keeps paying back investors. Eventually, the new users would pay Elisa and Wes back for their blocks. Or my sister could use those blocks to get into in a new house."

"And if the house had gained in value because Elisa and Wes improved it, it would rent for a higher amount, and the original investors would get paid back faster," Leon supplied.

"Yes!" Alex said.

"Interesting," Leon mused. "*Iiiiiinteresting...*" He looked at Alex. "Let me see if I get this straight," Leon said. "You're suggesting that there be some sort of not-for-profit foundation that holds a bunch of assets, like a vault. And then people could still *use* those assets, like your sister would use the house. And as they pay to use the assets, those payments are actually helping them build value, which they can financially transact with."

"BOOM," Alex said, and tossed the Yoda figure up into the air.

Sovereign Assets Explained Further

We will be devoting Chapter 9 to explain in greater detail how Sovereign Assets work. However, in order to fully appreciate the machinations that enable the usage of Sovereign Assets and the storage of value, it's important to understand the technology that supports them. For that reason, we're introducing the concept here briefly, then will explain them further after introducing some of the necessary technology required in Chapter 8.

Very briefly, then, here are some of the fundamental elements of an asset, once it's donated to the foundation:

- The asset becomes **self-owned**, hence the name "sovereign." This simply means it is owned by no one and therefore is no longer private property.
- A Sovereign Asset **can still be used**. The users pay a monthly fee for the right to use the Sovereign Asset, like Alex's sister and husband would pay rent. This would enable people like Elisa and Wes to begin building up long-term savings in real estate when that option would have previously been denied them because of the steep barrier(s) to entry discussed at the start of this chapter.

- The **monthly fee** is split into several "pots."
  » The majority of the payment is paid to the micro-investors who helped make the asset sovereign by moving it into the vault. This can be done either via donation, as in the example with Leon's dad, or via a crowd-funding campaign, which we'll illustrate in Chapter 10. Once the asset is "paid off" (like if all the investors for the San Jose house were paid in full, with interest), this portion of the monthly payment would go into a *treasury fund*. That treasury fund would make all the "Lego blocks" attached to that home worth more.
  » Another portion of that monthly payment is put into a *sustainability fund*. The Sustainability fund is specifically related to environmental provisions, to make the asset a "**good earth citizen**." This money might be used to invest in clean energy products, reduce the asset's carbon footprint, or ensure that the asset is disposed of in a "clean" way when the asset can no longer be used.
  » The third portion of the monthly payment goes into the *operation fund*. This money goes to the local SASTO to help cover costs related to paying taxes, provisions to pay accountants, insurance money, and so on.
- The **value of a Sovereign Asset is published by the Universal Ownership Vault DAO**.
- A Sovereign Asset's **value is determined by the market**. For instance, the hypothetical house that Elisa and Wes lived in would be worth whatever a comparable home in San Jose would sell for. Its rental value would be comparable to a similar home's rental value in the same area. This means the value of an asset is determined by whatever real people deem it is worth rather than manipulated by governments or politics.

Altogether, Sovereign Assets would help reinvent private property, create greater equality, incentivize environmental sustainability, allow for greater

Person to Person interactions, allow for greater flexibility and personal "sovereignty" in asset holdings, and still allow for the storage of value.

Is the Juice Worth the Squeeze?

The foundation, the SASTOs, the Sovereign Assets—is all this *really* necessary? We discovered it was by going through this process personally.

When we set about trying to turn the Experience Center property in France into a Sovereign Asset, we tried starting with a crowdfunding process, intending to eventually tokenize the asset and publish the tokens online. However, we ran into problems. The banking laws in France required that we get a banking license to do that; moreover, we discovered that the laws in every country have different requirements.

For five years, we consulted with lawyers, trying to find a way through legal snags and hindrances. We would hear things like, "You need to go to a notary" or "That runs up against confiscation laws." We also realized that, even if we were to tokenize the Experience Center property, we would still ultimately be acting as the manager of all the tokens, which—once again—could lead to power plays. The current systems built to support private property simply don't allow for this kind of universal ownership.

After five years of working through this conundrum, we've found this construct—with the foundation, SASTOs, and decentralized autonomous organization—to be the solution that will work in today's world and help us build a bridge to a "metaverse," which will allow us to engage with the value and usage of an asset more freely.

We've already discussed a number of advantages this "reinvention" could allow, but there are several more worth mentioning:

- **More people will care about more pieces of the planet.** People are often highly invested in the neighborhoods in which they live; they want to make that area a nice place to be and will work to support improvements in that area. Likewise, if people own value in assets all over the world—"Lego blocks," for instance, in France, and the US, and Colombia, and Brazil—people will care more about the stability, sustainability, and prosperity of those regions. This will help create a more connected global population that cares to collaborate for greater good, not compete.

- **There will be less of a focus on profits and a greater focus on sustainability.** This financial environment is not about personal enrichment or profit. Assets are not owned by traditional companies and managed for the sake of profits; now assets are *used* by companies but owned by "themselves" via the foundation. For example, a fracking company renting a Sovereign Asset could still drill and make profits from the oil. However, sustainability concerns would be a part of their model. Will this hurt innovation? No—but it would even out the excesses. A fracking company could still extract oil and make a profit but wouldn't be allowed to do that by wrecking the land for future generations.

- **You can't be evil.** The legal and technical frameworks behind Sovereign Assets mean that you have to play fair. You can't *buy* the fracking land; you can only rent it. As groups of people renting Sovereign Assets will likely be collaboratives, formed around a Collaborative Agreement—like the JALL group we've illustrated—their bylaws will be guided by the principles of quality of life. Could people still find a way to use this financial environment for evil? Probably—people are amazingly inventive at finding ways to engage in corruption. However, this environment is aimed at good and is a powerful step in the right direction. Private entrepreneurship can still be robust, but goods can only be *used*—they can't be squeezed.

- **The Person to Person environment discussed in previous chapters will inform how Sovereign Assets are handled.** We have taken great care to describe the collaborative environment that would dictate interactions in the Person to Person world. Remember: the Person to Person recommendations are built to help us avoid the tragedy of the commons. Sovereign Assets would be handled and stewarded by collaborative organizations in the Person to Person environment.

But wait—there's one major element we haven't discussed yet in this conversation about the Universal Ownership Vault. How would the assets be secured? We can't pull another Fort Knox. So how *do* we secure all these assets? That will be Alex and Leon's last consideration for the day.

THE NEED FOR A TECHNOLOGICAL PLATFORM

Leon and Alex set their Lego people down and stared at the world they had created on the table.

"I mean, I think we're brilliant," Alex said. "Which world leader should I call first?"

Leon stared at the Lego house, his brow furrowed. "Wait—there's still something we haven't figured out yet. We *might* be able to convince the world's greedy kids—that is, people like my dad—to donate their toys to the giant preschool vault. But who is going to secure the vault? Any human in that position would be corrupted by absolute power." Leon found the Darth Vader Lego person and made it do an evil laugh. "Muah hah haaaah."

"Mmm," Alex nodded in agreement. "How do we find uncorruptible people? Everyone is a little sinister at the core. If *I* had all the world's toys, *I* would be corrupted." They paused thoughtfully. "We need to find aliens; that's what we need. If we could find perfectly moral aliens to run this preschool, Earth might have a fighting chance at creating a better world."

Leon laughed. "I can't tell if you're kidding or serious."

Alex looked at him piercingly. "I'm always serious about aliens." They sighed. "But it might take a while to get them to Earth. And who knows if they'd be the world-dominating kind or the Vulcan kind." Alex stood up from the couch and stretched. "Oh man, *that's* what we need! We need Spock! Someone who functions with perfect logic and isn't affected by emotions like fear or greed. Spock could govern over the world's toy vault with integrity." They went over to the chalkboard and started doodling Spock.

Leon's eyes widened. "Wait—we don't need aliens. We don't need Spock." He got to his feet. "Alex—the world already *has* something that can operate free of emotion. Technology can, like blockchain and smart contracts. A DAO!"

"Woah, woah, woah, science fiction boy." Alex waved him off. "I've seen that movie. It's called *The Terminator*, and it doesn't end well for humans. Robots take over the world and destroy everything."

"Science fiction boy," Leon scoffed. "*You're* the one talking about aliens. Besides, blockchain is way different than AI. Listen: we need another form of safe keepers, right? We need security guards who won't create power structures but will provide safety. Well, blockchain *enables* safety, but since it's all just technology, it can't be corrupted like people can. Alex—we can use *tech* to innovate! Blockchain—Web3—it would turn the vault into an aquarium!"

Alex looked at him dubiously. "I think I would prefer Spock." Alex sighed and turned back to the chalkboard. "Well...our private property reinvention was a nice little rabbit hole to jump down for a while. I'll be sure to tell my sister all about it. Too bad it probably can't happen in reality."

Suddenly Leon slapped his forehead. "Oh my gosh, Alex. I'm an idiot! I've been looking for apps on Web2 to help us manage the draw for our group, but I should have been looking on *Web3* this whole time! I bet there's something on Web3 that could enable us to store all the numbers for our Future Value, and Collaborative Points, and all that." He looked at Alex in disbelief. "Web-fricking-THREE, not Web2! Leon, Leon, Leon..." he shook his head and stood up, grabbing his backpack. "I've got to go. I have so much web-searching to do."

"But I don't understand anything you just said," Alex said soberly. "Come back to the Lego table. Explain Web3 to me using toys."

"Can't right now! Gotta run!" Leon began jogging toward the stairwell.

"I enjoyed our bonding time!" Alex called after him. "Thanks for indulging my anarchy!"

Leon did an about-face and jogged back to Alex. He gave them a big hug. "Me too. Thanks for sharing your Nutella and Legos. I'd reinvent the global economy with you any day." Then he raced down the stairs and back to his dorm.

EXPLORE FURTHER

If you'd like to learn more, discuss this content with others, or access tools for your own application, go to the interactive section of the book using this QR code.

CHAPTER EIGHT

THE TECHNICAL TOOLBOX

Web3 Technology Enabling Person to Person Interaction

> *There is an opportunity to recreate the*
> *financial world as we know it in the parallel universe*
> *that is the blockchain. We are writing rules*
> *for this whole new universe.*

—Patrick M. Byrne, founder and CEO of Overstock.com

Leon grinned ear to ear as he sent the text to Alex: *THE VAULT EXISTS.*

His phone buzzed almost immediately with Alex's response, which was a run of profanities, all in caps. He laughed and put his phone in his pocket. Up ahead in the cafeteria line, he saw Jake and hurried to catch up with him. "Dude! I found it! I found what we need," Leon said exultantly, raising his voice above the dull roar of other students eating, chatting, and clattering their trays.

"Yeah?!" Jake asked, sliding his tray along the metal buffet bar. "What is it?"

Leon shook his head. "It's complicated. I want to wait until we're sitting down with Alex and Lana. They're meeting us here, right?"

"It's Taco Tuesday," Jake said. "Everyone on campus is here right now." Leon laughed in agreement.

The two young men gathered their food, checked out, and found Lana and Alex in a booth. Jake slid in next to Lana, and Leon sat next to Alex.

"DUDE," Alex said to Leon, and began hitting him in excitement.

"I know!!!" Leon said gleefully.

"The preschool?" Alex asked.

"Sooooo much better than the preschool!" Leon said. They both turned to Jake and Lana, across the table.

Jake looked puzzled at their exchange. "Do you have any idea what they're talking about?" he asked Lana.

She gave him a kiss on the cheek. "No, but I think it's cute that they're bonding." She looked at them. "What *are* you talking about?"

"Okay." Leon took a deep breath. "I'm so excited, I don't even know where to start. *So*, Alex and I were talking about this massive, worldwide preschool that holds all the world's toys so that all the kids can share, and we were calling it a vault, and then I realized that blockchain technology could actually *enable* a vault like that—you know, because it's distributed and transparent and blah, blah, blah—and so I started looking around on Web3 and it *exists*!" He looked at Jake and Lana, delighted with himself. "The vault *exists*!! And I found an app that *uses* all the information in the vault that will help us do all the functions we were doing in our Contribution Sessions, without needing to deal with our Excel spreadsheets and calculators!"

Alex was shaking their head. "No. No, no, no. Leon. I told you, we *can't* scare them with all that right out of the gate."

"I'm not scared, mainly because I didn't understand anything that you just said," Lana quipped.

"But...it sounds like you have an app that will help us do all our collaborative stuff?" Jake asked.

"Okay, yes, let's start there," Leon said. His eyes got big, and he waggled his eyebrows. "Are you ready?" He spoke with a heightened sense of drama. "The app is called...the *Collaborative Cloud*."

The rest of the group looked at him in silence. Leon turned hesitantly to Alex. "Was that too scary?"

Alex waved their hand in a circular motion. "Say more, lion cub."

"Okay, hear me out. This app—first of all—will do all that we want it to do. It's going to provide all of us with a way to transparently see all the value we've generated, *and* it will let us divvy up money according to our Collaborative Points!"

"Really?" Jake asked. "There's actually an app that will work with our point system?"

"Yes!" Leon said. "We can each input our points, and then the money is distributed into each of our accounts, according to what we entered. But here's something even cooler about it—the app is all open source, so I can actually contribute to the code and add features that we want. So—like, our future money. I could write that in. And if the Collaborative Points mechanism isn't exactly how we want it, I can just tweak it."

"Well, that's rad," Alex said. "So we each get our own accounts? Is this like a banking app?"

"Um...sort of, but not really. It works kind of like a bank, but instead of a bank behind it, there's a Universal Ownership Vault, connected to a DAO."

"Too scary," Alex interjected. "Simplify."

Leon sucked in his breath. "Okay—basically, there are a bunch of other people using these tools. They're all in collaboratives like ours. They operate in similar ways, they have group agreements like we do, they're using points to separate time and effort, and they even want to manage their finances like we do."

"What?!" Lana asked. "And here I thought we were being so original. I can't decide if I'm happy about this or offended."

"I think it's worth celebrating," Jake said.

Leon continued. "So the way they're doing their finances is by digitizing their assets. I think it's brilliant!"

"Is cryptocurrency involved?" Jake asked.

"Yes," Leon said defensively.

Jake grinned. "That's why you think it's brilliant."

"It's brilliant for a lot of reasons," Leon said. "There's no middleman—no bank fees, no one telling us what we can and can't do with our money, no debit cards . . . just people working with other people. Assets that are fluid and fungible."

"Fungible?" Lana asked, making a face. "*Fungible*? What does that even mean? It sounds like fungus. Plus, a ball. Fungi ball. Gross."

"Fungible means you can exchange it," Alex explained. "It's something that's basically interchangeable with another unit in its same category. So— like, you could trade a ten-dollar bill for a five and five ones. Or you could trade one barrel of oil for another barrel of oil."

"If you can't exchange it, then it's not as much funge," Jake teased Lana. She threw a tortilla chip at him.

"Where does the vault come in?" Alex asked. "Is the Collaborative Cloud the vault?"

"No," Leon said to Alex. "The Collaborative Cloud is a DAO that can interact *with* the vault, but it's actually a different system entirely. But let's not get into that quite yet." He glanced at Alex and whispered conspiratorially, "Hashtag dontscarethechildren." He turned back to Jake and Lana, who were looking annoyed. "The most important thing to know about the Collaborative Cloud is that it's built on a blockchain, like Bitcoin. That means it's decentralized."

"Again—you're saying words, but there's no comprehension happening over here." Lana waved her hand over her face.

"Okay, fair enough," Leon said. "You're right—there's a lot of tech concepts that are kind of complicated. Let me talk you through them. Um . . . we'll start with blockchain."

THE UOV AND THE COLLABORATIVE CLOUD

In our last chapter, we explained the need for a Universal Ownership Vault (UOV) that could safely house assets and publish their value on a secure network. The only way to do that is via a blockchain network, which makes all data publicly available, is resilient against hacks or corruption, and allows for distributed governance without power plays. We'll explain more about how blockchain accomplishes that in a moment, when we say more about technology. First, let's explore how this new system could interact with the vault, discussed in Chapter 7.

Remember Leon's father's Malibu beach house? Leon and Alex speculated what might happen if Leon's dad donated his house to the foundation associated with the UOV. Here's what they had discussed so far:

- The house would be donated to the foundation, and Leon's dad would get a receipt for its exact accounting value. In the United States, this would serve him as a tax write-off and/or reduce his capital gains on the property.[98] He would also relinquish management of the property.
- The asset would now be held in the UOV, under the stewardship of a local SASTO. Its value would be published on the internet and made available to rent on the Collaborative Cloud marketplace. The house would now be available for tenants like Alex's sister.

But what does Leon's father do with the receipt? Previously, we had implied that Leon's father could retain the *value* of his asset. That's what the Collaborative Cloud would allow.

Here's how that might work: Leon's dad could go to the Collaborative Cloud with his receipt, and one of the tools on the cloud would affirm that

---

[98] This is true as of writing in December 2021; see IRS, "Charitable Contribution Deductions," updated August 18, 2021, https://www.irs.gov/charities-non-profits/charitable-organizations/charitable-contri bution-deductions.

the value represented by the beach house had not yet been claimed. Using his receipt, Leon's father could claim that value. We can assume the house is worth around $5 million, which was Leon's ballpark estimation. Leon's father then would have 50,000 non-fungible tokens (NFTs), each worth $100, representing the value. Essentially, Leon's father has "tokenized" the asset of his beach house and now can transact with its value.[99]

We're going to explain how that would work in the second half of this chapter. For now, understand simply that:

- The UOV holds the assets and publishes their data.
- The Collaborative Cloud makes use of the information exposed by the UOV.
- The Collaborative Cloud provides tools to interact (via blockchain technology) with the value published by the UOV. Although the two are separate, the financial applications on the Collaborative Cloud reference the UOV's data.

And just what exactly is the Collaborative Cloud? The Collaborative Cloud can be thought of as a toolshed: it offers a number of Web3 tools that are useful for collaboratives. (More on Web3 in a moment.) It allows members to explore and find each other, collaborate, exchange value, and share the joy of the collaborative experiences. Some of the tools make use of financial information published by the UOV, adding a layer of additional functionality to the assets in the UOV. The distributed set of services provided by the Collaborative Cloud extend community into the digital space. It is open source, built *by* people of collaboratives, *for* people and collaboratives, using tools that exist on the decentralized web.

And yes—it's real. At the writing of this text, the Collaborative Cloud is accessible at https://qol.to/collaborativecloud. It contains the tools allowing for

---

[99] The NFTs are Web3 standard NFTs, so Leon's father could use them on ANY dApp or NFT marketplace available on the internet. All imaginable Web3 deFi tools and services on the internet can make use of them.

some of the functions described in the following chapters and accommodates new users' development. If collaboratives have specific needs, they can develop and publish that functionality. Alternately, they can provide a description of the requirements and provide a grant for someone else to develop it.

The Collaborative Cloud does more than just facilitate the exchange of cryptocurrency; it brings together all actors in the collaborative network. When creating their own Collaborative Cloud account, users choose which tools they will want to regularly use personally and/or for their collaborative, such as Collaborative Points or Future Value. And—since the Collaborative Cloud is open source—if a collaborative has a particular need that does not have a feature created for it yet, users can do their own software development to build new tools, as Leon mentioned.

Here are some of the potential functions enabled by the Collaborative Cloud:

- *Network capabilities:*
  - » Find people with talents or skills needed in one of the collaboratives you are engaged with.
  - » Find investors for your projects.
- *Collaborative capabilities:*
  - » Keep track of data relevant to each collaborative you participate in, such as Collaborative Points, QOL scores, personal finance, development plans, commitments, etc.
  - » Vote on the global guidelines for your collaborative, according to your collaborative points.
- *Personal capabilities:*
  - » Keep track of your personal finance.
  - » Participate in the buying and selling of financial assets in different markets.

This person-centric, decentralized network relies on some very specific technological tools to work. In our next section, we're going to explain some of those tools—as briefly and clearly as possible. If you're not interested in the technological mechanisms (or if you are already familiar with these terms), feel free to skip this section. With that said, however, the material that follows in subsequent chapters will make more sense with a basic grasp of this technology.

THE TECHNICAL STACK

In this section, we're going to briefly cover blockchain, Web3, dApps, smart contracts, and DiDs. These are some of the tools that enable the Collaborative Cloud DAO to function.

Since blockchain is a complex idea but a fundamental one, we're going to let the teaching expert in the JALL group, Jake, break it down via a simple metaphor.

Blockchain

Lana turned to Leon. "Can you please explain blockchain to us? Don't 'mansplain,' though—just *explain*."

Leon hesitated. "How do I know if I'm mansplaining?"

"Wait—let me see if I've got this one!" Jake said. "Leon's been geeking out about this stuff in our dorm every time he deals with his cryptocurrency. I think I finally understand what a blockchain is." He looked at Leon. "Do you mind?"

Leon grinned, relieved. "Be my guest. But don't mansplain."

"I don't think it would be possible for me to mansplain on this one because I'm still figuring it out too. Okay..." Jake studied the various condiments on the booth's tabletop, then grabbed a large sugar container. "Let's say that this sugar container is a centralized system, like Facebook or Google or Uber. Or even a banking or lending system, like Fannie Mae or Freddie Mac. You've got one company controlling everything that the people who come to it experience."

Jake raised one of his pointer fingers and mimed the finger hopping toward the sugar container. He made his finger bow toward the sugar container and said in a high voice, "Oh, great sugar container! Give me some sugar!" Jake wiggled the large sugar container and spoke loudly. "NO! YOU DO NOT GET ANY SUGAR." He set the container down. Jake made his other pointer finger hop up to the sugar container and in a high voice said, "Most powerful sugar container! May I please have some sugar?" He lifted the sugar container again and boomed out, "YES! But only since you asked nicely."

Alex grinned. "I like when Jake is able to explain things to us."

"So, clearly," Jake said, "the sugar container is all-powerful. It controls whether or not you get sugar, that is, money. It controls the algorithms you get served. It controls the listings that come to the top of your search results. It controls everything."

"I kind of hate this sugar container so far," Lana observed.

"Good! That's the point," Jake said. "And besides the fact that it's all-powerful—which is clearly problematic—watch what happens when a hacker gets to it." Jake made his right hand slink toward the sugar container, making a diabolical cackle as he did so. He pushed the sugar container over. It fell onto the table and sugar gushed out. Slowly, it rolled toward the edge of the table, spilling sugar all over. It stopped at the rim along the edge in front of Leon.

"You're kinda making a mess, babe," Lana noted.

"Exactly. One centralized system is vulnerable. If hackers get to it, the whole system is compromised and it makes a giant mess for everyone whose data is stored on that centralized system. Not to mention the whole system can just be *down* and you have zero control over when it comes back up because you're at the mercy of the all-powerful sugar container."

"Like when Facebook and Instagram and WhatsApp just went down that one day," Lana said.[100] Leon nodded emphatically.

"So then, explain a *de*centralized system," Alex said.

---

[100] Mike Isaac, and Sheera Frenkel, "Gone in Minutes, Out for Hours: Outage Shakes Facebook," *The New York Times*, October 4, 2021, https://www.nytimes.com/2021/10/04/technology/facebook-down.html.

"Right, that's what a blockchain is," Jake said. He picked up the sugar container, set it aside, and deftly swept the spilled sugar into a napkin, which he put on his plate. "Okay, so a blockchain is built out of many little blocks, chained together," he said. He took some paper sugar packets and laid them in a row along the table. "Each of these blocks contains some data. We can say that the sugar inside is the data. So that's like—your identifying information, um..." He paused and looked to Leon for help.

"On Bitcoin, the data would be like the sender, receiver, and amount of coins," Leon said.

"Okay, there you go," Jake said. "So the block contains the data. And on the *outside* of the block are two hashes."

Lana mused, "I assume you're not talking about hash browns."

"I wish he were," Alex said to Lana. They both snickered.

"Attention, please," Jake said. "A hash is like a digital fingerprint. Like—you know when you share a Google Doc, and you get that link with a super-long list of letters and numbers? That's a hash."

"A hash is time-stamped," Leon added. "You can't backdate it."

"Okay, got it," Jake said. He held up the sugar packet. "Each block has two hashes. It has its own hash, and it also has the hash of the previous block that it's chained to. So it's like each block is sort of holding hands with the previous block in the chain."

"Or they're just chained together," Leon said, dryly.

"Wait, I have an idea," Alex said. "You said it's like a fingerprint, right? Hang on." They reached into their bag for a packet of markers. "Here..." Alex colored their own pointer finger with red marker and pressed it onto a sugar packet. It left a distinct red fingerprint.

"Ooo! Can I?" Lana asked. She colored her finger purple and pressed it on the back of Alex's packet.

"Okay, good—so that would mean that your two blocks are chained together. Lana, do another purple fingerprint on that packet, and Leon, you do a fingerprint on the back of hers. And then, Alex, you do another red fingerprint on this one, and I'll do a blue fingerprint on the other side."

They busied themselves coloring their fingers and making their prints on the packets. Two fraternity guys walked by the table and shared a scoffing laugh.

Leon said, "Can I be the genesis block?" He held up the last packet, with his own single green fingerprint.

"What's the genesis block?" Alex asked.

"That's just the first one that starts the chain. Sure, buddy," Jake said. He lined up the packets on the table, starting with Leon's. "So each one of these blocks has the unique identifying information of the previous block *and* its own identifying hash on it. That's how they're all linked together. Now—if you were to try to change the data inside..." He dipped his finger in his water glass and let some drips fall onto the sugar packet with Alex and Lana's prints on it. Alex's red fingerprint began to smear.

"Hey!" Lana said indignantly. "That's our block!"

"Your reaction is perfect," Jake said, grinning. "If you change the data *inside*, it messes with the hash on the *outside*, and that alerts the other block it's chained to because now the tampered hash on this block—" He pointed to the smeared print. "—doesn't match the hash it's linked to anymore." He pointed to Alex's pristine print on the packet with his own fingerprint. "So then, that alerts *all* the other blocks because they're all chained to each other."

"That's what the nodes do," Leon chimed in. "The nodes are like the security alert system if anyone tries to mess with the chain."

"Ah. So that's why it's more secure than a centralized system?" Alex asked.

"Right," Leon said. "It's much harder to tamper with because there's that built-in alert system."[101]

"But couldn't a good hacker just successfully tamper with *all* the blocks in the chain?" Lana asked.

---

[101] This is because all participants in the Bitcoin network can run a node. The role of the node is to make sure the chain is valid. Running a node results in rejecting any block that does not meet the consensus rules.

"Actually, no, because there's a safety mechanism called 'proof of work,' a.k.a. consensus," Leon explained.[102] "There's a delay every time you want to change a block. Like, if you want to make a new block or if you were to try to tamper with a block, it takes ten minutes—that's the proof of work. Also, there are literally thousands of people all over the world, using thousands of computers, all competing to create the next block in the blockchain—that's called mining. If someone wanted to hack the blockchain, they'd have to beat out *all* those other miners, *six* times in a row. Which would basically require the energy power of a small country. The amount of energy and computing power required to do that makes it practically impossible."

Lana squinted her eyes. "I am trying to comprehend what you just said, and I'm *almost there*."

"Basically, the more people who compete to make the next block in the chain, the more secure it is." Leon paused, looking at Lana. "It's really, really secure."

"Roger that," Lana sighed.

Leon looked at Jake. "This was brilliant. Can I add a few more details?"

"Sure!" Jake said.

"So the other thing that's super cool about a blockchain is that it's distributed. There's no one company overruling the whole thing—"

"No fascist sugar container," Lana said.

"Exactly," Leon laughed. "It's distributed among *all* the different people that use it. That means if I want to send money to someone in Antwerp, I just send it right to them—person to person. There's no middleman; there's no banking system or wire agency that has to mitigate it all; it's just one person to another."

"But then how do you know it's not going to turn into the Wild West?" Alex asked. "Like—how can we trust that people will come through with payments if there's no agency ensuring accountability?"

---

[102] The mechanism is called consensus. Proof of work is one of the possible consensus mechanisms, famous for being used in Bitcoin. In Bitcoin's case, it is done by so-called "Miners." Proof of Stake is another consensus mechanism used in eth2 and Cardano.

"Because every transaction is public, transparent, and immutable," Leon explained. "Like, you're not relying on five-star reviews to tell you that you can trust someone. The tech itself[103] ensures that people have the assets they say they do, or that they are who they say they are. It actually allows for way less sleaziness than something like eBay." Leon pulled out his phone and pulled up the Collaborative Cloud window. He began scrolling through the different windows while speaking. "Plus, remember that *everyone* is helping to safeguard the system. Everyone has access to the same information and is monitoring it. That means no outages...no power plays..." Leon looked up from his phone. "It's basically going to change the world."

"So...the Collaborative Cloud is similar to Bitcoin?" Lana asked.

"It uses the same kind of technology," Leon said. "And it has the same advantages of being transparent, person to person, distributed, decentralized —all of that. But it's not just about monetary transactions. It does a lot more than that." He looked back down at the app he had pulled up on his phone. "Look, guys—I think we should move forward with this. I recommend we start sending the money we make to the Collaborative Cloud and do most of our financial stuff via this app."

Blockchain: Additional Details

As the JALL group helped illustrate, the blockchain technology that supports the Collaborative Cloud offers several advantages:

- **No power plays**: Because the network is distributed among its users, no one person, company, or entity can take it down. Only a majority of over 50% of users would be able to alter a blockchain, which is highly unlikely. Since there is no controlling company or institution in the middle, the applications are censorship-resistant, so people can keep on using them independently of government approval.

---

[103] One of the main mechanisms that allows for this is the DiD, a decentralized ID, which is described in the "How Does it Work" section.

- **More secure transactions**: As Jake helped illustrate through the sugar packets, the nature of a blockchain is more secure than a centralized system. Because blockchain uses consensus and nodes to create immutability, the details of a transaction can't be fudged or lost. Also, for a transaction to go through, the technology needs to be able to identify that each member of the transaction has sufficient funds to make it go through. There are no "bad checks" in a blockchain transaction. Users can trust one another in transactions— not because of composite data, like reviews and credit scores, but because of the mechanisms of the blockchain itself. As entrepreneur and venture capitalist Adam Draper said, "The blockchain... replaces third-party trust with mathematical proof that something happened."[104]

- **Immutable**: Any new bit of data added to a blockchain—that is, any new block—is permanently time-stamped and recorded. This record is shared with every user of the blockchain. As a result, there is a permanent and unforgeable register of who owns what and who transacts what, secured by cryptography. This public registry is shared across the entire blockchain network. We used to rely on institutions like banks to provide security for our financial exchanges, but because of the immutable, public, and cryptographically secured nature of a blockchain, that security is provided solely through technology. Many of the problems that used to be caused by the presence of humans—like mistakes, coercion, oppression, injustice, embezzlement, and so on—are simply a nonissue on a blockchain technological network.

- **More secure data**: Although it's not completely immune to hacking, the linked-hash mechanism, along with the fact that so many eyes

---

[104] Marisa Kendall, "Whatever Happened to Bitcoin? Adam Draper Has the Answer," *The Mercury News*, November 12, 2016, https://www.mercurynews.com/2016/11/11/whatever-happened-to-bitcoin-adam-draper-has-the-answer.

are helping to monitor the presence of potential bad actors, makes a blockchain database far more secure than typical centralized systems. Data is not kept on a central server but in the user's own digital wallet. Every bit of information is encrypted and can only be decrypted by the user's private key (associated with the DiD) so even if data were to be grabbed, it would still be unusable to the hacker. (We'll explain this more when we discuss DiDs.)

- **Transparent**: Unlike an empire such as Facebook, which closely guards their company secrets (to the possible detriment of their users), some networks that use blockchain technology, such as Bitcoin, Ethereum, and Cardano, are open source and transparent. Anyone can participate. Also, every transaction has identifying information about the user and sender.[105] Although this information is encrypted for security, the identifying information cannot be erased.

- **Person to person**: One reason blockchain technology is said to be so disruptive is because of how it negates the need for "middleman organizations" to mitigate transactions. Blockchain technology enables near-instant global cryptocurrency transaction exchanges, with very little fees. In the past, if Alex's mother wanted to send her father in Samoa money from the US, she would have needed to go through a wire exchange, paying fees to the organization arranging it. Now Alex's mother could send that money easily, cheaply, and near instantly via a blockchain network. This Person to Person network is good for more than just financial exchanges—it will also allow for the rich Person to Person community exchanges described in this book.

Blockchain is the most important concept to grasp as we move forward with the Collaborative Cloud. However, it's actually a derivative technology,

---

[105] This information can be as little as a digital-wallet-address. This is what is called pseudo-anonymity.

made possible by other tech. Let's turn now to Web3—the "parent" that begat the blockchain child.

Web3

The easiest way to explain Web3 is in contrast to Web2.

Web2 encompasses most of the centralized platforms we're familiar with on the internet—sites like Facebook, Google, Uber, Amazon, and so on. In our narrative, Web2 was illustrated by the large sugar container. In Web2, the company controls the site and all its mechanisms; for instance, Facebook is in control of all the algorithms it produces. If a Web2 company suffers an outage or a hack, the entire system is "down." Web2 profits off its users by collecting their data and using that data for marketing purposes. The code for most Web2 platforms is closed.

In contrast to this, **Web3 is *decentralized*.** There is no one person or company that controls it or governs it; instead, the network is created and facilitated by millions of users using millions of computers. As discussed, this makes it far more stable because if anyone attempted to tamper with it, they would actually have to take down a network with millions of different nodes—rather than attacking one centralized system. Web3's code is open source, which means there are no secrets: its mechanisms are visible to everyone. Finally, Web3 is managed and facilitated by its users. Rather than being a commodity that is manipulated for financial gain, Web3 users are in the driver's seat. We can think of Web3 as being a more evolved Web2. Cryptography is the revolutionary technology making Web3 possible.[106]

In October of 2021, Naval Ravikant tweeted this elegant description, comparing Web2 and Web3:

---

[106] Kasperky's definition of Cryptography: "the study of secure communications techniques that allow only the sender and intended recipient of a message to view its contents... Here, data is encrypted using a secret key, and then both the encoded message and secret key are sent to the recipient for decryption." From "Cryptography Definition," Kapersky, accessed January 30, 2022, https://www.kaspersky.com /resource-center/definitions/what-is-cryptography.

Web 2: Users are the data, corporations own the platform, and the code is closed.

Web 3: Users own their data, contributors own the platform, and the code is open.[107]

Web3 can operate the way it does through revolutionary cryptography technology. It is composed of dApps instead of classic centralized applications like Uber or Instagram.[108]

So—what is a dApp?

dApps

In Web2, we have "websites." In Web3, we have "dApps," and the collected body of dApps that exist form Web3.[109]

dApps are decentralized applications or programs that exist and run on a network of computers instead of a central server. In many ways, they function just like many of the apps or websites we already use on a daily basis, but they are outside the purview and control of a single authority.

Because Web3 dApps don't run via a centralized server, there is no need for a company or corporation to centralize power. The dApps are just there: transparently spread across thousands of computers across the internet. Each one of those individual machines is called a "node," together forming the network's foundation.

---

[107] Naval Ravikant, Naval, Twitter, October 12, 2021, https://twitter.com/naval/status/1448089151 677603846.

[108] A deep dive into the history of Web1 moving to Web3 can be found in Nader Dabit, "What is Web3? The Decentralized Internet of the Future Explained," freeCodeCamp, September 8, 2021, https://www .freecodecamp.org/news/what-is-web3.

[109] Another major technology underpinning Web3 and enabled by cryptography is interplanetary file system (IPFS) which deals with file and data storage. This would be capable of replacing the Google drive, database and web server of Web2.

The Collaborative Cloud DAO itself is a collection of dApps. When Leon, Jake, Alex, and Lana register on the Collaborative Cloud, they will be offered a menu of dApps to attach to their accounts, such as a dApp to track their Collaborative Points, their Future Value, their financial accounts, and so on. We'll explore this more later in the chapter.

Many blockchain networks—Ethereum and Cardano, for example—are building smart contracts *on top* of their blockchain network to allow for a richer feature set.

Smart Contracts

A smart contract is basically a tiny computer program that is built into the code of a dApp and executed by the nodes of the blockchain network. Its job is to automate processes that fall into the specific conditions determined by the contract. A smart contract can automate many of the administrative tasks that used to fall to lowly interns, for example—or even diligent administrative assistants.

Here's an example to illustrate. In Chapter 6, we saw the JALL group members laboriously calculate their different Collaborative Points, then apply those numbers to their entitled short-term cash, *then* figure out their Future Value, and so on. However, a smart contract would do much of that work for them. For instance, if Leon sends $300 to their collaborative, that $300 could be automatically distributed among the colleagues once they enter their Collaborative Point totals. That automatic distribution is accomplished via a smart contract written into the code. (In fact, we're going to illustrate this very thing in our next section of narration.)

Smart contracts operate via a simple formula: *If/when* _____, *then* _____. For this JALL group example, that formula is programmed with the information the colleagues choose: *If/when* [money is sent to the JALL brand asset], *then* [it should be distributed according to Collaborative Point percentages].

In sum, **a smart contract is a self-executing contract with the terms of the agreement between market participants directly written into lines of code**. The code controls the execution, and transactions are trackable and irreversible.

And who are the people using these dApps and smart contracts? The users of a blockchain system will all operate with a DiD: our final tool to discuss.

DiDs

A DiD is a decentralized digital ID that is required to engage on the Collaborative Cloud (and indeed, any blockchain network). Here, too, it is helpful to contrast the DiD with its Web2 counterpart: a username and password.

On most Web2 platforms, the central organization holds all the user's data. For instance, if you are an Amazon Prime customer, Amazon holds not only your username and password, but also your financial information, your buying history, your search history, your reviews, and so on. That's a lot of data about you that you're entrusting to a behemoth corporation.

This is problematic for two reasons: number one, the corporation holding your data is able to use your data to manipulate you. Not only can they manipulate your buying habits, but—as reports about Facebook have revealed—they can even manipulate your beliefs.[110]

Number two, when all your data is held by these corporations, the information you trust to them is vulnerable if *any* of those organizations is hacked or targeted. There have been so many data breaches that many websites exist just to help people determine whether or not their information has been compromised. The website haveibeenpwned.com records 11,595,885,292 leaked accounts, as of October 2021. Facebook alone accounts for 509,458,528 of

---

[110] Ariel Zilber, "Mark Zuckerberg 'Resisted Changes' after Facebook Officials Warned of 'Toxic' Algorithm," *Daily Mail*, September 16, 2021, https://www.dailymail.co.uk/news/article-9993981/Mark-Zuckerberg-resisted-changes-Facebook-officials-warned-toxic-algorithm.html.

those data breaches.[111] That's over *11 billion* leaks from companies that claim to keep our data safe. (They don't.)

DiDs attempt a solution to this problem. Using cryptography, they function as a digital identity wallet, holding all of your information inside. Every time you go to use a new platform, you choose what forms of ID—called "claims"—you will take out of your wallet to share with the platform. Everything else remains safely hidden within the wallet.

Here's an example. Let's say a certain site wants to verify that you are over eighteen before giving you access. A typical Web2 site would request (and store) your birthday. Even worse, some might actually read your photo ID and store that information. However, a DiD would protect all that private information. With a DiD, your wallet would submit the claim "Yes, I'm older than eighteen." The site could then transparently verify that claim against an authoritative third party (like the government, for example).[112] In this case, no information except the fact that you are older than eighteen is shared with the website, and the website has more certainty over the veracity of the claim than if they had just asked for your birthday.

Your own key to this DiD identity wallet is essentially a hash: a very long collection of letters and numbers. That key is the only thing that anyone will be able to see of you on the internet, unless you opt to open the wallet and provide additional information about yourself. That string of numbers and letters is the public key that verifies the veracity of what is *in* your wallet, while at the same time keeping the information inside private. Your DiD would allow you to buy and sell, giving full assurance to your transaction partners that you are "good" for the transaction, while still keeping most of your personal information private.

The JALL group members would be prompted to create a DiD when registering on the Collaborative Cloud. When logging in, the cloud would

---

[111] You can use that website to check if your email or phone number has been compromised and is found in one of the leaked databases.

[112] The third party only validates if the claim is true or false; it does not provide any other data.

prompt them to "connect my DiD." If it was Leon signing in, he could then choose to share his alias (like a username) to the cloud, which would identify him as he engaged on the network with others—for instance, his Collaborative Cloud alias might be CptnLion. Then the group members would choose the dApps they want to use (the collection of sub-applications) in operating their collaborative.

The main advantage of using a DiD is that it enables users to avoid the major privacy problems generated by data leaks and data misuse that characterize so many Web2 apps.

The Technical Stack: Quick Definitions

- **Web3** is a more evolved version of the internet as we currently know it. It is made of decentralized apps (dApps) instead of websites. Users own their data, contributors own the platform, and the code is open.
- **dApps** are decentralized applications or programs that exist and run on a network of computers and on the users' own browsers.
- **Blockchain** is made possible by the same cryptography that makes up Web3 and creates an immutable, secure, and transparent ledger of transactions. Rather than being managed by a central server, blockchain is maintained across many computers linked in a person to person network.
- **Smart contracts** are self-executing contracts with the terms of the agreement between market participants directly written into lines of code. They operate according to a formula, "*If/when [this happens], then [this happens.]*"
- **DiDs** are decentralized digital IDs that help keep data private and are used to engage in a Web3 environment, such as the Collaborative Cloud.
- A **DAO** is a decentralized autonomous organization. It's an organization that operates according to rules embedded within its transparent code, it is controlled by its own members, and it is not influenced by a central government. Both the

UOV and the Collaborative Cloud are DAOs. Each collaborative that is created in the Collaborative Cloud becomes a sub-DAO in the main Collaborative Cloud DAO.

On the Blockchain Revolution

That's a lot of new technological ideas to digest—especially if you're new to the blockchain world. But whether it's new information or whether you've been on the blockchain wagon ever since it got started in 2008, this major world development won't be disappearing anytime soon. In fact, it's just getting started.

The impact of Bitcoin and the blockchain technology in general is compared to that of the internet or even that of the invention of the printing press.[113] It is regarded as the separation of money and state because it does not rely on any central authority to wield control over people (at least in terms of data collection and financial control). Instead, blockchain puts that control in the hands of the people themselves.

For the state, this separation has caused uneasiness. Governments and governing authorities around the world are scrambling to determine the best way to handle blockchain technology. One technological pioneer, Naval Ravikant, has noted, "Nation states that are used to imposing capital controls will face a quandary: ban cryptocurrencies and live in the technology dustbin; enable them, and this virus—this religion, this protocol—will enable the free flow of money and language, along with packets, around the globe." This free flow of money, language, and assets across all borders offers incredible opportunities to build a world that allows for greater connection, freedom, and quality of life.

---

[113] For an excellent read comparing the Bitcoin revolution to the reformation that took place in Europe in the 16th the 17th century, check out Tuur Demeester's report, "The Bitcoin Reformation." Tuur Demeester, "The Bitcoin Reformation," Adamant Research, https://bitcoinwords.github.io/assets/papers/investment/Tuur%20Demeester%20-%20The%20Bitcoin%20Reformation.pdf.

Granted, with any new technology, there will be people who seek to abuse it for their own personal gain or power. The printing press, after all, was used to print *Mein Kampf,* even as it was used to print editions of the Bible, the *Complete Works of William Shakespeare,* and many other sacred works. However, technology and human evolution should not be halted simply because of those bad actors. People may misuse blockchain technology, but that reality in and of itself does not make the technology evil. In fact, this technology has the power to create a more distributed and equitable society, one that allows us greater rights and a louder voice in determining our own destinies. What's important to remember, for all those who wish to evolve as humans, is that we must harness this powerful new tool in meaningful and mindful ways.

Consider the point made eloquently by Allen Farrington in his essay "Bitcoin is Venice":

> Bitcoin is often framed as "competing" with fiat currency. This is true in a sense but I fear there is a rhetorical danger of invoking the wrong kind of "competition." It is not a fight, for example. There is no conflict. Bitcoin is not trying to damage or sabotage its opponents, because it isn't trying anything and it knows no opponents. It has no awareness whatsoever of who might oppose it or why. It is simply an alternative; an exit valve; an opt-out. It is competing only insofar as it is proving to be a far superior alternative. It is not a sword for Theseus to fight the Minotaur, but a thread to follow to exit the labyrinth. Bitcoin is Ariadne.[114]

The ecosystem we are unveiling in this book could not exist if it weren't for the blockchain technology. Granted, the technology required for the Collaborative Cloud and UOV is new and even nascent (from a technical,

---

[114] Allen Farrington, "Bitcoin Is Venice," Medium, September 17, 2021, https://allenfarrington.medium.com/bitcoin-is-venice-8414dda42070.

legal, and societal standpoint); however, this doesn't diminish the potential of what is to come. There is no stopping an evolutionary environment built around experimentation.

Here's the takeaway: the technological tools are there to facilitate the Person to Person environment. Most people using the Collaborative Cloud will not need to know about the smart contracts or the blockchain technology enabling it; they'll simply use dApps like the ones we're about to describe in the JALL narrative, such as a cash account, investment account, and so on. (They might not even know what they're using is called a "dApp.") The most important point to take away from this section on technology is simply that there are legal and technical frameworks to support the Person to Person machinations we're describing—whether or not you choose to "geek out" about them, as Leon does.

Still, perhaps this "brave new world" strikes you as unnecessary, or gives you pause. Is this really the best way forward? Is this really the only way to continue the journey toward greater quality of life? Could it potentially create a dystopia?

Of course, it's not the *only* way. Surely there are many ways to invest in greater quality of life. However, we believe the mechanisms described in these chapters do more to extend quality of life to the maximum amount of people than anything else we've discovered. At the same time, they provide a way to step out from underneath oppressive organizations that do much to hinder people's quality of life. In fact, the path that we are currently on in our use of technology seems more dystopian than the alternative we're proposing. Megacorporations like Meta, Google, and Amazon, which currently assert dominance and control over the internet, could not wield that power in a decentralized world. People are too little aware that the worst-case scenario is already in the making. So why not explore the enormous potential of a technological landscape that allows for greater security, freedom, and equality? In essence, these tools help widen the crack in the box and give people a chance to explore lives of greater freedom outside it.

With that in mind, let's check back in with the JALL group, who have some inhibitions of their own.

Peering into the Rabbit Hole

"So are you guys game?" Leon asked. "Should we set it up?"

Jake looked at his watch. "What does that involve? Are we just doing a quick app download? I have class starting in fifteen and still need to go grab my books."

"Um...no," Leon admitted. "You have to set up a DiD to interact on Web3. And you also have to accept the email invites I sent you to affirm you're all colleagues of our JALL Collaborative."

"I have to go too," Lana said. "I have Psych of Leadership. Plus, I still don't feel like I've fully wrapped my head around this. I want to talk about it more before we all commit. Is that okay?" She began gathering things into her backpack and preparing to leave.

"Yeah, of course," Leon said. "Meet at our dorm room at, what...sevenish? Alex—will you be out of your black holes class by then?"

Alex leaned back and stretched. "Introduction to Galactic and Extragalactic Astrophysics? Yes indeed."

"Alright. Seven o'clock it is," Leon responded.

Jake put his hand in the middle of the table and motioned for the others to do the same. "Ready? Three, two, one—BREAK!"

Lana grinned. "We are nerds," she said.

EXPLORE FURTHER

If you'd like to learn more, discuss this content with others, or access tools for your own application, go to the interactive section of the book using this QR code.

CHAPTER NINE

THE COLLABORATIVE CLOUD

A Platform for Collaborative Finance

Changing the world is about creating an engine to allow for people to change it themselves.

—Charles Hoskinson, founder of Cardano
and co-founder of Ethereum

At 7:15, Jake got a call from Lana. "Hey, what's up? You and Alex still coming?" he asked. "Leon is frothing at the mouth to get us hooked up with this Collaborative Cloud." He paused and listened. "What's wrong? Are you okay?"

Leon looked up sharply. "What's up with Lana?"

Jake waved his arm at Leon, shushing him. "Yeah. Yeah, we can totally come to your place. No problem. Okay, see you soon."

Leon perked up. "We get to go to the girls' dorm? I've always wanted to go a girls' dorm."

Jake hung up and grinned sympathetically at Leon. "Aw, buddy. You've never been to a girls' dorm before?"

Leon bristled. "I mean, I sort of have." He looked sheepishly at Jake. "In my mind. I imagine it's all very plush and nice-smelling." Jake laughed and grabbed his jacket.

When they arrived at Lana's dorm, Alex greeted them at the door and began walking with them upstairs. "So, what's going on with Lana?" Jake asked. "She sounded super depressed."

"She read an article," Alex said, and raised their eyebrows significantly.

"Oh?" Jake asked, confused. "She read...an article? That's why she sounded like her dog had just died?"

"She was trying to rally to come to your place, but she kept vacillating between despair and rage. Every time she picked up her jacket she would end up throwing it at something. Ha!" Alex laughed. "I finally just told her we should have you guys here."

Leon was looking curiously around him at the beige hallways. "So far, I'm a little underwhelmed, to be honest."

"This must have been some article," Jake mused. When they got to Lana's room, they found her sitting on her bed, grumpily munching popcorn.

"Hi guys," she said dismally. "Thanks for coming here. I was trying to rally, but...Anyway, sorry to be a diva."

"We don't mind coming here," Jake responded. "Where's Ashley?" Ashley was Lana's roommate.

"Rehearsal," Lana said, waving a hand dismissively. She sighed heavily.

Leon seemed pleased as he took in the décor in Lana's room. "Relatively plush," he observed quietly to Jake. "And it smells like girl. They even have a plant!" he whispered excitedly.

Jake sat down on the bed next to Lana and took her hand. "Babe. *What* was this article? Was it about...the destruction of the coral reefs? Human trafficking? Uyghur camps?"

"It was basically as bad," Lana said gloomily. "Did you know that Warren

Buffett paid 0.1 percent income tax last year? He gained over $24 billion in wealth and paid a measly $23.7 million! *Zero-point-one percent.*"

She blinked at Jake, waiting for his outrage to match hers. Instead, he looked back at her with a puzzled expression. This was not what he had expected from Lana. But that was turning out to be a relatively common experience for him.

Lana tried to emphasize her point. "Do you want to know what I'm paying in taxes working at the café? Like 15 percent! How is it legally okay that schmucks like me are dutifully paying 15 percent out of our itty-bitty paychecks, and Warren Buffett is only paying 0.1 percent??" She tapped the printed-out article vehemently. "And they all do that! Bezos, 0.98 percent. Bloomberg, 1.3 percent. Freaking Elon Musk, 3 percent."[115]

"Bastards," Leon said gravely, with just a hint of irony. Alex nodded soberly. Lana waited for a similar response from Jake. She cleared her throat loudly.

"Assholes!" he finally ejected.

"I know!" Lana said to him, glad that he was finally showing some outrage. "And it's *legal.* They never cash out any of their assets, so they have almost no income to declare—I mean, compared to the wealth they're actually creating. They live off loans they take out to fund their lifestyles, which are collateralized with all their fancy assets, so then they get tax *credits* for all those loans! Which means they pay even less tax. And some of the loans are taken out from their own companies, meaning they're just paying themselves back!"

"Seriously?" Jake asked. "Can I see that?" He picked up the article on the bed. It was highlighted and annotated with vigorous curses.

"I read it too," Alex verified. "The research is all legit. It's pretty crazy."

Lana huffed furiously. "Anyway. I basically never want to pay taxes again. Why should I pay my fair share if none of the wealthiest people in the world

---

[115] The article that Lana is reading is "The Secret IRS Files." See Jesse Eisinger, Jeff Ernsthausen and Paul Kiel, "The Secret IRS Files: Trove of Never-before-Seen Records Reveal How the Wealthiest Avoid Income Tax," ProPublica, June 8, 2021, accessed October 11, 2021, https://www.propublica.org/article/the-secret-irs-files-trove-of-never-before-seen-records-reveal-how-the-wealthiest-avoid-income-tax.

are paying theirs? Besides, our government seems perfectly happy to just print as much money as they want anyway. Why should anyone bother paying taxes if we're just going to keep on raising the debt ceiling indefinitely?"

Alex grinned at Leon and Jake. "I love that this woman has gone from being a socialist to a libertarian in the span of an article." Lana huffed at this. "It's okay," Alex said. "You contain multitudes. Here—I'll make us all hot chocolate. Hot chocolate makes everything better." They pulled several mugs off of Lana's bookshelf and began ripping open cocoa packets that they took out of a plastic container.

"Um—if I could interrupt—" Leon said. "Lana, I really think you're going to love this Collaborative Cloud app I found to manage our money." He looked for a spot to sit down and moved tentatively toward a purple suede beanbag.

Lana sighed. "Leon, I know you want us to plug into the app, but I'm not quite finished ranting about the billionaires."

"That's the thing, though—it's going to enable us to do some of the tricks that the billionaires do!" Leon said excitedly. Gingerly, he sat down in the beanbag.

"Wait—really?" Lana asked.

"*Yes*, it levels the playing field. I can explain all of it," Leon said. "You guys all created a DiD this afternoon, right? And you got my email invites?" Changing his mind about the beanbag, Leon heaved himself up and went over to the desk swivel chair.

"I did all that," Jake said. "But... I don't know, man. It's a banking app, but it's not a bank? I'm not sure it sounds legit. Maybe we should just stick with what we've been doing."

"We *can't* keep doing what we're doing," Leon said. "It's just not sustainable. Look: we've developed a good system for the short-term money stuff. Cash comes in; we figure out our relative points and the draw and all that; then I send everyone their money to their Venmo accounts. But all the money for our future investments—that $300 we set aside—that's just sitting in my personal checking account. And so is the money for each of our draws, and the money I use to pay for our operational costs. It's all just in my own account. I mean, I've set it aside—I'm not about to *do* anything with it. But that doesn't mean I *couldn't* just take it from you all." Across the room, Alex snapped their fingers in agreement and nodded, remembering the conversation they'd had with Leon about his dad in the art room.

Jake shrugged. "True, I guess. But we trust you."

Leon waved off the comment as though it were irrelevant. "But I *could*; that's the point. Besides, I don't want the burden of being the group's financial steward. I'd rather focus on the IT stuff. Me having that money in my account, is not good for anyone."

Alex, who had comfortably settled in the beanbag after distributing hot cocoa, spoke up. "I agree. We need to get Leon free from the burden of managing all the financial stuff."

"It's only $300," Jake said. "If you don't want the responsibility of it, you could just send it to someone else in our group, and we'd hang on to it."

"Buddy, that's no way to scale," Leon protested. "We're going to have more money to deal with soon, and it's just a bad idea for it to all be sitting in someone's personal account. Plus—what about our Excel spreadsheets? Our points, our QOL scores, our Future Value—all those numbers are just plugged in on Excel right now. Wouldn't it be nice to have something that could house all that with more clarity and transparency?"

"Maybe we do the app for the points and the quality of life," Lana suggested, "and we just stick with our regular old bank accounts for the money. I've been working on setting us up as an LLC, so we could create a shared company account for our investment money. That way, we'd all have access to it, and Leon wouldn't have the burden of all our group money sitting in his account."

"Really?" Leon asked, surprised. "You're setting us up as an LLC?"

"Yes," Lana said, with a mixture of pride and woe. "Partly to earn myself some unrealized potential and partly because I *felt*—past tense, *felt*—very strongly that we should be paying taxes on the cash we all withdrew."

"Former socialist," Alex said matter-of-factly.

"Well, I was listening to a lot of Bernie Sanders YouTube videos, okay?" Lana said. "But now—" She jabbed her finger at the article. "I don't want to pay taxes anymore. So maybe I'll stop with the LLC process. Unless it would help us to have the company account?"

Leon reached over and took some of Lana's popcorn, crunching it thoughtfully. "Well—it would still be awesome to get set up as an LLC because it makes the most sense. It would limit our liability, legally, and it would help us streamline things with our advertisers. And if we did have a company account, I could use it for the cash we need for our day-to-day operations, like what I pay to our video promoters. An LLC company account would allow me to do that rather than pay those bills out of my personal account."

Lana sighed. "Fine. I'll do it for you. And I'll do it for the unrealized potential, but not for the IRS. So, in that case, does that mean we don't need the Collaborative Cloud app?"

"We *do* still need the cloud. Ideally, we'd only keep the bare minimum needed in that traditional company account. That means we should use the cloud for everything else—our long-term investment money, our Future Value—or, in your words, our 'unrealized potential.' I've heard my dad complain about how much of a pain company accounts are, practically. Every investment move has to be a group decision, and then you get power plays because the people with the most money or power get to be the ones who make the decisions."

"I don't see that happening with our group," Jake said. "Our whole setup and our Collaborative Agreement protects us against people making power plays. Besides, wouldn't it be a good thing that we make every investment decision together?"

"That's easy enough now, as a group of four, but what if we grow? And what happens when we graduate or someone moves on? What happens to all the money *they* helped contribute to the shared account? How would we pay them out? Or what about if we do grow and make a lot more money, like we're hoping, and it's time to cash in on our Future Value—how is that going to get distributed? And when?"

Alex leaned forward. "Is this Collaborative Cloud going to help us resolve all these issues?"

"Yes, I think so," Leon said. "It will hold all of the value that we've generated, which is kind of like a company account—it's going to act as the repository of the money we've made, instead of my bank account. Which, frankly, makes *me* feel better. But because it's automatically distributed among us, we still have autonomy over what we do with it. We can reinvest it in ourselves, but each of us also has the freedom to invest in other projects. If and when one of us has to leave the group to go do something else, the value we generated goes with us. It's more fair; it's more flexible; it's more stable...It's just better."

Long-Term Investments:
The Case against the Current Models

In Chapter 6, we saw how Jake, Leon, Lana, and Alex were able to figure out a collaborative financial environment that worked for their day-to-day collaboration. They were able to use the collaborative finance talks to help separate power and money; as a result, they were able to make the transfer of effort into money an open, fair, and human process. They honored each person's contribution, sought to meet each person's needs, and helped fuel each person's quality of life.

This process, however, only captures that energy in the short term. To capture energy as it translates into finances for the long term, different tools are needed. Alex and Leon began exploring some of the possibilities of reinventing private property in Chapter 7, and we'll return to the concept of the Universal Ownership Vault at the end of this chapter. But there are other problems with the current options available for long-term financial investment as well.

In most current systems, the long-term store of human energy and effort is dehumanized. It shows up largely in two ways:

- **The balance sheet of companies**: Think about how we call people "human resources," for example. People's effort and energy—their hours working late at night, after getting the kids to bed; their effort to complete the project on time for the sake of their team; their risk of injury as they take on challenging physical work—is measured as a *resource*. The Oxford Languages dictionary defines "resource" as "a stock or supply of money, materials, staff, and other assets that can be drawn on by a person or organization in order to function effectively." Nowhere in the definition of "resource" is there an acknowledgment of the striving human that produces the assets used by the organizations they serve. "Human resources" are harnessed for an institution that ultimately centralizes wealth for the sole benefit of a few shareholders. Additionally, the hierarchical layers in most institutions create a great distance between the producer of the effort and the one wielding its power. This distance between those who produce the effort and those who wield the most organizational power can easily lead to several gradations of exploitation. It also fuels an overall disregard of people's quality of life. This does not help foster human connection or quality of life for the vast majority of people.

But what about people who don't work for a profit-driven company? What about entrepreneurs, or Uber drivers like Jake, or gamblers, or people who work for the government or nonprofits? These people are not dehumanized via a company balance sheet. However, we still see their situation as problematic. Anyone who gets paid in government-issued currency experiences the second dehumanizing effect of the current financial systems, represented by:

- **The country's GDP**: A country's GDP is used to fund our current currency system (fiat)—dollars, euros, pesos, yen, and so on.

Usually, these currencies are disconnected from a physical resource, like the gold standard. Instead, the value of currency is established by the country's own set of institutions, like central banks. Those institutions broker global-scale deals behind closed doors, which serve the needs of an even smaller set of individuals. The result is a lack of transparency, a lack of person to person connection, and certainly a loss of personal agency. There are many stories of people's wealth evaporating when a country's GDP goes up in smoke. For instance, in 2013, one US dollar was equal to 6.29 Venezuelan bolivars. In 2019, however, due to Venezuela's hyperinflation, one US dollar was equal to *20,197* bolivars. For many Venezuelans, their life's savings—the representation of years' worth of hard work —simply disappeared.

The first step toward freedom is better money.[116] Bitcoin and other digital currencies might form a possible solution—and, indeed, those are an integral component of the solution we propose. Digital currencies like bitcoin have value that is determined independent of any country's GDP and does not need to be facilitated by a middleman, like a bank or credit card company. Because bitcoin cannot be coerced by government, its value is the pure representation of the market. It's flexible to use even across country borders, and also cheaper because the middleman companies aren't taking a cut. Also, payments are guaranteed by the transparency of the system, so it's impossible to "double spend." In other words, no one can pay with a bad check; transactions are secure. However, digital currency by itself does not prevent dehumanizing effects or corruption. That's why it's necessary to consider a method of arranging business transactions that will incentivize fair play and Person to Person interactions.

---

[116] *The Fiat Standard* and *The Bitcoin Standard* make a strong case for this. See Saifedean Ammous, *The Fiat Standard: The Debt Slavery Alternative to Human Civilization* (The Saif House: 2021); Saifedean Ammous, *The Bitcoin Standard: The Decentralized Alternative to Central Banking* (Hoboken, NJ: Wiley, 2018).

But let's say you're not particularly concerned about the dehumanizing nature of being paid in dollars, euros, or any other sort of currency. You're mostly just interested in getting *paid* and building your business. In that case, you'll face the same dilemma that Leon was confronted with: do you store the long-term investment money in a company account or a personal account? Here, too, we run into some issues.

- **A company account is problematic** for some of the reasons Leon identified: it's practically cumbersome, requiring that a majority consensus be achieved before any investment decision. Alternately, a few people at the top—those with the most money and/or power—get to say where the money goes, which results in a power play that ignores the rest of the people whom the decision affects. If and when a shareholder wants to pull out of the business, it's a complicated and lengthy process to pay that person out. Even in a best-case scenario, like if a group seeks to honor all members by requiring a 100% consensus for decisions related to the company account, there can be problems. A single holdout can tyrannize the rest of the group by withholding their "Aye," preventing growth by systematically rejecting any investment proposal. Finally, since value is captured in a typical company via shares, there's no good or easy way to leave that company other than cashing out your shares and paying taxes.

Although a company account will be necessary to legally represent the collaborative, we believe it should contain just enough to handle day-to-day transactions: buying goods, paying suppliers, ensuring there's enough liquid cash to facilitate the daily operations, and so on. A **Collaborative Checking Account** would receive all money coming in from customers and hold the money used in the draw. However, it would not hold any group investment money. In our narrative, this is the LLC company account that Lana is working to set up; it would hold the $100 they need to pay their monthly fees to their video promoters. This group account is not geared for growth;

it is mainly used to pay bills. However, as an investment account for larger, long-term goals, the company account poses problems.

So why not just keep all the money in a trustworthy individual's account, as Jake suggested? That would be called a personal account, but that, too, poses practical issues.

- **A personal account is problematic** for tax reasons. If all the company's money were deposited into a person's individual account, their personal taxes would explode. This is especially true in Europe, where the middle and top tax brackets are expected to pay over 50% in taxes. Although a personal account might allow for greater flexibility, no businessperson would be able to get rich by funneling all their company's profits into a personal account. Also, as Leon suggested, a personal account poses the issue of potential power plays: the person owning the account has the ultimate decision power.

If both the company and personal accounts pose problems, then what is the best way for a collaborative to arrange long-term investment money? What about Future Value and Collaborative Points? Neither a personal nor a company account can handle those needs well.

The Collaborative Cloud seeks to enable tools that will accommodate those needs in a way that allows working groups to function efficiently but also enables individuals to operate with freedom and autonomy. Not only will these tools allow for the separation of effort and money, through the representation of Collaborative Points; they also support a Future Value feature, provide total transparency, and allow for radical personal agency and independence in financial dealings, even within a collaboration. It also opens up its users to the network of people around the globe who—like them—want to collaborate and invest in one another, person to person.

ELEMENTS OF THE COLLABORATIVE CLOUD

"Have I convinced you?" Leon asked the others. "Are you down to try this Collaborative Cloud?"

Jake, Lana, and Alex all looked at each other. They seemed to come to silent agreement. Alex looked at Leon. "Let's do it."

"Okay!" Leon said, excited. "Then all of you need to accept the invites I sent you to join our collaborative. Oh—and you should also have gotten an email asking you to cosign the creation of the JALL brand asset. That way, we all have access to it."[117]

Jake pulled up his email. He read aloud. "Leon Kilroy has invited you to join the JALL Collaborative as a colleague." He began typing into his phone, following the instructions on the screen. Alex and Lana pulled out their phones and opened Leon's invitation.

"Now it wants me to sign in with my new DiD..." Jake observed.

"That's the decentralized ID you told us to set up, right?" Lana asked. Leon nodded. "I feel so hip with the crypto lingo," Lana commented to Alex. "Look at me, with my DiD..."

"She don't tiptoe with the crypto, gets it easily..." Alex rapped. Lana grinned and pumped her fist.

"Okay—once it's loaded, you should see three different accounts pop up on your home screen," Leon instructed. "Here, I can show you how it looks on my account." The other three paused and looked at Leon's phone. "So here..." Leon said, clicking through his home page. "There's our collaborative that I created: The JALL Collaborative. That's our landing page for doing all our Collaborative Points stuff. And connected to that is our brand asset... That's where we send the money we make from the YouTube videos. I've already sent it the $300 that we decided to set aside the other day."

---

[117] When co-signing the creation of their collaborative, each group member would affirm that they are the JALL collaborative and have the right to administer and use the DAO. They would also likely submit their Collaborative Agreement and register their brand.

"How does that work?" Alex asked.

"After we figure out our Collaborative Points and how much money we want to budget for growth and do the draw, et cetera, we decide how much money to send to the brand asset. Then, once I send the money, the app automatically distributes that money to our different accounts, based on our Collaborative Points."[118]

"Huh. So we'll still do a normal Contribution Session before getting into the Collaborative Cloud?" Lana asked.

"Right," Leon said. "Because that's how we're going to determine our Collaborative Point percentages and how much money we want to save long term, how much we need in short-term cash, and so on. We have to plug all that information into the Collaborative Cloud so that it knows what to do."

"Mine has finished downloading," Jake said. He pulled up the app. "Hey—I see that JALL Collaborative screen too! Cool."

"Yep, you'll all see that JALL Collaborative screen. Okay now…" He leaned over and looked at Jake's phone. "You need to pick which dApps you want to use. So choose 'Manage My Points,' and 'Accounts,' and 'Contribution Session.' That should be good for now." Jake followed his instructions. Leon then clicked on the Accounts app, which brought up a new screen with three options: Free Cash Account, Investment Account, and Asset Account. The other three leaned in and peered down at Jake's phone.

"Woah. Nifty," Lana said.

"Sick, I see those three accounts too," Alex remarked.

"You'll even see some money in the Investment Account, once we all enter our Collaborative Point percentages," Leon said. "Okay—let's start with the Free Cash Account. That's probably the most straightforward."

"*Free* cash?" Jake asked. "I like the sound of that. 'Would you like some cash for free, good sir?' Why yes, I would."

"It *moves* freely," Leon said. "But you're right; 'free cash' has a nice ring to it."

---

[118] This automatic transfer occurs via a smart contract.

The Free Cash Account

Leon took another handful of popcorn and munched it while talking. "So right now, our payments from YouTube advertisers are all direct-deposited into my normal checking account. And after that happens, we figure out our points, do our draw, and I can send money to the Venmo accounts of anyone who needs cash in hand—"

"So far, that sounds like what we've been doing already," Jake observed.

"Right, but there's an alternative: you *could* send the money you need in the short term to this Free Cash Account rather than your Venmo. The Free Cash Account is almost exactly like a checking account or our Venmo accounts, except it only holds digital currency. So, remember when we each withdrew a certain amount of money for our short-term needs? Jake, you needed $200 to pay your bills, and Lana wanted $50 for concert tickets. Alex, you needed $100 for—"

"Stardust and moonshine," Alex supplied. Lana stood up and went to the microwave to pop more popcorn.

Leon laughed. "Sure—all of your stardust bills. Anyway, so next month, I could send all of the money you need for the short term to the Free Cash Account. It's like a wallet with digital currency."

"Only digital currency? What if I just want actual dollars?" Jake asked.

"Then I just send money to your Venmo account instead of sending it to the Collaborative Cloud app," Leon said. "Exactly like we've been doing already. So you don't *have* to use the Free Cash Account—but you might want to. You can pay for pretty much anything with digital currency these days."

Alex spoke up. "Speaking of banking apps, I think we should all start using Strike instead of Venmo. The Strike app uses the Bitcoin network so you can pay or receive money in digital currency *or* cash. Like—*any* country's cash, any currency. It's a way to take a stand against the financial system and all the effed-up corporations supporting it. Rebellion without violence! It's pretty badass."

Lana waved her hands. "Hold that thought, Alex; one new app at a time. I'm already struggling to keep up." Alex shrugged and pulled up some music on their laptop. Pink Floyd's "Money" started to play through the speaker over the noise of the popping popcorn in the microwave.

"Good choice, DJ," Leon said approvingly to Alex. Alex winked at him good-naturedly. "Okay, that's pretty much all you need to know about the Free Cash Account," Leon said to the others. "Let's move on to the Investment Account." Lana tossed Leon his own bag of popcorn and put another into the microwave. He looked at it, delighted. "Hot chocolate *and* my own bag of popcorn? I love this place."

> The **Free Cash Account** works like a typical checking account, except it only holds digital currency.[119]

The Investment Account

"Am I doing this right?" Lana picked up her phone again and looked from her screen over to Leon's. "Okay, so far, so good." She studied Leon's screen. "Wait, what's the Investment Account?" Lana asked.

"That's where all of our long-term value is held," Leon responded. "Here, let's get some money in it. We're all good now, right? You've all got the apps pulled up, and you selected those same three dApps I told Jake to get?"

"Yes—we're all registered and we've all cosigned as colleagues," Jake said.

"Okay, good. Then I'm going to start a Contribution Session." He pulled up a new screen on his phone. "This is where we'll enter our points, and short-term cash allotment, and Future Value, and all the rest. So just enter

---

[119] These accounts are also described in brief on our website, for the reader's easy reference. Please see this chapter's QR code.

your Collaborative Points for now. Once you do that, you'll see your own Investment Account has some money in it." They all punched numbers into their phones.

"Cool! My Investment Account has $264 now," Leon said.

"Why do you have $264 in that account?" Alex asked.

"Good question," Leon said. "So first of all—you guys remember how we set aside $300 to invest in our brand? To save toward a future marketing campaign and grow it? Well, I've deposited the $300 that we set aside for that future investment into our JALL brand asset. That $300 makes up our asset's treasury, and whatever is in the treasury is programmed to get distributed into each of our Investment Accounts, based on the Collaborative Point totals that we enter. Since I had 38% of our Collaborative Points, I got an extra $114 in my Investment Account."

"That's 38% of $300," Alex mused. "Got it."

"And when you entered *your* Collaborative Point percentages, the asset should have sent you your own portion. Does that all make sense so far?" Leon asked.

Lana leaned over and studied Leon's phone. "It says $264, Leon. Not $114."

"Right, because my Investment Account *also* holds any money that we decide to set aside for long-term investments. Do you guys remember how I didn't withdraw any of my entitled $150 during the draw? I kept it all. So that $150 is here also."

"You are spinning fast and loose with these numbers, my man," Alex commented.

"I've got mine pulled up," Jake said. "Let's see, I have ... zero dollars in my Free Cash Account. Sounds about right. I entered my Collaborative Point percentage: 21%. So now ... when I go to my Investment Account, I have ... $63! Nice! So that's my portion of the $300?"

"Yes, that's 21% of $300. But hang on, buddy, you still had $3.85 left that you didn't withdraw, remember? That should be added to your Investment

Account, so hang on...I'll send that now." He pulled up a different app. "That's still sitting in my personal checking account, but now that you're good to go on the cloud, I can send it to you."

A new number registered on Jake's screen: $66.85. Jake looked at Leon with a grin. "Dude. I love that you are so committed to making sure I keep track of that $3.85."

"I want you to see what happens to it when it's earmarked for long term!" Leon said.

"My turn," Alex said. "I have zero in the Free Cash Account—all of us have zero in the Free Cash Account, right? Because you just sent the money to our Venmos last time."

Leon nodded. "But next time we do the draw, I could send your short-term money to the Free Cash Account."

Alex held up their phone. "I have 23% of our group's points and $69 in my Investment Account." Alex raised their eyebrows at Leon. "Getting kinky on me, cloud man?"

"Hey, woah—that's 23% of $300, no one's getting kinky. That's what you're entitled to, based on your Collaborative Points. Now here—let's add the $38.46 you set aside..." He typed into his phone. "Boom. It should say $107.46."

Lana had been studying her phone as well. "And 18% means...$54 for me. Woo hoo! Leon, could you send me the $57.69 I didn't withdraw earlier? I want to see that too."

"You got it," Leon said. He looked down at his phone, plugged in some numbers, then looked up. "It should say $111.69 in a second."

"It does!" Lana crowed. "I have some nice, pretty money. Watch out billionaires." She looked up. "Wait, how does this help me take on the billionaires again?"

"Well, for starters, you can't withdraw it," Leon explained. "Once we deposit money into the Investment Account, it's converted to digital value, and it can't be withdrawn. It can only be invested."

"Hold up," Alex said. "Hooooold up. Are you telling me we can't cash this money out?"

"That's right," Leon said. "Because I'm actually sending our money to the Universal Ownership Vault. The money becomes part of the treasury of the SASTO that holds our brand account. So—technically, the money doesn't belong to us anymore. But the Collaborative Cloud registers the value we've contributed and lets us invest with it."

"Aaaaaah!" Alex said. "I effing love this vault, Leon. Although it bugs me a little that we can't withdraw this."

"Um, yes—that actually feels like a *huge* problem to me," Jake commented. "Why would we want to invest in something if we don't get real money out of it?"

"Okay, it *is* real money, first of all," Leon said. "But if you invest it and don't cash it out, then..." he tapped the article that Lana had printed out. "You do things like the billionaires do. If you don't ever withdraw cash from your account, then you don't pay taxes on it. You use the value in your Investment Account to invest in other things. There's also a way to leverage your value as collateral for taking out loans."

"Aaaah!" Lana's eyes opened wide and she grinned. "So *that's* why you said this cloud app is going to make me feel better about the asshole billionaires!"

"Yes!" Leon said. "*And* I think it's so awesome how value is distributed according to our Collaborative Points. Money is personal—and value should be personal. The fact that all the value is split between our different Investment Accounts means we have personal agency over what to do with it."

"Yes, yes," Lana said. "All of the above. But can we go back to the billionaires part?"

"Sure," Leon grinned. "Let me take a sec to explain more about how it works."

How the Investment Account Works

As the JALL crew illustrates, the Investment Account shows value representing the asset's treasury; funds for that treasury come in via two sources:

1. Each colleague's voluntary "long-term cash"—in other words, whatever they opted to *not* withdraw from their entitled money during the Contribution Session.
2. The distribution of the money that they determined to set aside for their company, which is split according to their Collaborative Point percentages. In our narration from Chapter 6, we showed Leon voicing the suggestion to contribute $300 to this "pot," and the others agreed.

Now wait a second, you might be thinking. *What is the point of setting aside money to invest in the business if it ends up being split among individuals anyway?*

This is how we solve the problems posed by the company account versus personal account dilemma. As discussed earlier, a company account is cumbersome, must be ruled by the majority (in which case the minority simply loses), and if a person leaves the business, they simply forfeit whatever money they helped earn that may be stuck in that company account. A personal account is nimbler but can also easily be corrupted.

A third option is required: one in which money can be set aside for future investment in a business but still remains individual and autonomous. That's what we can accomplish via the Investment Account.

Colleagues agree to store the money that is distributed to them via the Investment Account, but they ultimately have a final say over how that money is invested. Most colleagues will likely choose to invest that money in their own collaboration's work—but they can choose to invest in other ways as well. These are *personal* Investment Accounts, meant to aid collaboration and autonomy at the same time.

The **Investment Account** references the value of the asset's treasury in the UOV and allows colleagues to steer that value into investments. It represents long-term cash that a person chooses to voluntarily store (similar to a savings account); it also holds a person's distributed allotment (according to their Collaborative Points) of whatever money a group has set aside to invest in their business—that is, the treasury. Since money in the Investment Account is actually stored in the UOV, it cannot be withdrawn as cash; it is represented value that can only be invested in other assets in the UOV. These transactions occur on the Collaborative Cloud.

Once money goes into this future-oriented Investment Account, it can be invested in assets held by the UOV. Value in your Investment Account might be devoted to your own collaborative's assets or directed to those facilitated by another collaborative. In either case, value from an Investment Account would always be transferred via a Request for Investment (RFI) auction, which will be illustrated in our next chapter. These accounts are funded by actual money, but that money is converted to value.

Remember: the assets in the UOV are worth real money and funded by real money, but since all those assets become "sovereign" once in the vault, they can't be bought or sold. No one gets to put their hands in that cookie jar. However, the money *in the treasury of* those assets can be used as value in the Investment Account. That's why you can transfer money and invest it, but it can't be withdrawn.

As the JALL colleagues put to Leon: why on earth would it be a good thing to *not* be able to withdraw your hard-earned money? This is when we return to Lana's billionaires. The billionaires of the world have managed to leverage their enormous wealth to build even *more* enormous wealth—and one of the main ways they do that is by withdrawing very little money. Any money that is withdrawn is taxed. However, by leveraging their assets, they're able to take out loans to fund their lifestyles—often earning tax credits by doing so. And by leaving their assets untouched, those assets are able to keep growing and growing, earning compound interest and funding new investments, which lead to greater wealth. The Elon Musks and Jeff Bezoses of the worlds do not have their checking accounts filled with billions. They're billionaires, but they don't have that in their bank accounts. They have that in shares, and overseas companies, and so on. They use their assets as part of a long-term strategy that enables them to build more wealth.

The Investment Account and the Asset Account, which we'll discuss in a moment, make those same benefits available to everyone—not just the super wealthy. They level the playing field and incentivize long-term investing, helping people who have long struggled in the rat race of poverty or low to middle class get a leg up in building a robust financial future.

Let's say more about that.

Why Prioritize Long-Term Investing?

What keeps people in poverty? There's no end of thoughtful dialogue on this point, but surely one major factor is the fact that poverty causes people to prioritize their short-term needs at the expense of long-term savings. This makes sense: how is someone supposed to save for the future if they're struggling to put food on the table? However, when we maintain a focus on resolving short-term needs, we are prevented from saving and thus kept in a cycle of poverty. There is no building of assets. There is no accumulation of equity. There is no compounding interest or dividends. There is only next week's paycheck and a stack of bills.

So how do we solve this? People can be given choices that they don't currently have. They should be allowed to build equity when they pay their rent check. They can be enabled to earn long-term value even if they don't have spare cash to invest—even if all they have to give is some spare time or elbow grease, some as yet "unrealized potential." People are incentivized to engage in a financial environment that promotes long-term investment. They are given access to some of the same tools that the billionaires use, which can lead to greater wealth building, equality, and security. We've touched on some of these ideas already and will explore others further in future chapters.

But how realistic is it to think that a person in dire straits will choose to *not* withdraw their full entitled amount during a Commitment Session? Wouldn't anyone in Jake's shoes—a little hard up, a little short on cash, with wants that outweigh the dollars in their wallets—withdraw everything they could and forget about the opportunities represented by the long-term Investment Account?

Let's consider Jake's scenario—which, admittedly, is a best-case scenario. Jake does not currently have any addictions or nefarious connections to the underworld. He also is not in a destitute or war-torn situation. He's just a broke college student who'd like enough money to pay his bills, take his girl-friend out, buy a junker car, and ideally help his family back home. Could he meet those needs and wants via the long-term financial tools available via the Collaborative Cloud?

We already saw in Chapter 6 how Jake can trade his Collaborative Points for cash to pay his bills, so we can assume the bills are taken care of. If he needs additional money to fund certain aspects of his lifestyle, he could opt to use the value in his Asset Account as collateral for a loan (more on this in a moment). He could use a car as a Sovereign Asset and save the value that he pays toward the car every month for his own long-term investments (we'll discuss this more in the next chapter). And if he wants to help his family back home, he could use the money in his long-term Investment Account to invest in their business or help them get an apartment.

We have yet to explore fully most of these possibilities, but the point is: the financial tools created within the Person to Person financial environ-ment allow for *options*. They allow for *choices*. And many of those choices allow for long-term investments, which have the potential to make more money, which can then be invested in new assets, which can then generate more value.

This does require that we think differently about our money. It's not uncommon for people to fit their lifestyle to their income. If they make less, they buy less. If they make more, they buy more. If they make even more, they expand their palate for luxury.

However, we began this journey by pressing each person to consider what it is they really want out of life. What does quality of life look like for you? What would be a life worth living? By *starting* with a long-term vision—a clear idea of purpose and goals and desired legacy—we can help ourselves snap out of the overconsumption that many of us instinctively go toward. A richly qualitative life asks that we don't just consume today, but instead, we think about where we want to go in the future. That line of thinking can help us operate differently, in a way that sets us up for the life we want.

And it *is* possible to snap out of overconsumption. In Chapter 6, we discussed the company Semco, which has its employees determine their own salary. Consider what happened when one of its managers was encouraged to take a higher salary than he currently earned:

> Jose Violi, who was a Semco employee during that period, took everyone by surprise when he rejected the company's offer to increase his pay.
>
> The market research showed that his salary was well below the market average for his position and the company wanted to close the gap. However, he declined their offer saying he was perfectly happy and comfortable with his current salary. Despite the management insisting upon giving him the raise, he was the only employee who refused to accept it. Today [as of March 2020], he is one of the main shareholders of the Semco Partners Holding.[120]

It's amazing to think of what we could learn from a person like Jose Violi or how we might be influenced when the majority of people in our circle are thinking with a long-term vision for their future rather than a short-term

---

[120] "What Happens When Employees Choose Their Own Salaries," Semco Style Institute.

goal of consumption. The Person to Person network fostered by the Collaborative Cloud will promote this community, one that allows global dialogue and collaboration to happen. That's what our JALL group will discover next.

The Network: Person to Person

"You said, 'invest in other things,' Leon," Lana said. "What do you mean, 'other things'?"

"Other projects. Other collaborative groups or other investments on the network," he responded.

Alex leaned forward. "Like what?"

"There are tons of projects and investment opportunities connected to other people on the network. Like—here, Lana, you'd like this one: there's a coffee roasting project down in Nicaragua. There are building projects in France... There's a muralist—you'd like that one, Alex—and there's one for building a school for refugee kids in Pakistan... Or we can each use our Investment Accounts to invest in our own JALL brand."

"Okay, slow down," Lana said. "I need to make sure I understand this. The Free Cash Account is like our own digital currency wallet. It's money we can use for whatever we want."

"For anything that can be bought with digital currency, yes," Leon said.[121]

"And then... the Investment Accounts help us keep track of our long-term savings and enable us to each invest in projects we're excited about, including our own." Lana looked at Leon questioningly. "I'm assuming a good investment will end up actually making us more money? So we could increase the money in our Investment Accounts?"

"Right," Leon said. "And the fact that we can't withdraw it means, number one, we get to use the same strategies that the billionaires do, and number

---

[121] With more and more companies like strike.me, crypto.com, blockfi.com, www.lolli.com, and nexo.io now supporting crypto, almost truly anything can be purchased with digital currencies. You can even use Twitter to tip another Twitter user. When, for example, you send $1, behind the scenes Bitcoin lightning is used to get the money from A to B, instantly and at no cost.

two, we're prioritizing our long-term savings." He looked at the other three. "Are we okay to move on to the last one?"

The Asset Account

Lana raised her eyebrows at Leon and took a big bite of popcorn. "Do you promise it's the last one?"

"For now, yes," Leon said. "Alex, you'll like this one. It works with the UOV."

"Hell yes!" Alex said.

"You'll like this one too, Lana. It's the Asset Account, which keeps track of our Future Value."

"What?!" Lana asked incredulously. "It keeps track of our unrealized potential?"

"Our Future Value, yes, but you can call it what you want. This Collaborative Cloud dApp keeps track of how people invest their *time and skills*, not just their money. Not everyone has the liquid cash to be a financial investor in something, but plenty of people have talents and time they could invest. Like all of us. So if you were to choose to invest your time and effort into a project, the app will keep track of your Future Value, a.k.a. your unrealized potential. Like, for instance—Alex, you could contribute marketing graphics for a coffee roaster in Central America. And rather than asking for monetary payment, you could earn Future Value."[122]

Alex clarified. "But in this case, the Future Value is hypothetical money. Not real money?"

"Right, it starts as hypothetical money, just like how we've thought about it as we've kept track of our Future Value with our own project," Leon answered. "But down the road, you can actually get 'reimbursed' for it—you

---

[122] To do that, Alex would become part of their collaborative, earn points, and get the split/draw/ investment money/future value, etc. as explained earlier in Chapter 6.

get something called 'Value Cards.' I'm still figuring those out. But that's the other function of the Asset Account—storing those Value Cards. I think Value Cards are basically 'realized' value. We can do cool stuff with them."

The Asset Account and Value Cards

The **Asset Account** notes **Future Value** that has been earned by the colleagues. That Future Value is tied to an asset (in the JALL group's case, it's tied to their brand asset). The Future Value will be converted to Value Cards in the future, once certain terms are met. (This will be explained in our next chapter.)

The Asset Account also holds **Value Cards**,[123] which represent realized value. A person could hold a number of different Value Cards for several Sovereign Assets in their account. Value Cards can be collateralized for a loan or sold.

Remember, in Chapter 6, Jake, Alex, Lana, and Leon determined the "Future Value" of the effort they had put into their work by determining the market value of their contribution; for instance, Alex had said they would have been paid $100 per hour for their videography work. The colleagues agreed to keep track of each other's Future Value so that, if their videos made more money in the future, they could fairly compensate each other. Lana referred to this Future Value as "unrealized potential," and they also called it "someday maybe money." The Asset Account documents and stores this Future Value.

In our next chapter, we'll show how an asset can be funded through a Request for Investment (RFI). This involves investors who will need to be

---

[123] Value Cards are non-fungible tokens (NFTs). Each Sovereign Asset has its own distinct Value Cards, which have their own distinct worth.

paid back. As they are paid back, the Future Value becomes *realized* value, and Value Cards will be issued. This will all be illustrated in Chapter 10.

In addition to noting Future Value, the Asset Account also holds these Value Cards. It's through the mechanism of Value Cards that people are able to donate their assets to the Universal Ownership Vault, yet still retain the value. Let's look at how that would work, returning once again to the illustration of Leon's father's Malibu beach house.

- After Leon's father donates his house to the foundation, the house becomes a Sovereign Asset. It is now held by the Universal Ownership Vault and can be used by tenants like Alex's sister. When they pay "rent"—that is, monthly usage rights—they will earn Value Cards.

- Likewise, Leon's father would earn Value Cards from the donation of this asset. After getting a receipt for $5 million from the Universal Ownership Vault, he could register that receipt on the Collaborative Cloud and earn 50,000 Value Cards worth $100 each. Essentially, he has tokenized this asset, making it portable, verifiable, divisible, and censorship-resistant.

- In general, Value Cards function as **non-fungible tokens**. In other words, they cannot be exchanged like cash. However, they can be used as collateral to get a cash loan (like the billionaires use their assets as collateral for loans) or can be sold to get cash.

So, what would the JALL group see when they engage with their Asset Accounts? As Leon mentioned to Lana, they would see their Future Value. They also would each get 1 Value Card just for creating the brand asset. (Since an Asset Account will always hold Value Cards, colleagues will get a single Value Card when they create their asset.) Here, once again, are the JALL colleagues' Future Value numbers:

JALL's Future Value and Value Cards

	New Point Total (Post-trade)	Collaborative Point Percentage (CP%)	Future Value (CP% * $10,000)	Value Cards
Jake	8,047	21%	$2,100.00	1
Alex	9,000	23%	$2,300.00	1
Lana	7,000	18%	$1,800.00	1
Leon	14,953	38%	$3,800.00	1
Totals:	39,000	100%	$10,000	4

Let's allow Jake, Alex, Lana, and Leon to talk through their own Value Card scenario.

The JALL Group's Value Cards

"Okay, everyone pull up the Asset Account dApp," Leon instructed. The others did so.

"Awww, there's my unrealized potential!" Lana crowed. "Eighteen hundred dollars. I just love that. Even if it's still pretend."

"Hey! I have a Value Card," Jake observed. "What is that?"

"So Value Cards are associated with our asset's treasury," Leon explained. "Do you guys remember how much we have in the treasury?"

Jake and Alex looked blank. Lana's hand shot up: "Three hundred dollars!" she burst out.

"Correct!" Leon said proudly.

"But I thought that $300 had been disbursed among us already in the Investment Accounts?" Jake asked. "Right?"

"Yes," Leon said. "The treasury will always show up in our different Investment Accounts, according to our Collaborative Points. That's because, on the Collaborative Cloud, money is always personal, and we have autonomy over what we contributed. But even with the treasury money as visible amounts in our different Investment Accounts, the fact is, our brand still has $300 behind it. That means we're worth $300. Our asset, specifically, is worth $300."

"Yes, so the *Value Card*...?" Jake prompted.

"Since our asset is worth $300 at the moment, and there are four Value Cards issued for our asset, each Value Card is worth $75. That's one-fourth of $300."

"Huh," Jake said. "What if we put more money in the treasury? Will they be worth more?"

"Yup," Leon responded. "The more money we put in the treasury, the more valuable our Value Cards will be."

"Can we get more Value Cards?" Alex asked.

"Yes—" Leon paused and hesitated. "We can do something called an RFI, which recruits external investors. But let's not get into that yet...I don't fully understand it still, and we've got enough to wrap our heads around right now."

"No kidding," Lana puffed. "I'm exhausted."

"Why does mine say 'JALL Value Card'?" Jake asked. "Why doesn't it just say 'Value Cards'?"

"Because you could have Value Cards related to other assets too," Leon explained. "Like—let's say Lana wants to invest in that Nicaraguan coffee roaster, and she sends them $200. She would have 2 Value Cards in the coffee roasting project too. Or, Jake, let's say that you start renting an apartment that is held by the Universal Ownership Vault. Every time you pay rent, you will get Value Cards in your Asset Account. Those might be titled '1053 Waring Rd Value Cards' or something."

"I'm already feeling so attached to this coffee roaster," Lana mused.

"So—we can earn them by investing in our own asset?" Jake asked. Leon nodded. "And we can also get them when we invest in other collaboratives' assets."

"Right. They just represent a portion of the asset's value. If you've got a card for that asset, you hold a portion of its value," Leon explained.

"Huh. What can we do with these Value Cards?" Jake asked. He took a slurp of cocoa.

"We can trade them for other Value Cards, or sell them for cash, or collateralize them for a cash loan." He looked over at Lana and grinned. "Like...the...*billionaires!*"

Lana raised her mug to cheers this remark and accidentally spilled cocoa on her sweater. "Damn it," she swore, handing off her cocoa to Jake.

"Why *would* anyone give us a loan, with just those hypothetical Value Cards as collateral?" Alex asked. "We're basically a brand-new baby enterprise. We'd be a huge risk for a lender."

Leon shrugged. "Maybe an investor asks for a high rate of return since we're a riskier bet and they think the risk could pay off. Or maybe our fans like what we're doing and want to be a part of it."

"I doubt that," Jake said skeptically. "How attached would a fan feel, just giving us a loan?"

"Well, remember, the Value Cards are like non-fungible tokens—as in, they're unique. Our JALL brand Value Cards are special to the work that *we're* doing. Like, Jake—you know that concert ticket you have posted on our dorm room bulletin board? The Thrice one?"

"Hell yes." Jake straightened up. "Summer of 2019, baby. Best concert of my life."

"Okay—that piece of paper has no monetary worth, but it represents something really meaningful to you. So the Value Cards that each of us has right now? Those are our group's *first* Value Cards. Think of the first shares that Apple produced! Can you imagine how special it would be to own one of the pieces of paper connected to Apple's *first* shares?" Leon asked.

"I love that you're comparing our little YouTube videos to Apple," Lana said wryly. "Truly, Leon, your ambition is epic."

"Hey—" Leon pointed at Lana with eyebrows raised. "Where's the faith? None of that back talk, young lady."

"Mansplaining," Lana and Alex both said loudly at the same time.

"Oh, damn it! I'm sorry," Leon said sheepishly. "The point is, with the Value Cards, people who believe in us might want them just because they want to feel connected with what we're doing."

"Could we give our Value Cards a unique design?" Alex asked. "Like, could I make a 'first edition' JALL Group Value Card graphic?"

"Yes! That would be awesome!" Leon responded. "*I'd* put that on Jake's bulletin board."

VALUE CARDS

Value Cards represent the value of a Sovereign Asset. Their worth is equivalent to the approximate market value of an asset divided by the number of Value Cards issued for that asset. (The asset's treasury helps to inform the estimated value of the Sovereign Asset.) So if a house was worth approximately $300,000 and there were 1,000 Value Cards attached to that asset, each Value Card would be worth $300. That value would raise or lower, depending on how the asset appreciates or depreciates in value.

A Value Card is free to be traded, sold, or collateralized. In the latter case, a person could agree to give another person a cash loan in exchange for Value Cards as collateral.

A collateralized Value Card is tied to a debt and will therefore be "frozen" until the debt is repaid; it cannot be traded, sold, or further used as collateral.

"Wait a second..." Lana raised her hand. "I don't understand what is behind this whole Asset Account. And you said something about how the stuff in our Investment Accounts is tied to the asset treasury? I don't get it. What is behind this whole thing?"

"Sovereign Assets," Leon said. "Which are held in the Universal Ownership Vault."

"Also known as the giant preschool," Alex supplied.

"Giant preschool?" Lana asked. She rubbed her forehead. "I'm so confused."

"Sorry," Alex said. "The preschool helps me connect the dots, but that was probably confusing."

"I'm confused too," Jake said. "Could someone break down this concept of a Sovereign Asset?"

HOW DO SOVEREIGN ASSETS WORK?

In order to fully understand the Asset Account and its related Value Cards, we need to return to the concept of Sovereign Assets, first introduced in Chapter 7. A Sovereign Asset, as we initially described it, is an asset that is donated to the Universal Ownership Vault or created through funding (as we'll illustrate in our next chapter); the asset becomes "self-owned." People pay to use it and earn Value Cards with their payments.[124]

A Sovereign Asset can be many things, both tangible and intangible—a property (like the Malibu beach house), a brand (like the JALL brand), a truck, a bitcoin, a piece of art, a coffee roaster, a patent, and so on. For the sake of simplicity, we're going to return to our original example of a Sovereign Asset: a beach house. What would the life span of this Sovereign Asset look like?

Inception

How does a Sovereign Asset begin? In Chapter 7, Leon and Alex discussed the possibility of Leon's father donating his beach house to the UOV. But it's also interesting to consider how a Sovereign Asset might be built from the ground up.

---

[124] As the Value Cards represent the value of a Sovereign Asset, they are initially in the hands of the people that helped create the SA: the people *donating* the asset or *funding* its creation. Gradually, as users begin to pay those investors back, the Value Cards would move towards the one(s) *using* the asset.

Let's say there's a group of colleagues who decide they want to build this beach house. However, they don't have the capital to buy or build a beach house outright. So this group of colleagues writes up a business plan. They determine they will need $500,000 to build it and can pay approximately $40,000 per year to use it. In addition, they have found a collaborative group of builders who have agreed to contribute approximately $50,000 worth of unpaid effort for a stake in the property. The colleagues take their business plan to the Collaborative Cloud marketplace and make a Request for Investment (RFI) at an online auction. (We'll be discussing the online marketplace, auctions, and RFIs in our next chapter.)

Funding

The auction takes place, and the $500,000 is raised from about one hundred different investors. In exchange for the money they contributed toward the beach house project, the investors get Value Cards, each worth $100. If an investor gave $1,000 toward the house, they would hold ten cards. These cards represent a portion of the house's value, so each investor holds a portion of the asset's value. To clarify: they don't own the house itself; they just hold a portion of its value.

Generally, there will be three groups of people who interact with the Sovereign Asset:

- **The users** are the people in one or more collaboratives that run and operate the asset. In the case of a beach house, this might be the people living there. Alternately, if the beach house was being rented out like an Airbnb, the users might be a collaborative providing hospitality, dealing with cleaning and maintenance, and so on. All the collaboratives using the asset have some sort of usage rights and pay a price for that usage. The effort of the people working to produce these services is translated into Collaborative Points, as we have discussed in previous chapters.

- **The investors** are the second group of people involved in the inception of a Sovereign Asset: the people who participated in the auction and contributed money to bring the Sovereign Asset into existence. At the end of the auction, these investors will be ranked according to mathematical equations that factor in who gave how much and their expected rate of return. If an investor ends up being on the bottom of the list, they will need to wait awhile to get that money back. The ranking is transparent, and investors will have a clear idea of when they will be paid back and at what rate, and will also have information about how the asset is expected to appreciate over time. There are several different kinds of investors; these will also be discussed in our next chapter.

- **The builders** are the third group, who represent anyone who participates in the creation of a Sovereign Asset through unpaid effort. Let's say this group of builders is paid $50,000 in cash but also contributes an additional $50,000 worth of effort in exchange for Value Cards. We can imagine that their contribution directly impacts the market value of the house, making it worth $550,000, rather than $500,000. In that case, their effort is immediately compensated with Value Cards, worth $100 each—so they would have 500 Value Cards to split among them. In this case, their Value Cards are exactly the same as the cards the investors hold; whereas the investors made a contribution in cash, the builders invested via effort.

Creation

The process of building the house transforms the $500,000 cash plus $50,000 worth of contribution effort from the builder collaborative into $550,000 worth of real estate property.

When the Sovereign Asset is created, the contract of the Sovereign Asset will be established. The contract of a Sovereign Asset uses smart contracts, a tool introduced in Chapter 8. This means the contract must adhere to the code written into the Sovereign Asset's prime directives, which center around a few key principles:

- The **purpose** it was infused with at creation. A house, for example, has the purpose of providing its dwellers with a stable and comfortable place to stay.
- The **operational fund** provides money for administrative and legal costs, along with insurance. A Sovereign Asset like a house would have premium insurance, which would ideally take care of major repairs that may be needed from a catastrophe.
- The **sustainability fund**: there should be some capital available for the end-of-life recycling cost, and so on.

In other words, the smart contract of the Sovereign Asset is focused on balancing quality of life for the people that use and invest in the Sovereign Asset, along with the asset's impact on the environment that supports its life cycle (i.e., the planet, the community, etc.). It also seeks to provide a reliable, predictable, and sustainable way to store value for the people who have invested in it.

There is no fund for maintenance, such as fixing or improving the house. These costs would be paid by the users directly (similar to what a homeowner would be responsible for).

Use

Now the house is built, the contract is in place, and the house is ready to house its first tenants. The collaborative group of colleagues that first conceptualized the house might move in; these are the users. The Sovereign Asset would make an agreement with the collaborative of users; this agreement would detail who will be the steward(s) and caretaker(s) of the house. (In this case, that would likely be the collaborative of people renting the house.)

At the end of the year, the users would have paid—as they agreed—$40,000 usage rights. Essentially, this is their "rent." Out of that monthly rent, the Sovereign Asset would have taken a portion[125] of the money and put it into the sustainability and operational funds..

However, unlike typical rent, which is described as "money flushed down the drain," this $40,000 payment money enables the users to earn value. For every $100 they pay back to investors, the colleagues get a Value Card (distributed in terms of their Collaborative Points) in exchange. That $40,000 of repaid cash translates to 400 Value Cards, each worth $100.[126]

Assuming the house is still worth $550,000, there is now $40,000 of debt-free value. This value appears as Value Cards in the Asset Account of the users, distributed according to their respective points.

Let's say the users put in some "sweat equity" to maintain the property—for instance, keeping the garden looking nice or making needed repairs. That effort could be noted as Future Value. If they make an investment in the house that directly impacts the market value—for instance, redoing the kitchen—that investment could make their Value Cards worth more.[127] Alternately, if a major rehab were needed and the users did not have the capital for it, they could submit a Request for Investment and raise the money for the improvements from investors. (This might be similar to the process of getting a home equity line of credit from a bank, but in this case, the process is purely person to person.)

---

[125] The exact percentage amount is fixed at inception and dictated by the type of Sovereign Asset (house, car, etc.).

[126] We have stated this simply for the sake of illustration, but in reality, the $100 payments would not directly translate to a Value Card of the same value, because a portion would be devoted to provisions for the funds.

[127] If the users invest effort that does not directly relate to an increase in the asset's value, they could earn Future Value.

Fast-Forward

Let's skip ahead twenty years and assume that all investors have now been paid off with their agreed-upon rates of return. The collaborative colleagues running and operating the house are still paying their usage rights of approximately $40,000 per year. However, since there's no more debt to be repaid, that "rent" now becomes the treasury in the Sovereign Asset. That treasury appears in the Investment Account of each colleague, again distributed according to their respective points.

When that happens, the colleagues can use the money in their Investment Accounts to invest in other Sovereign Assets, or they could collateralize their Value Cards to get a cash loan; that money could then also be invested. (This is the billionaire strategy that Lana described.) Investing in new assets would enable them to continue building wealth in sustainable projects they believe in without getting hit with the burden of taxes.

End of Life

As with most assets, a time would likely come that would signal the Sovereign Asset's "end of life." For the sake of our illustration, let's imagine that the beach house has fallen into disrepair and is further damaged in a fire. The building needs to be torn down so a new house can be built.

Sovereign Assets are created with a focus on sustainability, so there is real attention devoted to the end-of-life recycling of the asset. For example, let's say the beach house property has contaminated soil from a leak in the fuel tank installed with the initial construction of the house; a new law doesn't allow for a new house to be built on contaminated soil. Before a new house can be built, the ground should be cleaned. The sustainability fund would take care of that cleaning cost or any cost required to prioritize environmental considerations.

What happens to all the people still holding Value Cards in that asset? If a Sovereign Asset became unusable or destroyed, then the people holding the Value Cards would hold the value of whatever the asset—in this case, the land—is worth, plus the amount in the treasury. Fortunately, the loss would be less acute for each investor since the Value Cards would be spread out across a number of people and not concentrated as one person's main source of wealth.

If, at the end of the Sovereign Asset's life cycle, there is still money remaining in the asset's funds, that money would be distributed to the asset's treasury.

When a Sovereign Asset Changes Users

Let's say that the Kim family has been "renting" out the beach house in Malibu as a Sovereign Asset. They've taken good care of the house and done a good job maintaining its value. Eventually, however, they decide they want to move. What happens next?

When they're ready to move, the Kim Collaborative ends their usage contract, and they move.[128] They will still hold many Value Cards connected to the beach house asset, which means they have the same incentives as owners to "leave well." They will do their best to ensure the house looks as nice as possible so that the new users will pay the most competitive market value. The Kims might choose to contact a real estate agent or a professional photographer to take pictures of the home so that it goes to market well.

Once they end their usage contract, the Sovereign Asset, via smart contracts, puts itself on the market. The Sovereign Asset can use any documents the users may have generated via a photographer, for example, to create a listing; that listing will be visible in the Collaborative Cloud and advertised to new potential users. A "usage auction" occurs in which different collaboratives bid to be selected as the new users. The Sovereign Asset will make a new contract with whatever collaborative makes the best offer.

---

[128] The Kims can choose to move to another Sovereign Asset, but that's not mandatory. They can sell their Value Cards at any time and "cash out," even if they still occupy the property.

THE FUNDAMENTAL CHARACTERISTICS
OF A SOVEREIGN ASSET (SA)

1. The SAs are essentially self-owned, that is, sovereign. Although they are legally held by the SASTOs, that legal requirement is as minimal a constraint as possible to remove the "private" from "private property."

2. The Sovereign Asset's value is represented via Value Cards that are distributed among investors and users.

3. The asset itself exists to serve its created purpose; that is, a house exists to provide a comfortable place to live.

4. There are two main groups of people who interact with a Sovereign Asset: the users and the investors. A third category of builders may also interact with the Sovereign Asset but—depending on the nature of their contribution—would fall into either or both of the first two groups.

5. As users pay back investors, the Value Cards are given to the users. These Value Cards can be either made liquid through being sold or collateralized to get a loan.

6. The SA is focused on sustainability, not mass consumption. The decisions around its use and development will be guided by principles set forth by the community in the UOV DAO.

COMPENDIUM

Let's sum this all up.

A Person to Person financial environment can be made possible through two platforms: the Universal Ownership Vault and Web3 applications such as the Collaborative Cloud. Both platforms are decentralized and distributed among all their different users. This means there is no middleman or middling party that can censor or hinder interactions. A network of decentralized applications is powerful and is resistant to any individual or group wielding absolute power: it does not care about jurisdictions, has no company behind it, has no CEO to hold accountable, and is therefore challenging to regulate. It's built *by* people, *for* people, in an effort to better serve their needs.

The use of cryptocurrency lends itself to this financial system. Any sort of fiat money (i.e., conventional paper currency) is strictly regulated. The world of fiat currency is one where banks, governments, and local institutions hold a firm grip. Navigating this environment is complex, expensive, and at the mercy of regulation. Cryptocurrency, on the other hand, is a medium of exchange that is determined by the open market, is secure and transparent, transcends borders, and resists regulation. All of that works well with a Person to Person environment, which resists power plays and seeks to optimize direct connections between human beings.

The Universal Ownership Vault is a physical and legal place, with a real identity in the world. When the dApps on the Collaborative Cloud gather the information made public by the UOV, it becomes possible to:

- Build true personal finance
- Participate in the growing decentralized finance (a.k.a. DeFi) space[129]
- Fund your projects
- Become an investor
- Build wealth
- Get liquidity through collateralized loans
- Get fair access to using the assets

---

[129] In the Web3 decentralized financial world, you can essentially do anything you would otherwise do in the traditional finance world. There are lending dApps, such as AAVE (aave.com). There are saving dApps, such as Compound (compound.finance). Finally, there are exchange dApps, such as Uniswap (uniswap.org).

In short, it becomes possible to establish financial security in both the short and long term. However, because assets in the Person to Person environment are no longer private property but are rather held by the UOV, this allows for the separation of value and usage, meaning people are able to experience the freedom, flexibility, sustainability, and greater equality that Alex and Leon were dreaming about in Chapter 7.

The foundation network guarantees that whatever is put in the vault will stay there and that it will be handled in accordance with local regulations. Because of the way it is built, the vault is owned by everyone, and therefore no one, at the same time. The vault is stable, predictable, and transparent. Once you put something in the vault, you donate it; it's not yours anymore and will never be again.

And yet, because of the transparency of the UOV, someone like Leon's father could donate an asset, watch it be tokenized, and then experience the incredible freedom and benefits found in the Collaborative Cloud. People can now use the same financial constructs the billionaires use to invest and grow their money, but instead of one person possessing a billion dollars, you have a billion people with one dollar—all making their few dollars work for them.

Additionally, the Collaborative Cloud offers a solution to the problems posed by the company versus personal account. It allows for everyone to operate independently, as individuals. People's finances will not be tied to a group's entrepreneurial venture, and if or when a person chose to leave a business, they will walk away with the fair value that they put into it. There is no "group money"; all accounts are strictly personal.

Finally, the dApps available through the Collaborative Cloud allow for the full fruition of a truly collaborative environment. This technology smoothly enables all of the needs that the JALL group identified in Chapter 6: a way to track Collaborative Points, do a draw, calculate Future Value, and so on.

In sum: these are the financial and technical apparatuses that will allow for a Quality of Life World.

CLOUD PEOPLE

Jake breathed a sigh and shook his head. "This is crazy aligned with what we want to do," Jake said. He put his phone down, turned toward Lana, and half-tackled her. She shrieked with laughter, and they flopped horizontally onto the bed.

"I know!" Leon said. "And what's especially cool is all the people on this network are interested in collaborating in similar ways, exchanging their talents. So...it's a way to access funding to help us grow our brand; it's a way to build wealth and invest, the same way the billionaires do; it can function as a company account that still gives us the freedom of a personal account...But we're also building quality of life—we're connecting with other people around the world. There's more transparency; there's more equity. There's more trust and justice."

Lana propped herself up on her elbow and turned to Alex. "You were right. Leon is a smart cookie."

Alex stood up and stretched, grinning, then went and flopped down on top of Jake and Lana. "We are *all* smart cookies," Alex crowed. "We are macadamia nut cookies, bitches!"

Leon stood and stepped tentatively toward the dogpile on Lana's bed. Jake looked at his roommate with a smile. "I can't believe this is the same guy I met in September who was glued to his video games and seemed like such a doofus."

"Only a doofus would use the word 'doofus,'" Leon said. He took another hesitant step toward the bed.

"Oh my gosh, Leon, just hop on!" Lana called out, laughing. She, Jake, and Alex reached out and grabbed Leon, pulling him into the tangle of arms and legs. He whooped and piled on, finally settling on the end of the bed, where Jake and Lana's legs made a space.

"For real, though, this whole thing has been pretty cool. Like—kind of life-changing." He grabbed a teddy bear on Lana's bed and hugged it. Then he raised his head and grinned at Jake. "Smells like girl," he whispered.

EXPLORE FURTHER

If you'd like to learn more, discuss this content with others, or access tools for your own application, go to the interactive section of the book using this QR code.

PART FOUR

OPPORTUNITIES CREATED BY THE PERSON TO PERSON ENVIRONMENT

Only one who attempts the absurd is capable of achieving the impossible.

–Miguel de Unamuno

CHAPTER TEN

THE AUCTION

How the Tools of the Collaborative Cloud Can Facilitate Investment

See, the world is full of things more powerful than us.
But if you know how to catch a ride,
you can go places.

—Neal Stephenson, American writer

Jake's phone buzzed. Across the dorm room, Leon's phone dinged.

"It's from Lana," Jake said. He read it aloud: "*It's done. Emailing it to you now.*"

Leon stepped over to his desk and opened his email. "Yes! Here it is. Our project description for the auction." He read the document title: "Request for Investment."

"Are you sure we're ready for this, man?" Jake asked. "We're going to be on the hook for $10,000 if this works."

"We're ready," Leon said confidently. "Our videos are picking up speed every day. And that PSA one that you and Lana did together about self-care for gamers has practically gone viral. We've gotten so many new ad requests just from that one alone. If we can invest in a solid promotional campaign, we're just going to keep blowing up. Besides—I've told you there are more safeguards for borrowers on the Collaborative Cloud than with a bank, right?"

"Tell it to me again," Jake said.

"When we're repaying our loan, there's no specific amount we have to pay every month—we just have to commit to paying a *percentage* of our profits."

Jake nodded, trying to internalize the information Leon had given him before. "So even if we have a bad month, there's no big problem, right?" he asked.

"Right," Leon said. "I mean, our interest keeps running, but they're not going to seize our brand or anything. The only time a Sovereign Asset would intervene is if its sustainability is threatened, but that's more relevant for a house or something. That's not really going to happen with our brand, as long as we're working on it. Does that make you feel better?"

"Yes, a little. I still feel nervous about it—I don't want to let anyone down." He looked over Leon's shoulder at Lana's document on the screen. "Well, let's print it out and read it in the quad. I could use some air," Jake said. Leon nodded and sent the document to the printer, which hummed and whirred out two copies of Lana's project description.

"I'll bring chips." Leon grabbed a fistful of snacks and tossed two Gatorades to Jake. "You carry those."

"Good," Jake said. He loaded the drinks into his bag. "I can't believe we're going to recruit investors through an auction. This feels crazy to me." He went to his closet and grabbed a Frisbee. "I'm bringing the Frisbee too. I'm going to need to throw something around to work out my nerves."

"I suck at Frisbee," Leon complained.

"I know; that's why it will help me feel better," Jake quipped.

The trees in the quad had all lost their leaves, but the rare winter sunshine had brought many other students outside to study and chat. Jake and Leon found a sunny spot near several students who were walking on a slackline between two trees.

"Okay," Leon said, throwing a beach towel down on the ground. "Let's see what we've got." They settled into a comfortable position, each with their own copy of Lana's write-up. "Woah, there are pictures," Leon observed.

"Yeah! She incorporated some of Alex's graphics from the videos. Cool, right?" Jake asked.

Lana's project description did everything it needed to do to bring their group's investment proposal to the marketplace auction. It was titled "Request for Investment: The JALL Brand Asset." She'd provided a description of their collaborative group, outlined their work, and chronicled their growth.

"Did you see how she described each of our roles?" Leon asked. He read aloud. "'Leon Kilroy: Chief Strategist, Facilitator of Finance, Director of Marketing and IT, *Lion Tamer*.' Lion tamer?!"

"Read mine," Jake said with a grin.

"Jake Ramirez: Content Writer and Director, Project Manager, On-Screen Talent, Voice of Caution, General Eye Candy."

"What?!" Leon laughed. Jake struck a model's pose and flexed his biceps.

"I wasn't crazy about the voice of caution part—although I guess it's true. But I like the eye candy part." He grinned. "I came up with Lana's," Jake said. He read: "Lana Aarden: Head of People, Communications Director, Group Therapist, Miner of Unrealized Potential, Pirate Queen."

"Pirate Queen. Nice," Leon said.

Jake responded, "You know, because she's suddenly not into paying taxes. Can't you picture her dumping boxes of tea into the Boston Harbor? Pirate Queen."

Leon finished: "Alex Faumuina: Graphic Design, Videography, Content Editor, Head of I&D"—he broke off. "What's I&D again?"

Jake supplied "Inclusivity and diversity."

"Ah, right," Leon said. "Very important." Jake nodded. Leon finished up: "'... Executive of Snack Distribution, General Badass.' That's pretty accurate."

"Is it okay that we had a little fun with the descriptions? And that she included Alex's graphics?" Jake asked.

"It definitely wouldn't fly if we were applying for a bank loan," Leon said. "But here, the main goal is to get the attention of investors and appeal to them. So—it might actually work in our favor. Let's read the rest."

Lana had noted how much the group could commit to pay investors back every month—$500. There was an explanation about why they believed a marketing ad campaign could increase their revenue, and it described the promotional company the group had selected, along with research they'd found about that company's track record of marketing success. She had noted their targeted investment amount: $10,000, measured as 100 Value Cards, each worth $100.

Lana had also made note of the JALL group's current economic trajectory, citing statistics like the current daily views for their videos and the "CPM"—a Google advertisement metric. She also noted each group member's hourly contributions, along with the comparable economic compensation for their work: $9,000. There was also a description of how their investors would be ranked, related to the amounts they contributed and their expected rate of return. Additionally, Lana had made it clear that the colleagues all had skin in the game, explaining that—via the Future Value Card creation mechanism[130]—their ability to personally reimburse themselves for their effort required that they make their collaborative financially profitable. She'd ended the document with a conclusion that sold them, basically, as a cool group doing cool things and worthy of investors' confidence.

"I think she makes us sound pretty good," Jake remarked. "I don't see any changes that we need to make."

"Yeah, she hit all the boxes she needed to. She's a great writer," Leon observed.

"Lana got a full ride to our school. Did you know that? Anyway. She *must*

---

[130] The Future Value card creation will be explained at the end of the chapter.

be a good writer, because even I'm feeling convinced that this is a good idea now." Jake took a swig of coffee out of his thermos and stood up. "Come on, throw the Frisbee with me."

"Wait, let me text Lana back first." Leon read his text aloud as he typed. "*Read ur doc Pirate Queen, looks rad. lets submit 2 marketplace & schedule auction.*"

"What about Alex?" Jake asked. "They need to read it over too."

Leon added to his text. "*. . . if Alex is cool.*"

Leon stood up and stretched. His phone dinged a quick response. He looked. "It's from Alex," he said. "*Fully preheated. Ready to cook. Macadamia nut cookies 4lyfe.*" He paused and studied the phone. "I think that means they're on board."

There was another ding from Leon's phone. "Lana says . . . *Submitted. Auction date is Friday the 12th, pending approval.*"

Another text came through from Alex. *I'm hosting.*

Jake and Leon looked at each other. "Was that sarcastic?" Leon asked.

Jake said, "That was probably serious. Alex's place is epic. It will be the perfect spot to tune into the auction. Haven't you been there?"

"No. Why? Have *you* been there?" Leon asked defensively.

"That's where we've filmed most of the videos. Alex has a single, so it's perfect. And seriously, it's *epic*. You'll see. Come on," Jake said, and slapped the Frisbee against Leon's chest. "Let's see those lion-taming muscles in action."

GOING TO AUCTION

One of the unique aspects of the Collaborative Cloud network is the marketplace, where collaboratives and investors can connect with one another and support each other's goals.

What is this marketplace? As a matter of fact, there are several marketplaces on the Collaborative Cloud. Although these marketplaces mainly serve an operational purpose (similar to Craigslist or Opendoor), they have the potential to be developed into spaces of connection and discovery, similar to how people connect and dialogue on the Collaborative Cloud. The marketplaces are all related to the workings of the Sovereign Assets:

- There is a marketplace where the SAs that *require fresh capital* will be listed. This is where visitors will find the current and upcoming RFIs, and this is the marketplace featured in the JALL auction. Unlike the typical red tape a person would normally experience when seeking a loan or investment capital, this Person to Person marketplace poses no barriers to anyone who wants to request investment. Both investors and those seeking investment are free to make decisions about who they want to connect with, what assets to invest in, and in what way.

- There is also a marketplace where the SAs that are *looking for new collaboratives* to steward them will be listed. This is where visitors will find the current and upcoming usage auctions. For instance, this is where an SA house might be listed if it was seeking new tenants.

- There is a marketplace where SAs looking for *service* will be listed. For example, if an SA needs to contract an accountant, the Sovereign Asset's DAO would publish a contracting request explaining the need. This is where people in the marketplace will find current and upcoming tenders that they could apply to fill.

When a collaborative needs money to grow their operations or increase the value of their asset, they can make a Request for Investment on the Collaborative Cloud. This pitches their project to all of the potential investors represented on the network.

RFI: Request for Investment

Lana's project description was the first step for anyone bringing a **Request for Investment (RFI)** to the marketplace. A project description does what a typical bank loan application might do: it's meant to introduce the collaborative to potential investors, explain the collaborative's work, demonstrate the colleagues' credibility, and showcase their likelihood of providing their investors with a good return.

As Lana's colorful introduction of the group members illustrates, there is more flexibility in how an RFI presents itself to the Collaborative Cloud network than in how a small business would present itself to a bank. That's because this is a person to person interaction: it's one group of people appealing to other people, acknowledging themselves as unique humans.

THE MAKINGS OF A SOLID RFI[131]

1. A description of the collaborative, detailing the colleagues' work, their purpose, and the colleagues themselves.

2. The amount of money the collaborative will pay for the usage rights of the Sovereign Asset for which they are seeking funds, that is, the monthly "rent." (The SA, in turn, reimburses investors.) A collaborative pays this usage fee for any Sovereign Asset, whether that's a tangible asset, like a house or truck, or an intangible asset, such as the JALL brand.

3. The reasons detailing why the investment is safe and/or worthwhile for investors.

4. The amount of money the collaborative hopes to raise, noted in Value Cards.

5. Details about how Value Cards will be ranked and distributed, according to the expected rates of return.

6. The amount of Future Value that is tied to the RFI. (This will be explained at the end of the chapter.)

---

[131] This information is also provided on our website, for the reader's easy reference. Please see this chapter's QR code.

How Are Value Cards Ranked?

After securing investors for their project, the collaborative's Sovereign Asset will pay the investors back via monthly payments. (Essentially, the collaborative pays the Sovereign Asset a monthly usage "rent," and then the SA sends that money on to investors.) But who gets paid back first? Who gets paid back last? That's all determined via the Value Card ranking, which happens in real time during the auction.

There are three ways to invest in a collaborative:

- **Debt investments** are the investments that hold Value Cards as collateral and expect a percentage yield—that is, an interest rate.

- **Value investments** are investments where investors don't expect a percentage yield but, rather, want a buyback when a Card reaches a target value, for example 2× the purchase price. In our next segment of narration, this is the approach that Leon's dad uses. Generally, these investments are put at the bottom of the ranking.

- **Collectible investments** have no expected rate of return or buyback obligation; essentially, these cards are bought at a 0% interest rate. This is the strategy Jake's grandmother uses for one of her cards because she wants to support her grandson. Although collectible card holders might choose to hang on to their cards as a collectible, these cards could still be sold, similar to how shares can be bought at one price and sold at another. Generally, collectible investments will also be listed first in the ranking order of the cards.

The ranking order of the investments determines who gets paid back first; those pledges listed in the first few spots will see a quick return on their money, whereas investments ranked toward the end of the list will need to wait awhile before getting their money back—although they will have gained substantial interest by waiting. The collaborative will determine the rules for this ranking ahead of time. Almost always, the collectible investments will be listed first in the ranking order; from there, the collaborative can choose a number of options in which to rank the rest of their cards.

For instance, the JALL group might say that cards with low interest rates will be given priority in the ranking; so 5 cards worth $500 at 3% interest would be ranked before the same amount of cards at 4% interest. That rule would incentivize their investors to ask for a low rate of return, since cards with low interest rates would be paid back the fastest. That would be great for the JALL group: they wouldn't have to pay back a huge amount of interest. However, it also might make their project less appealing to investors. Additionally, it means all the pledges that asked for a high rate of return—listed at the end of the ranking order—will have months and months to build up substantial interest.

Alternately, the JALL group might say that they will prioritize cards that ask for a larger rate of return. In this case, 5 cards at 4% would be ranked *before* 5 cards at 3%. This would be a strategy to encourage many "grassroots" investors to sign up: people who don't want to risk a large amount of money, but still want to be paid back quickly and have their investment be worth their while. For a group like the JALL Collaborative, with an asset's worth mainly based on the strength of the business plan and the trustworthiness of the team (i.e., a risky investment), this would be a way to incentivize people to go out on a limb for them. This strategy would also be a smart way for the group to pay off investors quickly and get rid of the highest interest payments before the interest had much time to grow.

Investors can choose to mix and match their pledges. For instance, an investor might bid on 2 cards with 5% return and 2 cards with 2% return; this would position the investor in two different places in the overall ranking.

Lastly, investors could choose to use a venture capitalist strategy, the "value investments." In this case, the investor doesn't request a rate of return, but they do require the opportunity to sell back the Value Cards once they have increased in value, up to a certain amount—let's say, double the original amount. This strategy is good for the investor—they get the opportunity to potentially double their money, so long as the collaborative is successful. It can also be helpful to the project collaborators doing the work: since the interest isn't running on the value-only investments, it gives them more time to build up their project.

However, if the brand goes wild and achieves success quickly, the group will end up losing a large portion of their profits in their obligation to sell the Value Cards back at double their value to the Value Only Investors. For this reason, a collaborative would probably limit the number of Value Only Investment cards they sell.

Each collaborative can determine their own strategic rules for the card-ranking ahead of time and will define those rules using an algorithm. The algorithm is determined in advance and is published for potential investors so that investors have the opportunity to read them over ahead of the auction and form their investment strategy. The algorithm will define the way pledges are ranked, which will happen in real time during the auction.

One Example of a Ranking Algorithm

Collectible investments would be listed first by default. From there, a collaborative could establish an algorithm that ranks their cards according to the specifications below.

1. Rank 1: Minimum 20% to maximum 100% of the total RFI amount dedicated to collector investors

    a. *For instance: The JALL group specifies that they will accept as many collectible cards as they can, up to 100%. By saying they need a 40% minimum, this ensures the collectible cards will be prioritized at the top of their ranking list, ahead of the "0%" minimums noted in ranks 2 and 3. Their auction will only be successful if 20% of the $10,000 comes in without a required interest rate.*

2. Rank 2: Minimum 0% to maximum 50% of the total RFI amount dedicated to debt investors

a. For instance, the JALL group says they will take up to 50% of Value Cards with an interest rate, in case there aren't as many collectible investors to help them reach their goal of $10,000. They don't want to have 100% of their Value Cards require an interest rate because that interest will build up quickly if their brand takes a long time to grow.

3. Rank 3: Minimum 0% to maximum 50% of the total RFI amount dedicated to value investors

a. For instance, the JALL group specifies that they won't sell more than 50% of Value Investor Cards. Capping the Value Investor Cards at 50% helps ensure they have a diversity of debt repayment obligations. This is a safe strategy.

When the total amount of money is raised, the auction ends and the position of investors becomes final. If the amount of money does not meet the minimal amount by the end of the auction, the funds are returned to the investors' originating account via a smart contract. (This is a similar mechanism used by the Kickstarter campaign website.) So, for example, if the JALL group doesn't secure $10,000 worth of investments, the auction would "fail," and the money would be returned to the cloud accounts of the investors who had bid on the project.

But let's assume that the auction is successful. What would happen then? In a moment, we're going to see the different people who bid on the JALL colleagues' auction. Spoiler alert: Jake's grandmother, Lucy, turns out to be even more tech-savvy than Jake's parents and sets herself up with a DiD and a Collaborative Cloud account so that she can support her grandson. Let's imagine that Jake's grandmother, Lucy Ramirez, commits to buying 1 Value Card as a collectible investment and a second at 4% interest.

- Once Lucy has made a bid to invest, the funds would be moved out of Lucy's account—either her Free Cash Account or her

Investment Account—and be transferred to the JALL Collaborative's auction account.[132]

- When the auction has successfully concluded, the funds are sent to the JALL brand Sovereign Asset. The JALL colleagues can now contract with a marketing agency for the $10,000 sum to do their marketing campaign; they will send the invoice to the Sovereign Asset. Essentially, this involves preparing an order for the smart contract of their SA to execute. The JALL group is taken care of then— but what happens with the investors' cards?

- Let's consider Grandma Lucy again. Lucy would receive 2 Value Cards from the JALL group as a pledge for the cash she contributed. Although they are not yet worth real cash, they do have value: they represent a piece of the asset she bid on, in this case, the JALL group's brand.

- The collectible investment card will serve Lucy as a collectible item that carries personal meaning. In the same way that a valuable baseball card has both personal worth and financial value, Lucy can choose to hold on to one of the first Value Cards of her grandson's entrepreneurial venture as a keepsake. That collectible investment card would allow Lucy to hold the value of a tiny piece of the JALL brand as long as she chooses to keep the card. However, she could also choose to sell this card at any time.

- The second card Grandma Lucy bought is a debt investment card, which she asked to be paid back at 4% interest. When the JALL group sends money to their Sovereign Asset to pay back Grandma Lucy, she will make a profit on this investment. At that point, the card would leave her Asset Account and go to theirs. Value Cards

---

[132] Some technical details on how this works: The auction account is a smart contract. Each smart contract has a specific pledging address where funds can be deposited. When the RFI has raised money for something tangible—like, say, a work truck—those funds would create a tangible Sovereign Asset. In the JALL group's case, they are raising money for something intangible: a marketing campaign. After raising the $10,000 they need, their sovereign brand asset will give the collaborative access to the necessary cash to purchase the marketing campaign.

live in Asset Accounts because that's what they are: financial assets. However, Grandma Lucy will not be able to sell or collateralize this 4% card until the JALL colleagues pay it off. The 4% card will be locked by the debt contract until the debt is fully paid.[133]

- When the JALL group repays Lucy's investment at 4%, she will get the $100 she originally spent on the card plus 4% interest. That money would go into Lucy's account;[134] now she can use that money to make new investments. The JALL Collaborative receives the Value Card, meaning they now "own" more of their brand and are steadily building up its realized value.

Why Value Cards?

But why bother with Value Cards? Why not just do all this with currency like dollars, euros, or bitcoin? Wouldn't that be easier?

First of all, let's remember that the Collaborative Cloud is not like a bank. It does not "hold" money, nor can it disburse or distribute money. All money, treasury, and assets that inform dealings on the Collaborative Cloud are actually housed in the Universal Ownership Vault—and thus no longer belong to anyone; as discussed in previous chapters, they are Sovereign Assets. However, in exchange for creating a Sovereign Asset in the UOV, the Collaborative Cloud generates *tokens* referencing the value of the Sovereign Asset. These tokens can be sold, traded, or collateralized. They are non-fungible tokens[135] that take the form of Value Cards.

---

[133] We will discuss what happens to these cards if the debt is defaulted on later in the chapter.

[134] This would usually be returned to a person's Investment Account, but in some cases—depending on the mechanics of the crowdfunding campaign and the legal set-up—the money might be returned to a person's Free Cash Account.

[135] A quick reminder of the definition of a non-fungible token, supplied by Wikipedia: "A non-fungible token is a unique and non-interchangeable unit of data stored on a digital ledger. NFTs can be associated with easily-reproducible items such as photos, videos, audio, and other types of digital files as unique items, and use blockchain technology to give the NFT a public proof of ownership." "Non-fungible token," Wikipedia, accessed November 29, 2021, https://en.wikipedia.org/wiki/Non-fungible_token.

Perhaps Value Cards seem less appealing than cold, hard cash or flexible digital currency. However, remember what Lana discovered when she read the article about the tax habits of billionaires: when people *withdraw* cash from an asset, they pay taxes on that cash. However, if investments and loans are made simply using forms of *collateral*, then taxes are not required. This enables people from any walk of life to use the same financial tools that enable the super wealthy to get ahead—regardless of what a person is starting out with in their bank accounts. They can invest in long-term financial assets and secure loans, mainly using forms of collateral.

The Value Cards are a convenient form of collateral and also offer ways to house value. Investors buy them with real cash money, which means they have a real financial value—but all that value remains within the UOV, made visible in the Collaborative Cloud. There are no withdrawals and therefore no taxes.

There's a strong Person to Person element to Value Cards as well. When you hold the Value Card of an asset held by another collaborative, you are allowed to access an "insider" feed, like a social network for people involved in the project. You also have access to key financial details concerning that asset. In a sense, holding Value Cards for a Sovereign Asset allows you to become "part of the gang," gaining exclusive entry to an online "party" held by people doing work you admire.

Not only do Value Cards enable people to have access to the same financial tools as the super wealthy; they also increase the flexibility of any asset. For example, many middle-class people have most of their personal wealth tied up in the home where they reside. Depending on how much a person has paid down their mortgage loan, home equity may be a sizable financial asset. But it's also a cumbersome one. In order to access that equity, you have to remain attached to that pile of bricks: you must sell it, which is a major process; you must rent it out, which can be challenging; or you must take a loan out on your equity, which requires that you still remain involved in taking care of that pile of bricks.

It would be easier and more convenient to simply not own the pile of bricks at all, yet still hold the value of all the money you've invested in it over the years. Sovereign Assets, as discussed in previous chapters, enable that freedom—you no longer own the pile of bricks. Value Cards represent the worth: you still own all the value. Together, these tools allow for increased equality, freedom, and wealth building.

We introduced the basic elements of Value Cards in Chapter 9, but let's do a quick review of how they work since the rest of this chapter deals with them heavily. As discussed in Chapter 9, when money flows into the Sovereign Asset via investors, Value Cards are created. They will initially be valued at the amount of money that investors purchase them for; in our narrative example, each Value Card is bought for $100. However, from there, the Value Cards will fluctuate in value, just like the price of shares in a company fluctuates on the stock market. If the JALL Collaborative gets more successful and becomes more lucrative, the Value Cards will increase in value. If the JALL Collaborative starts struggling, on the other hand, the worth of the JALL Value Cards will drop.

The approximate worth of the Value Cards for any Sovereign Asset is the total value of that asset divided by the number of Value Cards issued for that asset. So let's imagine that a Sovereign Asset house is built with $300,000, using 3,000 Value Cards, each purchased for $100. But then, imagine that the house increases in value—say the "Zestimate" provided by Zillow puts it at $360,000. Now each Value Card is worth approximately $120; that's $360,000 divided by the 3,000 Value Cards held by investors. However, just like a Zestimate can't predict the true value of a home until it's sold on the market, a Value Card's true worth won't be known until it is sold on the marketplace.

Let's return to Jake and the rest of the group to see how their own auction experience plays out.

JALL GOES TO AUCTION

On Friday night, Jake, Lana, and Leon all showed up at Alex's dorm. They buzzed Alex's room number and waited for the doors to unlock. Leon was feeling left out.

"Am I the only one of us who hasn't already seen Alex's place?" he demanded. The door buzzed and the three headed into the lobby. Jake led them toward the stairwell.

Lana shrugged. "How have you *not* been here already? Alex and I study together all the time," she said. "And sometimes I get to be a fly on the wall when Jake and Alex are filming." She smiled cheerfully at Leon. "You're going to like it. It's epic."

"So I hear," he said, grumpily. They climbed out at the third-floor landing and found Alex's door. Jake rapped out a musical knock—*shave and a haircut...two bits.* He grinned at Leon. Leon rolled his eyes.

Alex opened the door and gestured inside. "Welcome, my cookies."

Leon had intended to play it cool when walking in, but he couldn't hold back his surprise. "Woah..." he said.

Alex had transformed their room into outer space. Massive canvas drop cloths hung from the ceiling, which Alex had painted entirely black, they had created a universe of stars and swirls, nebulae, and planets and moons. In one corner of the room was a prism lamp, which cast out changing colors; another lamp shone patterns of colored light onto the ceiling. Alex's bed was lofted above the desk; on the ceiling above the bed, there were hundreds of scraps of paper posted to the ceiling that contained scraps of poetry, quotes, and drawings. The desk underneath the bed was clearly not being used as a desk: instead, it was crammed full of books and containers of various art supplies. There were two beanbags on the floor. On the opposite wall, there was a long, narrow table beneath two large-screen monitors. On one screen, Alex had pulled up the group's auction page. The other showed the group members' different accounts on the Collaborative Cloud.

"This is unreal. Your place is incredible," Leon said in awe.

"Thanks," Alex said with pride. "I lucked out, getting a single. Turns out that declaring yourself as gender-fluid on your intake paperwork is a pretty good way to get a room to yourself. Do you guys want food?" Alex gestured to some platters of cheese, crackers, fruit, and wine over on the long table.

"Ooo, classy spread, Alex," Lana said approvingly. "You should host all our meetings."

"All hail the executive of snack distribution!" Jake cheered. "True to form." He turned to Leon. "So how is this auction going down?"

Leon checked his watch. "We're live at 6:00 p.m. Two minutes away. Do you all have people showing up?"

"Oh man, it was so hard to get my parents to figure out the Collaborative Cloud," Jake said, rolling his eyes. "I think they're good now, but it took forever. Still, I guess I should be proud of them. My mom wasn't even texting three years ago. I've recruited some others too—all the other mentors at the after-school program I used to teach at."

"And your grandma is coming," Lana elbowed him. "That's my favorite part." She turned to the others. "She got the hang of it faster than his parents, actually. I have a crew. My folks, my mentor, three of my teachers from high school, my old soccer coach, some relatives, my big brother . . . Plus, some of the other baristas from the café."

"Cool," Leon said. "My dad is coming." He rolled his eyes. "I mean, I guess it's a good thing."

"Aw, honey, that's dope," Alex said. "He's supporting you."

"Yeah—whatever," Leon said. "Anyway—he's got a few of his golf buddies coming too. And my mom will be there, and my aunt."

"I have sixty people coming," Alex volunteered.

"What?!" the others asked, incredulous.

"Basically my whole extended family. I have a lot of cousins." Alex shrugged. "We're Samoan; that's how we do it."

"Oh my gosh, it's starting!" Lana said. The screens on the wall were changing. "Hurry, grab some food! I call a beanbag."

Three bids came in almost simultaneously:

1.	TopDawg86:	100 cards	$10,000 @ *Sell when worth $200/card*
2.	LucyRamirez:	1 card	$100 @ *collectible*
3.	LucyRamirez:	1 card	$100 @ *4% interest*

"Aw, Abuela's an investor!" Jake cried, cheered to see his grandmother's name.

"One of the first ones, *and* she put in two different types of bids! Damn, Jake, she is *fast* on the draw," Lana said, impressed.

"And she's doing a collectible card." Jake said happily. "Abuela's the best!"

"Abuela's also pretty savvy," Leon observed. "She's getting herself a decent rate of return too."

"Hold up—" Alex said. "Not to take away from Grandma Lucy's glory or anything, but TopDawg86 just basically funded our whole project. Who is that?"

"My dad," Leon said, sighing.

"What does it mean—'Sell when worth $200/card'?" Lana asked.

"It means he doesn't want to be paid back with interest, but he wants to sell us back all the cards once they've doubled in value. It's a venture capitalist strategy," Leon explained.

Jake asked, "Is that good? I mean—I guess it's good that he thinks we'll double his value, right? That means he believes in us."

"Yeah—I mean, it's definitely a vote of confidence." Leon smiled, which caused Lana to gasp.

"Oh my gosh—this is totally a bonding moment between you and your dad!" She stood and hugged him. Alex waved cheering hands from the other beanbag.

Leon waved them off, trying to tamp down their enthusiasm. "Not so fast; we wouldn't want him to fund the entire thing. That would sap our cash flow down the road because we'd have to pay him back double. But we planned for that—let's see how he responds when our algorithm changes his investment." Leon raised his eyebrows at the others. "Dad might not be happy with that."

"There it goes. Look—" Alex said. "The order is changing."

1.	LucyRamirez:	1 card	$100 @ *collectible*
2.	LucyRamirez:	1 card	$100 @ *4% interest*
3.	TopDawg86:	50 cards	$5,000 @ *Sell when worth $200/card*

"My abuela is on top?" Jake asked. "And your dad is down to 50 cards. Why is that?"

"Our algorithm prioritizes investors with low interest rates first. Any investors using Dad's strategy go to the bottom of the ranking order, and our algorithm only allows us to do 50% of value investment cards. So Dad can't buy more than 50% with that strategy."

Leon's phone buzzed. "Dad texted. I bet he's pissed off." He read the text aloud: "*Only 50% VI? Smart strategy.*" Leon smiled again. "That's cool. He actually approves."

Lana squealed. "So many warm fuzzies from a ranking algorithm!" she crowed.

"Hey, Auntie Talia!" Alex said, drawing everyone's attention back to the screen. "At 1% interest. Aw, she's basically giving us the money for free."

"And Mr. Henderson!" Lana said. "My old soccer coach. Dang, he's going for it. We gotta make good for that guy."

Two more bids had appeared, and once again the order rearranged.

1.	LucyRamirez:	1 card	$100 @ *collectible*
2.	Talia777:	1 card	$100 @ *1% interest*
3.	LucyRamirez:	1 card	$100 @ *4% interest*
4.	RHenderson:	10 cards	$1,000 @ *5% interest*
5.	TopDawg86:	50 cards	$5,000 @ *Sell when worth $200/card*

"Can we bid?" Lana asked. "How do we bid?"

"Yes, damn—I should have explained all that before. I'm so sorry guys," Leon said. "Okay, look at the screen with our accounts." He pointed at the other screen, which showed each group member's accounts on the Collaborative Cloud. "Alex, can you bring up our Investment Accounts?" Alex went to their computer and did so. The screen showed:

```
JakeR:  $66.85
AlexF:  $107.46
LanaA:  $111.69
LeonK:  $264
```

"Okay, great—so remember, that's the divvied up value from the $300 we put into our asset's treasury to build the brand plus the money that each of us elected to hold back during the first draw. So it looks like Alex and Lana could each buy 1 Value Card. I could buy two."

"I don't even have enough for one?" Jake said, dismayed. "WTF?! Can I deposit some money to get $100 in my account? I can't miss out on this."

"Yeah, you can send some money to your Free Cash Account to make up the difference. Do you have $46 to spare?" Leon asked.

"Barely, but yes," Jake said, getting out his phone. "I'll pull a couple of Uber all-nighters if I have to. I'm not missing out on getting one of our first Value Cards."

"So how do we bid, Leon?" Lana asked impatiently. "I want a piece of this pie!"

"Here—I'll show you," Leon said. "I want to go all in with mine, so I'm going to pledge $200. And let's say...4.5% return. That way we pay back Grandma Lucy before me." He pulled out his phone, brought up his Collaborative Cloud app, and began typing. "Look—you go to our JALL auction page, and then just do this..."

Suddenly, Leon's name appeared on the auction screen, ranked in the number three spot below Grandma Lucy:

3. LeonK: 2 cards $200 @ *4.5% interest*

"Cool," he said. "Okay—now look at my totals on the other screen." On the screen showing the group members' Collaborative Cloud accounts, Leon's Investment Account now showed:

LeonK: JALL 2 Value Cards pledged

"There!" he said happily. "Once the auction is done—assuming it's successful and we get the money we need—those cards will move out of my Investment Account and into my Asset Account. Then they'll show up as 'Locked.'"

"Okay, my turn!" Lana said impatiently. She pulled out her phone. "Pulling up the Collaborative Cloud account... Going to our auction page..." She looked at Jake. "I have to pledge it to our brand asset, right? I'm not going to accidentally pledge to something else?"

Leon said, "Actually, you could choose to invest that money in a different collaborative. It's great if you want to invest in us, but it's your call. In some ways, that's the beauty of this model—you have the freedom to do what you want with that money. You could choose to invest that money in the Nicaraguan coffee roaster if you wanted to."

"Okay, I do *love* that Nicaraguan coffee roaster—but I definitely want my first Value Card to be for our brand. I'll come back to the roaster. How do I make sure I'm bidding on us?"

"Here," Leon said. He directed Lana to the JALL auction page on her phone and she typed in her bid.

Alex spoke up. "I'm planning to invest in an Iranian muralist. I found her on the cloud network—her work is incredible. It's totally subversive."

"Woah," Jake said. "That's cool. So—you're going to invest in her instead of us?"

"Don't worry, JALL baby comes first," Alex said. "But I put $300 in my Free Cash Account from some freelance work I got paid for. I've got enough for two cards for JALL and two for the muralist."

Lana's name appeared on the screen at the number two ranking.

> 2. LanaA: 1 card $100 @ *3% interest*

"There I am!" she cheered. "I'm number two!"

"Ahead of Abuela," Jake observed, raising one eyebrow.

"Only because I'm taking a lower interest rate," Lana said, a bit defensively. "Anyway, I'll make Grandma Lucy some cookies. She likes me."

"Alex, you should go next," Leon prompted. "And bid on that Iranian muralist too—then you can see what happens to your Asset Account when you've invested in multiple collaboratives."

Alex punched numbers into their phone, pledging $200 at 4.5% to their own JALL Collaborative, then pledging their remaining $200 to the Iranian muralist as a collectible investment.

"No return from the muralist?" Jake asked. "Why 4.5% from our group but a collectible investment for the muralist?"

"Because I don't want money from the artist," Alex answered. "I just want to support what she's doing because I think it's rad and I want the inside scoop on her work. Besides, if she ends up becoming famous, my Value Cards connected to her work would become hella valuable on the market. But I do want money from *our* group. I deserve it." Alex grinned.

"Okay—Alex, can you bring up your Investment Account now?" Leon asked. Alex navigated to their Investment Account on the big screen. It showed:

> AlexF: JALL Brand Asset 2 cards pledged
> Tamana: 2 cards pledged

"Tamana, that's the muralist, yeah?" Leon questioned. Alex nodded. "Okay, so when both auctions end—assuming they're successful—then your Investment Account is basically going to look empty, but those cards will show up in your Asset Account as 'Locked.'"

"When do they get *unlocked*?" Alex asked.

"Your collectible ones for Tamana are free to sell anytime, although you might want to hang on to them. But since you've got a debt contract with our collaborative, the JALL cards will be freed when we pay you back," Leon explained. "Then you'll get that money back into your Investment Account, plus interest."

"What happens if we never pay Alex back?" Jake asked. "Do the cards stay locked forever?"

"No—if a collaborative defaults on a loan, then those cards would be unlocked by the Sovereign Asset. Then you would try to sell them on the marketplace and hopefully make up some cash."

"Okay, well hopefully that's not going to happen." Jake took a deep breath and grinned. "I've got $100 between my Investment and Free Cash Accounts now. My turn?"

"Go Jakey! Go Jakey!" Lana and Alex chanted together. He began punching numbers into his phone.

"Hey Leon, what else can we do on this Collaborative Cloud marketplace?" Alex asked, swirling their wine.

OTHER TYPES OF
MARKETPLACE OPTIONS

In addition to the RFI, there are several other types of marketplaces that Collaborative Cloud users can access.

Collateral for Cash

As discussed in the previous chapter, one of the ways that the very wealthy avoid paying taxes is funding their lifestyles through loans. They're able to secure these loans because of all their assets—there's no shortage of collateral to reassure their lenders. When they get cash via loans, then they have liquidity to buy things in a manner that is completely disconnected from income. Since income taxes are only paid on income, cash from loans is tax-free. In fact, sometimes, there are even tax credits for loans.

However, there's an even bigger benefit to this approach than simply paying less in taxes: the ability to continue building *long-term value* but still have access to cash in the short term. The reason that many people stay stuck in a cycle of poverty is because they are so strapped for cash for their short-term expenses and thus never begin investing in long-term investment vehicles.

For instance, imagine that Jake earns around $400 per month from his Uber driving. The majority of that goes toward his dorm room rent, which is partly offset by a modest scholarship and housing stipend; the rest usually needs to go toward his cell bill. That leaves him with almost nothing left for food off campus, dates with Lana, clothes, coffee, and so on.[136] It certainly doesn't leave him with enough to set up a long-term investment vehicle. However, the financial tools available via the Collaborative Cloud provide people with a variety of options to pursue greater financial health—especially when it comes to long-term strategies.

In Chapter 6, we saw Jake sell some of his Collaborative Points to Leon to get the cash he needed for the short term. Now we'll discuss another option for Jake: Value Cards can also provide a way for Jake to get short-term cash, and if Jake felt confident that his Value Cards would appreciate quickly, this might be an even better option for him to get short-term cash than trading away some of his Collaborative Points.

On the Collaborative Cloud, Jake could use his Value Cards as collateral to gain access to short-term cash without actually selling his cards. This means he can make strategic investments in *long-term* wealth-building strategies

---

[136] Thankfully for Jake, the money he's now making through the JALL Collaborative is helping him earn money for some of these things.

while still having the cash he needs for his day-to-day needs.[137] Here's how that would work:

Jake would go to the marketplace and make a collateral for cash request; let's say he asks for $100. The person funding his loan will ask for a loan-to-value ratio (in addition to an interest rate) based on how solid Jake's Value Cards appear to be. For instance, a Value Card associated with a house in the UOV would probably be viewed as a very solid form of collateral, so an investor might ask for a 1-to-1 loan-to-value ratio: "I'll hold on to one of your Value Cards and give you $100 cash at 5% interest."

However, in Jake's case, his Value Cards are tied to the JALL Collaborative brand, which is a fledging enterprise and therefore a riskier investment. The person funding Jake's RFL is more likely to ask for a 2-to-1 loan-to-value ratio: "I'll fund you the $100 at 5% interest, but I want two of your Value Cards as collateral." Jake would then have to contribute double the Value Cards for the cash he's asking for—basically $200. They make the exchange; Jake would send 2 Value Cards to the person funding him, and he would get $100 in his Free Cash Account.

Now what happens? Let's see how this plays out in three different scenarios.

1. Scenario 1: Jake is able to pay the investor back the next month, plus interest: $105. He gets his 2 Value Cards back.
2. Scenario 2: Jake continues to pay the interest but doesn't pay back the $100 principal. So long as he keeps up with the interest payments, he can keep the $100 forever.
3. Scenario 3: The debt-to-value ratio becomes imbalanced, either because Jake can't keep up with the interest payments or because the Value Cards' worth as collateral drops (like if the JALL Collaborative starts struggling). Jake's debt is now bigger than

---

[137] Obviously, it's best to continue building your long-term investments *without* the need of loans. Since loans need to be paid back with interest, they work out better for the lender than the borrower. For this reason, loans should be viewed as a necessary evil, rather than a Plan A—even on the Collaborative Cloud network.

the 2-to-1 loan-to-value ratio they had agreed on, and something needs to happen to rebalance the debt. There are two options now:

» Jake gives some money to diminish the debt, to maintain the 2-to-1 ratio: "Here is $50 to pay for half of my debt. Since my 2 Value Cards are worth $150 right now, you have plenty of collateral to cover the 2-to-1 ratio on the remaining $50 debt."

» However, if Jake doesn't do that, then the smart contract takes one of the Value Cards and puts it in a Dutch Auction.

In the event that Jake's Value Cards actually increase in value while collateralized, nothing unusual happens. Jake will still pay the interest while the Value Cards are collateralized and will receive the Value Cards back if or when he decides to pay down the debt. In the meantime, he can feel good about his decision to collateralize the Value Cards rather than sell, and his investor can feel good that he made a solid investment.

Dutch Auction

A Dutch Auction exists to offer protection to lenders against defaulting loans. This is a way to liquidate the Value Cards being used as collateral, in case the user defaults on the loan or the collateral drops in value.

Here's how a Dutch Auction works. We're going to call Jake's lender BbRuth. In the event that Jake defaults on his loan, here's what would happen:

• The smart contract that governs Jake's loan from BbRuth puts up one of Jake's collateral cards for auction. As mentioned before, the Value Card's estimated value is determined by the Sovereign Asset it is associated with, divided by the number of Cards issued for that SA. So let's say the JALL Collaborative's cards have an estimated value of $80 each.

Once you put a card in the Dutch Auction, the bidding starts at $100. One minute later, it would go to $99.99; one minute later, it would go to

$99.98. If there are multiple bidders for the $100 card, it simply goes to the fastest bidder. (Although that's unlikely to happen, because if the cards were worth more than $100, it wouldn't go to the Dutch Auction.) Essentially, this is a liquidation process. The most likely people bidding on Value Cards in a Dutch Auction would be brokers using a strategy of buying and reselling to make a profit.[138]

The Dutch Auction would be repeated with other Value Cards until the loan-to-value ratio requirements are met. It's possible that the Dutch Auction wouldn't be able to sufficiently reimburse the lender if the lender didn't ask for a realistic loan-to-value ratio at the start. For instance, if BbRuth gave Jake a 1-to-1 loan-to-value ratio, he would have only had one card to sell as collateral in the Dutch Auction.[139] If that one card ends up selling for $70, BbRuth would end up $30 short of the $100 he loaned Jake. However, in this scenario, the 2-to-1 value ratio meant BbRuth has two cards to sell. If they both sell at $70 in the Dutch Auction, the debt would be repaid, plus interest. The remainder goes back to the borrower, so in this case, back to Jake's Free Cash Account.

Selling Value Cards for Cash

There's another way that Jake could get cash if he needed it: rather than doing an RFL, which would result in a loan, he could simply sell one of his own Value Cards on the market. If someone was willing to pay $70 for it, then that $70 would go right into Jake's pocket. However, this is more of a short-term strategy, and it wouldn't benefit Jake in the long run.

---

[138] More information about Dutch Auctions, including the financial strategy behind them, can be found in the FAQs section connected to this chapter, accessible via the chapter's QR code.

[139] In this case BbRuth could choose to bid on the auction himself, if he knew that the depreciation of the asset was only temporary and he didn't need the cash now. He could buy back the asset for $70 and then wait for it to reappreciate before selling it on the open market.

Here's why: once Jake sells his Value Cards, it's like cashing out your shares in the stock market. Not only would Jake have to pay taxes on that $70; he would also lose any opportunity to gain additional value in the future by holding on to that card. We can safely assume that Jake, Leon, Lana, and Alex all believe in their brand and intend to work hard to make it more successful. Their cards might be worth around $100 today, but in several years, there's a good chance their cards will be worth $200.

It would be smarter for Jake to take out a loan through an RFL. Over the next three years, he might have to pay around $50 in interest, but by then, his cards might be worth $200 each, and he would still possess that value.

These financial tools incentivize people to play fair. Even if two people don't know or trust each other well, the checks and balances provided through the smart contracts running on a blockchain ensure all transactions go through the way they're supposed to.[140] As a result, people are able to maintain a sustainable quality of life by getting the money they need in the short term while still building long-term value.

FUTURE VALUE

There's one more element at play in these auction scenarios: Future Value. We've waited to explain this component because it adds some complications. However, it enables greater quality of life for everyone involved because it rewards effort and contribution. It's also a way for people to gain long-term value, even if they don't start out with any spare financial capital with which to participate in auctions or investments.

In the current models at work in the world, effort and contribution often go unrewarded. Take the JALL Collaborative, for instance. People starting up

---

[140] As the working of a smart contract is defined upfront and because of the fact that the blockchain guarantees an immutable execution of such algorithm, both parties can be sure that whatever they've agreed on will come to pass.

a business like Jake, Alex, Leon, and Lana will often work eighty-hour weeks, with little to show for it. Sometimes the founding members get ownership shares, but people who come on later or are in lower positions may never see their effort rewarded. Instead, all their work hours serve to make the people at the top even richer.[141]

We can consider Alex, for example. In Chapter 6, Alex estimated they had contributed a total of twenty unpaid hours for the JALL Collaborative. Based on the conversations that the JALL group had during the draw, Alex identified their hourly rate as $100 per hour; their twenty unpaid hours are worth $2,000. But clearly, the actual cash the group had on hand to pay Alex was far below what Alex actually contributed in terms of economic value.

This can be rectified by tying Future Value to the Value Cards created during a Request for Investment (RFI). Let's see how this would play out by returning to our example.

- Because the JALL Collaborative is essentially a startup, the group members agree that Future Value is a major component of what's been poured into their brand. They agree to tie Future Value to the Value Cards that get created whenever money is sent to their brand asset.

- Leon sets that up via the Collaborative Cloud: using smart contracts, rules are set in place that will create an additional Value Card whenever an investor's card is paid off. These additional cards will compensate them for their Future Value—making their "unrealized potential" realized.

- The JALL group has set out to raise $10,000 for their brand asset, which will result in 100 Value Cards, each worth $100. Jake, Alex, Lana, and Leon estimate their Future Value at $9,000.

---

141 Pim de Morree, "Today's Capitalism Sucks. Here's More Evidence," Corporate Rebels, August 3, 2021, https://corporate-rebels.com/capitalism-sucks.

- The JALL group tells investors that they have tied $9,000[142] of Future Value to the investment goal of $10,000. Investors know, going in, that there will be additional Value Cards generated to compensate for that $9,000. This is both a pro and a con for investors: the additional 90 Value Cards generated for the Future Value will dilute the worth of their own Value Cards. (This is explained further in a moment.) However, it also means they're investing in a collaborative made up of people with skin in the game. Investors will know that the JALL colleagues will be incentivized to make their work profitable because, ultimately, the worth of the Value Cards *they* hold will be defined by the value of their asset.

- Assuming the auction is successful, the JALL group will have raised $10,000, and 100 Value Cards would have been issued, each worth $100.

- When the first Value Card is paid back with $100 from the JALL Collaborative, that Value Card is "freed" from its frozen debt status and is sent back to the JALL Collaborative. The $100 value of the card is disbursed according to the group members' Collaborative Points. (So Leon, at 38%, would get $38; Lana, at 18%, would get $18, etc.)

- Upon this Value Card being paid back, a smart contract issues a *second* Value Card to the JALL group to compensate for Future Value. This card would go to whichever JALL group member's turn is next. One Future Value Card might go to Alex in one round; in the next round, the Future Value Card would go to Lana, and so on. If a $100 Value Card were credited to Lana's Asset Account, the amount still "owed" to her in Future Value would be diminished by $100. This process keeps up until the full $9,000 of Future Value

---

[142] Realistically, the JALL group might only tie $4,500 to this first RFI so as not to deter investors and try to collect additional Future Value down the road with other RFIs. (Future Value can *only* be repaid by tying it to an RFI.) However, for the sake of maintaining consistency with numbers, we'll stick with the $9,000 Future Value for our narrative.

has been compensated for[143] and each group member has been rewarded for the effort they put in.

- These additional Value Cards *dilute* the worth of each of the Value Cards associated with the JALL brand asset. For instance, although 100 Value Cards were initially issued from the $10,000 investment, each worth $100, the total 190 cards that would eventually be issued would only be worth $52.63. (That's $10,000 divided by 190.) This prospect would probably be unappealing to investors.

- *Unless, that is,* the JALL group works hard to make their brand more profitable—which, in this case, they will. In fact, more profitability was the entire reason for raising the $10,000 in the first place. If they have succeeded in making their brand more profitable, they may have established a market value of $20,000—twice what they started out with. That means each of the 190 Value Cards would have actually *increased* in value, to $105.26. (That's $20,000 divided by 190.)

These first-edition Value Cards associated with the JALL brand may have also grown in appeal as a collector's item if the JALL brand attracts a following. They might have become valuable tokens to sell and/or collateralize.

What about additional Future Value that the colleagues might generate through unpaid effort? Will that Future Value ever have a chance to be realized?

Yes—through future RFIs. Future Value will always be bound to an RFI, but the colleagues won't necessarily always need to fund an RFI via outside investors. If the collaborative is doing well and the investors are paid back, the JALL brand Sovereign Asset would be growing the treasury. This would result in money building up in the Investment Accounts of the JALL colleagues. If they decided to do an RFI later on and tie more Future Value to the money raised, the members might be able to fund the entire RFI themselves.

---

[143] Or, until someone's Future Value balance is less than $100.

This way of rewarding Future Value through Value Cards means that people can build long-term financial capital, even if they don't start out with any capital at all. For instance, let's imagine that a single mom has no extra money to invest in long-term savings vehicles; she's using every spare dollar to pay for her family's necessities. But she does have some *effort* to spare. Perhaps her neighbor has started up a collaborative project and needs someone's help watching his kids. The single mom agrees to watch his kids for free after school and earns Future Value attached to her neighbor's Sovereign Asset. That translates to Value Cards. As the neighbor's project becomes more lucrative, the single mom's Value Cards increase in their worth. Down the road, she has the opportunity to use her Value Cards to collateralize or sell.

The same is true for Jake. With every month that Jake puts effort into the JALL Collaborative, he will gain in Collaborative Points and Future Value; these can translate to Value Cards.

Rewarding Future Value with Value Cards would only be applicable for startups like the JALL group who find themselves putting in lots of unpaid effort. The mechanism creates equitable rewards, can build confidence for investors, and can generate long-term investment vehicles for people who would otherwise be unable to create them. It also ensures that colleagues are fully and equitably compensated for their contribution, even after they leave a collaborative. For instance, if Alex moved on from the JALL Collaborative but still had Future Value that had not been compensated yet, a new RFI would still generate Value Cards for Alex until their Future Value had been completely rewarded.

FULLY FUNDED

After close to two hours, the amount of money raised for the JALL group's marketing campaign neared $10,000. Many bids had come in from their network of friends, family members, and supporters; they were also surprised and pleased by how many of their YouTube followers had made small contributions.

Jake's parents were the last to submit their bids, and only managed to do so after several tech-support calls with their son and Grandma Lucy. Finally, their names appeared in the number five slot:

5. G&JRamirez: 3 cards $300 @ 5% interest

The numbers total shifted to "$10,000," and the screen issued a burst of confetti with the words "FULLY FUNDED." All four JALL group members jumped up and cheered, hugging each other and dancing around the room. Alex grabbed the bottle of wine and began pouring it into various glazed pottery cups.

"I seriously can't believe we made it all the way to $10,000!" Jake said, grinning in disbelief.

"Believe it, baby!!" Lana cheered. She threw her arms around Jake and kissed him on the lips. "People believe in *us*!" They flopped down onto a beanbag and began making out.

Alex had turned on bumping techno music and was dancing. Leon just stood there, grinning, taking it in. His phone buzzed with a text. When his face noticeably changed as he looked at his phone, Alex slid over next to Leon to peer down at the screen. "From your dad?" they asked. Alex read aloud: "*Cool to see you finding your own path, son. Proud of you.*"

Alex looked at Leon. "That's good, right? Papa Bear is proud of you."

Leon shrugged and smiled grimly. "Because I'm raising money. I'm acting like an entrepreneur. He can't express love when I strike out at the state baseball championship, but he can tell me he's proud when I recruit investors."

"Hey now," Alex said. "Maybe finance is the only language your dad knows how to love in. You know? That doesn't make it any less significant. Love is love. Proud is proud."

"Maybe," Leon grudgingly acknowledged. "It just means he's an idiot about expressing love in every other context."

"And that's pain, and that sucks. But maybe you can find your way toward each other," Alex urged. "Like you and me—right, MAGA man?" Leon gave a dry laugh.

Alex continued. "Finance is an area you two have in common. Maybe it's not what you *wish* you had in common . . . but it's something."

Leon shrugged again. "True, I guess. There's a sliver of overlap in the Venn diagram."

"Embrace the center of the Venn diagram!" Alex urged. "Papa Bear is gonna change slowly, and you're going to accept slowly, but that still means the center of the diagram is expanding. Right?" Alex lifted their mug of wine and held out one to Leon. "And we're celebrating tonight. This auction was epic, and we did good. Cheers to us!"

"Cheers to us." Leon smiled and bumped Alex's mug with his.

"And cheers to the center of the Venn diagram!" Alex raised their cup again, sipped, and started grooving.

"Alright, alright, alright." Leon lifted his cup and drank. "I'll drink to that." A new song came on: "Rags2Riches." "Oh yes! I know this one!" Leon said.

Jake had broken out of his tangle with Lana and sat up. "I know this one!" he cried.

The two young men leapt up and started doing the moves they'd learned on TikTok, stacking their fists and shaking their heads. Lana laughed and waved her fingers. "Sparkles!" she cried.

"Wait!" Alex said. They grabbed a glitter container off the desk and shook it over Jake and Leon. "You are both sparkle men. Think happy thoughts. Now you can fly."

"I've got all kinds of happy thoughts tonight!" Jake said.

Leon was grooving in a circle and spread out his arms. "Second star to the right, and straight on 'til morning." He looked at the rest of them and grinned. "We've got the money to fly, people. Let's do this."

CHAPTER ELEVEN

QOLIHOP: QUALITY OF LIFE HOUSING PROJECT

Exploring Possibilities Enabled by the Person to Person Environment

Housing is absolutely essential to human flourishing. Without stable shelter, it all falls apart.

−Matthew Desmond, American sociologist and principal investigator of Princeton University's Eviction Lab

Jake groaned as he tried to close the hatch of the 2016 Ford Fiesta he had bought six months ago. Leon's duffel wasn't so bad, but Lana had brought along a giant suitcase with early Christmas presents for his family, and Alex—newly into oil painting—had asked to bring along an easel. He stared at the small trunk, wondering how to shift the bags to squeeze in his snack cooler.

Two years had passed since the JALL group had successfully raised the $10,000 for their marketing campaign via the RFI. In the time since, the group had managed to grow their following of video gamers on YouTube with the marketing push. However, the biggest growth of their brand occurred once they decided to make a series of videos showcasing the philosophy, spirit, and logistical workings of their own collaborative. Jake had made a video sharing the story that began the group's whole endeavor, when he retreated to the library to journal about his personal essence and goals. Lana made a video describing how to engage in frictionless Commitment Sessions. Sometimes Leon and Alex got in front of the camera as well, role-playing their former selves to show how their group got started. They showcased how they'd developed their Collaborative Agreement, worked out their Contribution Sessions, and found new financial opportunities on the Collaborative Cloud. The online following for JALL has increased to eighty thousand followers. Jake and Lana have even developed their own fan base, especially as they've made videos together and allowed their personal relationship to inform their banter.

As a result of their successful brand growth, the JALL group had managed to successfully pay off their investors with interest. Now the group members held the entirety of the cards connected to their brand asset. With the brand steadily growing in profitability, the JALL Value Cards had a market value between $175 and $215. Jake had collateralized a number of his to purchase the car. And now he was taking his best friends home for a Ramirez family Thanksgiving.

"Ramirez, why don't you just let me drive the Rav?" Leon asked. "It has a big trunk that could easily fit everything."

"No way," Jake grunted as he finally managed to close the hatch. "I've been riding shotgun in your Rav long enough. It's my turn to drive. Besides—" he wiped his forehead. "I wouldn't trust a Californian on the turnpike in November." He grinned.

Leon rolled his eyes. "Californians are the best drivers in the country, amigo. We drive fast because we kick ass."

"Yeah, except in the rain and never in the snow," Jake retorted.

Lana and Alex came out of Lana's dorm, where they had made one more bathroom stop before the long drive. "I'm so ready to be out of this dorm next year," Lana remarked as they all climbed into the car. "It's fun being an RA to the little froshies and all, but I am sooooo ready for my own place." Alex connected their phone to the car's sound system and began playing Silk Sonic.

"I'm getting my own place," Alex said cheerfully. "Michelle and I are moving in together."

"Whaaaaat?!" the others cried out. Michelle and Alex had been dating for the past year, and the rest of the group had become close with Michelle, a literature student.

"Where??" Lana asked. "Alex! This is huge!"

"She found us this awesome apartment on Fourth, near the transit stop. We're splurging on a two-bedroom so I can have my own studio." Alex grinned. "Moving in January." Alex let out a rare squeal. "Eeeee! I'm so excited."

"On Fourth?" Lana asked, her attention piqued. She looked over at Jake from the passenger seat. "That's not at all far from Mrs. Crumble's house in Prospect Place . . . We could *do* it, baby . . ."

"What's this?" Leon asked. He leaned forward from the back seat. "Isn't Mrs. Crumble the old lady that brings her pig to your café, Lana?"

"Yes, she's my bestie. And the pig, Carol—named after Carol Burnett, which I find hilarious—loves me too. I always give it a bran muffin. Mrs. Crumble has seen all of our YouTube videos and is a little obsessed with Jake." Lana grinned and pinched Jake's cheek. "She says he's a 'real looker.' Which I agree with. Anyway, she wants to sell her house to us."

"Woah!" Leon cried out. "Seriously, Jake? You never told me about this."

"That's because it's not happening," Jake said. "There's no way I can buy a house right now; are you kidding? What bank would qualify *me* for a loan? I still have all my student debt, I don't have much of a credit history, there's that little juvie episode on my record—"

"From eighth grade!" Lana protested.

"—And there's still the down payment issue." Jake made eye contact with Leon in the rearview mirror. "Pretty sure I don't have enough Collaborative Points to trade with you for a down payment."

"What about all the money you've saved up in Value Cards?" Leon asked. "Lana's got plenty of Value Cards too."

"A lot of mine are currently collateralized so that I could get the car," Jake pointed out. "And okay, yes, I've been able to save a lot from our JALL Collaborative work, but I've still got my student loans to pay off...And I've got grad school in mind too. Basically, the money I've saved is spoken for. I don't have anything close to a down payment. And I'm not about to ask Lana to fund the whole thing on her own." He looked back over at Lana and spoke gently. "Listen, babe. I love the idea of living together, and Mrs. Crumble's place seems great—her offer is amazing. But I just think buying it outright is totally beyond us right now." He shifted to a conciliatory tone. "Maybe we could rent to own if she really likes the idea of selling it to us?"

Lana sighed. "I've told you; Mrs. Crumble can't afford to rent-to-own because she wants to move into a retirement community that is crazy expensive. She needs to actually sell her house so that she has all that cash to get into her next place."

Jake shrugged and his face hardened. "Well, we're not her people, then."

"Gah!" Lana threw up her hands and appealed to Alex and Leon in the back. "Can you believe this opportunity that's just been *handed* to us? Mrs. Crumble could be our only chance to buy our own place in this kind of crazy market. And Jake won't even—"

"Why don't you turn it into a Sovereign Asset?" Alex piped up. Alex turned to Leon and bumped his arm. "Remember my sister and Wes and the Lego house? This is literally what we talked about." Alex paused. "Except I don't think we ever figured out *how* they would get into the Lego house."

"I was thinking the same thing; you could totally Sovereign Asset it!" Leon said. He leaned forward toward Jake and Lana. "Listen: you could crowdfund via an RFI, just like we did with our marketing campaign money.

Then Mrs. Crumble donates the house to the UOV, converts it to a Sovereign Asset, and you two become the first users. You earn Value Cards with every month's payment."

Lana looked back at Alex and Leon, her face radiant. "We could *do* that?"

"Crowdfund what—the cost of the *house*?" Jake's voice cracked. He cleared his throat and lowered his voice. "Peeps, we're talking several hundred thousand dollars."

"Probably between $310,000 and $330,000," Lana supplied. "I've been researching comparable two bedrooms in the area with similar square footage, built around the same time. That's about what they're going for."

"Three hundred and twenty *thousand*?" Jake asked, incredulous. "You think we can raise $320,000 on a crowdfund?!"

Lana furrowed her eyebrows at Jake. "You're thinking with a scarcity mindset again, Jakey. Think of all the good things the universe wants to give you. Think abundance." She leaned over and rubbed his chest. "Take some deep breaths. I can tell you're getting flooded."

Jake compliantly began taking deep breaths, and Alex leaned forward. "There's an artist who made over $300,000 in the past ten months selling NFTs of her artwork on Web3," Alex said.[144]

"Seriously?!" Jake asked, dropping the deep breathing.

"Lana Denina. Her style isn't totally my flavor, but I still think she's badass."

"That's chump change," Leon said. "Did you guys hear about the DAO that was created to buy a copy of the US Constitution? They raised 47 *million*."[145] He shrugged. "They still got outbid by a billionaire—"

"Damn billionaires," Lana muttered.

---

[144] Taylor Locke, "This 24-Year-Old Artist Has Made over $300,000 in 10 Months Selling Nfts: 'I Hope to Inspire More Creatives Who Look like Me'." *CNBC*, December 3, 2021, https://www.cnbc.com/2021/12/03/24-year-old-artist-made-over-300000-dollars-in-10-months-selling-nfts.html.

[145] Nilay Patel, "From a Meme to $47 Million: ConstitutionDAO, Crypto, and the Future of Crowdfunding," *The Verge*, December 7, 2021, https://www.theverge.com/22820563/constitution-meme-47-million-crypto-crowdfunding-blockchain-ethereum-constitution.

"But the point stands: there is some wild stuff happening in the DeFi world." He translated himself: "Decentralized finance. For the noobs in the car."

"And there are tons of people out there looking for good things to invest in," Lana said. "Real estate is a *great* investment. Did you know that wealthy people in Europe start getting negative interest rates from banks if they have too much money just sitting there? My wealthy uncle in Belgium is literally losing money every day his euros sit in a bank.[146] He's chomping at the bit to find a different investment vehicle." She looked over at Jake. "I bet he would bid $20,000. Easy."

Leon leaned forward toward Jake. "Seriously—$330,000 is not out of the question. You just have to get the word out."

Lana looked at Jake, her eyes shining. "Jake, we have eighty thousand followers on YouTube. Plus, we have all of our friends and family. That's a major network of people who care about us. If we pitched this to our You-Tube network, I think there are a ton of people who would be game to do this. We could also try to expand our social media presence to TikTok and Twitter and Instagram . . . Besides, we're not asking for their charity—they would be investors, and they'd get paid back, just like we paid our investors back from the first auction."

Jake took a deep breath. "Okay, so *if* we raise the money . . . What then?"

Lana smiled and twinkled her fingers. "Okay. We'd need to pay the monthly usage fees, which would be like our rent. I've already played around with numbers, and Zillow says a mortgage payment would be around $1,700 per month for a $320,000 twenty-five-year loan around 3.75%.[147] But a two-bedroom *rental* would actually usually go for around $2,000. So, actually,

---

[146] Gregory Claeys, "What Are the Effects of the ECB's Negative Interest Rate Policy?" Monetary Dialogue Papers, European Parliament, Directorate-General for Internal Policies of the Union (June 2021), DOI: 10.2861/041324.

[147] These numbers are based off average property values for a two-bedroom/two-bath homes in the Prospect Park neighborhood of Minneapolis, Minnesota as of December 2021.

if we were to live in this place as a Sovereign Asset, we'd not only be earning value, we'd also be getting a better deal than if we rented."

Alex spoke up from the back seat. "Yeah, but keep in mind that you have to add like $500 to whatever Zillow says would be your monthly payment to cover insurance, taxes, all that," Alex said. "The fees for the Sovereign Asset funds would probably be comparable. Plus, you might want to do some updates or repairs. So your monthly payment would probably need to be around $2,000 anyway. Or even $2,200."

Lana looked at Jake, her enthusiasm temporarily dampened. "Huh. I don't think we could swing $1,100 apiece." She sighed, crestfallen. "Damn it. Oh man, I was so convinced we could make this work."

"You could get a roommate," Alex offered.

Jake and Lana looked at each other. They both spoke aloud at the same time: "Leon!"

"What?!" Leon protested. "No. Nooooo, no, no. I'm not interrupting this honeymoon."

"Leon, come on!" Lana cried. "It'd be fun! And you'd be earning Value Cards instead of throwing your money away on renting!"

"Dude, this is seriously a good idea," Jake said. "I'd be living with my best friend and my girlfriend. You and I could still go on runs and play hoops together all the time."

"Come on, you two are going to want to walk around naked and stuff," Leon protested. "This is like the *definition* of third wheel."

"Leon, we'd have our own bedroom with a *door*," Jake said. "Do you have any idea how much of an improvement that is over our current situation? That's one small step for man, one giant leap for nudity."

"Well, *now* someone's starting to sound excited," Lana observed, amused. She turned back toward Leon. "I practically live with you two anyway. But now we'd have more space, and we'd all be earning value with our payments. And we can do Commitment Sessions when things get challenging... We *know* how to do this; we will be great roommates!"

Leon turned to Alex for help. "Alex. Tell them this is a bad idea."

"I think it's a great idea, actually," Alex said. "Jake and Lana are good for you. And there's no pressure if it doesn't work out. If it's a Sovereign Asset, then it's not like you're signing a mortgage loan with them. You can leave anytime you want. But in the meantime—like Lana said—you're earning Value Cards. It's smart. In fact, I wish Michelle and I had thought of it." They grinned. "We'll get in on the action by investing in your RFI."

"I don't know..." Leon said, reluctantly. "Aren't you all forgetting that I can be a pain in the ass sometimes?"

Alex leaned over toward him. "Brother. You're listening to those lies again. Thinking that people don't want you. Thinking that people don't love you. Look at these people." Alex gestured to the front seat. Lana was facing Leon with a pleading smile, holding up prayer hands. Jake was looking at Leon earnestly in the rearview mirror. "These people love you," Alex said firmly.

"Buddy," Jake said. "One of my main reservations with pursuing this with Lana is that I didn't want to leave you high and dry. Seriously—we would love for you to live with us."

Leon looked at them tentatively. "Really?"

"Really, really, really, really!" Lana crowed. "Say you're on board. Let's do it. And Alex and Michelle can come over every week for family dinners. Pleeeease."

"Okay," Leon said, grinning in spite of himself. "What the hell."

"YES!" Jake said, pumping his fist. "Oh man, I feel so much better knowing that Leon is in this too. Now I *know* it's going to work out."

Leon began to tick off to-do items. "We need to start crunching numbers to write up the RFI proposal. And we should make some videos for the YouTube channel, explaining Sovereign Assets to our followers. Let's think of other ways to get the word out and drum up interest—I can reach out to my crypto community. And we should all tour Mrs. Crumble's place." He thought for a moment and then grinned. "I call the pig's room."

PROBLEMS AT HOME

Lana has good reason for feeling excited about living in Mrs. Crumble's home as a Sovereign Asset. Let's think through the alternatives they would be looking at otherwise, regarding their housing plans.

Renting is problematic, mainly because it's "throwing money away," as the two already discussed. It's the only real option for anyone who can't afford to buy a home, but unfortunately, it's often a reason why many people stay in poverty. With high rental costs, it can be a struggle to save up enough for a down payment, keeping people stuck in rentals and barred from the opportunity to build long-term wealth via real estate. What's more, in urban centers like where Jake and Lana want to live, rent continues to rise as inventory drops. That's a factor being exacerbated by companies like Airbnb, which have caused many potential rental properties to be taken off the market to be listed as vacation rentals instead.

Purchasing a home is also problematic, especially for a couple like Jake and Lana—and, for that matter, the vast majority of first-time home buyers. Buying a home is more expensive and more challenging than at any time in recent memory. In fact, home ownership among millennials below thirty-five is at its lowest level in thirty years. Among the ages of thirty-five to forty-four, home ownership rates have dropped even more significantly.[148] Millennials are typically shouldering a greater debt burden than previous generations, which makes it particularly challenging to save money for a down payment.[149] They also don't always have a substantial credit history to qualify for a loan.

---

[148] Medha Agarwal, "The next Billion Dollar Company Will Reinvent Home Ownership for Millennials," LinkedIn, December 3, 2018, https://www.linkedin.com/pulse/next-billion-dollar-company-reinvent-home-ownership-medha-agarwal.

[149] Tyler Durden, "Millennial Renters Abandon Their Plans to Buy a Home," ZeroHedge, accessed December 9, 2021, https://www.zerohedge.com/personal-finance/millennial-renters-abandon-their-plans-buy-home.

Even if someone were to finally be in a position to buy a modest home, there are often Goliaths competing against them for the same property. As Alex and Leon discussed in Chapter 7, there are Wall Street hedge funds buying up properties in the California Bay Area to help secure their pension funds. Other anonymous shell companies do the same thing, paying cash. In highly competitive real estate markets, the typical middle-class person or family doesn't stand a chance.

Another problem with home ownership is that it impedes flexibility—that's a problem for people like Jake and Lana who are just starting out in their adult lives. The standard advice when buying a home is to stay in it for roughly five years so that you can begin to experience the advantages of building equity after paying off mostly interest for the first few years. For anyone who knows they don't want to live somewhere longer than, say, two years, that's an issue. The standard default alternative is simply to rent if you want flexibility, but that brings us back to the same issues with renting we just discussed.

As the world continues to populate, urban centers continue to experience increased demand for more housing, and working people continue to seek out flexibility in their movement as more work goes online—this is simply not a sustainable model.

In a Person to Person environment—one that would allow more quality of life—this is what we might hope for:

- A way to enjoy the flexibility of renting while still being able to earn long-term value with your monthly payments.
- A platform to find sustainable and affordable housing, no matter what your economic status.
- A way to connect and collaborate with other people in a meaningful way, throughout the home ownership process.
- An economic environment that facilitates collaboration and responsible, autonomous participation.
- A focus on human quality of life, in balance with ecological sustainability.

That is what the QOLiHoP vision is all about, which stands for Quality of Life Housing Project. The Person to Person environment, when applied to housing, allows for all these "wish list" items to become a reality, through turning properties into Sovereign Assets and connecting collaboratives who will make good use of them—like Jake, Lana, and Leon—to those Sovereign Assets.

QOLIHOP: THE PERSON TO PERSON ENVIRONMENT APPLIED TO HOUSING

In order for QOLiHoP to get started, several things need to happen:

1. A Current Property Owner Decides to Convert Their Property to a Sovereign Asset

This is what Mrs. Crumble has decided to do for Jake, Lana, and now Leon, which means she agrees to "sell" her house via the Collaborative Cloud, on an RFI auction, then donate the property to the Universal Ownership Vault.[150] The process of donating her property to the UOV would only start *after* the RFI is successful. So there is no financial risk for Mrs. Crumble. In the worst case, should the RFI fail, she would only have lost a couple of weeks in her timetable to sell her home.

Because the money for the home will be generated via a crowdfunding process, this may be a lengthier selling process than what typically happens when a real estate agent brings a home to market. This is a choice by the homeowner to prioritize quality of life over speed and greed.

As Mrs. Crumble illustrates, the QOLiHoP process is a way for established property owners to help others get a leg up in the world and collaborate with them in doing something profoundly meaningful. They're helping to restore

---

[150] The Universal Ownership Vault was introduced and described in Chapter 7.

greater equity to one of the world's most inequitable systems. In the process, they also open themselves up to a number of tax advantages, as discussed in previous chapters, while still ensuring they get paid a fair price for their home.

In our book's introduction, the two of us described a property in France, in the town of Ginoles les Bains, that helped inspire our journey in dreaming up the Person to Person environment. We lovingly dubbed it the Experience Center and have converted the large property into a Sovereign Asset. The property is available to be used by one or several collaboratives who will steward the property for connection, gathering, healing, community, and rest, therefore fulfilling and restoring the purpose of the property. It is our dream to bring the property into new revitalization through dedicating it as a Sovereign Asset, allowing it to serve as a platform for people to experience greater quality of life.

2. The Sovereign Asset Finds a Collaborative to Use It

In our example, Jake, Lana, and Leon would be the collaborators who will be the first users of Mrs. Crumble's house. The collaborators should be intent on using and stewarding the Sovereign Asset in a way that will help the asset fill its intended purpose. In QOLiHoP, the Sovereign Asset's purpose is very straightforward: this is a property that needs people to live in it and/or run it as a business. (The property's purpose is *not*, on the other hand, to secure pension funds of a giant corporation in another state.)

Shortly after making this agreement, the original owner and the collaborators should work together to arrange for an appraisal and inspection of the home, similar to what would happen in a normal property sale. This information will help inform the next step—determining the fair purchase price —and provide necessary information about aspects of the property that may need repair.

3. The Original Property Owner and the Collaborative Agree on a Fair Price

Lana's research has determined that a fair purchase price for Mrs. Crumble's house would be around $320,000; we can assume Mrs. Crumble agrees to that number as well. But what about the interest factor? As Alex had pointed out, the monthly payment for a Sovereign Asset should factor in interest, payments to the sustainability fund and operations funds, and additional money that might be needed for repairs. So, when all is said and done, what should the monthly payment be? Exactly how long will a Sovereign Asset be receiving monthly payments until all investors are paid off?

In Europe, a standard mortgage lasts around 20 years; in the US, it's common to arrange for a 30-year mortgage. On the shorter end, then, we're dealing with 240 months; on the longer end, we're dealing with 360 months. Splitting the difference would be a 25-year mortgage, which equals 300 months.

To determine a fair purchase price and a monthly payment, additional calculations need to be made on top of the time frame of repayment. The SASTO (i.e., the legal organization that will technically own the property[151]) needs the amount to be right so that they have not overextended themselves for a property worth less than its purchase price; investors need it to be right so that their investment is correctly collateralized; the collaborative needs it to be correct too, so that they don't pay more than the property is worth in their monthly usage fees. These calculations are an important step to protect everyone in the process.

1. How much a property should cost, plus taxes, registration fees, and potential initial repairs. This number would determine the initial RFI crowdfund target.

2. Additional monthly costs: namely, the money required for the Sovereign Asset's sustainability and operations funds. (These cover costs for insurance, taxes, environmental sustainability factors, etc.)

3. How much the collaborative can afford in a monthly payment. This payment should align with a comparable monthly rent for other similar properties in the area. This number can be multiplied by

---

[151] We introduced and described SASTOs in Chapter 7.

300 to determine if the monthly payments will completely pay down the home within twenty-five years with interest and sufficiently cover the added monthly cost of the funds.

Let's take a look at how all these numbers might play out in Lana, Leon, and Jake's situation with Mrs. Crumble's house:

THE NUMBERS FOR
MRS. CRUMBLE'S QOLIHOP SCENARIO

The RFI target to crowdfund from investors:

- **Purchase price**: Mrs. Crumble wants $320,000 for her property.
- **Taxes**: The property taxes to make the purchase are $30,000.
- **Repairs**: The group wants to make some repairs approximating $30,000.
- **The total amount of money requested in the RFI would be $380,000.**

Payment calculations:

- **Average interest rate**: After running the RFI, the average annual interest rate requested from investors works out to 3.75%
- **Monthly payment**: Lana, Jake, and Leon are able to pay $2,200 a month. We can assume that approximately 70% of that amount will be used by the SA smart contract to repay investors ($1,540) and 30% ($660) will be devoted to the SA's funds.
- **Repayment timeline**: Given those parameters, the Value Cards ranked last would be paid back in approximatively thirty years.[152]

---

[152] However, given the likelihood of subsequent users paying a *higher* "rent" (usage fee) as the property value increases, there is a good chance investors would be paid back more quickly than this original 30-year repayment estimate.

Given the above calculations, Jake, Lana, and Leon's original determination that they could afford to use Mrs. Crumble's house as a Sovereign Asset is correct.

It's important to note: this is only one way of doing things; the QOLiHoP is not a system or a model with set rules; it's a vision for how the Person to Person environment could apply to housing. This is an idea that can be adapted and evolved according to the unique needs of any particular situation. However, both collaboratives and owners should take steps to ensure they can afford to use the Sovereign Asset, in the same way that there are checks and balances in place from mortgage lenders to evaluate what kind of loan a would-be homeowner would qualify for.

The collaborators should ensure that they can afford to use the Sovereign Asset (i.e., pay the appropriate rent) and have a plan about how they intend to steward the asset well, in a sustainable fashion. For instance, if Jake, Lana, and Leon realized that Mrs. Crumble's house *should* rent out for $3,000 per month, they would need to find a more affordable Sovereign Asset to QOLiHoP with. If there were a significant price discrepancy between what Jake, Lana, and Leon were paying and what anyone else would pay for a comparable home in the neighborhood, that discrepancy would, among other things, deter investors. In general, it's better to stick with a rent that is a good representation of the normal rental price of a similar property in the neighborhood.

If they intend to make repairs or update, those changes should be clarified in their proposal when they bring the property to auction; alternately, they may do separate RFIs later on, when they decide they want to do a big update.

Just like a typical pair of college students would start out looking for a cheaper rental and gradually look for a larger property down the road, when they were more established in their careers and/or had expanded their family, QOLiHoppers would also seek different types of Sovereign Assets to live in, according to their financial budget and stage in life. The beauty of living in a Sovereign Asset, however, is that you're earning value from day one while still enjoying the flexibility of being able to move to a different property whenever you're ready, without going through the hassle of selling your property.

In brief, here is a summary of the steps related to determining the Sovereign Asset's monthly usage fee:

- Rent can be chosen by the collaborative making the RFI. In that sense, investors know the initial timeline, as that is the one they subscribe to. The collaborative should choose a monthly rent that is relatively consistent with market prices to attract investors.
- Rent changes every time a new collaborative takes over the usage rights of the Sovereign Asset as the result of the usage auction. In most cases, we assume the rental price is at par with market conditions.
- Investors' repayment timeline can be *altered* by changes in the rental price of a Sovereign Asset. That isn't necessarily a problem because they are free to "sell" their "investment" at any time if the new timeline doesn't fit their personal plan.
- As far as real estate Sovereign Assets are concerned, given the current market conditions, usage rights are more likely to become *more* expensive with each usage auction, shortening the investors' initial timeline.

4. The Collaborative Prepares to Go to Auction

Similar to what we saw in Chapter 10, Leon, Jake, and Lana would now need to write up their proposal for how they would use the Sovereign Asset. Their proposal, ideally, will help attract and reassure investors that they will be trustworthy stewards of the Sovereign Asset. Here is the kind of information they might want to provide:

THE MAKINGS OF A STRONG QOLIHOP PITCH[153]

- The collaborative's plans for use: both in terms of how long the collaborative intends to stay in the house and what their plans are for doing updates to the house. They might even include a design page(s) where they provide pictures showing their aesthetic and intended style updates.
- An inspection report detailing the home's structural soundness
- An appraisal report with an approximate estimation of the property's value
- The collaborative colleagues might choose to volunteer their credit history and provide additional financial details. For Lana, Jake, and Leon, investors would likely also be reassured by evidence about their work history and work prospects as they prepare to graduate college.
- The colleagues' dreams: Lana, Leon, and Jake should describe how and why this opportunity to live in a Sovereign Asset would help them make a better start in life. For instance, Jake could honestly attest to the fact that he would not be able to afford home ownership without an opportunity like this. He could also emphasize the benefits of QOLiHoP: decreasing debt, building capital, strengthening people, building sustainability, breaking the cycle of deprivation, and realizing more equity. Lana could discuss how they plan to use the asset to increase its value, make it more environmentally sustainable, and serve the community around them. Leon could describe the flexibility of the QOLiHoP housing situation and talk about the close friendships the three share. All three could highlight the ways they would be able to invest in their community as a

---

[153] This information is also provided on our website for the reader's easy reference. Please see this chapter's QR code.

result of the QOLiHoP opportunity. For instance, instead of taking a lucrative corporate job mainly for its high pay, Lana could feel free to invest her considerable talents in an area that she feels is more directly tied to increasing quality of life, like social work. Jake could pursue his teaching career with energy and focus rather than worrying constantly about high mortgages and financial stress. Leon could continue to research and scale the possibilities of the Collaborative Cloud through experiencing living in a Sovereign Asset firsthand. And finally, they could describe their dream of building quality of life in each other's company.

Now Jake, Leon, and Lana are ready to go to auction.

5. The Sovereign Asset Is Featured in an RFI Auction (Spearheaded by the Collaborative) to Raise Funds for the Full Purchase of the Asset

This would essentially be a similar process to what you read in the auction chapter, only it would likely last much longer—possibly a month or two—to raise the full amount needed.[154] Lana and Jake would use this time to expand and leverage their network to recruit investors. When QOLiHopping, your network is the single most important prerequisite to successfully purchase the value of a home. Luckily, Lana, Jake, and Leon have amassed a substantial network through their personal connections and large YouTube following. But what about people who aren't YouTube or TikTok stars?

---

[154] Depending on local jurisdiction rules and/or the seller's needs, they could also choose to raise a *partial* amount of the cost of the property, and the original owner would hold Value Cards for the remaining amount. A similar scenario is illustrated later in this chapter when we look at how Jake's parents might convert their bodega to a Sovereign Asset.

This is where we invite "Heroes" to play a role. Heroes are influencers, and in the QOLiHoP world, they act as a kind of real estate agent—only instead of selling properties, they're selling cards. These Heroes promote a Sovereign Asset property to their followers to attract potential investors. Using their network of social media followers, Heroes help collaboratives secure funding for their RFI, enable owners like Mrs. Crumble to get their money more quickly, and experience meaning and belonging in the process. They are compensated in Value Cards, which would be specifically designated as "Hero Card" NFTs.

6. The Legal Maneuvers Occur

The money has been raised: now it's time to legally transfer ownership and convert the property to a Sovereign Asset. Because the RFI is a smart contract, the subsequent legal transfer of the home *only* occurs once the full funds have been raised. The algorithm would go something like, "When [this much money is raised], then [the SASTO purchases the home and converts to an SA]."

The actual legal process could occur as either an acquisition or a donation, depending on the jurisdiction. For example, in Belgium, there is no tax benefit to donating property to charity. The legal transfer would likely occur via an acquisition: after sufficient funds were raised for the purchase of Mrs. Crumble's house via the RFI, the UOV would supply sufficient cash to the SASTO; the SASTO would buy the house from Mrs. Crumble; and Mrs. Crumble would receive the cash. However, in the US, it might make more sense to donate the house to take advantage of possible tax benefits; then she would get Value Cards and could sell those to investors for cash. This would all take place after the RFI had successfully raised funds for the full purchase of her house.

In either case, the UOV creates the legal vehicles to do the purchasing. The UOV publishes all the data related to that property, including its appraisal value. With that data made available, Value Cards can be minted on the Collaborative Cloud.[155] Although this sounds complicated, Jake and Lana would only experience this as a couple of clicks on their Collaborative Cloud apps.

Let's check back in with the JALLers as they share their QOLiHoP news with Jake's parents and brainstorm ways to expand and excite their own network of people.

RECRUITING A NETWORK

By the time Jake parked the car on the curb in front of the bodega, it was after dark and the shop was closed. The four college students lugged their bags up the outer stairwell to his parents' second-story apartment and rang the bell. Julia, Jake's mother, flung the door open.

"Jakey's home!" she cried. She began waving them in, giving hugs, taking bags, and motioning to her husband to get them settled. "Lana, baby! Oh my goodness, you're prettier every time I see you. And Leon! Give Auntie a hug. Come in, come in! And you must be Alex! Alex, I've heard so much about you; *welcome* to our home!"

"It's gonna be tight and cozy, kids!" Gabe said. "Sammy's home with a friend too, so they're in his room. You can all cram in Jake's room, or you can take over the living room once we go to bed and spread out there. We made up an air mattress and a camping cot, so just... make yourself at home!"

"It's past our bedtime, so now that you're all here safe and sound, we're heading to bed," Julia said. "I'll be up early to get the turkey going."

The next day was full of baking, cooking, and planning. Lana eagerly filled in Julia and Gabe about their plans for next year, telling them about

---

[155] Since Jake, Lana, and Leon are using an RFI to purchase Mrs. Crumble's home, the Value Cards would be minted and distributed to the investors by a smart contract after the RFI target goal has been met, at which point Mrs. Crumble would also receive the purchase price money. A different process would ensue if Mrs. Crumble had instead elected to donate her property to the UOV first.

Mrs. Crumble, her home, and the idea to turn it into a Sovereign Asset, with Leon jumping in to answer technical questions. Jake and Sammy were put to work cooking up their family's classic Thanksgiving dishes, which were a blend of traditional American and Puerto Rican options. Alex, Gabe, and Sammy's friend Luke started up an epic cribbage tournament. Finally, midafternoon, the dinner was ready. Julia and Gabe added a card table to the end of their kitchen table, stretching the setup into the living room. Julia covered both tables with a long white tablecloth and Lana set out candles. Alex made napkin swans, the Ramirez sons set out the food, and Leon and Luke helped Gabe gather chairs and stools for everyone.

Leon held up his phone. "Say hi to Kimbree, everyone!" Kimbree was Leon's long-distance girlfriend, whom he'd met via his online gaming community.

"Hi Kimbree!" everyone called.

"Okay, Ramirez rules: no phones at the table. I gotta go. I'll call you later," Leon said. He hung up the phone, flushed and smiling, and settled into his seat.

"*There*," Julia said. "Hold hands, everyone. Gabe, baby, bless the food for us." Gabe said a brief prayer. Finally, they all began to dig in.

"So...I'm intrigued by this Sovereign Asset idea," Gabe said, carving up the turkey. "But I still want to know exactly how you three plan to raise $320,000."

"We're up to $380,000 now, actually," Leon quipped. "I ran a bunch of numbers, and based on what Lana said about needed updates, that's what we should shoot for to cover taxes, insurance, repairs, et cetera."

"Sure, why not add another sixty grand?" Gabe said, grinning. He raised his eyebrows and looked around at all those gathered. "This is an industrious, innovative group, no denying it. So, what's the plan?"

"Good question, Gabe," Lana said, passing him the salad. She looked at Jake and Leon. "We talked about this a ton on the way up. Our first step is to tell our families about it, which I did earlier today. I also checked in with Mrs. Crumble and made sure she's on board for all of this. She's super excited. She wants Jake and me to sit down with her financial advisor and explain everything to him, so we're going to do that." Lana took a bite of the stuffing. "Mmm! Julia, this Puerto Rican stuffing is *amazing!*"

"You can thank your boyfriend for that," Jake said, bumping against her.

"I'm so excited to cook together with you," Lana said.

"I talked to my parents about it this morning too," Leon shared. "Mom didn't fully get it, but Dad was on board. He wants in." Leon grinned. "Told us to schedule a call with him to talk dollars."

"And now Julia and I know, so you can check that off your list," Gabe said. "What next?"

"Lana and I are going to put together a YouTube 'tutorial' about how the Sovereign Asset process would work. That way, all of our followers can get on board," Jake said. He looked over at Alex and grinned. "Alex is going to let us film in the art building so we can use their Lego illustration to explain the whole thing."

"And don't forget, I'm going to design your NFT," Alex said. "I'm envisioning a caricature of Mrs. Crumble and sweet, sweet Carol with her bran muffin." Alex raised their wine glass in tribute to Carol.

"Ha!" Lana laughed. "Oh my gosh, *please* do that. Yeah—and actually, I think Jake and I are going to need to film a couple tutorials. Because we'll have to explain Value Cards and the repayment process and all of that. So, once we fully explain how this Sovereign Asset housing scenario would work on the YouTube videos, we're going to do a video introducing Mrs. Crumble and doing a tour of her house..."

"I already can't wait for the Mrs. Crumble videos," Alex said.

"I know! See?" Lana exulted. "Alex knows Mrs. Crumble from the café."

"Does she really have a pig?" Sammy asked. "Pass the gravy, please."

"She really does," Alex said. "This woman has all the makings of a YouTube and TikTok star. She's sarcastic and blunt and hilarious. I can hear her now: 'I like you, Jake. But more importantly, the pig likes you. That's important. Carol has telepathy.'"

Lana imitated Mrs. Crumble in the same voice that Alex had used: "'You can do a close-up. I've had my wrinkles freshly pressed.' She actually says that! She is so funny."

"We should post videos throughout the auction process too," Leon said. "Giving updates. We can interview investors, and they can explain why they're choosing to invest in the Sovereign Asset. You know, some might say they want to be on the front edge of a new real estate trend that promises more access and equity... Some are doing it as a long-term financial strategy."

"Some people might just like your story," Julia said. "You three are all so cute."

"Fanks, Ma," Jake said, his mouth full of mashed potatoes.

"You should expand to TikTok too," Luke said. "Everyone I know is on TikTok."

"I could edit together some amazing Mrs. Crumble dance videos for TikTok," Alex offered. "If she's up for it."

"I bet she'd get a kick out of that," Lana said. "And we'll do Twitter. We should lean hard into our network and try to get some big names to retweet us."

"Maybe the final video should end with a proposal!" Julia suggested, opening her eyes wide at Jake and Lana. "I love shows that end with proposals." Julia took a sip of her wine and smiled. Alex whooped and Sammy and Luke both began to laugh and cheer.

"Alright, alright, alright," Jake said, waving them off. He leaned over and kissed his mother's cheek. "I know you'd prefer we do things the old-fashioned way, Mama," he said. "Don't you worry. I'm not letting this girl get away." He winked at Lana, who blushed. "But the proposal idea is great. Leon, maybe you could fly Kimbree out for it."

Leon laughed. "Actually, I was thinking it would be a great last video to film Mrs. Crumble getting into her new retirement community, and showing the three of us getting settled into the house. Kind of a homecoming video."

"I love it!" Alex said. "I'll film Mrs. Crumble walking Carol around the pool at her new retirement place. And you hanging up your posters in the pig's old room. Ha!"

"Well, it's an ambitious plan," Gabe said. "But we're behind you. And I'm glad, for Mrs. Crumble's sake, that the RFI needs to be fully funded before anything legal occurs." He raised his glass. "A toast! To new possibilities. To our bright, successful sons—" He looked at Jake and Sammy. "And the wonderful people they surround themselves with." He smiled at Lana, Alex, Leon, and Luke. "To my wife, and her love, and her wisdom. And because we have all plenty to be thankful for."

"Hear! Hear!" everyone else chorused, and clinked and sipped from their glasses.

ADDITIONAL QOLIHOP NOTES

We'll leave the cozy Ramirez apartment for a moment to discuss additional logistics of the QOLiHoP scenario. Let's tackle a few other elements about how this process might play out.

Types of Investors

Similar to what was illustrated in Chapter 10, there are three ways to invest in a QOLiHoP property:

- **Debt investment**: these Value Cards are bought with a specific interest rate, which would be similar to a mortgage loan being extended at 3.5% or 4%. For instance, if you bought $300 in Value Cards at 3.5%, then when Jake, Leon, and Lana (via the Sovereign Asset) pay you back, they would owe you your $300 plus 3.5%

annual interest, compounded monthly[156] over the duration of the time you've held your card.

- **Value investment**: these Value Cards *do not* have an interest requirement; however, investors require that the cards be purchased back by the Sovereign Asset smart contract once the value of an asset has reached a certain amount. If you bought $300 of Value Cards at a 1.2× buyback, for instance, then Leon, Jake, and Lana (via the Sovereign Asset) would buy those cards back for $120 each, once the value of their asset had reached that level.

- **Collectible investment**: in the previous chapter, we described a "collectible" investment as one where an investor buys a Value Card in an asset with no repayment expectation. However, when the asset is a piece of real estate, the Value Cards in this third category function like a piece of equity, in addition to a collectible NFT. If a property raises in value, a collectible investment Value Card attached to it would also raise in value. If the property declines, a collectible investment Value Card would also decline.

The different options will appeal to different investor profiles. From an investor's perspective, a value investment or a high-yield debt would be better than a collectible investment, but those cards would also score lower in the RFI auction. Depending on an investor's goals and their relationship to the collaborative sponsoring the RFI, an investor will make a bid that best suits their goals.

The nature of the RFI also bodes well for the collaborative of users, as the "competition" around the auction will make sure the best deals are on the table for them. The result should be a market-driven price, providing the best possible allocation of capital for the investor and the best possible deal

---

[156] One twelfth of the yearly interest is added to the principle each month and used as the new principle the next month.

for the user, since the RFI's algorithms would try to achieve (in economic terms) a *perfect competition condition*.

Altogether, the combination of investment styles will allow more equitability, accessibility, and flexibility for anyone who wants to experience the benefits of living in their own home and gaining long-term value.

Do I Have to Wait Twenty-Five Years before Seeing My QOLiHoP Investment Repaid?

Let's say you invest $500 in Leon, Lana, and Jake's QOLiHoP house at 4% interest. You find yourself in the lower half of the ranking, which—when you do the math—means they're not scheduled to pay you back for another fifteen years or so. Do you have to wait all that time before seeing your money back with interest?

Yes—*if* you want. For some people, this could be a long-term financial strategy, similar to target-date mutual funds that you plan to cash out in forty years. For instance, if you waited fifteen years to see your $500 back at 4% annual interest (compounded monthly), you'd get a return of $1,056.85.

Or, no—*if* you prefer. Investors can also choose to sell their debt-investment Value Cards at any time, similar to how banks can sell mortgage loans. If you have a QOLiHoP Value Card that brings 2% per year that is due to be repaid in the next five years, you could go to the marketplace with that card and put it up for sale: "I am holding this debt-investment Value Card. Would anyone like to buy it for cash?" Your debt might then be exchanged between people who need short-term cash and people who would prefer a long-term investment. None of these transactions would need to involve the users of the QOLiHoP property. This means investors can actually have a liquid investment in a real estate property. Normally, real estate properties are prized for their stability but are considered a difficult asset to get in and out of. However, investing in a QOLiHoP property would mean investors aren't trapped in their investment; they can make it liquid at any time.

Do Investors Get a Say over Updates, Remodels, and So On?

Let's say that Lana's mom buys $5,000 worth of real estate investment Value Cards—but tells Lana and Jake she has one condition: "I want full creative ownership over the kitchen remodel." If Mama Aarden holds the value of a large piece of the house—does that mean she gets a say over what happens to it? Do any of the investors get that privilege?

The answer is no, and Lana's mom has no more influence in this matter than *any* mother would have over the decorating decisions in her child's first home. When investors commit to a QOLiHoP Sovereign Asset, they choose the underlying asset first, since their investment will be tied to the asset long after the first user collaborative has moved on. However, the first user collaborative will also be an indication as to the appeal and stewardship of the asset. That's why Jake and Lana would have published information about their intended updates in their initial RFI. If you are a collaborative using a Sovereign Asset house—for all intents and purposes, that's *your* house. You choose the kitchen updates. You install a security system. If there's a plumbing problem, you can arrange to get that fixed. And yes: you're going to need to mow that lawn.

What Is the Repayment Schedule?

There is much more flexibility with a QOLiHoP repayment schedule than with a typical bank loan. If you've had a windfall month—like if you've received an inheritance—in a QOLiHoP scenario, you could choose to buy back 300 cards that month and wipe out all those interest obligations.

By the same token, if you've had a bad month—for instance, if you lose your job because of a worldwide pandemic—you're not obligated to pay anything for a time, so long as the Sovereign Asset remains sustainable. The smart contracts that help operate a Sovereign Asset make sure that the investors are paid back and the asset is adequately serving the users, and checks that the asset itself is ecologically sound, receiving money into its sustainability and operations funds, and so on. If all those boxes are being checked, you could foreseeably coast through a challenging time and wait to pay the monthly usage fees until your income had picked up again. (Granted, debt-investment Value Cards would continue to accrue interest that entire time.)

If the Sovereign Asset determines that it is no longer being sustainably used (for instance, if the sustainability and operations funds have not been receiving payments), then it will initially remind the collaborative about what they need to pay, in the same way that a landlord would. If nothing changes, the Sovereign Asset will put itself back on the marketplace for new users. Once a new collaborative of users is in the house, investors will continue to be repaid with those monthly payments.

Let's say that the users are making payments on time—but they're also letting their nine cats spray urine on the property and seriously damaging the building's value. How does the Sovereign Asset intervene in that case?

It doesn't—because the technology behind the SA wouldn't smell the cat urine. However, a cat spraying all over the house would not endanger the Sovereign Asset's sustainability. The worsened living conditions might impact the rental price for future collaboratives, but that in turn can present new opportunities. For example, a skilled laborer might elect to take over the SA for a while at a very low or even symbolic rental price; that person could fix the property in exchange for Future Value. (We discuss this scenario in greater depth in our section on other QOLiHoP scenarios.) Once fixed, a new collaborative could take over at "normal" market prices again, which would unlock the skilled laborer's Future Value.

The previous inhabitants would damage their reputation as a collaborative and lose the Value Cards that the Sovereign Asset had held as a security deposit.

In any case, there cannot be an SA "administrator" serving in a landlord capacity, as this would mean the asset is no longer sovereign. The above processes are fully automated, predictable, and community-driven.

What about Squatters?

What happens in the instance that a Sovereign Asset determines the QOLi-HoP collaborative should leave, but the people living in the house don't want to go? Who evicts those people? If necessary, other outside collaboratives could be contracted to initiate the legal process necessary to evict a collaborative of users that were trying to abuse this flexibility. But there are a number of reasons to believe that a QOLiHoP scenario would only rarely get to that point.

First of all, in the big picture, no one can get "conned" because the Sovereign Asset is in the middle. Investors are protected: if users managed to live rent-free for a year in a Sovereign Asset, the fundamental arrangement would still exist; the next users would continue to pay back the investors. Additionally, in the same way that a traditional landlord would collect the first and last months' rent as a deposit, the Sovereign Asset might hold the first two months' Value Cards as a deposit to safeguard against defaulting.

However, the "squatters" would damage their reputation on the Collaborative Cloud. It would be difficult to get away with defaulting on your responsibility long term. Because everyone on the Collaborative Cloud uses a DiD,[157] your reputation as a negligent "squatter" would follow you if you were to try to take advantage of the flexibility of the system. The next time you tried to get into a Sovereign Asset house, the SA would evaluate your inconsistency and choose a different user collaborative. You might be able to get away with defaulting once or twice, but eventually, your bad credibility would mean game over.

And once again, we return to the importance of collaboratives operating themselves in the manner we described in Part 1 of this book. Transparency, openness, and a commitment to one's own personal responsibility take away a lot of the nastier sides of an eviction scenario. The mindset and ideas that

---

[157] DiDs were discussed in Chapters 8 and 9.

define the Sovereign Asset's "ecosystem" will generally ensure that the people who step in are mostly doing it for the right reasons.

No system will be the Garden of Eden, and there will always be bad actors—however, the QOLiHoP has many checks and balances in place to get the right people involved, set them up to function at their best, and maintain full transparency and protection for colleagues in the collaborative.

What Happens Once the House Is Paid Off?

If all investors are paid off, then the Sovereign Asset's treasury will continue to receive users' monthly payments and accumulate money. That money is split into the Investment Accounts of the colleagues in the collaborative using the asset and contributing to it.

Because a Sovereign Asset will always receive monthly payments, a property is never "paid off." This might sound like a disadvantage to people who like the idea of getting a break from housing expenses once they have paid off a loan. However, this creates a scenario where people are able to amass multiple properties, which often exacerbates inequality. Maintaining monthly payments ensures that a Sovereign Asset is sustained well and still works as a viable financial asset, since—once investors are repaid—the monthly payments are received into the SA's treasury. The users submitting those monthly payments would have the option to direct the funds from the SA's treasury into more "liquid" SAs and sell the Value Cards, which in effect would be like paying themselves. Although this would induce taxes and reflects a short-term financial strategy, it could be meaningful in some scenarios.

What If the Asset Is Destroyed?

Let's say an asset is burned badly in a fire or is destroyed in some other way. In that case, most insurance companies would replace the building with a new build, after which the SA could resume hosting users. Alternately, the property could be sold, and the money from the liquidation would appear in the SA's treasury. The Value Cards attached to that asset would be defined by the remaining funds in the treasury.

Plenty of assets wouldn't have land to sell or liquidate, though—so what happens in that case? Let's say that Jake's car—a Sovereign Asset—is totaled in an accident. (Don't worry; everyone is okay.) In that case, after liquidating the physical parts of the vehicle, the remaining money would be in the SA's treasury. At that point, the SA would start to behave more like an intangible SA since there is no longer a "real-world" asset backing it. The worth of its Value Cards would be tied directly to the remaining funds in the treasury.

Ultimately, the QOLiHoP ecosystem is meant to be tried out and experimented with. In fact, we hope people experiment the hell out of it. The scenarios we've described should not be thought of as a system or a model. Rather, QOLiHoP starts as a mindset. We've sought to provide a framework that will allow people to pursue home "ownership" with a different kind of approach, one that allows for more equity and accessibility. This is not just a financial strategy to get money; it's a way to allow for more human connections and quality of life.

Other QOLiHoP Scenarios

Jake, Leon, and Lana finding a great house to live in for their senior year of university is only the beginning. There are many ways that this Person to Person housing scenario could help create a Quality of Life World. Here are just a few:

Skillful User with Little Financial Capital

Cody Maxwell is a rehabilitated ex-con who is a great handyman. He's found an affordable manufactured home that he'd like to buy and fix up, but he can't get a housing loan for it. In a QOLiHoP scenario, Cody could raise an RFI, posting pictures of his past work, and recruit a network of his customers who know him and trust his skill. His RFI would probably be mostly based on value-only investments, trusting that Cody would do a great job fixing up a place and therefore dramatically increase its value. Cody could take on a three-year "lease" so that he wouldn't pay rent until the second year. In the worst-case scenario, if Cody defaulted, the investors would get stuck with the manufactured home and the SA would look for a new renter. Cody could choose to post pictures of his work to the community of investors as he lives there. If Cody is really a good guy and genuinely wants to get back on his feet, then he's going to keep his word. In the event that he does, the next time he does an RFI, people will be fighting over him.

Smaller Needs

Let's say that Jake's younger brother, Sammy—now a freshman at college—wants to share a car with his buddies. They could do an RFI to have a "collective car," sharing costs and benefits, without the hassle of arranging shared ownership. If and when one person in their group doesn't need the car anymore, the others could either agree to increase their share of the monthly usage fees or find another friend to take over the payments. In the meantime, each of the users is earning Value Cards with their monthly payments—*and* enjoying a flexible car-sharing situation.

College Alumni–Sponsored Housing

Perhaps an alumni board of a college is looking for new ways to attract students to their campus. They hear about the QOLiHoP benefits that can help students like Jake, Lana, and Leon; thinking that this might be a selling point to prospective students, they put their resources together to invest in a number of QOLiHoP properties. When touring students find out that they could actually earn long-term value for themselves through paying their monthly rent for student housing, the number of applications to the college jumps. The college continues to invest in QOLiHoP housing, and this financial benefit to students becomes a major draw.

Elderly Communities

QOLiHoP allows for many flexible community-living scenarios. For example, let's say that you have seven elderly friends who all make a small pension. They can't afford to buy a house, and they also can't afford to get into a wealthy retirement community. However, they *could* afford to function as a collaborative and pay for a house that they all live in together. They are able to experience community and friendship in each other's company and help take care of each other. They also recruit a younger healthcare worker who agrees to live with them, "rent-free," who earns Value Cards via the Collaborative Points they earn from their effort.

Any number of possibilities are made available through the creative and flexible options generated by the Person to Person environment. And on that note—why stop at housing? What else might the Person to Person financial environment enable? Julia and Gabe are about to discover what Sovereign Assets might hold in store for them.

Arranging Inheritance: The Family Cabin

Let's imagine that Lana's family, the Aardens, is trying to figure out an inheritance scenario. Her grandparents, Paul and Paisley Aarden, bought a family cabin in the mountains in the 1960s, and it's been the center of the extended family's gatherings for decades. After Paisley's passing, Grandpa Paul passed along trusteeship of the cabin to his two children, Brad (Lana's dad) and Betsy. Paul has also created a bank account for the cabin and deposits $1,000 every month so that there are funds to complete needed updates. Brad and Betsy have been faithfully taking care of the cabin, doing updates as needed and putting in the work to maintain the property. However, they're now in their sixties, and they're starting to think of how to pass the property on.

No one wants to sell it—the family cabin holds too many memories. However, passing along the cabin to the six grandchildren feels logistically unrealistic. The simplest option would be for one or two of the children to buy the cabin outright, take responsibility for the maintenance, and then share the usage of the cabin as it has always been shared. However, there's no obvious candidate for who that would be.

Among the grandchildren, there's a range of financial stability, proximity, and emotional attachment to the cabin. For instance, Lana is close enough to the cabin that she could go often, and she is also very attached to the property. However, she doesn't have much practical home ownership experience, nor does she have the financial capital to buy it outright. Her wealthy cousin Matt has the financial capital to buy it outright, but is the least emotionally attached to the cabin since he owns one himself already. Lana's older brother, Dylan, loves the cabin and would make a great steward, but he lives far away from the cabin and can only visit twice a year.

Betsy and Brad know that asking the six grandchildren to share the finances and/or responsibility could potentially open up sources of conflict. And even if the six are willing to work together *now* to share the costs and responsibility of the cabin—what might happen down the road? If one of the grandchildren wanted to sell off their stake in the cabin, would the other grandchildren be obligated to buy that stake to preserve the family ownership? What if they couldn't afford to do that? Could these financial complications threaten the family's harmony or lead to them lose the cabin eventually?

Ideally, the six cousins would be able to share the use, responsibilities, and cost of the cabin in a way that still honors each person's autonomy and protects the property. But how? Let's explore how they could resolve these issues by converting the cabin to a Sovereign Asset.

- As Brad and Betsy don't want immediate "cash" for the cabin, they would turn it into a **Sovereign Asset** by donating it to the UOV. This would "automate" the financial obligations and transactions of the cabin's ownership, which would remove the burden of responsibility from any one of the grandchildren while also mitigating the possibility for conflict.

- After the legal transactions (creating the SASTO and adding it to the UOV), the DAO publishes the value. At that point, Brad and Betsy can redeem the Value Cards on the **Collaborative Cloud** using their donation receipt.

- Betsy and Brad are the initial recipients of the **Value Cards**, and they decide to add a buyback option[158] to those cards; doing so would make it easy for the grandchildren to buy one another's cards if one or more of them wanted to "sell" their share to the other cousins. It also means the grandchildren could choose to sell their Value Cards to outside investors; however, this would not threaten the family's exclusive lease on using the Family Cabin, as we'll explain more in a moment. As it is for family purpose, let's assume the buyback option is set at 1× (so equal to the initial value, $100 per card).

- As Brad and Betsy want to treat all the children equally, they **distribute** the Value Cards in eight equal parts: one part for each of them, as they help their children transition into the stewardship role, and six equal parts divided equally amongst the children.

- **Sustainability** is a prime directive for Sovereign Assets; therefore, the cost of usage (rental price) would need to cover, at minimum, the provisions for:

  » The operational fund, like insurance and taxes for the property

  » The sustainability fund, making sure that the SA maintains sufficient funds to be able to sustain itself in case the collaborative of

---

[158] A reminder: in a buyback option, each Value Card has a smart contract that can instruct the SA (at the Value Card holder's instigation) to buy the card back when there's $100 in the treasury. When the SA buys back the Value Card, the Value Card's worth is distributed among the Collaborative Point holders, according to their percentages. Once this has been done enough times that a colleague has $100 worth of a Value Card, they have that new Value Card in their wallet. This means that the people putting in the most effort to the Family Cabin also hold the larger share of Value Cards.

grandchildren defaults or loses interest in maintaining the cabin as users. (This would cover costs for disconnecting from the grid, preparing for winter, etc.) Although the grandchildren in this scenario are unlikely to default, this sustainability provision is made "just in case."

- Ideally, the **rental price** would be close to the market price for a similar rental in the area; we'll explain why in a moment.

That's how the financial and legal processes might go—but how would the grandchildren manage the usage and stewardship responsibilities? How would they sort out who pays what in monthly fees? If one grandchild does most of the upkeep, could they pay a smaller monthly amount? Let's consider now how the grandchildren might operate as a **collaborative**.

- Brad, Betsy, and the children all form the **Family Cabin Collaborative** that gets the initial lease for the cabin. This means—regardless of who holds the Value Cards—the family members are the only ones with usage rights to the cabin. The grandchildren are free to sell or collateralize their Family Cabin Value Cards without threatening the rest of the family members' usage rights, allowing for greater flexibility and less potential for conflict. The collaborative commits to paying for the monthly usage rights of the Family Cabin SA.
- On a human level, the colleagues form a **Collaborative Agreement**. They assess their collaboration against the CDPs through using the ACT matrix, for example. They ask: What is the shared purpose of our Family Cabin Collaborative? Why is being a member of this collaborative important to me/us? What are possible setbacks or hinderances we might experience as a collaborative? What is needed to serve our purpose? How will we act, contribute, and handle ourselves in the best interest of the collaborative? How will we resolve conflicts and keep each other accountable? By going through all these questions, the grandchildren help to ensure they will work together well, prepare themselves to steer through potential conflicts,

and maintain their family closeness while working together.

- The family members discuss an **appropriate monthly usage fee** that they will all contribute to, ensuring the fee meets the following standards:

  » There is sufficient income to pay the minimal sustainable monthly rent to the SA to cover its funds.

  » There is a little extra money in the collaborative account for maintenance.

  » All the grandchildren feel it is an equitable arrangement.

  » The grandchildren might choose to pay *more* than the bare minimum as a monthly fee, as that would increase the worth of their Value Cards. In doing so, their Value Cards would be more attractive to investors, and each grandchild's Value Cards could become a financial asset to either sell or collateralize. Additionally, paying more than the bare minimum into the SA's treasury would mean each colleague has that extra money distributed into their Investment Account, creating a kind of "slush fund" that could be used for the cabin's projects. If and when the family cabin needs a larger update—like redoing the porch, for example—the grandchildren could start a "Porch-Fixing RFI" and choose to fund that RFI using the money in their Investment Accounts. Each person would be free to invest in this or not. Those who *did* choose to invest would end up with more Value Cards in the Family Cabin SA as a reward for their investment.

- As a final step in setting up their collaborative, the Aarden family members would now come up with a system for **Collaborative Points**, devising a way to reward effort in a Contribution Session. For instance:

  » Vacuuming the cabin and cleaning the bathrooms is worth 500 points.

  » Doing a once-a-year deep clean of the cabin is worth 1,500 points.

  » Dealing with administration issues is worth 50 points per hour.

  » Checking on the status of the cabin is 100 points per check.

  » Arranging firewood for the winter season is worth 700 points.

  » Contributing $1 to the SA's treasury equals 1 point.

To help with the maintenance budget, the family might say that if a member of the collaborative uses the cabin, they should pay $50 for a day. This would give them 50 points (as a $1 contribution is also worth 1 point), but—since they are also "consuming" the service of being there and enjoying the SA—it would also *cost* 50 points per day. In most cases, this would work out to be a neutral effect; however, it would allow for some members of the family to contribute money without using the cabin; alternately, someone could take on a "stewardship" task for the cabin, such as raking up leaves, that could earn sufficient points to make the stay "free." Here's one example: Lana's wealthy cousin Matt, who has his own mountain cabin, might want to contribute to maintaining the family cabin, as he enjoys seeing everyone else enjoy it so much, even though he himself won't be going there. In that case, he would just get 1 point for every contributed dollar. This ensures he maintains a voting "voice" over the cabin's future and stays connected with his family, without the obligation to take responsibility of its upkeep.

The flexibility of the finances also can help someone in Matt's situation, who might want to minimize his stake in the family cabin or eventually exit it entirely. For example, as Matt is the least connected to the cabin, he might request to sell off his Value Cards. Brad and Betsy could arrange for Matt to have the Value Cards that are bought back first. When the SA treasury has $100 in it, the SA would automatically buy back one of Matt's cards and distribute it to the other colleagues, via their Collaborative Point percentages. This way, Matt gets "cash" in his Investment Account, which he can direct to other investments as he chooses, and his Value Cards are distributed to the other family cabin colleagues. The grandchildren who are more invested in the family cabin would be able to slowly earn a larger portion of Value Cards in the cabin over the following months.

This is only one way in which the Aarden family could use the Person to Person tools to arrange their inheritance scenario. By separating property ownership from its value and from its usage through the Sovereign Asset arrangement, there are myriad possible scenarios that would accommodate any wish on the family's collaborative side.

The result is a group effort to maintain the family cabin that is equitable, logistically feasible, and helps ensure that harmony among the family continues. It arranges for stewardship of the family cabin to continue, along with enjoyment of its use. If and when one or more family members choose to exit the Family Cabin Collaborative, they have the option to sell their Value Cards to anyone without jeopardizing the rest of the family's ability to maintain their use of it. The cousins who want to stay and use it are free to do so and maintain an exclusive lease, even while the others trade and exchange their value. This setup helps the family avoid power-play scenarios and continue in loving relationships with one another. Finally, because the family has formed a collaborative, they have an incentive to remain connected with one another and the tools to pursue their collaboration in an intentional, frictionless way.

OTHER POSSIBILITIES

Julia set down her wine glass. "I just need to be sad about one thing," she said. "I'm so happy that everyone's happy, but I need to get one sad thing off my chest."

"What is it, Mama?" Jake asked.

She sighed. "Well, thanks to the amazing success of our boys and their meaningful career plans—cheers to Sammy, by the way, who just got accepted into the nursing program. We haven't made enough of a fuss over that." Everyone paused and cheered for Sammy. Jake leaned over and ruffled his little brother's hair. Julia smiled and continued. "Well, thanks to the success of our boys... Gabe and I don't know who we're going to pass on the bodega to." She comically stuck out her bottom lip. "Which means we don't know how we're going to retire."

Gabe shrugged in acknowledgment. "We'd love to retire in the next five years, once we get Sammy through school. But we don't have anyone to sell our business to."

"Oh man, Dad, that sucks," Jake said. "The bodega is such a neighborhood hub—especially since you've opened the café and deli."

"It's even better since the vacant lot next door was turned into a community garden," Sammy said. "Mom and Dad's shop is the place to be now. It's where everyone catches up and shares the news."

"You can't think of anyone who would buy it?" Jake asked.

Gabe grimaced. "The only potential buyer is Roland Moody." Julia made a face. Roland Moody was a man in the neighborhood with a notorious reputation for running seedy establishments.

"We just don't have the energy to keep it going much longer," Julia sighed. "We've thought about renting it out—I think Otis and Tara would love to run it. But if they run it, then they should really live in this apartment, which means we'd need capital to get into somewhere new…And honestly, if we're going to set ourselves up as retirees, we really need—like—some *decent* capital. I just don't know how we'd do that without selling the business."

"Who are Otis and Tara?" Alex asked.

"Otis and Tara are a young married couple," Julia explained. "Otis worked at the bodega all through high school and calls us his uncle and auntie—but neither Otis nor Tara has enough money to buy it outright."

Leon, Jake, Lana, and Alex gave each other knowing looks. "Mom…Dad…" Jake said. "Join the club here. You could convert the bodega into a Sovereign Asset. Raise the money you need, set up a steady monthly payment for your income, and pass on the bodega to Otis and Tara to operate."

Gabe and Julia looked at each other across the table. Julia raised her eyebrows at him. Gabe turned to Jake. "Go on. I'm listening."

Converting the Bodega: A Retirement Scenario

Let's assume Gabe and Julia own both the property (the grocery shop and the apartment above it) and the business, making two assets. Here's how Gabe and Julia could undertake Jake's suggestion:

- **Step 1:** Jake's parents donate the bodega (both the real estate and the business) to the Universal Ownership Vault (UOV).[159] The value of the donation is estimated using traditional but realistic valuation methods. They get two **receipts** for their donation.
- **Step 2:** On the Collaborative Cloud, Gabe and Julia create a **collaborative** of the two of them.
- **Step 3:** Gabe and Julia's donation creates two **new Sovereign Assets in the UOV**.
- **Step 4:** Gabe and Julia can use the receipts to **mint NFTs representing the value of the donation** in the Collaborative Cloud. These NFTs are $100 Value Cards. The amount of NFTs Gabe and Julia get is equal to the value of the donation divided by 100.
- **Step 5:** Gabe and Julia now have all the Value Cards in their personal **Asset Accounts**. As they are the ones who gave birth to the Sovereign Assets, their collaborative also holds the **initial rental agreement**.
- **Step 6:** Should they continue to run their business as before, they would now **pay a monthly rental usage fee** for it. The value of the rent, minus the Sovereign Asset funds provisions, would appear in their personal Investment Accounts. This additional money would **increase the SA treasury**, as there is no Value Card buyback registered in the Sovereign Asset. (In other words, since there are no investors who need to be paid back, their monthly payments go into the SA's treasuries and increase the value of their Value Cards. Essentially, they're paying themselves.) The money in their Investment Accounts can be used to invest in RFIs and acquire new Value Cards from other Sovereign Assets, enabling Gabe and Julia to potentially increase their financial capital and/or set up long-term investments before retiring. Alternately, their Investment Account money might

---

[159] Gabe and Julia would donate the assets, rather than crowdfund as in the earlier example, as they would still be using it themselves for a while.

simply increase the value of their existing Value Cards when the profit returns to the SA treasury. (This would depend on the type of investment they chose in the RFI.)

Let's say five years go by, and now Gabe and Julia are ready to hand over the reins of running the business. Ideally, they would like to get some immediate cash from this exchange that could help them get set up in a healthy retirement situation; they can do this by selling off some of their Value Cards. They don't need to sell them all outright (especially because their preferred new owners couldn't afford to do that), but they'd like at least 30% of the value immediately, and a priority buyback for the remainder of their cards (meaning they would be the first investors reimbursed by the monthly payments). All of this means it's time to do another RFI, which means it's time to recruit Otis and Tara.

Otis and Tara agree they want to commit to running the bodega, and they're excited about the possibility of earning value as users of a Sovereign Asset. As Gabe and Julia noted, Otis and Tara don't have the money to buy the business and property outright, but they think they can crowdfund up to the 30% amount Gabe and Julia have requested.

To do that, Otis and Tara would start a collaborative in the Collaborative Cloud. Once they are able to raise Gabe and Julia's requested terms of 30% of the value and a priority buyback for the rest of the cards, they will obtain the lease currently held by Jake's parents' collaborative. Then they'll officially be the new users of the bodega asset and property.

Otis and Tara, as a new collaborative, would start an RFI. The RFI would:

- Put 30% of the Value Cards held by Jake's parents up for sale.
- Assign a priority buyback at 1× value for the remainder of the cards, per Gabe and Julia's terms. In other words, Gabe and Julia would get paid back first with the monthly payments. The 1× value means they aren't looking for more than the initial value they agreed on, which ensures they are put at the top of the ranking list.

- The Sovereign Asset would transfer the lease upon successful completion.

Let's assume the RFI is successful.

Jake's parents would now have 30% worth of value in their Free Cash Account, which can be converted to dollars at any point. The investors would have the purchased Value Cards in their Asset Accounts. The lease would be in the hands of Otis and Tara, the new collaborative—along with any other colleagues they want to partner with. The new people start working at the bodega and pay the monthly rent.

With every rental payment, Jake's parents get money in their Investment Accounts and Otis and Tara get Value Cards in their Asset Accounts.

Since Jake's parents would likely need real cash, they might choose to invest the cash in their Investment Account in a very liquid Sovereign Asset, such as a bitcoin fund, for example. Once they own a Value Card from a bitcoin fund, they will be able to trade that for immediate cash.

In this way, Jake's parents have sold their business with a 30% down payment and a monthly buyback. If they wish to do so, they could even join the new collaborative for a short while to transfer knowledge. That would get them some points in the process, ensure a smooth transition, and help them leave in a frictionless way, whenever the moment comes.

QUALITY OF LIFE WORLD

That night, Jake, Lana, Leon, and Alex all piled into Jake's old room together for a sleepover. Lana lit some candles and instructed the others to sit in a circle.

"What are we doing?" Leon asked, amused. "Is this a séance?"

"No, dodo, we're going to share what we're thankful for. If you were at the Aardens' house for Thanksgiving, this would have been the entirety of our dinnertime conversation. And it's my favorite part of Thanksgiving. So we're going to do it."

Jake nudged Lana. "You first, then, Beauty."

She smiled. "I'm thankful for all of you—my dearest and best friends. I'm super excited to think about living with Jake—*and* Leon—next year." She grinned and nudged Leon with her foot. "I feel like I'm finding new ways to help other people find quality of life, which is my life's goal. I do that as a resident advisor in the dorms, but more and more that's happening via our YouTube channel... And I'm super excited about finding ways to do that as a career. Now that we've got this housing thing figured out, I feel less stressed about finding a super-high-paying job, and I feel like I can look for meaningful work that really excites me." She paused. "Okay, someone else's turn."

Alex spoke up. "I'm thankful for Michelle. She rocks my world." Alex grinned at them. "I'm thankful for youuuuu." They paused. "I've basically built a career's worth of freelance work at this point. Like, I'm working and getting paid well as an artist. So that's pretty rad. I'm still learning a shitload about black holes and quantum physics. And I'm happy." Alex smiled. "Who's next?"

"Me," Jake said. Lana rested her head on his shoulder. "I love my teaching internship right now. And I love that I can think about pursuing a career in teaching without feeling all the stress that I used to feel about money. I love that I get to teach on YouTube all the time about stuff that feels meaningful." He looked at them all in wonder. "Like—how crazy is it that Lana and I are YouTube 'stars'? It's ridiculous." He looked over at Leon on the air mattress and smiled. "Thankful for my brother." He looked over at Alex. "Alex is my family." Alex smiled. "I love *my* family," Jake said, nodding toward the rest of the apartment. "And I love this woman." He looked at Lana, who lifted her head to look at him. "I intend to marry you one day, you know," Jake told her matter-of-factly. "I hope that fits your plans."

"Good," she said, and smiled. "I like long-term investments."

"And unrealized potential," Leon said, grinning.

"That's right," she said. "Your turn, big guy."

Leon sighed and sat up on the air mattress. "Well, I'm thankful that I'm finding a way to be successful that still lets me have a healthy work/life balance. And I'm figuring out ways to grow and scale our collaborative model, which is super exciting. I mean—guys—people are contacting me on the Collaborative Cloud to consult with them on how to run their own groups. It's unbelievable."

"And you're thankful for Kimbree..." Lana prompted.

Leon grinned. "Yup. Very thankful to finally have a girlfriend. Even if she lives in Atlanta. And a very cool girlfriend at that." He paused. "I'm thankful to have a better relationship with my dad."

"Aww..." Alex said softly.

"Yeah," Leon said, looking over at Alex. "Remember how you told me that he might not have a whole lot of languages to communicate love in? Well...I kind of rolled with that and just started inviting him into the conversation more as I was figuring out our collaborative and the money and all that. Turns out it's been a great way to bond." He shrugged. "He still has a pretty low emotional IQ. But...I guess I'm learning to recognize the ways he tries to connect with me. And I actually feel like there's love there. We don't actually say the word 'love' much...but it's there, and that feels big."

Alex leaned over from their camping cot and fell on top of Leon in a big bear hug. They rolled off the air mattress and up against Jake's bed. Lana and Jake took the opportunity and piled on top of them.

"I looooove us!" Lana sang.

Leon grunted from the bottom of the pile. "I think I was on top the last time we dogpiled."

They each extricated themselves and held hands. "You guys," Jake said, shaking his head in wonder. "My mom and dad are going to be able to retire without sacrificing the bodega. That means my neighborhood stays healthy and stable, and my parents get taken care of. And *we*—" He motioned to Leon and Lana. "—are moving in together, just up the road from Alex. Every time we pay rent, we're going to get Value Cards and be saving up for the future...I get to pursue my dream job without feeling financially stressed."

He paused, overwhelmed. "Did we seriously just ... *do that* in the last three years?"

Leon grinned and nodded. Lana kissed Jake. Alex slung both of their arms around the group. "We are large, my lovelies. We contain multitudes."

These are the kinds of quality of life opportunities made available through a Person to Person environment. There is greater equity, the chance to get ahead, the ability to weigh quality of life *in balance* with financial needs, and the opportunity to work together with others to find a solution that suits everyone's purpose. It allows for greater connection, greater fairness, greater sustainability and kindness. It equips people with the agency to pursue their own best life. It allows for more connection, richer connection, person to person.

In short: this is how we move toward a Quality of Life World.

EXPLORE FURTHER

If you'd like to learn more, discuss this content with others, or access tools for your own application, go to the interactive section of the book using this QR code.

CONCLUSION

BEGINNINGS

We are born makers.
We move what we're learning from our heads
to our hearts through our hands.

—Brené Brown

And so, even as we steer this book toward an ending, we find a beginning instead.

In that way, we're not unlike our college students. As Jake, Lana, Alex, and Leon consider life after university, they are beginning again. They're seeking avenues of purpose, choosing the people they want to be close to, and finding ways to build financial security—just like they were at the start of this journey. However, they are not the same people as they were freshman year. As a result of the Person to Person journey they've taken and tools they've found, they have changed. Each of them can be more confident in the quality of life they're working toward as they venture into their new beginning.

So, too, the conclusion of this book ends back where it began—but with many new ideas.

Specifically, we circle back to a swimming pool. In our book's introduction, we described the conversations we'd had while standing in the empty pool of the Experience Center—that special place in Ginoles les Bains. Vines grew down the side, while shrubs grew up from the bottom. It felt like such a shame that a property this beautiful—with so much potential as a destination for community gatherings and rest and connection—was going unused. The beauty of the place inspired us to begin imagining what it might become.

It's the place where *our* Person to Person journey started—even though her own journey started years before we arrived.

The Experience Center sits in one of the most picturesque parts of the Aude region in Southern France, La Haute Vallée, nestled at the base of the Pyrenees and close to major cities such as Toulouse and Perpignan, near the border with Spain. The place still bears all the signs of her rich history: the hotels and bathhouse echo her days as a resort in the 1920s; the hot springs still carry all the medicinal properties that caused the site to become a destination for healing; and the swimming pool points to her its most recent iteration—as Joeri had experienced in his childhood—as the community pool. She has always been a place of gathering and friendship.

And always—even well over a century ago—the site of the Experience Center has been focused on quality of life and equitable arrangements for people from a variety of economic standings. During her hotel era, different rooms were offered at different price ranges; wellness center services were provided as well as access to the outdoor pools. The thermal station was an important place of gathering for young and old. In the entire country of France, Ginoles les Bains was the only thermal station open to women and children in addition to men. The place has always been unique and accessible to all people, men and woman, young and old, locals or tourists, rich or poor. She's a place that seeks to welcome anyone into her lovely environment, where people can enjoy services according to their needs and budget.

She is less glamourous now. These days, the site's famous pools have filled in with overgrowth. The buildings are dated and in need of repair. But the place still emanates a powerful sense of peace. The gardens invite wandering and exploration beneath the ancient sycamore trees and the rows of palms. You can hear the springs' bubbling water—still crystal clear and potable. When you lift your eyes, you see the French Pyrenees watching over the valley like guardians. The place energizes, even as she calms.

From the beginning, we saw the potential that the Experience Center held as a place of rest, healing, connection, and gathering. She seemed to have a purpose and an identity of her own: to bring people together, provide a restful place for rejuvenation, and foster connection.

As we crafted our ideas for a Quality of Life World, we envisioned this location playing a key role in demonstrating how a Person to Person environment could help people reconnect with ancient paths while building new quality of life. We knew her history, we had played a role in her present —but what would be her future? It was in answering this question that we followed the same journey we have sought to take you through in the chapters of this book.

THE PATH TOWARD PERSON TO PERSON

The Person to Person vision started off like a massive knot we needed to untie. At the start, we mainly experienced the tension of that knot. We tried to consider ways to make the Experience Center equitable, profitable, sustainable, and a center for quality of life, but it was like we were yanking on the knot, expecting it to loosen and instead seeing it grow tighter. While considering traditional business models, we ran into restrictions, frustrations, and economic impossibilities. The conflict we experienced between the property's state of disrepair and the enormous amount of effort and means it would take to rebuild it and make it useful for the community felt insurmountable.

However, rather than despair, we decided to take hope from German sociologist Georg Simmel and consider this conflict as a normal process.

Georg Simmel wrote that the existing conditions in any society contain the seeds of future social changes.[160] According to him, conflict is a permanent feature of society, not just a temporary event. It's something we can expect and even embrace—not interpret as a reason for despair. He also made the point that working through conflict can bind people together—it can encourage people of similar interests to unite in order to achieve their objectives. Continual conflict in this way keeps society dynamic and ever changing.

So we asked ourselves: how can this tension help us discover seeds of future change? Can we somehow connect with others and strengthen our resilience to unlock this place's potential? And if so—how?

We sought to explore the world of possibilities. By expanding our imaginations, perhaps we could envision what this might become.

In this book's narrative, we depicted the JALL group encountering similar challenges, ones that led them to invent, create, and evolve along a similar trajectory that we took. The narrative arc is accurate but features a very condensed version of the training we sought out in reality and the answers we arrived at after much trial and error. As we navigated our way toward the Person to Person vision, we completed trainings on Prosocial, the Holacracy© model, and co-ownership; we talked with legal experts, researched quality of life, and learned about cryptocurrency, bank licenses, and financial models. We even built a company in Estonia with a bank license and minted a Quality of Life crypto coin, before shelving that as yet another trial and error. Throughout each new training, our ideas were informed by Pim's background as a therapist and Joeri's background in IT, management, and entrepreneurship.

Our first project was to research **quality of life**. We asked: how can people increase quality of life, even within the limitations of their context and situation? People *do* have agency over their quality of life but also need

---

160 Lewis A. Coser, *Masters of Sociological Thought: Ideas in Historical and Social Context, Second Edition* (New York: Harcourt Brace Jovanovich, 1977), excerpted in "The Significance of Simmel's Work," George Simmel Online, accessed January 7, 2022, https://socio.ch/sim/work.htm.

to accept that there are limitations to what can be changed. We learned about the quality of life domains: the areas of life in which people can make an impact to increase their well-being and satisfaction. There is almost always *some* action you can take to build up greater health in one domain. We also learned that people can powerfully complement our efforts toward quality of life—provided we collaborate in positive ways.

The **Person to Person** vision came about from the realization that, although we live in a world that prioritizes lots of man-made constructs like companies and governments, ultimately, those are a distraction from what is truly meaningful. The "business of living" often takes us further away from truly living. We've gotten so used to those constructs as a matter of fact that we don't question them anymore. But maybe we should. How can we evolve from human "doing" to human *being*? How can we get back to people? In the end, all we are is people, living together with other people, figuring out ways to do that in the most peaceful, productive, and sustainable way possible. Unless you're wealthy enough to construct your own isolated bubble, you need communities to make things work. For the 99.9% of "ordinary people, community is a way to become stronger and access opportunities that would be otherwise unavailable. So—how do we optimize community?

The answer begins with **mindset**: people need enough self-awareness and sufficient understanding of others to form genuine, values-aligned connections. How can we construct a society that exists apart from hierarchies and power structures, where people are still productive? You need to understand what you most deeply care about so that you are intrinsically motivated to do your best work with other like-minded people. This requires awareness of your own purpose, gifts, and hang-ups. Awareness comes before anything else; it's a requirement in order to empathize with others, consider their needs, advocate for your own, and recognize your own pitfalls and areas of contribution. When we adopt a mindset that is willing to consider the needs of others, even as we consider ourselves, then collaborations can align and effectively work. The Core Design Principles (CDPs), based on

Elinor Ostrom's seminal work, identify the critical elements of productive, sustainable collaboration.

But even the most principled collaboratives built on the CDPs are still made up of humans who will struggle. Therefore, people need **tools to optimize collaboration**. We learned the necessity for these tools firsthand as we traveled throughout Europe and then to California to explore collaboration with other people. Many of those encounters informed the work in this book, such as Paul Atkins; Brian Robertson from Holacracy©; Matt Prewitt and Jennifer Morone from Radical Exchange; Jose Leal, Matt Perez, and Kelly Jackson from RadicalPurpose.org; Audrey Tang, digital minister of Taiwan; and Kim Wright and Jacqueline Horani from Conscious Contracts. Yet in spite of our common ground, we struggled to communicate our ideas in a comprehensible way. We wanted to jump across the chasm and get everyone else to jump with us but hadn't yet learned how to build a bridge to help others across. (We hope we have built something of a bridge with this book.) As a result, we were frequently met with their questions, skepticism, and impatience. Forming a shared identity as a group and finding a common purpose is hard. People need tools to identify problems, mitigate challenges, and overcome obstacles. We need to know how to meet each other helpfully on both the good days and the bad days. With that in mind, we made an inventory of tools that will help people continue good work in their collaboratives rather than quit.

But it's not enough to talk about it; that's why a **Collaborative Agreement** is necessary. When there are no hierarchies to regiment people's roles, each individual in a group needs to commit to make things work. This topic led us to take a course on Conscious Contracts and explore how dialectical behavioral therapy could play a role in helping group members take personal agency over their contribution. In collaboration with José, Natasha, and Laura of Radical Purpose, we also began developing a sample Collaborative Agreement that could serve as a legal document but was written in plain language with visuals; our colleague Fernanda began taking on a Portuguese translation.

With that groundwork laid, it was time to return to the economic component of the knot we sought to untie and consider **collaborative finance**. There were two sides to explore. One: how do you represent contribution and effort, apart from money? Other people, such as Mike Moyer of "Slicing Pie"—were already looking into this. One solution presented itself: Collaborative Points, which allowed for many other collaborative finance possibilities. Two: how do you store long-term value in order to generate stability and a good life for yourself in a manner that does not promote injustice or power plays? The only precedent seems to be shares—but fundamentally, there is no way to make money (even via shares) neutral and free from power. There will always be people fighting over it. But there's also no easy way to "get rid" of money—people still need to go grocery shopping, and pay their bills, and so on. The dilemma posed by this second aspect of finance prompted us to start inventing.

Our chapter on the **reinvention of private property** explores how to get out of the box. The invention of bitcoin and the blockchain revolution provided a possible solution of how to do money differently—but we still wanted to deal with real-world assets properly and legally. On one side, we were studying legality, regulations, and licenses; on the other side, we were witnessing "Wild West" freedom and possibilities of the blockchain world. This tension prompted experimentation. We asked: how do we marry the two sides? After some trial and error, the answer was ultimately the Universal Ownership Vault DAO. The UOV is compliant with laws but also revolutionary: it separates money and power but still allows people to build long-term wealth. This first symbolic stone in the UOV was the Quality of Life World Foundation (in Belgium), created for the public good.

In order to implement all of this, **technical tools** were needed. We found practical technologies such as smart contracts, DAOs, blockchain, the Collaborative Cloud, and so on to actualize and support the collaborative finance concepts.

And now, at last, came the fun part: exploring **opportunities and applications**. We asked: How can we reinvent financial processes using these new constructs and tools? How can people get capital? How does someone buy a house? How do you build long-term value? How can Collaborative Points translate to value? How do we ensure the control of money stays free of any small group's control? The answers to many of these questions came in the form of RFIs, Sovereign Assets, collateral for cash, and some of the other concepts we explored in Chapter 10. In this stage of our trajectory, we also saw the formation of one of the first real-life collaboratives, Au P'tit Plaisir, and helped them convert their café coffee trucks into Sovereign Assets.[161]

The most obvious initiative to explore in greater depth was the Quality of Life Housing Project, or **QOLiHoP**: a specialized application of the Person to Person environment that has widespread impact. Our world has a major housing problem. Could this new way of participating in housing reduce the indebtedness of people? Could it allow people to enter into home "ownership" earlier? What other kinds of social problems could we solve? The possibilities for application are vast and exciting.

This journey taught us that *every step* that's represented in this book is key for greater quality of life. Don't skip one; you need them all! They are deliberately built one on top of the other. You can't jump ahead to QOLiHoP without first building a healthy collaborative; you can't build a healthy collaborative without first building self-awareness. In order to build a Person to Person environment, people need to start from the inside and slowly work out—just as we've sought to illustrate.

The JALLers' Contribution

As we began to articulate this path toward greater quality of life, we realized that we needed people to "try on" the concepts and walk around in them. So while our own acquaintances began to slowly build fledging collaboratives, we also built a narrative of Jake and his friends applying these concepts from

---

[161] The story of Au P'tit Plaisir is shared in greater depth on our website: https://QOL.to/auptitplaisir.

start to finish, pursuing their own "Quality of Life World."

These college students started the journey by taking action toward stronger personal agency. Jake began small, identifying his own personal essence and considering quality of life as it related to his life domains. Then Jake joined Leon, Lana, and Alex as they began to work together, moving beyond personal reservations and insecurities to forge deep, authentic connections with each other. The quality of life focus expanded as they reconfigured the personal dynamics of their working collaboration to honor each other's effort and contribution. Finally, the JALLers went *really* big, exploring personal finance on the Collaborative Cloud, starting a Sovereign Asset business, and living in a Sovereign Asset house. At the end of it all (at the beginning of it all), we see them experiencing stronger relationships, more purpose and meaning, and ultimately, greater quality of life.

This narrative was necessary to illustrate the comprehensive arc of the Person to Person journey. Jake, Alex, Lana, and Leon's story is meant to demonstrate the various ways we can *all* begin to work toward an environment that prioritizes quality of life and sustainability over the toil for wealth, power struggles, and the pursuit of short-term comfort at the expense of long-term sustainability. Ultimately, we hope the story inspired you, piqued your curiosity, and led you to imagine the ways these ideas could play out in your own context.

THE EXPERIENCE CENTER: THE FIRST SOVEREIGN ASSET

But the story keeps going—and the Experience Center waits to play her part.

In the five years since first purchasing the property, the vision for a Person to Person environment has developed and evolved. The collaborative recommendations have been honed; the Experience Center has been converted to a Sovereign Asset, and Value Cards have been created; the Collaborative Cloud is online, dressed in her first outfit—and the book is written.

Now it's time to pass the baton so that others can carry the vision forward.

You see, that's the thing about a Sovereign Asset: once it becomes sovereign, it doesn't belong to you anymore. The Experience Center is no longer "our" project. She has her own purpose; she extends her own invitation. Her future shape and form will not be determined by the person with the biggest bankroll or the shareholders with the greatest power, but by the people who have the vision and effort to determine her direction—by those brave, inspired, entrepreneurial souls who know there must be something more and are willing to put in the work to achieve it.

And what might these "Person to Person" people do at the Experience Center? Set up a music recording studio, perhaps? Open a fab lab for artistic expression? The upper floors of the hotels could become QOLiHoP apartments; the ground-level spaces could be used by healthcare providers as offices and clinics. Several collaboratives might return the Experience Center to a therapeutic retreat—even one where people take a break from the hustle and bustle of their nine-to-five existence and intentionally reflect on their goals for the eight life domains. Artists might turn the former bathhouse into an art gallery space; restaurateurs could convert the ancient mill into an eatery, café, or bar to help foster community connection. Event-planning cooperatives could use the chapel as a venue for ceremonies or large events; farming cooperatives could use the grounds for a working farm and sustainable agriculture—a site for green care.

Or perhaps the Experience Center would become a destination for people who have caught the Person to Person vision. It might welcome new collaboratives to a place where they can meet together and work through their Collaborative Agreements or discuss best practices with other groups. Maybe others would explore best practices in the working of Sovereign Assets. Or maybe the Experience Center will simply serve as a place of reflection, rest, and regeneration where people could take a big drink of quality of life before heading back into the world they've grown accustomed to.

Our hope for this place is that it will offer a small representation of how the Quality of Life World could look in other contexts. This could be a living heterotopia, functioning, as one writer puts it, "as a world within a world, mirroring and yet upsetting what is outside."[162]

But ultimately, we hope the Person to Person vision doesn't remain within the boundaries of a property in France. There are Person to Person people on every continent who can actualize this vision in their own places and context. Every single person can choose to begin to pursue greater quality of life in their own corner of the world.

ARE YOU ONE OF THEM?

And in that respect, the Person to Person vision is just as "sovereign" as the Experience Center: it is no longer ours. The Person to Person ideas are meant to be taken up by others, passed around, questioned, attempted, and evolved as they should. We are not protective or jealous over these ideas. We have never sought to present ourselves as experts or owners. Instead, these concepts have been written down simply so that they can be more readily shared and inspire others.

The Person to Person vision—like the Experience Center—waits like a would-be mother, ready to adopt a brood of children. All that is needed now are people to actualize the vision.

And what sort of people would they be? As the first collaboratives in our acquaintance began to form, we paid attention to the kind of people that were willing to step out of the box and try life in the Person to Person environment.

These are people with the courage to become entrepreneurs: people willing to wield the responsibility that comes with freedom, willing to make the hard decisions enabled by autonomy. The Person to Person vision needs people brave enough to cut themselves loose from the security of a monthly

---

[162] Heterotopia is a concept elaborated by philosopher Michel Foucault. See "Heteretopia (space)," Wikipedia, accessed January 31, 2022, https://en.wikipedia.org/wiki/Heterotopia_(space).

paycheck and let go of a traditional backup plan, like retirement benefits or other familiar forms of a safety net.

These are people willing to deepen their own self-awareness in the company of other collaborators, in the interest of building a strong team, people who seek to articulate their skills, recognize their limitations, and align in complementary ways with others. There is room for people with all kinds of different personalities, talents, and skills, yet we know that people in a Person to Person environment need to share some common traits: a willingness to get to know each other, show up, build trust, make agreements, and honor their commitments.

These are people willing to persevere, people who can get creative, people who will take initiative when confronted with the inevitable hurdles posed during a collaboration, such as resolving conflicts.

Like our JALL colleagues, these are people who will take agency as problem solvers. They will be willing to show up as whole humans to their collaboration—something that is often hard but leads to continual growth.

It will be hard, certainly. Any new beginning is challenging. It takes time to build momentum and multiple iterations to get something right. But we also trust that these people will remain motivated—as we are—by the quality of life that might be cultivated in a Person to Person environment:

- Work feels like home; colleagues feel like friends. People are comfortable showing up as their whole selves.
- Tools replace rules and enable people to work with the abilities and within the limitations that life offers us.
- It's a place that blurs the lines between physical and digital space, one that fosters connection and understanding among people that might have otherwise remained divided or disconnected.
- This environment allows us to live and work in the place of our choosing, somewhere we love to be that feeds our creativity and innovation.

- Here, we can engage in the community of practice as other like-minded people seek to connect and participate in the Person to Person vision.

CONNECT/COLLABORATE/BEGIN

The story continues. The Experience Center waits to play her part. But whether or not there's a happy ending in store for the Person to Person vision—or rather, an auspicious beginning—is not up to us anymore.

It's up to you.

We invite you to pick up this idea. Turn it around; mull it over; evolve it a little. Talk about it with your friends and neighbors. Explore https://qol.world and ask questions to us and others. On this site, you'll find pages with descriptions of other collaboratives at work, real examples of Sovereign Assets, answers to FAQs, a forum for dialogue, channels to discuss specific topics and chapters, and links to the UOV and the Collaborative Cloud.

Try beginning a Person to Person environment of your own—following the example of the JALL students, start small and watch the journey unfold from there. Start building your own Quality of Life World, whether that's through visiting the Experience Center in the South of France or exploring the Collaborative Cloud from your own bedroom from https://qol.world. We hope you've gotten just enough of a taste of these ideas from this book to begin imagining how to apply these concepts to your own situation. Can you catch the vision? We welcome you to engage, join, participate, and collaborate.

Change is needed. The world is a hurting, broken place. Our trajectory is not sustainable—not for people, not for society, and not for the planet. Let us not ignore the seriousness of what's at stake—we must look up.[163]

---

[163] *Don't Look Up*, directed by Adam McKay (Netflix, 2021).

All of us have a choice about how we respond: we can despair, we can become numb, or we can try to light a spark and put something in motion.

We can *hope*—and we can do something about it.

Shall we begin?

ABOUT THE AUTHORS

JOERI TORFS

Joeri Torfs is the operational director of the Quality of Life World Foundation. He has spent his career as an entrepreneur, software developer, and enterprise architect. In the latter role, he assesses the needs of an organization and then constructs a technological system that will best suit their requirements, a job that allows him to build structure from chaos and regularly challenge the status quo. Joeri is driven by knowledge and learning; he considers himself allergic to rules and authority. His purpose is to free humanity from the enslavement of society by building and using systems, frameworks, and tools capable of converting human intuitive behavior and collaborative instincts into constructive outcomes. He's convinced that, together, we can increase our quality of life by accepting life's challenges, building trust, letting go of control, and pursuing frictionless collaboration in a framework that can evolve with societal needs.

PIM AMPE

Pim Ampe is the constitutional director of the Quality of Life World Foundation. She also works as a drama therapist, specializing in dialectical behavioral therapy and solution-focused therapy, as well as serving as a Prosocial facilitator. Her current roles build off her lengthy experience in the mental health and welfare sector, where she worked in a variety of therapeutic positions, using a breadth of methods and frameworks. Pim cares deeply about the well-being of others and loves coaching and supporting people. Her life's purpose is to help people increase their quality of life by expanding their ability to adapt and self-manage in the face of life's challenges. She is a passionate learner and loves spending time with her family.

GRETA MYERS

Greta Myers is a writer, editor, and book coach with Scribe Media. Although she has helped many authors translate their ideas into written form, Joeri and Pim are the first collaborators who insisted she share authorship credit with them on the cover of their book—a fact that emphasizes their deep commitment to their principles and one that has also endeared them to Greta forever. She considers *Person to Person* to be one of the most challenging and meaningful projects of her life. Before joining Scribe Media in 2017, Greta enjoyed a career as a high school English teacher. She loves connecting with people, learning from them, and finding ways to make compelling ideas interesting and accessible to others. Her purpose is to use words to bring hope. Greta lives in Southern California with her sweetheart, Jeff, and their daughters.

ACKNOWLEDGMENTS

PIM'S ACKNOWLEDGMENTS

Writing a book was something I never saw myself doing. It was Joeri who taught me to be audacious, to be bold and brave enough to speak out loud, and to write down my experiences and ideas in words. So, thank you Joeri for this daring and intense experience. I don't know if I would do it again, but you offered me a great learning experience, like you offer me plenty in our relationship.

It was Greta who had the talent to transform our words into a readable book. I am forever grateful for the time she spent with us and the dedication she had toward the creation of this book. It was a pleasure to meet her, Jeff, Ramona, and Gloria on this journey.

Barbara engaged herself as the editor of our book; she challenged us with questions and offered us her experience and ideas, which helped us to complete the process of writing the book. Meeting her family in the process was a plus.

We had the pleasure and privilege to have some early supporters during the making of this book, so thank you to Lola and Enrico for being on our side all along this process. Thank you, Lisa and Passi for showing an interest in the content of this book from day one and spending hours walking and talking with us about the material and the challenges that came along with it during the process of creation.

This book found parts of its origin in the work I've been doing for twenty-two years now as a therapist. Some people taught me enormously during that process, so thank you to Ann for being my mentor (and BFF), and thank you to all my clients, who trusted me to be their collaborator on the daring path of therapy.

JOERI'S ACKNOWLEDGMENTS

To the saying "It takes a village to raise a child" I would add, it takes people to make a journey. The content of this book came to be as a result of the encounters and the experiences I have had—the good ones, but also the bad ones. I'm therefore thankful for everyone I crossed paths with for the exchanges, the lessons, and the learnings each one of them brought.

A special mention goes out to Pim, who helped me become a human being.

Additional thanks go to the following:

Jose Leal, for the countless hours spent exchanging ideas and poking holes in theories.

Greta, for her creativity and patience in turning a lifetime of ideas into a digestible format.

Benoit Spitaels, Marlies Van de Poel, Iuliana Babei, and François Barre, for their legal guidance.

Emiel De Smedt and Pieter Truyen, for their accounting insights.

Molly Goodman and Elise Torfs, for their research on quality of life.

Jennifer Morone, for her genuine interest and support.

Oana Bogdan and Leo Van Broeck, for their early embrace of our concepts and collaboration. Thank you for your commitment to sustainable living and quality of life.

Vitalik Buterin, for writing the foreword for our book.

A special acknowledgment to Satoshi Nakamoto, who unleashed the technology making the revolution possible.

GRETA'S ACKNOWLEDGMENTS

When I first heard about Pim and Joeri's book topic to guide people in building a Quality of Life World, I had one major question: "How?" With all of people's inherent flaws and with all the world's brokenness—how on earth could humans realistically join together to do better?

I'm so thankful I took the risk to sign on to this book and learn their answer to that question of *how* over the past year. Pim and Joeri: thank you for your patience in explaining your ideas, your high standards for how we convey them, your warmth and friendship, and opening my mind to these amazing, epic ideas. Thank you for so eagerly welcoming my questions, diving down into the rabbit holes, and climbing up out of them again. Thank you for choosing hope and action over complacency and despair. I am richer for our collaboration!

Thank you to Jeff for taking care of our girls during all the early-morning calls, and for being one of the book's earliest readers and commenters. Thank you to Ramona and Gloria for sparing Mama so that I could take time to learn about how to build a better world for you.

Thank you to Barbara Boyd, for your invaluable insight, wisdom, encouragement, and support. Thank you to Emily Gindlesparger for your mentorship.

Made in United States
North Haven, CT
09 July 2022

21093203R00295